STRUCTURED FORTRAN 77
FOR ENGINEERS AND SCIENTISTS
third edition

D. M. ETTER

Dept. of Electrical & Computer Engineering

University of New Mexico, Albuquerque

The Benjamin / Cummings Publishing Company, Inc.
Redwood City, California · Fort Collins, Colorado · Menlo Park, California
Reading, Massachusetts · New York · Don Mills, Ontario · Wokingham, U.K.
Amsterdam · Bonn · Sydney · Singapore · Tokyo · Madrid · San Juan

To my family, Amy Marie and Jerry Richard.

Sponsoring Editor: Alan Apt
Production Editor: Laura Kenney
Text Designer: Linda M. Robertson
Cover Designer: Victoria Ann Philp
Photo Researcher: Sarah Bendersky
Compositor: Progressive Typographers
On the Cover: Photograph of Very Large Array (VLA) radio telescopes by Gregory Heisler, © The Image Bank.

Library of Congress Cataloging-in-Publication Data

Etter, D. M.
Structured FORTRAN 77 for engineers and scientists/D. M. Etter—3rd ed.

1. FORTRAN 77 (Computer program)   2. Structured programming.
I. Title.
QA76.73.F25E85   1990
620'.0028'55133—dc20   89–17533
                                                              CIP

ISBN: 0-8053-0051-1
ABCDEFGH-DO-8932109

The Benjamin/Cummings Publishing Company, Inc.
390 Bridge Parkway
Redwood City, California 94065

Preface To
The Instructor

We've designed this introductory text in FORTRAN 77 specifically for an audience of engineering, science, and computer science students who will be using the computer as a tool in college courses, in activities outside of school, and in their careers. The material is therefore framed in real-world applications so that students can immediately begin to see the usefulness of the computer. However, knowing a computer language is to no avail if students cannot break down a problem solution into the properly ordered steps that a computer can perform; to that end, we stress a top-down design approach to problem solving throughout the text. Our objectives in this text are the following:

1. To acquaint students with the capabilities of computers and the types of problems that computers can solve.
2. To teach complete standard FORTRAN 77 so that students can use the computer to solve problems they encounter in both academic and nonacademic environments.
3. To establish good problem-solving techniques applicable to any problem, whether computer related or not.
4. To use practical, real-world engineering and science problems while accomplishing the first three objectives.

NEW FEATURES

Although our objectives have remained the same, we've enhanced this edition in several ways.

New Engineering Applications We've added new engineering-oriented examples, exercises, and problems throughout the text. A number of special application sections have been added to include new problems related to areas such as biomedical engineering, manufacturing engineering, and optical engineering.

Software Tools Algorithms for common techniques are presented and reinforced through a variety of applications. Sorting and searching have been expanded in this edition. Sort algorithms are provided for selection sorts, insertion sorts, and bubble sorts. Search algorithms for searching both ordered and unordered lists are presented with sequential and binary searches. Algorithms for inserting and deleting with ordered lists are also covered. These algorithms are then developed into functions and subroutines so that students can refer to these software tools in other programs. The reuse of existing software tools is stressed throughout the text.

Structure Charts The addition of structure charts provides a graphical picture of the modular structure of a program. Structure charts are included for all programs that contain subroutines and/or functions. Pseudocode and flowcharts still graphically illustrate the logical flow of the steps in an algorithm.

Expanded Numerical Techniques Numerical techniques have been expanded. For example, there is a new section on Gauss elimination, which is implemented in a new application related to deformable mirrors used in optical engineering and astronomy.

DISTINGUISHING FEATURES

A number of features distinguish this text from other FORTRAN texts.

Engineering and Science Applications Over 500 examples and problems that have been developed over a period of 15 years represent a wide range of engineering and science applications. Such topics as equipment reliability, quality control analysis, cryptography, terrain navigation, water treatment, sensor data, and spacecraft data analysis are included. Many of the solved problems contain sample data and corresponding output from actual computer runs.

Problem-Solving Design Process Used throughout the text, the five-phase design process is introduced in Chapter 1. These five phases are:

1. State the problem clearly.
2. Describe the input and the output.
3. Work the problem by hand for a specific set of data.
4. Develop an algorithm using top-down techniques.
5. Test the algorithm with a variety of data sets.

This design process is used consistently with all complete programs.

Engineering Case Studies A set of 32 engineering case studies comprise the application sections. Each case study includes a detailed development of the problem's solution along with sample data to illustrate testing the algorithm.

Numerical Applications and Techniques In this introduction to numerical applications, we discuss some of the common numerical techniques (approximations, iterative solutions, and matrix operations) used in solving engineering and science problems, and we present some suggestions for avoiding or minimizing precision errors. Complete applications are solved using linear modeling, numerical integration, roots of polynomials, and solutions to simultaneous equations. Additional problems (including numerical differentiation and interpolation) are included in the problems at the end of the chapter.

Complete FORTRAN 77 Coverage Complete coverage of FORTRAN 77 makes this book not only suitable for the first-time computer user but also as a valuable reference for the experienced user. In addition, only standard FORTRAN 77 statements and structures are used, so all programs and statements are compatible with any FORTRAN 77 compiler. Another advantage of using only standard FORTRAN 77 is that all programs will work properly on the new version of FORTRAN that is close to adoption because the new version is upward-compatible. The previous edition of this text included special appendices to show the differences between standard FORTRAN 77 and that used in the common personal computer compilers; these appendices have been deleted from this edition because the microcomputer compilers now are typically full standard compilers.

Motivational Problems as Chapter Openers Each chapter begins with a specific problem that cannot reasonably be solved with the FORTRAN statements presented up to that point; hence, we establish motivation to develop new elements of the language in order to solve the described problem. The introductory problem is solved after the new topics are covered.

Early Programming This book assumes no prior experience with computers; it therefore begins with an introductory chapter that explains many terms associated with computing. This chapter also introduces the five-step process for developing problem solutions. The presentation of FORTRAN statements begins with Chapter 2. By the end of Chapter 2, complete programs have been written.

Top-Down Design Techniques The five-step design process that appears throughout the text stresses top-down design techniques. A problem is first decomposed into general steps shown in a block diagram. Then, using stepwise refinement, the steps are translated into a computer language. Both pseudocode and flowcharts contribute to the development of the stepwise refinements so that students become acquainted with both techniques. Structure charts illustrate the modular structure of programs.

Structured Programming Approach To promote simplicity in solutions and reduce the time spent in testing and debugging programs, all problem solutions use structures with one way into the structure and one way out of the structure. All programs are implemented as either WHILE loops or iterative loops (DO loops). Thus, GO TO statements are used only to implement WHILE loops.

Software Tools Algorithms for common techniques are presented and used in numerous applications. Several forms of algorithms for averaging data and determining maximums and minimums are developed. Sort algorithms are presented for selection sorts, insertion sorts, and bubble sorts. Search algorithms for searching both ordered and unordered lists are presented with sequential and binary searches. Algorithms for inserting and deleting from ordered lists are also included. After subroutines and functions are covered, these algorithms are all developed into modules so that students can refer to these software tools in other programs. The reuse of existing software tools is stressed throughout the text.

FORTRAN Statement Summaries Each chapter contains a summary of the FORTRAN statements presented in that chapter. The summary contains the general form of the statement, specific examples of the statement, and a brief discussion of the rules for using the statement.

Self-Tests and Solutions The self-tests in chapters 2 – 9 allow students to check their understanding of the new material. Students can immediately determine whether they are ready to proceed to the next section by checking their answers to all the self-tests against the solutions included at the end of the text.

Style/Technique Guides Each chapter after the introductory chapter contains a style/technique guide to promote good programming habits that stress readability and simplicity. Although entire books are devoted to programming style and technique, this topic is included in each chapter on the premise that developing good style and technique is an integral part of learning the language. In addition to this special section at the end of each chapter, a number of examples in the text have multiple solutions, thereby exposing students to different approaches to solving the same problem. If one of these solutions has better style or technique than the others, it is pointed out in the accompanying discussion.

Debugging Aids Debugging aids are included in every chapter after Chapter 1. This section outlines efficient methods for locating and correcting program errors relevant to the programming techniques described in the chapter. With guidance from this section, students learn consistent methods for spotting and avoiding the common errors associated with each new FORTRAN statement. In addition to debugging aids, a number of examples in the text include an incorrect solution to a problem along with the correct solution. The incorrect solution is used to highlight common errors, thus helping students avoid making the same mistakes.

Key Words and Glossary A list of key words appears at the end of each chapter. For easy reference, the definition of each of the key words is in the glossary at the end of the text.

Large Number of Problems Over 400 problems are included in the self-tests and end-of-chapter problems. These problems vary in degree of difficulty, from simple to more challenging problems. Solutions to all of the self-tests and to many of the end-of-chapter problems are included at the end of the text.

Emphasis on Interactive Processing Although both batch processing and time-sharing are discussed, the emphasis is on time-sharing with interactive terminals. Conversational computing is also emphasized in many of the examples.

I/O Flexibility List-directed input statements and simple formatted output statements are used throughout the text. This choice provides maximum flexibility in the form in which data is entered and maximum control over the form of output data. We encourage the use of list-directed output for the testing and debugging phases, but we always use formatted output in our final programs.

Use of Color Color is used throughout the text to emphasize important material. Pedagogically, the use of color in emphasizing certain statements within a computer program is especially significant. Without using arrows or lines or distracting symbols, we can clearly stress the use of a new statement or point out the differences in two similar program segments. All pseudocode and flowcharts are highlighted in color for easy reference. End-of-chapter problem numbers appear in color to indicate that the solution is included at the end of the text.

ORGANIZATION

We recommend that chapters 1–7 be covered sequentially because these first seven chapters contain material that provides students with a thorough knowledge of the fundamentals of the language. Then, material can be selected from the last three chapters as time permits. Also, a few sections have been marked in the table of contents as sections that could be omitted without loss of continuity. The text is intended for an audience of engineering and science students who have no prior computer background. Calculus is not required, but knowledge of college algebra and trigonometry is assumed.

SUPPLEMENTS

Instructor's Guide An instructor's guide is available on request from the publisher. This supplement contains suggested course syllabi for both semester and quarter courses, viewgraphs, new computer projects, and complete solutions to the end-of-chapter problems. The new computer projects (along with their data files and solutions) and the complete solutions to the text end-of-chapter problems are available in diskette form from the author.

Test Bank A test bank is also available on request from the publisher. This supplement contains 150 quizzes that are printed one per page to allow simple copying of the pages for use in the classroom. Midterm and final exams are also included for class distribution as actual exams or practice exams. Solutions to the quizzes and exams are included. This material is also available in diskette form from the author.

Software A diskette that contains all the programs and corresponding data files from the application sections is available to instructors. With these, students can run the programs to be sure they understand how the programs work; the students can also easily make modifications and test them. This process emphasizes hands-on experience with the programs as they are being studied. Ideally, instructors should request the software supplement from the publisher and then load the files into a computer library that students can access directly from their terminals.

ACKNOWLEDGMENTS

After writing several textbooks, I appreciate more than ever the suggestions, guidance, and criticism provided by reviewers. The group of especially helpful reviewers that Alan Apt (Executive Editor) assembled for this text were Professors Jeanine Ingber, Betty J. Barr, W. F. Beckwith, and Lawrence J. Genalo. Reviewers of previous editions were Professors John Cowles, Mike Manry, Josann Duane, Ronald Danielson, William Holley, John Goda, Lee Maxwell, John R. Zimmerman, Susanne M. Shelley, Ted Wagstaff, Glen Williams, Edward T. Ordman, Elizabeth Unger, Joe Jefferis, Robert Aiken, Enrique A. Gonzales, and William Harlow. I also want to thank the following people at the Benjamin/ Cummings Publishing Company who are as excited and enthusiastic about this new edition as I am: Alan Apt, Mark McCormick, and Mary Ann Telatnik (Editorial); Laura Kenney (Production); and Lisa Judy and Colleen Dunn (Marketing). Special thanks also go to my husband Jerry (a mechanical engineer) who not only helped with the proofreading but also helped develop some of the new engineering applications. Finally, I want to express my appreciation to Caryl Peterson for her assistance in testing the many programs and solutions.

PREFACE TO
THE STUDENT

HOW TO USE THIS BOOK

The influence of computers on our lives grows with each new technological advance. Whether we use this influence to our advantage depends a great deal on our understanding of the computer's abilities and limitations. Assuming no previous computer experience, this text is designed to begin your computer education by introducing you to the process of problem solving with the computer language FORTRAN 77.

Chapter 1 is an introduction to computers and the types of problems they can solve. A color section shows some of the many different engineering and science applications that use computers as tools. If you have some prior computer experience, you will find that you can cover this chapter quickly.

Beginning with Chapter 2, we present the features of FORTRAN that make it such a versatile and powerful language. Our presentation includes many examples, with an emphasis on the problem-solving technique presented in Chapter 1. Chapters 2–7 should be covered sequentially. Each key section is followed by a short self-test. Complete each self-test after reading the corresponding section, then check your answers with the complete set of answers in the back of the text. If you have trouble completing a self-test, reread the section before continuing on in the text.

Chapters 8–10 contain a number of topics that may be useful in special applications. Chapter 8 contains discussions of three additional data types: character data, double-precision data, and complex data. Chapter 9 is a detailed discussion of advanced file-handling statements and techniques. Chapter 10 presents some of the common numerical techniques used in many engineering and science applications.

Color Color is used to identify pseudocode solutions throughout the text. In addition, key statements in FORTRAN programs are highlighted in color. We've printed all FORTRAN statements, output from programs, and data file contents in a special typeface to distinguish them clearly from the other material.

Debugging and Style Each chapter contains a debugging section and a style/technique section. The debugging section points out errors commonly made with the FORTRAN statements presented in the chapter and makes suggestions for avoiding them. The style/technique section includes guidelines for developing a programming style that stresses readability and simplicity. It is a good idea to review these sections periodically as you progress through the text.

Key Words and Glossary A list of key words appears at the end of each chapter. The definition of each of these key words is included in the glossary at the end of the text for easy reference.

FORTRAN Statement Summary At the end of each chapter that presents new FORTRAN statements we have included a statement summary that gives the general form of each new statement, examples of the statement, and a discussion of the rules associated with the statement. These statement summaries appear at the end of the chapter, and a color bar at the bottom edge of these pages helps you locate them easily.

Problem Solving Programming, like most skills, becomes easier with practice. A large number of problems appear at the end of each chapter. Solutions to selected problems appear at the end of the text; those problem numbers are in color. A special five-phase design process for solving problems, presented in Chapter 1 and illustrated throughout the text, allows you to begin decomposing a problem solution into smaller and smaller pieces, thus simplifying the overall solution.

BRIEF CONTENTS

DETAILED CONTENTS

Each chapter begins with an opening problem and an introduction and ends with a summary and key words. Chapters 2–10 also contain:
- *debugging aids*
- *style/technique guides*
- *problems*
- *FORTRAN statement summaries*

Asterisks indicate sections that can be omitted without loss of continuity.

ENGINEERING AND SCIENCE APPLICATIONS

AERONAUTICAL ENGINEERING

BIOMEDICAL ENGINEERING

CHEMICAL ENGINEERING

CIVIL ENGINEERING

Beam Analysis (Probs.4.26–4.27,p.185).
Earthquake Measurements (Sec.5–5,p.213; Probs.5.6–5.10,p.235).
Tremor Averages (Prob.5–29,p.237).

ELECTRICAL ENGINEERING

Energy Conversion (Ex.2–14,p.46; Probs.2.1–2.5,p.60).
Equipment Reliability (Sec.2–9,p.54; Probs.2.21–2.25,pp.62–63).
Parallel Resistance (Prob.2.31,p.64; Ex.4–1,p.146; Ex.4–2,p.147).
Circuit Inspection (Prob.3.27–3.28,p.135).
Diodes (Prob.3.33,p.138).
Communication Channels (Prob.5.38,p.240).
Electric Circuit Model (Sec.8–6,p.386; Probs.8.11–8.15,p.393).
Transfer functions (Probs.8.20–8.22,p.394).
Voyager Spacecraft Data Analysis (Sec.9–3,p.407; Probs.9.1–9.5,p.432).
Power in Frequency Bands (Sec.10–3,p.449; Probs.10.6–10.10,p.488).
Electrical Current Analysis (Sec.10–7,p.471; Probs.10.16–10.18,p.489).

ENVIRONMENTAL ENGINEERING

Timber Regrowth (Sec.3–7,p.115; Probs.3.11–3.15,p.133).

MANUFACTURING ENGINEERING

Critical Path Analysis (Sec.4–2,p.153; Probs.4.1–4.5,p.181).
Quality Control (Sec.4–6,p.173, Probs.4.11–4.15,p.182).
Equipment Maintenance (Prob.5–32,p.238).

MECHANICAL ENGINEERING

Cable Car Velocity (Ex.3–4,p.87; Sec.3–8,p.119; Probs.3.16–3.20,p.133).
Solar Device (Prob.4.16,p.182).
Fuel Analysis (Probs.4.21–4.22,p.183; Prob.8.26,p.395).
Temperature Distribution (Sec.8–4,p.375; Probs.8.6–8.10,p.393).
Materials Testing (Probs.9.23–9.27,p.434).
Coil/Deflection Model (Sec.10.2,p.442; Probs.10.1–10.5,p.488).
Robot Arm Stability (Sec.10–5,p.457; Probs.10.11–10.15,p.489).

OPTICAL ENGINEERING

Deformable Mirrors (Sec.10–8,p.476; Probs.10.19–10.21,p.490).

PETROLEUM ENGINEERING

Seismic Drilling (Probs.4.23–4.25,p.184).
Oil Well Production (Sec.6–6,p.270; Probs.6.6–6.10,p.293).

METEOROLOGY

PHYSICS

SOCIOLOGY

STATISTICS

APPLICATION — Experimental Data Analysis

The analysis of laboratory data often involves time-consuming computations that must be performed before the final results of an experiment can be determined. Many of these computations can be performed quickly and easily with a computer. Therefore, one of the benefits of learning to use the computer is that you can then use this tool to help you with other tasks and in other coursework. In this chapter, we use the familiar problem of computing an average from a set of measurements to illustrate the steps in the development of a FORTRAN solution to a given problem. (See Section 1 – 4 for the solution.)

1

AN INTRODUCTION TO FORTRAN 77 AND PROBLEM SOLVING

INTRODUCTION

Problem solving is an activity in which we participate every day. Problems range from analyzing our chemistry lab data to finding the quickest route to work. Computers can solve many of our problems if we learn how to communicate with them in computer languages such as FORTRAN 77. Some people believe that if we describe a problem to a computer, it will solve it for us. Programming would be simpler if this were the case; unfortunately, it is not. Computers only perform the steps that we describe. You may wonder, then, why we go to the effort of writing computer programs to solve problems if we have to describe every step. The answer is that although computers can perform only simple tasks, they perform them extremely accurately and at fantastic rates of speed. In addition, computers never get bored. Imagine sitting at a desk analyzing laboratory data for eight hours a day, five days a week, year after year. This is a pretty dismal thought, and yet thousands of laboratory results must be analyzed every year. Once the steps involved in performing a particular analysis (such as computing an average) have been carefully described to a computer, however, it can analyze data 24 hours a day, with more speed and accuracy than a group of technicians.

We must not forget that someone must first describe the steps to the computer using proper computer language statements before the computer can be used to solve the problem. We will spend much of this text teaching you the FORTRAN 77 language, but any computer language is useless unless you can break a problem into steps that a computer can perform. Therefore, techniques for problem solving will also be presented and illustrated in each chapter.

In this first chapter we discuss the different types of computers, from the supercomputer to the personal computer. We compare different computer languages and discuss some of the reasons why there are so many languages. We then present a design process for problem solving that we will use throughout the text. This design process will be illustrated by the problem of computing the average of a set of data values mentioned in the introductory chapter application.

1 – 1   COMPUTER ORGANIZATION

Computers come in all sizes, shapes, and forms, as illustrated in the color section in this chapter. All these computers have a common internal organization, shown in the block diagram in Figure 1 – 1. Each part is likely to be physically distinguishable from the others in large computer systems. In a microcomputer or minicomputer, all the parts within the dotted line may be combined in a single, integrated circuit chip.

The processing unit or *processor* is the part of the computer that controls all the other parts. The processor accepts input values and stores them in the memory. It also interprets the instructions in a computer program. If we want to add two values, the processor will retrieve them from the memory and send them to the *arithmetic logic unit* or *ALU*. The ALU performs the desired addition, and the processor then stores the result in the memory. If we desire, we may also direct the processor to print the result on paper. The processing unit and the ALU use a

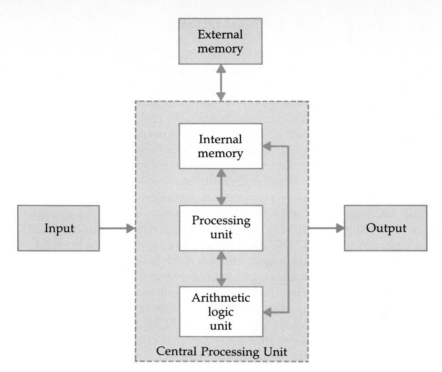

FIGURE 1-1 Block diagram of a computer.

small amount of memory, the *internal memory*, in their processing; most data is stored in *external memory*. The processor, internal memory, and ALU are collectively called the *central processing unit* or *CPU*. Thus, a microprocessor is a CPU, but a microcomputer is a CPU with input and output capabilities.

The size of a computer system needed to solve a particular problem depends on the type and number of steps required to solve a problem. If the computer is to be part of a home security system, a microcomputer is sufficient; if the computer is to handle airline reservations for a major airline, then a large computer system may be required. Because FORTRAN 77 is available on most computers, we will be able to use a variety of computers for our programs.

When working with computers, you will often hear the terms *software* and *hardware*. Software refers to the programs that direct computers to perform operations, compute new values, and manipulate data. Hardware refers to the physical components of the computer, such as the memory unit, the processor, and the ALU. A person who works with software might write computer programs, and a person who works with hardware might design new components or connect devices. For example, a hardware engineer might design the interface equipment necessary to connect a microprocessor to an input terminal.

1 – 2   COMPUTER LANGUAGES

Computer hardware is based on two-state *(binary)* technology; that is, computers are built from components that have two values (such as open or closed, on or off, plus or minus, or high or low). These two values can be represented by the numbers 0 and 1. Thus, computers are often defined as machines capable of interpreting and understanding sequences of 0's and 1's, called binary strings.

Because we have been trained to think in terms of English-like phrases and formulas, we use English-like languages such as FORTRAN 77 to tell the computer the steps we want it to perform. A special program called a *compiler* then translates the FORTRAN 77 program into binary strings that the computer can understand. This compilation procedure is discussed in Section 1 – 3.

FORTRAN (FORmula TRANslation) was one of the first computer languages. Originally developed in the 1950s for technical applications, FORTRAN 77 is a specific version of FORTRAN based on a set of standards established in 1977. These new standards greatly improved the language by adding new features and structures that allow us to write powerful yet readable programs. COBOL was designed to handle business-related problems and file manipulations. BASIC, a language similar to FORTRAN, is commonly used with minicomputers and personal computers. ALGOL, PL/I, Pascal, and Modula-2 are other more recent languages that are *structured languages* because of special structures included in the language. (FORTRAN 77 is also a structured language, but the original FORTRAN was not.) Ada is a new language designed for the U.S. Department of Defense for use in technical applications. All these languages are considered high-level languages because their instructions are in English words as opposed to binary strings.

Learning a computer language is similar to learning a foreign language. Each step that you want the computer to perform must be translated into "computer language." Fortunately, computer languages have small vocabularies and no verb conjugations; however, computers are unforgiving in punctuation and spelling. A comma or letter incorrectly placed will cause errors that keep your program from working properly. You will discover that you must pay close attention to many such details.

We have discussed *high-level languages* (such as FORTRAN 77) and *low-level languages* (binary or machine language). At another level are *assembly languages*. Assembly languages are between high-level and low-level languages and do not require a compiler to translate them into binary code. A smaller program, the *assembler*, translates the assembly language into machine language.

Most assembly languages do not have many statements, which make them inconvenient to use. For example, you might have to add a series of numbers to perform a single multiplication. You would also have to understand certain elements of your computer's design to use an assembly language. For these reasons, when given a choice, most people prefer to write programs in a high-level language. Assembly language is used primarily when it is necessary to minimize a program's memory requirements and its execution time.

Some of the statements in various high-level languages are illustrated in Table 1 – 1. Each section of code represents the calculation of a water bill based on

---

the number of gallons of water used. In order to encourage conservation of water, many communities charge a higher rate per gallon if the usage is over a specified amount. In this example, we assume that one rate is used if the number of gallons is less than or equal to 5000; another rate is used for each gallon over 5000. The different names used to represent gallons used, water rates, and total water bill reflect the various rules within the individual languages. Also note the differences in punctuation among the various languages.

TABLE 1-1 Examples of High-Level Languages

Language	Example Statements
FORTRAN 77	```IF (GALLNS.LE.5000.0) THEN BILL = GALLNS*RATE1 ELSE BILL = 5000.0*RATE1 + (GALLNS - 5000.0)*RATE2 ENDIF```
Pascal	```IF GALLONS <= 5000.0 THEN BILL := GALLONS*RATE1 ELSE BILL := 5000.0*RATE1 + (GALLONS - 5000.0)*RATE2;```
C	```IF (GALLONS <= 5000.0) BILL = GALLONS*RATE1; ELSE BILL = 5000.0*RATE1 + (GALLONS - 5000.0)*RATE2;```
Ada	```IF GALLONS <= 5000.0 THEN BILL := GALLONS*RATE1; ELSE BILL := 5000.0*RATE1 + (GALLONS - 5000.0)*RATE2;```
BASIC	```IF G > 5000.0 THEN 200 LET B = G*R1 GO TO 250 200 LET B = 5000.0*R1 + (G - 5000.0)*R2 250```
COBOL	```IF GALLONS IS LESS THAN 5000.0 OR GALLONS IS EQUAL TO 5000.0, COMPUTE BILL = GALLONS*RATE1 ELSE COMPUTE BILL = 5000.0*RATE1 + (GALLONS - 5000.0)*RATE2.```
PL/I	```IF GALLONS <= 5000.0 THEN BILL = GALLONS*RATE1; ELSE BILL = 5000.0*RATE1 + (GALLONS - 5000.0)*RATE2;```

1-3 RUNNING A COMPUTER PROGRAM

In the previous section, we defined a compiler as a program that translates a high-level language to machine language. This compilation step is the first step in running a computer program. As the compiler translates statements, it also checks for *syntax errors*. Syntax errors, also called compiler errors, are errors in the statements themselves, such as misspellings and punctuation errors. If syntax errors (often referred to as "bugs") are found, the compiler will print error messages or diagnostics for you. After correcting the errors ("debugging"), you must rerun your program, again starting with the compilation step. Once you have compiled your program without errors, a *linkage editor* program performs the final preparations so that it can be submitted to the execution step. It is in the execution step that the statements are actually performed. Errors can also arise in the execution step; these are called *logic errors*, run-time errors, or execution errors. These errors (also called "bugs") are not in the statement syntax but are errors in the logic of the statements, which are detected only when the computer attempts to execute the statement. For example, the statement

$$X = A/B$$

is a valid FORTRAN 77 statement that directs the computer to divide A by B and call the result X. The statement contains no syntax errors. Suppose, though, that the value of B is zero. Then, as we try to divide A by B, we are attempting to divide by zero, which is an invalid operation; we will get an execution error message. Logic errors do not always generate an error message. For instance, if we were supposed to divide by 0.10 and instead we multiplied by 0.10, no error would be detected by the computer although our answers would be wrong.

A computer program is often called the *source program*. After it is converted into machine language by the compiler and prepared for execution by the linkage editor, it is in machine language and is now called the *object program*. A diagram of this *compilation-linkage-execution process* is shown in Figure 1-2.

It is uncommon for a program to compile, link, and execute correctly on the first run. Do not become discouraged if it takes several runs to get your answers. When you do get answers from your program, do not assume they are correct. If possible, check your answers with a calculator, and always check to see if the answers make sense. For example, if the answer represents the weight of a

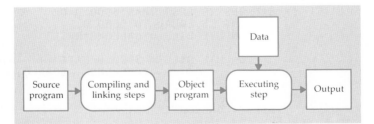

FIGURE 1-2 Compilation-linkage-execution process for running a computer program.

boxcar, then 5 pounds is not reasonable and suggests that you have given the computer incorrect information or an incorrect program to execute.

Two methods are used for running computer programs: *batch processing* and *time sharing*. In batch-processing systems, the computer stores the program in its memory and compiles and executes it completely before executing another program. In time-sharing systems, the program is typed into the terminal, followed by a command such as RUN, which immediately begins the processing. This technique is called time sharing because the computer does a few steps of a program from one terminal, then a few steps of a program from another terminal, and so on until it is back to the first terminal. The computer then performs another cycle of steps in each program. We usually do not notice the time between cycles because the computer executes statements so quickly. We seem to have the undivided attention of the computer, although we are actually sharing it with many other terminal users. Interaction with either type of system is generally by means of a terminal. Hard-copy terminals use paper to record the input and output from the computer, and CRT (cathode ray tube) terminals use a video screen to display the input and output.

Most time-sharing systems allot each user a specified amount of memory to be used as a workspace in the computer. This workspace is usually divided into a temporary workspace and a permanent workspace. As you enter programs or data into the temporary workspace you can edit the information, which means you can add to it, delete portions of it, or modify it with the use of an editing program (called an editor). When you have the program or data in the form that you want, you can save it in the permanent workspace. You can then clear the temporary workspace and begin entering new information or you can "log off" the terminal. The next time you "log on," you can load any information that was previously saved in your permanent workspace into your temporary workspace.

Time sharing or using a personal computer is called *interactive computing* because we are interacting with the computer more than in a batch-processing system. This increased interaction results in more efficient use of your time — you have fewer delays.

We can also interact with computers using workstations. A *workstation* is a computer that can do many types of processing by itself, and thus can function as a standalone computer. However, a workstation is also connected to other computers via a *computer network* that allows the computers to communicate with each other. The access to the network can be used to increase the resources available to the workstation. For example, a workstation may have a dot-matrix printer attached to it for general printing. If the user wishes to print an important report on a laser printer attached to the network, the workstation can request that the information be transmitted across the network and printed on the laser printer. Workstations can also share programs or data files with other computers on the network. For example, instead of every computer on a network maintaining its own FORTRAN 77 compiler, the compiler could be stored on one computer and then copied to other workstations that wanted to use it. After each user finished using the compiler, it would then be deleted from all the individual workstations, but it would still be retained on the original computer system.

1–4 TOP-DOWN DESIGN TECHNIQUES

Having discussed computer hardware and software, we now turn to developing a procedure for solving problems using the computer. Our procedure has five phases; we will use it each time we present a complete problem solution. Understanding the phases will be easier if we go through them using a familiar problem, such as computing an average. This problem arises when we are computing our homework average in one of our courses or when we are summarizing experimental data from a lab experiment.

The first phase of our design process is to state the problem clearly. It is important to give a clear, concise statement of the problem to avoid any misunderstandings. For our example, the problem statement is

Compute the average of a set of experimental data values.

The second phase is to describe carefully any information or data needed to solve the problem and then describe how the final answer is to be presented. These items represent the input and the output for the problem. Collectively, they are called *input/output*, or *I/O*. In our example, the input information is the list of experimental data values. The output is the average of these data values.

The third phase is to work the problem by hand or with a calculator, using a simple set of data. An example of a set of data values and the computed average is

LAB MEASUREMENTS   4/23/89

NUMBER	VALUE
1	23.43
2	37.43
3	34.91
4	28.37
5	30.62
Sum	154.76

Average = Sum/5 = 30.95

The fourth phase is to describe, in general terms, the steps that you performed by hand. The sequence of steps that solves the problem is called an *algorithm*. The procedure that we use in our algorithm development is called *top-down design*. Top-down design is composed of two techniques: *decomposition* and *stepwise refinement*. We break the problem into a series of smaller problems (decomposition), and address each smaller problem separately (stepwise refinement). Decomposition is a form of "divide and conquer" in which each part of the overall problem is described in general terms. Stepwise refinement begins with this general description and successively refines and describes each step in greater detail. The refining continues until the solution is specific enough to convert into computer instructions.

The advantage of decomposition is that we can initially think of the overall steps required without getting lost in the details. Details are introduced only as we begin the refinement of our algorithm. We will show the decomposition in block diagrams to emphasize that we are breaking the solution into a series of sequentially executed steps. Two tools assist us in refining the general steps of the decomposition: *flowcharts* and *pseudocode*. A flowchart shows the steps in an algorithm in graphic form, and pseudocode presents algorithm steps in a series of English-like statements. For the development of our example solution, we will describe the steps in a longhand form similar to pseudocode. The details of flowcharts and pseudocode are presented in Chapter 3.

Applying the concept of "divide and conquer," or decomposition, to our problem of computing an average, we first break the problem into a series of smaller problems.

DECOMPOSITION

Read data values and sum them.
Divide sum by the number of data values.
Print the average.

The second part of top-down design is to refine each step in the decomposition into more detailed steps. As you read the following algorithm, remember the steps you just performed in the longhand example; they should be similar to these steps:

ALGORITHM FOR COMPUTING AN AVERAGE

Step 1. Set the sum of the values to zero.
          Set a count of the values to zero.
Step 2. As long as there are more data values, do the following:
          Add the next data value to the sum.
          Add 1 to the count.
          When there are no more values, go to the next step.
Step 3. Divide the sum by the count to get the average.
Step 4. Print the average.
Step 5. Stop.

Once the solution steps, or algorithm, are detailed, they are ready to be converted into FORTRAN 77. The statements for solving this problem will not all be presented until Chapter 3, so there are items in the solution that you probably won't understand at this time. We present the solution here so that you can see how similar it is to the refined steps previously described. We assume that a data value of zero is used to indicate that we have reached the end of the data values.

```
*----------------------------------------------------------------*
      PROGRAM   COMPUT
*
*  This program computes the average of
*  a set of experimental data values.
*
      INTEGER   COUNT
      REAL   X, SUM, AVERG
*
      SUM = 0.0
      COUNT = 0
      READ*, X
   1  IF (X.NE.0.0) THEN
          SUM = SUM + X
          COUNT = COUNT + 1
          READ*, X
          GO TO 1
      ENDIF
      AVERG = SUM/REAL(COUNT)
      PRINT 5, AVERG
   5  FORMAT (1X,'THE AVERAGE IS ',F6.2)
      END
*----------------------------------------------------------------*
```

The fifth phase of problem solving is to test the solution steps (or algorithm) that you have just described. Testing an algorithm is not easy. We can usually find data for which our algorithm works correctly, but it is just as important to determine if there are sequences of data that cause our algorithm to fail — so that we can correct the steps in the program. A correct algorithm to average data should work properly for any set of data. If the data from our longhand example were used in the FORTRAN program presented here, the output on our terminal screen would be

THE AVERAGE IS   30.95

Algorithm testing is discussed further in later chapters.

These five phases for algorithm development are used in the special application sections throughout the rest of the text.

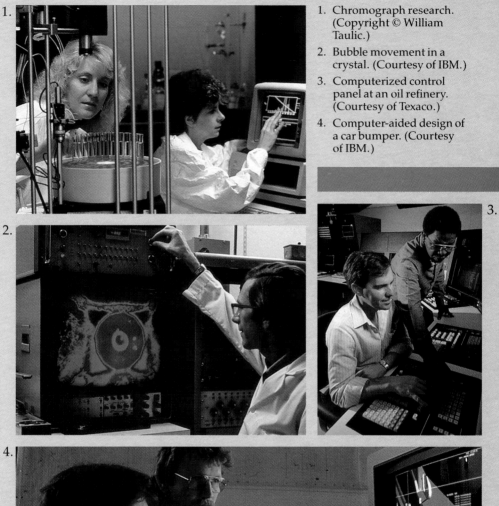

1. Chromograph research. (Copyright © William Taulic.)
2. Bubble movement in a crystal. (Courtesy of IBM.)
3. Computerized control panel at an oil refinery. (Courtesy of Texaco.)
4. Computer-aided design of a car bumper. (Courtesy of IBM.)

5.

6.

7.

5. Computerized monitor-
   ing of traffic. (Copyright
   © Alan D. Levenson.)

6. Laptop computer being
   used in an oil field.
   (Courtesy of Texaco.)

7. Computerized quality as-
   surance testing. (Copyright
   © Lawrence Migdale.)

8. Aircraft testing. (Copyright
   © Peter Menzel/Wheeler
   Pictures.)

8.

9.

10.

11.

12.

9. Manufacturing and testing of fiber optics. (Copyright © Hank Morgan/Rainbow.)

10. Analysis of meteorological data. (Copyright © Lawrence Migdale.)

11. Electron microscope display. (Copyright © Lawrence Migdale.)

12. Computerized tracking of lightning with data from remote weather stations. (Copyright © Rich Frishman.)

13.

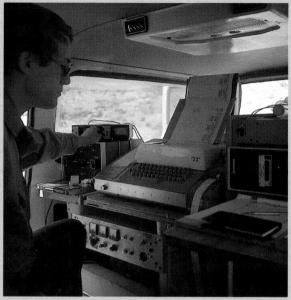

14.

15.

16.

SUMMARY

In this chapter we discussed the fundamental concepts of computers. The process of converting a computer program into a form the computer can understand and execute was described, and the five-phase procedure for developing problem solutions (algorithms) was presented. The five phases are

1. State the problem clearly.
2. Describe the input and output information.
3. Work the problem by hand (or with a calculator) for a specific set of data.
4. Develop a solution that is general in nature.
5. Test the solution with a variety of data sets.

The solution is developed using top-down design. Decomposition assists in describing the general steps that have to be performed to solve the problem. Stepwise refinement guides us in refining the steps and adding necessary details.

KEY WORDS

algorithm
arithmetic logic unit (ALU)
assembler
assembly language
batch processing
binary
bug
cathode ray tube terminal (CRT)
central processing unit (CPU)
compilation
compiler
computer network
data
debug
decomposition
design phases
diagnostic
editor
execution

FORTRAN 77
hardware
high-level language
input/output (I/O)
interactive computing
logic error
machine language
memory
object program
problem solving
processor
program
software
source program
stepwise refinement
syntax error
time sharing
top-down design
workstation

APPLICATION — Equipment Reliability (Electrical Engineering)

If you have a personal computer, or if you have a friend who has one, open the back of the computer system and look at the computer board(s) that contain its circuitry. Each board contains a large number of components. You might wonder how computers can be so reliable when so many different components could malfunction. Much of their reliability is due to the quality control maintained during their manufacture. Also, during the design of the computer, or any other complicated piece of instrumentation, the reliability is analyzed. This analysis depends both on the reliability of the individual components and on the manner in which the components are connected. Write a FORTRAN program to compute the reliability of a design with many components connected serially. (See Section 2–9 for the solution.)

2

ARITHMETIC COMPUTATIONS

INTRODUCTION

Arithmetic operations (adding, subtracting, multiplying, and dividing) are the most fundamental operations performed by computers. Engineers and scientists also need other routine operations, such as raising a number to a power, taking the logarithm of a number, or computing the sine of an angle. This chapter discusses methods of storing data with FORTRAN 77 and develops the statements for performing arithmetic calculations with that data. We also introduce statements for simple data input and output. With this group of statements, we can write complete FORTRAN 77 programs.

Before we discuss which types of numbers can be stored in computers and some specific statements, we need to outline the proper form for entering FORTRAN statements. These rules generally apply to FORTRAN statements entered on both time-sharing systems and batch systems. Each statement is entered on a new line. We refer to specific positions within the line by column number: The first position in a line is column 1, the second position in a line is column 2, and so on.

1. Columns 1 through 5 are reserved for statement numbers (also called labels), which must be nonzero positive integers. Not every statement requires a number, but as you will see in later chapters, some statements need numbers so they can be referenced. If column 1 contains an asterisk or the letter C, the line is a comment line. Comment lines are used for entering general comments and are printed in a listing of the program; comment lines are not converted into machine language or used during execution of the program.
2. Column 6 is used to indicate that a statement has been continued from the previous line. Any nonblank character except a zero can be used in the second line in column 6 to indicate continuation. A FORTRAN statement may have several continuation lines if it is too long to fit on one line.
3. FORTRAN statements start in column 7 and can extend to column 72. In general, blanks can be inserted anywhere in the statement for readability. All information beyond column 72 is ignored.

These rules are summarized in Figure 2-1.

Some terminal editors require you to number each line. These line numbers are used in editing but cannot be referenced by a FORTRAN statement. If you are using one of these editors, all statements will have a line number, and statements referenced in your program will also have a FORTRAN label.

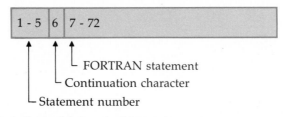

FIGURE 2-1 General form of a FORTRAN statement.

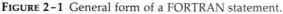

2-1 CONSTANTS AND VARIABLES

Numbers are introduced into a computer program either directly with the use of *constants* or indirectly with the use of *variables*. Constants are numbers used directly in FORTRAN 77 statements, such as − 7, 3.141593, and 32.0. Constants may contain plus or minus signs and decimal points, but they may not contain commas. Thus 3147.6 is a valid FORTRAN constant, but 3,147.6 is not. Constants are stored in memory locations but can be accessed only by using the constant value itself.

A variable represents a memory location that is assigned a name. The memory location contains a value; we reference that value with the name assigned to that memory location. We can visualize variables, their names, and their values as shown:

AMOUNT	36.84	VOLUME	183.0
RATE	0.065	TOTAL	486.5
TEMP	17.5	INFO	72

Each memory location to be used in a program is given a name and may be assigned a value using a FORTRAN statement. In the preceding example, the memory location named RATE has been assigned the value 0.065.

Each variable must have a different name, which you provide in your program. The names may contain one to six characters consisting of both alphabetic characters and digits; however, the first character of a name must be alphabetic. The following are examples of both valid and invalid variable names:

DISTANCE	Invalid name — too long
TIME	Valid name
PI	Valid name
$	Invalid name — illegal character ($)
TAX−RT	Invalid name — illegal character (−)
B1	Valid name
2X	Invalid name — first character must be alphabetic

Numerical values in FORTRAN can be one of four types: integer, real, double precision, or complex. Integer-type values are those with no fractional portion and no decimal point, such as 16, − 7, 186, and 0; they are also called fixed-point values. On the other hand, real-type values contain a decimal point and may or may not have digits past the decimal point, such as 13.86, 13., 0.0076, − 14.1, 36.0, and − 3.1; these real values are also called floating-point values. Double-precision values and complex values are discussed in Chapter 8.

A memory location can contain only one type of value. The type of value stored in a variable is specified by two methods: *implicit typing* or *explicit typing*. With implicit typing, the first letter of a variable name determines the value type that can be stored in it. Variable names beginning with the letters I, J, K, L, M, or N

---

are used to store integers. Variable names beginning with one of the other letters, A–H and O–Z, are used to store real values. Thus, with implicit typing, AMOUNT represents a real value and MONEY represents an integer value. An easy way to remember which letters are used for integers is to observe that the range of letters is I–N, the first two letters of the word integer.

With explicit typing, a special FORTRAN statement is used to specify the variable type. For example, the statements

```
INTEGER  WIDTH
REAL  ITEM, LENGTH
```

specify that WIDTH is a variable containing an integer value and that ITEM and LENGTH are variables containing real values. These *specification statements* have the following general forms:

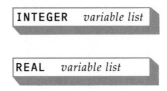

INTEGER *variable list*

REAL *variable list*

The variable lists in the previous statements contain variable names separated by commas. These statements are *nonexecutable* because they are used by the compiler to specify the type of value to be stored in a variable and are not translated into machine language. Specification statements are placed at the beginning of the program — before any executable statement.

It is helpful to select a variable name that is descriptive of the value being stored. For example, if a value represents a tax rate, name it RATE or TAX. If the implicit typing of the variable name does not match the type of value to be stored in it, then use a REAL or INTEGER statement at the beginning of your program to specify the desired type of value. Some programmers prefer to list all variables in specification statements, including those correctly typed by the implicit rules. In the example programs used in this book, all variables are included in specification statements. When individual statements are used as examples, you can assume that the variables are typed according to their names unless otherwise indicated.

SCIENTIFIC NOTATION

When a real number is very large or very small, decimal notation does not work satisfactorily. For example, a value that is used frequently in chemistry is Avogadro's constant, whose value to four significant places is 602,300,000,000,000,000,000,000. Obviously, we need a more manageable notation for very large values like Avogadro's constant or for very small values like 0.000000000042. *Scientific notation*, commonly used in science, expresses a value as a number between 1 and 10 multiplied by a power of 10. In scientific notation, Avogadro's constant becomes 6.023×10^{23}. Elements of this form are commonly referred to as the mantissa (6.023) and the exponent (23). The FORTRAN form of scientific notation, called *exponential notation*, expresses a value as a number between 0.1 and 1 multiplied by an appropriate power of 10. Exponential notation uses the letter E to separate the mantissa and the exponent. In exponential form, Avogadro's constant becomes 0.6023E24. Other examples of decimal values in scientific and exponential notation are

DECIMAL VALUE	SCIENTIFIC NOTATION	EXPONENTIAL NOTATION
3,876,000,000	3.876×10^9	0.3876E10
0.0000010053	1.0053×10^{-6}	0.10053E−05
−8,030,000	-8.03×10^6	−0.803E07
−0.000157	-1.57×10^{-4}	−0.157E−03

Although FORTRAN uses an exponential form with a mantissa between 0.1 and 1.0, it will accept mantissas beyond that range; for instance, the constant 0.16E03 would also be valid in the forms 1.6E02 or 0.016E04.

MAGNITUDE LIMITATIONS

There are limitations on the magnitude and precision of values that can be stored in a computer. All limitations on values depend on the specific computer. For instance, pi is an irrational number and cannot be written with a finite number of decimal positions; in a computer with seven digits of accuracy, pi could be stored as 3.141593. In addition to limits on the number of significant positions in the mantissa, there are also limits on the size of the exponent.

Table 2–1 compares the approximate range of values that can be stored in several large computers. Check a reference manual to find the ranges of real and integer values for the computer you will be using.

TABLE 2-1 Typical Ranges for FORTRAN Data Values

COMPUTER	REAL VALUE RANGES	MAXIMUM INTEGER
IBM 360/370	Mantissa: 6 significant digits Exponent: −77 to 75	2,147,483,647
VAX	Mantissa: 7 significant digits Exponent: −38 to 38	2,147,483,647
CRAY-1	Mantissa: 13 significant digits Exponent: −2465 to 2465	2.8×10^{14}
CDC 6000/7000	Mantissa: 14 significant digits Exponent: −293 to 322	9.2×10^{18}

This self-test allows you to check quickly to see if you have remembered some of the key points from Section 2–1. If you have any problems with the exercises, you should reread this section. The solutions are included at the end of the text.

Problems 1–10 contain both valid and invalid variable names. Explain why the invalid names are unacceptable.

1. AREA	2. PERIMETER
3. VOLUME	4. LENGTH
5. TAX-RATE	6. TEMP-A
7. F(X)	8. 2TIME
9. TIME2	10. AMT$

In problems 11–16, tell whether or not the pair of real constants represents the same number. If not, explain.

11. 2300; 2.3E04	12. 0.000007; 0.7E04
13. 1.0; 1	14. 110.0; 11.01E01
15. −34.7; −0.34E02	16. −0.76; 7.60E−01

2–2 ARITHMETIC OPERATIONS

Computations in FORTRAN may be specified with the assignment statement whose general form is

$$\boxed{variable\ name = expression}$$

The simplest form of an expression is a constant. Hence, if the value of pi is needed frequently in a program, we might choose to define a variable PI with the value 3.141593. We could then refer to the variable PI each time we needed the constant. An assignment statement that assigns a value to PI is

PI = 3.141593

The name of the variable receiving a new value must always be on the left-hand side of the equal sign. In FORTRAN, the equal sign can be read as "is assigned the value of." Thus, this statement could be read "PI is assigned the value 3.141593." The term "initialized" is often used to refer to the first value assigned to a variable in a program; this statement could also be read "PI is initialized to the value 3.141593."

TABLE 2-2 Arithmetic Operations in Algebraic Form and in FORTRAN

OPERATION	ALGEBRAIC FORM	FORTRAN
Addition	$A + B$	A + B
Subtraction	$A - B$	A − B
Multiplication	$A \times B$	A*B
Division	$\dfrac{A}{B}$	A/B
Exponentiation	A^3	A**3

It is important to recognize that a variable can store only one value at a time. For example, suppose the following statements were executed one after another:

```
WIDTH = 36.7
WIDTH = 105.2
```

The value 36.7 is stored in the variable WIDTH after the first statement is executed. The second statement replaces that value with the new value 105.2, and the first value is lost.

Consider these statements:

```
TEMP1 = -52.6
TEMP2 = TEMP1
```

The first statement stores the value -52.6 in TEMP1. The second statement stores the same value in TEMP2 that is stored in TEMP1. Note that the value in TEMP1 is not lost; both TEMP1 and TEMP2 now contain the value -52.6.

Often we want to calculate a new value using arithmetic operations with other variables and constants. For instance, assume that the variable RADIUS has been assigned a value and we want to calculate the area of a circle having that radius. To do so, we must square the radius and then multiply by the value of pi. Table 2–2 shows the FORTRAN expressions for the basic arithmetic operations. Note that an asterisk (instead of a $\times$) represents multiplication; this avoids confusion because AXB (commonly used in algebra to indicate the product of A and B) represents a variable name in FORTRAN. Division and exponentiation also have different symbols that allow us to write these arithmetic operations on a single line.

EVALUATING AN ARITHMETIC EXPRESSION

Because several operations can be combined in one arithmetic expression, it is important to determine the priorities of the operations (the order in which the operations are performed). For instance, consider the following assignment statement that calculates the area of a circle:

```
AREA = PI*RADIUS**2
```

TABLE 2-3 Priorities of Arithmetic Operations

Priority	Operation
First	Parentheses
Second	Exponentiation
Third	Multiplication and division
Fourth	Addition and subtraction

If the exponentiation is performed first, we compute PI $\times$ (RADIUS)^2; if multiplication is performed first, we compute (PI $\times$ RADIUS)^2. Note that the two computations yield different results. The order of priorities for computations in FORTRAN is given in Table 2-3 and follows the standard algebraic priorities.

Operations in parentheses are performed first. When executing the previous FORTRAN statement, the RADIUS is first squared, then the result is multiplied by PI—correctly determining the area of the circle. Remember that we assume that both PI and RADIUS have been initialized. The following statements also correctly compute the area of the circle:

```
AREA = PI*RADIUS*RADIUS
```

or

```
AREA = 3.141593*RADIUS*RADIUS
```

If a minus sign precedes the first variable name in an expression, it is computed on the same priority level as subtraction. For example, $-$A**2 is computed as if it were $-$(A**2) $-$A*B is computed as if it were $-$(A*B); and $-$A+B is computed as if it were ($-$A)+B.

When two operations are on the same priority level, as in addition and subtraction, all operations except exponentiation are performed from left to right. Thus, B $-$ C $+$ D is evaluated as (B $-$ C) $+$ D. If two exponentiations occur sequentially in FORTRAN, as in A**B**C, they are evaluated right to left, as in A**(B**C). Thus, 2**3**2 is 2^9, or 512, as opposed to (2**3)**2, which is 8^2, or 64.

A more complex arrangement is represented by the following expression for one of the real roots of a quadratic equation:

$$X1 = \frac{-B + \sqrt{B^2 - 4AC}}{2A}$$

Recall that A, B, and C are coefficients of the quadratic equation ($AX^2 + BX + C = 0$). Because computers cannot divide by zero, we assume A is not equal to zero. The value of $X1$ can be computed in FORTRAN with the following statement, assuming that the variables A, B, and C have been initialized:

```
X1 = (-B + (B**2 - 4.0*A*C)**0.5)/(2.0*A)
```

To check the order of operations in a long expression, you should start with the operations inside parentheses; that is, find the operation done first, then second, and so on. The following diagram outlines this procedure, using braces to show the steps of operations. Beneath each brace is the value calculated in that step:

$$X1 = \underbrace{(-B}_{-B} + \underbrace{\overbrace{(B**2 - 4.0*A*C)}^{B^2-4AC}**0.5)}_{} / \underbrace{(2.0*A)}_{2A}$$

$$\underbrace{}_{-B+\sqrt{B^2-4AC}}$$

$$\frac{-B+\sqrt{B^2-4AC}}{2A}$$

As shown in the final brace, the desired value is computed by this expression.

Parentheses placement is important. If the outside set of parentheses in the numerator in the previous FORTRAN statement were omitted, our assignment statement would become

$$X1 = \underbrace{-B}_{-B} + \underbrace{\overbrace{(B**2 - 4.0*A*C)}^{B^2-4AC}**0.5}_{\sqrt{B^2-4AC}} / \underbrace{(2.0*A)}_{2A}$$

$$\underbrace{}_{\frac{\sqrt{B^2-4AC}}{2A}}$$

$$-B + \frac{\sqrt{B^2-4AC}}{2A}$$

As you can see, omission of the outside set of parentheses causes the wrong value to be calculated as a root of the original quadratic equation. Omission of a different set of parentheses would result in the following expression:

$$X1 = \underbrace{(-B + B**2 - 4.0*A*C**0.5)}_{-B+B^2-4A\sqrt{C}} / \underbrace{(2.0*A)}_{2A}$$

$$\frac{-B+B^2-4A\sqrt{C}}{2A}$$

Again, the wrong value would be calculated. If all parentheses were omitted, the expression would become

$$X1 = \underbrace{-B}_{-B} + \underbrace{B**2}_{B^2} - 4.0*A*\underbrace{C**0.5}_{\sqrt{C}} / 2.0*A$$

$$\underbrace{}_{\frac{4A\sqrt{C}A}{2}}$$

$$-B + B^2 - \frac{4A^2\sqrt{C}}{2}$$

Still another incorrect value would be computed.

Omitting necessary parentheses results in incorrect calculations. Using extra parentheses to emphasize the order of calculations is permissible even though

---

they may not be needed. It is advisable to insert extra parentheses in a statement if it makes the statement more readable.

You also may want to break a long statement into several smaller statements. Recall that the expression $B^2 - 4AC$ in the quadratic equation is called the discriminant. Both roots of the solution could be calculated with the following statements after initialization of A, B, and C:

```
DISCR = B**2 - 4.0*A*C
X1 = (-B + DISCR**0.5)/(2.0*A)
X2 = (-B - DISCR**0.5)/(2.0*A)
```

In the preceding statements we assume that the discriminant, DISCR, is positive, enabling us to obtain X1 and X2, the two real roots to the equation. If the discriminant were negative, an execution error would occur when we attempted to take the square root of the negative value. If the value of A were zero, we would get an execution error for attempting to divide by zero. In later chapters we learn techniques for handling these situations.

We often use variables as counters in our FORTRAN programs. We first initialize the counter to a certain value and later, under certain conditions, change it to another value. For example, a counter named COUNTR, which we assume was listed in an INTEGER statement, is incremented by 1:

```
COUNTR = COUNTR + 1
```

This statement may look invalid because, algebraically, COUNTR cannot be equal to COUNTR + 1. But remember, in FORTRAN, this statement means "COUNTR is assigned the value of COUNTR plus 1." Hence, if the old value of COUNTR is 0, the new value of COUNTR after executing this statement is 1.

TRUNCATION AND MIXED-MODE OPERATIONS

When an arithmetic operation is performed using two real numbers its intermediate result is a real value. For example, the circumference of a circle can be calculated as

```
CIRCUM = PI*DIAMTR
```

or

```
CIRCUM = 3.141593*DIAMTR
```

In both statements, we have multiplied two real values, giving a real result, which is then stored in the real variable CIRCUM.

Similarly, arithmetic operations between two integers yield an integer. For instance, if I and J represent two integers, and if I is less than or equal to J, then the number of integers in the interval I–J can be calculated with the following statement:

```
INTERV = J - I + 1
```

Thus, if I = 6 and J = 11, then INTERV will contain 6, the number of integers in the set {6, 7, 8, 9, 10, 11}.

Now consider the statement:

$$LENGTH = SIDE*3.5$$

Assume that SIDE represents a real value and that LENGTH represents an integer value. We know that the multiplication between the real value SIDE and the real constant 3.5 yields a real result. In this case, however, the real result is stored in an integer variable. When the computer stores a real number in an integer variable, it ignores the fractional portion and stores only the whole number portion of the real number; this loss is called *truncation*.

Other computations with integers also give unexpected results. Consider the following statement that computes the average, or mean, of two integers, N1 and N2:

$$MEAN = (N1 + N2)/2$$

If we assume that all the variables in the statement are integers, the result of the expression will be an integer. Thus, if $N1 = 2$ and $N2 = 4$, the mean value is the expected value, 3. But if $N1 = 2$ and $N2 = 3$, the result of the division of 5 by 2 will be 2 instead of 2.5 because the division involved two integers; hence, the intermediate result must be an integer. At first glance it might seem that we could solve this problem if we called the average by a real variable named AVE (instead of MEAN) and used this statement:

$$AVE = (N1 + N2)/2$$

Unfortunately, this cannot correct our answer. The result of integer arithmetic is still an integer; all we have done is move the integer result into a real variable. Thus, if $N1 = 2$ and $N2 = 3$, then $(N1 + N2)/2 = 2$ and $AVE = 2.0$, not 2.5. One way to correct this problem is to declare N1 and N2 to be real values and use the following statement to calculate the average:

$$AVE = (N1 + N2)/2.0$$

Note the difference between rounding and truncation. With rounding, the result is the integer closest in value to the real number. Truncation, however, causes any decimal portion to be dropped. If we divide the integer 15 by the integer 8, the truncated result is 1, the integer portion of 1.875.

The effects of truncation can also be seen in the following statement, which appears to calculate the square root of NUM:

$$ROOT = NUM**(1/2)$$

However, since $\frac{1}{2}$ is truncated to 0, we are really raising NUM to the zero power; ROOT will always contain the value 1.0, no matter what value is in NUM.

We have seen that an operation involving only real values yields a real result and an operation involving only integer values yields an integer result. FORTRAN also accepts a *mixed-mode* operation, which is an operation involving an integer value and a real value. The intermediate result is a real value. The final result depends on the type of variable used to store the result of the mixed-mode operation. Consider the following arithmetic statement for computing the perimeter of a square whose sides are real values:

$$\text{PERIM} = 4*\text{SIDE}$$

The preceding multiplication is a mixed-mode operation between the integer constant 4 and the real variable SIDE. The intermediate result is real and is correctly stored in the real result PERIM.

Using mixed mode, we can now correctly calculate the square root of the integer NUM, using this statement:

$$\text{ROOT} = \text{NUM}**0.5$$

The mixed-mode exponentiation yields a real result, which is stored in ROOT.

To compute the area of a square with real sides, we could use the mixed-mode expression

$$\text{AREA} = \text{SIDE}**2$$

or the real-mode expression

$$\text{AREA} = \text{SIDE}**2.0$$

The result in both cases is real; but in this case, the mixed-mode form is preferable. Exponentiation to an integer power is generally performed internally in the computer with a series of multiplications such as SIDE times SIDE. If an exponent is real, however, the operation is performed by the arithmetic logic unit using logarithms; SIDE**2.0 is actually computed as antilog(2.0 × log(SIDE)). Logarithms can introduce small errors into the calculations; although 5.0**2 is always 25.0, 5.0**2.0 is often computed as 24.99999. Also, note that $(-2.0)**2$ is a valid operation, but $(-2.0)**2.0$ is an invalid operation — the logarithm of a negative value does not exist, and an execution error occurs. As a general guide when raising numbers to an integer power, use an integer exponent, even though the base number is real.

Mixed-mode expressions may still lose accuracy through truncation if operations between integers are embedded in the expression. For instance, assume that we want to calculate the volume of a sphere with radius R, where R represents a real value. The volume is computed by multiplying 4/3 times pi, times the radius cubed. The following mixed-mode statement at first appears correct:

$$\text{VOLUM} = (4/3)*3.141593*R**3$$

The expression contains integer and real values, so the result will be a real value. However, the division of 4 by 3 yields the intermediate value of 1, not 1.333333; therefore, the final answer will be incorrect.

Because mixed-mode operations can sometimes give unexpected results, you should try to avoid writing arithmetic expressions that include them. The only time that a mixed-mode expression is desirable is in an exponentiation operation in which an integer is raised to a non-integer power or when a real value is raised to an integer power.

UNDERFLOW AND OVERFLOW

In a previous section we discussed magnitude limitations for the values stored in variables. Because the maximum and minimum values that can be stored in a variable depend on the computer system itself, a computation may yield a result that can be stored in one computer system but is too large to be stored in another. For example, suppose we execute the following assignment statements:

$$X = 0.25E20$$
$$Y = 0.10E30$$

If we assume that we are using a VAX computer (see Table 2–1), both of these variables are within the range of real values that we can store (the exponent range is −38 through 38). Suppose we now execute the following statement:

$$Z = X*Y$$

The numerical result of this multiplication is .025E50. Clearly this result is too large to store in a VAX computer. The error is not a syntax error; the statements themselves were valid FORTRAN 77 statements. The error is an execution error because it occurred during execution of the program. This error is called an exponent *overflow* error because the exponent of the result of an arithmetic operation was too large to store in the computer's memory.

Exponent *underflow* is a similar error caused by the exponent of the result of an arithmetic operation being too small to store in the computer's memory. If we were using a VAX computer, the following statements would generate an exponent underflow error because the value that is computed for C has an exponent smaller than −38:

$$A = 0.25E-20$$
$$B = 0.10E+20$$
$$C = A/B$$

If you get exponent underflow or overflow errors when you run your programs, you need to examine the magnitude of the values you are using. If you really need values whose exponents exceed the limits of your computer, the only solution is to switch to a computer that can handle a wider range of exponents. Most of the time, exponent underflow and overflow errors are caused by other errors in a program. For example, if variables are initialized to an incorrect value or the wrong arithmetic operation is specified, exponent underflow or overflow can occur — but the source of the problem is elsewhere. If you consider the limits on values that can be stored in a VAX, for example, you will see that it is an unusual problem whose answer is greater than 10 raised to the thirty-eighth power or is smaller than 10 raised to the negative thirty-eighth power.

SELF-TEST 2–2

This self-test allows you to check quickly to see if you have remembered some of the key points from Section 2–2. If you have

---

any problems with the exercises, you should reread this section. The solutions are included at the end of the text.

1. What value is stored in Y after the following statements are executed?

```
REAL   X1, X2, X3, Y
X1 = 5.0
X2 = 5.0
X3 = 0.5
Y = X1+X2/X1-X2/X3
```

2. What values are stored in the variables A and K after the following statements are executed?

```
REAL   A
INTEGER   I, J, K
I = 8
J = 3
A = I/J
K = I/J
```

3. What value is stored in T after the following statements are executed?

```
REAL   R, S, T
R = 4.0
S = 10.0
T = 1.0/(1.0/S)+(1.0/R)
```

2-3 INTRINSIC FUNCTIONS

Algorithms commonly require many simple operations such as computing the square root of a value, computing the absolute value of a number, or computing the sine of an angle. Because these operations occur so frequently, built-in computer functions called *intrinsic functions* are available to handle these routine computations. Instead of using the arithmetic expression X**0.5 to compute a square root, we can use the intrinsic function SQRT(X). Similarly, we can refer to the absolute value of B by ABS(B). A list of some commonly used intrinsic functions appears in Table 2–4, and a complete list of FORTRAN 77 intrinsic functions is contained in Appendix A, along with a brief description of each function.

The name of the function is followed by the input to the function, also called the *argument* of the function, which is enclosed in parentheses. This argument can be a constant, variable, or expression. For example, suppose that we want to compute the cosine of the variable ANGLE and store the result in another variable COSINE. From Table 2–4, we see that the cosine function COS assumes that its argument is in radians. If the value in ANGLE is in degrees, we must change the degrees to radians (1 degree = pi/180 radians) and then compute the cosine. The following statement performs the degree-to-radian conversion within the function argument:

```
COSINE = COS(ANGLE*(3.141593/180.0))
```

TABLE 2-4 Common Intrinsic Functions

FUNCTION NAME AND ARGUMENT	FUNCTION VALUE	COMMENT
SQRT(X)	$\sqrt{X}$	Square root of X
ABS(X)	$|X|$	Absolute value of X
SIN(X)	Sine of angle X	X must be in radians
COS(X)	Cosine of angle X	X must be in radians
TAN(X)	Tangent of angle X	X must be in radians
EXP(X)	e^x	e raised to the X power
LOG(X)	$\log_e X$	Natural log of X
LOG10(X)	$\log_{10} X$	Common log of X
INT(X)	Integer part of X	Converts a real value to an integer value
REAL(I)	Real value of I	Converts an integer value to a real value
MOD(I,J)	Integer remainder of I/J	Remainder or modulo function

The inside set of parentheses is not required but serves to emphasize the conversion factor.

The REAL and INT functions may be used to avoid undesirable mixed-mode arithmetic expressions by explicitly converting variable types. For example, if we are computing the average of a group of real values, we need to divide the real sum of the values by the number of values. We can convert the integer number of values into a real value for the division using the REAL function, as shown in the following statement:

```
AVERG = SUM/REAL(N)
```

If the values were integers, then the sum would also be an integer. We would still probably want the average to be represented by a real value, which could be specified by

```
AVERG = REAL(SUM)/REAL(N)
```

It is also acceptable to use one intrinsic function as the argument of another. For example, we can compute the natural logarithm of the absolute value of X with the following statement:

```
XLOG = LOG(ABS(X))
```

When using one function as an argument for another, be sure to enclose the argument of each function in its own set of parentheses. This *nesting* of functions is also called *composition* of functions.

It is important to observe that an intrinsic function and its argument represent a value. This value can be used in other computations or stored in other memory locations. It does not of itself, however, represent a memory location. A function can never appear on the left-hand side of an equal sign; it must always be on the right-hand side. For example, to compute the square root of X, we can use the statement

$$ROOT = SQRT(X)$$

but we cannot reverse the order and begin the statement with SQRT(X) because SQRT(X) is not a variable name. The intrinsic square root function could be used in the computation of a root of the quadratic equation used in a previous example, as shown:

$$X1 = (-B + SQRT(B**2 - 4.0*A*C))/(2.0*A)$$

The type of value returned by a function is specified in Appendix A. Many of these intrinsic functions are *generic functions*, which means that the value returned is the same type as the input argument. The absolute value function ABS is a generic function. If X is an integer, then ABS(X) is also an integer; if X is a real value, then ABS(X) is also a real value. Some functions specify the type of input and output required. IABS is a function that requires an integer input and returns an integer absolute value from the function. If K is an integer, then ABS(K) and IABS(K) return the same value. Appendix A contains all forms of the intrinsic functions and identifies all generic functions.

SELF-TEST 2–3

This self-test allows you to check quickly to see if you have remembered some of the key points from Section 2–2 and Section 2–3. If you have any problems with the exercises, you should reread these sections. The solutions are included at the end of the text.

In problems 1–6, convert the equations into FORTRAN assignment statements. Assume all variables represent real values.

1. Slope of a straight line between two points:

$$SLOPE = \frac{Y2 - Y1}{X2 - X1}$$

2. Correction factor in pressure calculation:

$$FACTOR = 1 + \frac{B}{V} + \frac{C}{V^2}$$

3. Coefficient of friction between tires and pavement:

$$FRICTION = \frac{V^2}{30 \cdot S}$$

4. Distance of the center of gravity from a reference plane in a hollow cylinder sector:

$$\text{CENTER} = \frac{38.1972(R^3 - S^3)\sin A}{(R^2 - S^2)A} \qquad \text{where } A \text{ is in radians}$$

5. Pressure loss from pipe friction:

$$\text{LOSS} = F \cdot P \cdot \frac{L}{D} \cdot \frac{V^2}{2}$$

6. Equivalent resistance of a parallel circuit:

$$\text{REQ} = \frac{1}{\dfrac{1}{X1} + \dfrac{1}{X2} + \dfrac{1}{X3} + \dfrac{1}{X4}}$$

In problems 7–12, convert the FORTRAN statements into algebraic form.

7. Uniformly accelerated motion:

```
MOTION = SQRT(VI*VI + 2.0*A*X)
```

8. Electrical oscillation frequency:

```
FREQ = 1.0/SQRT((2.0*3.14159)*(1.0/XL*C))
```

9. Range for a projectile:

```
RANGE = 2.0*VI*VI*SIN(B)*COS(B)/G
```

10. Length contraction:

```
LENGTH = LI*SQRT(1.0 - (V/C)*(V/C))
```

11. Mass energy:

```
C = 2.99E10
ENERGY = 1.6747E-24*C*C
```

12. Volume of a fillet ring:

```
PI = 3.14159
VOLUME = 2.0*PI*X*X*((1.0-PI/4.0)*Y-(0.8333-PI/4.0)*X)
```

2–4 SIMPLE INPUT AND OUTPUT

The input and output of information are fundamental parts of a computer program. FORTRAN has two types of statements that allow us to perform these operations. *List-directed* input/output statements are easy to use but give us little control over the exact spacing used in the input and output lines. *Formatted* input/output, although more involved, allows us to control the input and output forms with greater detail. In this section, we present list-directed input/output and simple formatted output. For our example programs, we use list-directed input statements and formatted output statements—this allows us to be flexible about the form we use for information that we enter, and at the same time allows us to be specific about the form used to print the output from our program. Refer to Chapter 4 for more information on input and output statements.

LIST-DIRECTED OUTPUT

If we wish to print the value stored in a variable, it is necessary to tell the computer the variable's name. The computer can then access the memory location and print its contents. Generally, time-sharing output is displayed on the terminal screen and batch output is either displayed on the terminal screen or printed on computer paper. The general form of the list-directed PRINT statement is

PRINT*, *expression list*

The expressions in the list must be separated by commas. The corresponding values are printed in the order in which they are listed in the PRINT statement. The output from each PRINT statement begins on a new line.

In our examples, computer output is shown inside a terminal screen, as illustrated in Example 2–1.

EXAMPLE 2-1   WEIGHT and VOL

Print the stored values of the variables WEIGHT and VOL.

Solution

COMPUTER MEMORY

WEIGHT   35000

VOL   3.15

FORTRAN STATEMENT

```
PRINT*, WEIGHT, VOL
```

COMPUTER OUTPUT

```
35000   3.15000
```

The number of decimal positions printed for real values and the spacing between items varies depending on the compiler used. If a value to be printed is very large or very small, many compilers automatically print the value in exponential notation instead of in decimal form, as shown in Example 2–2.

EXAMPLE 2-2 Density Value

Print the value stored in the variable DENSTY.

Solution

COMPUTER MEMORY

DENSTY $\boxed{0.0000156}$

FORTRAN STATEMENT

        PRINT*, DENSTY

COMPUTER OUTPUT

    0.156000E-04

Descriptive information (sometimes called literal information or *literals*) may also be included in the expression list by enclosing the information in single quotation marks or apostrophes. This descriptive information is then printed on the output line along with the values of any variables also in the PRINT statement.

EXAMPLE 2-3 Literal and Variable Information

Print the variable RATE with a literal that identifies the value as representing a flow rate in gallons per second.

Solution

COMPUTER MEMORY

RATE $\boxed{0.065}$

FORTRAN STATEMENT

    PRINT*, 'FLOW RATE IS', RATE, 'GALLONS PER SECOND'

COMPUTER OUTPUT

    FLOW RATE IS 0.0650000 GALLONS PER SECOND

EXAMPLE 2-4 Centrifuge Information

Print the values stored in the variables RPM and FORCE using descriptive headings.

Solution

Computer Memory

RPM | 37.5

FORCE | 6.75

FORTRAN Statements

```
PRINT*, 'CENTRIFUGE RPM AND FORCE'
PRINT*, RPM, FORCE
```

Computer Output

```
CENTRIFUGE RPM AND FORCE
37.5000   6.75000
```

LIST-DIRECTED INPUT

We frequently want to read information with our programs. The general form of a list-directed READ statement is

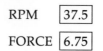

READ*, *variable list*

The variable names in the list must be separated by commas. The variables receive new values in the order in which they are listed in the READ statement. These values must agree in type (integer or real) with the variables in the list. If the program is run in a time-sharing mode, the system will wait for you to enter the appropriate data values when the READ statement is executed. If more than one value is being read by the statement, the data values can be separated by commas or blanks. For batch systems, the data lines follow the complete program. Batch processing usually requires extra information, called *job control information,* with your program. Typically, this extra information requires additional information lines before your program, between your program and its data, and after your program. A READ statement will read as many lines as needed to find new values for the variables in its list. Also, each READ statement begins reading from a new line.

EXAMPLE 2-5   Capacitor Charge

Read the beginning and ending charges for a capacitor.

Solution 1

This solution uses one READ statement; thus both values can be entered on the same line.

FORTRAN STATEMENT

```
READ*, BEGIN, ENDING
```

DATA LINE

```
186.93, 386.21
```

COMPUTER MEMORY

BEGIN | 186.93 |

ENDING | 386.21 |

The data values in this example could also have been entered on separate lines since the READ statement will read as many lines as needed to find values for the variables in its list.

Solution 2

This solution uses two READ statements; thus the values must be entered on different lines.

FORTRAN STATEMENTS

```
READ*, BEGIN
READ*, ENDING
```

DATA LINES

```
186.93
386.21
```

COMPUTER MEMORY

BEGIN | 186.93 |

ENDING | 386.21 |

FORMATTED OUTPUT

To specify the form in which data values are printed and where on the output line they are printed requires formatted statements. The general form of a formatted PRINT statement is

```
PRINT  k, expression list
```

The expression list designates the memory locations whose contents will be printed or arithmetic expressions whose values will be printed. The list of expressions also determines the order in which the values will be printed. The reference k refers to a FORMAT statement, which will specify the spacing to be used in printing the information. The FORMAT statement has a statement label k. A sample PRINT and FORMAT combination is

```
      PRINT 5, TIME, DISTNC
    5 FORMAT (1X,F5.1,2X,F7.2)
```

Recall that statement labels are entered in columns 1 through 5.

The general form of the FORMAT statement is

> *k* **FORMAT** *(specification list)*

The specification list tells the computer both the vertical and horizontal spacing to be used when printing the output information. The vertical spacing options include printing on the top of a new page (if the output is being printed on paper), the next line (single spacing), double spacing, and no spacing. Horizontal spacing includes indicating how many digits will be used for each value, how many blanks will be between numbers, and how many values are to be printed per line.

To understand the specifications used to describe the vertical and horizontal spacing, we must first examine the output from a line printer or terminal, the most common output devices. Other forms of output have similar characteristics.

The line printer prints on computer paper that is on a perforated, continuous roll so it is easy to separate the pages. A common size computer paper page is 11 inches by 14 7/8 inches. Typically, 55 to 75 lines of information can be printed per page, and each line can contain up to 132 characters. In our discussion of printed output, we assume that an output line contains 132 characters. Most line printers print either 6 lines per inch or 8 lines per inch. The PRINT/FORMAT combination specifically describes where each line is to be printed on the page (vertical spacing) and which of the 132 possible positions will contain data (horizontal spacing).

The computer uses the specification list to construct each output line internally in memory before actually printing the line. This internal memory region, which contains 133 characters, is called a *buffer*. The buffer is automatically filled with blanks before it is used to construct a line of output. The first character of the buffer is called the *carriage control character*; it determines the vertical spacing for the line. The remaining 132 characters represent the line to be printed.

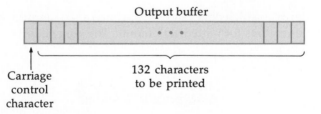

Output buffer

Carriage control character

132 characters to be printed

The following list shows some of the valid carriage control characters and the vertical spacing they generate. When needed for clarity in either FORMAT statements or buffer contents, a blank is indicated by the character b placed one-half space below the regular line.

CARRIAGE CONTROL CHARACTER	VERTICAL SPACING
1	New page
blank	Single spacing
0	Double spacing
+	No vertical spacing

Double spacing causes one line to be skipped before the current line of output is printed. When a plus sign is in the carriage control, no spacing occurs and the next line of information will print over the last line printed. On most computers, an invalid carriage control character causes single spacing.

When a terminal is used as the output device, the width of the line may be less than 132 positions. Although terminal systems do not always use carriage control, the internal buffer will contain one character more than the line width if carriage control applies. Because a terminal does not have the same capabilities as a line printer for spacing a new page, a 1 in the carriage control usually becomes an invalid control character and causes single spacing. If the terminal system does not use carriage control, then the entire contents of the buffer, including the carriage control character, will appear on the terminal screen.

We will now examine four FORMAT specifications that describe how to fill the output buffer. Commas are used to separate specifications in the FORMAT statement. Additional FORMAT specifications are included in Chapter 4.

Literal Specification The literal specification allows us to put characters directly into the buffer. The characters must be enclosed in single quotation marks or apostrophes. These characters can represent the carriage control character or the characters in a literal. The following examples illustrate use of the literal specification in FORMAT statements.

EXAMPLE 2-6 Title Heading

Print the title heading TEST RESULTS on the top of a new page, *left-justified* (that is, no blanks to the left of the heading).

Solution

FORTRAN STATEMENTS

```
      PRINT 4
    4 FORMAT ('1','TEST RESULTS')
```

BUFFER CONTENTS

```
1TEST RESULTS
```

```
        111
123456789012
```

```
╭─────────────────╮
│  TEST RESULTS   │
╰─────────────────╯
```

The buffer is filled according to the FORMAT. No variable names were listed on the PRINT statement; hence, no values were printed. The literal specifications cause the characters 1TEST RESULTS to be put in the buffer, beginning with the first position in the buffer. After filling the buffer, as instructed by the FORMAT, the carriage control is examined to determine vertical spacing. The character 1 in the carriage control position tells the computer to begin a new page. The rest of the buffer, 132 positions, is then printed. Notice that the carriage control character is not printed. The row of small numbers above the computer output shows the specific column of the output line: The first T is in column 1, the second T is in column 4, and the third T is in column 11.

EXAMPLE 2-7 Column Headings

Double space from the last line printed and print column headings 1988 kWh and 1989 kWh, with no blanks on the left-hand side of the line and seven blanks between the two column headings.

Correct Solution

FORTRAN Statements

```
      PRINT 3
    3 FORMAT ('0','1988 kWh        1989 kWh')
```

Buffer Contents

```
┌─────────────────────────────────┐
│01988 kWh        1989 kWh         │
└─────────────────────────────────┘
```

Computer Output

```
          11111111112222
12345678901234567890123
```

```
╭─────────────────────────────╮
│ 1988 kWh        1989 kWh     │
╰─────────────────────────────╯
```

The line shown is printed after double spacing from the previous line of output.

Incorrect Solution

FORTRAN Statements

```
        PRINT 3
     3 FORMAT ('1988 kWh         1989 kWh')
```

Buffer Contents

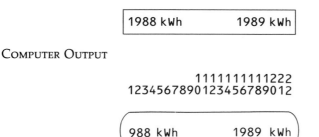

Computer Output

```
                1111111111222
     12345678901234567890 12

   988 kWh         1989 kWh
```

In this example we forgot to specify the carriage control. However, the computer does not forget: The first position of the buffer contains a 1, which indicates spacing to a new page. The rest of the buffer is then printed.

X Specification The X specification will insert blanks into the buffer. Its general form is nX, where n represents the number of blanks to be inserted in the buffer. An example using both the X specification and the literal specification follows.

EXAMPLE 2–8   Centered Heading

Print the heading EXPERIMENT NO. 1 centered at the top of a new page.

Solution

Because an output line contains 132 characters, to center the heading we determine the number of characters in the heading (16), subtract that from 132 (132 − 16 = 116), and divide that by 2 to put one-half the blanks in front of the heading (116/2 = 58).

FORTRAN Statements

```
        PRINT 35
    35 FORMAT ('1',58X,'EXPERIMENT NO. 1')
```

Buffer Contents

58 blanks

```
5666666666677777
9012345678901234
```

EXPERIMENT NO. 1

This heading could have been printed without the 58X specification by using a literal specification of 1 followed by a literal of 58 blanks and EXPERIMENT NO. 1.

I Specification The literal specification and the X specification allow us to specify carriage control and to print headings — they cannot, however, be used to print variable values. We will now examine a specification that prints the contents of integer variables: The specification form is Iw, where w represents the number of positions (width) to be assigned in the buffer for printing the value of an integer variable. The value is always *right-justified* (no blanks to the right of the value) in those positions in the buffer. Extra positions on the left are filled with blanks. Thus, if the value 16 is printed with an I4 specification, the four positions contain two blanks followed by 16. If there are not enough positions to print the value, including a minus sign if the value is negative, the positions are filled with asterisks. Hence, if we print the value 132 or − 14 with an I2 specification, the two positions are filled with asterisks. It is important to recognize that the asterisks do not necessarily indicate that there is an error in the value; instead, the asterisks may indicate that you need to assign a larger width in the corresponding I specification.

More than one variable name is often listed in the PRINT statement. When interpreting a PRINT/FORMAT combination, the compiler will match the first variable name to the first specification for printing values, and so on. Therefore, there should be the same number of specifications for printing values as there are variables on the PRINT statement list. (In Chapter 4 we will explain what happens if the number of specifications does not match the number of variables.)

EXAMPLE 2-9 Integer Values

Print the values of the integer variables SUM, MEAN, and N on the same line, single spaced from the previous line.

Solution

COMPUTER MEMORY

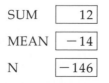

SUM	12
MEAN	− 14
N	− 146

FORTRAN Statements

```
        PRINT 30, SUM, MEAN, N
     30 FORMAT (1X,I3,2X,I2,2X,I4)
```

Buffer Contents

$$bb\,^{12}bb\,^{**}bb\,^{-146}$$

Computer Output

```
          11111
   1234567890123
```

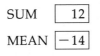

```
   12   **   -146
```

The computer will print SUM with an I3 specification, MEAN with an I2 specification, and N with an I4 specification. The value of SUM is 12, so the three corresponding positions contain a blank followed by the number 12. The value of MEAN, -14, requires at least three positions, so the two specified positions are filled with asterisks. The value of N fills all four allotted positions. The carriage control character is a blank; thus the line of output is single spaced from the previous line.

EXAMPLE 2-10   Literal and Variable Information

On separate lines, print the values of MEAN and SUM, along with an indication of the name of each of the integer variables.

Solution

Computer Memory

SUM | 12 |

MEAN | -14 |

FORTRAN Statements

```
        PRINT 2, MEAN
     2 FORMAT (1X,'MEAN = ',I4)
        PRINT 3, SUM
     3 FORMAT (1X,'SUM = ',I4)
```

Buffer Contents

$$b\,^{MEAN}b\,^{=}bb\,^{-14}$$

$$b\,^{SUM}b\,^{=}bbb\,^{12}$$

```
                    11
        12345678901
```

```
    ⎛  MEAN  =   -14  ⎞
    ⎝  SUM   =    12  ⎠
```

F Specification The F specification is used to print real numbers in a decimal form (for example, 36.21) as opposed to an exponential form (for example, 0.3621E+02). The general form for an F specification is Fw.d, where w represents the total width (number of positions) to be used in printing the real value and d represents the number of those positions that will represent decimal positions to the right of the decimal point. For example, the minimum size F specification that can be used to print 34.186 is F6.3, a total of six positions counting the decimal point with three positions to the right of the decimal point. Before the value is inserted in the buffer, the decimal point is located in the specified position; the form for F6.3 is thus

$$\text{decimal portion} = d$$
$$\underbrace{XX.\overbrace{XXX}}$$
$$\text{total width} = w$$

If the value to be printed has fewer than d decimal positions, zeros are inserted on the right-hand side of the decimal point. Thus, if the value 21.6 is printed with an F6.3 specification, the output is 21.600. If the value to be printed has more than d decimal positions, only d decimal positions are printed, dropping the rest. Thus, if the value 21.86342 is printed with an F6.3 specification, the output is 21.863. Many compilers will round to the last decimal position printed; in these cases, the value 18.98662 is printed with an F6.3 specification and the output would be 18.987.

If the integer portion of a real value requires fewer positions than allotted in the F specification, the extra positions on the left-hand side of the decimal point are filled with blanks. Thus, if the value 3.123 is printed with an F6.3 specification, the output is a blank followed by 3.123. If the integer portion of a real value, including the minus sign if the value is negative, requires more positions than allotted in the F specification, the entire field is filled with asterisks. Thus, if the value 312.6 is printed with an F6.3 specification, the output is ******.

If a value is between -1 and $+1$, positions must usually be allowed for both a leading zero to the left of the decimal point and a minus sign if the value is negative. Thus, the smallest F specification that could be used to print $-.127$ is F6.3, which would be printed as -0.127. If a smaller specification width were used, all the positions would be filled with asterisks.

EXAMPLE 2-11 Angle THETA

Print the value of an angle called THETA. Construct the Greek symbol for theta using a zero with a dash printed over it. The output should be in this form:

$$\theta = XX.XX$$

Solution

COMPUTER MEMORY

THETA | 3.184 |

FORTRAN STATEMENTS

```
      PRINT 1
    1 FORMAT (1X,'0')
      PRINT 2, THETA
    2 FORMAT ('+','- = ',F5.2)
```

BUFFER CONTENTS

| b⁰ |
| +-b=bb3.18 |

COMPUTER OUTPUT

123456789

(θ =   3.18)

The first PRINT statement printed a zero in the first position of the output line after single spacing from the previous line. The second PRINT statement had a plus sign in the carriage control, which caused no vertical spacing. The dash character is therefore printed on top of the character zero, giving the Greek symbol theta. The value of the variable THETA is printed on the same line.

EXAMPLE 2-12 Sine and Cosine Computation

Print the values of the sine and cosine of the angle THETA. Assume that THETA is in radians. Use descriptive literals.

Solution

THETA $\boxed{1.26}$

FORTRAN STATEMENTS

```
   PRINT 1, THETA, SIN(THETA)
 1 FORMAT (1X,'THE SINE OF ',F5.2,' RADIANS = ',F4.2)
   PRINT 2, THETA, COS(THETA)
 2 FORMAT (1X,'THE COSINE OF ',F5.2,' RADIANS = ',F4.2)
```

BUFFER CONTENTS

```
 b THE b SINE b OF bb 1.26 b RADIANS b = b 0.95

 b THE b COSINE b OF bb 1.26 b RADIANS b = b 0.31
```

COMPUTER OUTPUT

```
          1111111111222222222233333
 12345678901234567890123456789012 34
```

```
 THE SINE OF   1.26 RADIANS = 0.95
 THE COSINE OF   1.26 RADIANS = 0.31
```

Suppose that the value of THETA was 1.78 radians. Then the computer output for this set of FORTRAN statements would be:

COMPUTER OUTPUT

```
          1111111111222222222233333
 12345678901234567890123456789012 34
```

```
 THE SINE OF   1.78 RADIANS = 0.98
 THE COSINE OF   1.78 RADIANS = ****
```

The asterisks were printed instead of the correct value of -0.21 because the correct value requires a total of five positions instead of the four allotted with the specification F4.2. In order to have a solution that will work for all possible values of the sine and cosine functions, we should use an F5.2 format specification in both formats, as shown below:

```
   PRINT 1, THETA, SIN(THETA)
 1 FORMAT (1X,'THE SINE OF ',F5.2,' RADIANS = ',F5.2)
   PRINT 2, THETA, COS(THETA)
 2 FORMAT (1X,'THE COSINE OF ',F5.2,' RADIANS = ',F5.2)
```

E Specification Real numbers may be printed in an exponential form with the E specification. This specification is primarily used for very small values, or very large values, or when you are uncertain of the magnitude of a number. If you use an F format that is too small for a value, the output field will be filled with asterisks. In contrast, a real number will always fit in an E specification field.

The general format for an E specification is Ew.d. The w again represents the total width or number of positions to be used in printing the value. The d represents the number of positions to the right of the decimal point, assuming that the value is in exponential form, with the decimal point to the left of the first non-zero digit. The framework for printing a real value in an exponential specification with three decimal places is:

$$\text{decimal portion} = d$$
$$\overbrace{\underbrace{SO.\overbrace{XXX}ESXX}_{\text{total width} = w}}$$

The symbol S indicates that positions must be reserved for both the sign of the value and the sign of the exponent in case they are negative. Note that with all the extra positions, the total width becomes ten positions. Three of the ten positions are the decimal positions and the other seven are positions that are always needed for an E format. Thus, the total width of an E specification must be at least $d + 7$; otherwise asterisks will be printed. The above specification is then E10.3.

If there are more decimal positions in the specification than are in the exponential form of the value, the extra decimal positions are filled on the right with zeros.

If the total width of the E specification is more than 7 plus the decimal positions, the extra positions appear as blanks on the left side of the value.

EXAMPLE 2-13   TIME in an Exponential Form

Print the value of TIME in an exponential form with four decimal positions.

Solution 1

COMPUTER MEMORY

$$\text{TIME} \quad \boxed{-0.00125}$$

FORTRAN STATEMENTS

```
          PRINT 10, TIME
       10 FORMAT (1X,'TIME = ',E11.4)
```

BUFFER CONTENTS

$$\boxed{{}_b\text{TIME}_b={}_b-0.1250E-02}$$

```
                  111111111
         123456789012345678
```

```
┌─────────────────────────────┐
│  TIME = -0.1250E-02         │
└─────────────────────────────┘
```

Solution 2

COMPUTER MEMORY

TIME │ −0.00125 │

FORTRAN STATEMENTS

```
           PRINT 15, TIME
        15 FORMAT (1X,'TIME = ',E13.4)
```

BUFFER CONTENTS

```
┌──────────────────────────────────────┐
│  TIME =    -0.1250E-02                │
│ b    b bbb                            │
└──────────────────────────────────────┘
```

COMPUTER OUTPUT

```
              11111111112
         12345678901234567890
```

```
┌─────────────────────────────┐
│  TIME =    -0.1250E-02      │
└─────────────────────────────┘
```

Both of these solutions use an exponential format, but the second solution will place two additional blanks after the equal sign.

SELF-TEST 2−4

This self-test allows you to check quickly to see if you have remembered some of the key points from Section 2−4. If you have any problems with the exercises, you should reread this section. The solutions are included at the end of the text.

1. What is printed by the following statements? Show the exact location of any blanks.

```
        INTEGER  SECNDS
        REAL  DIST
        SECNDS = 23
        DIST = 57.829
        PRINT 5, DIST, SECNDS
      5 FORMAT (1X,F7.4,2X,I3)
```

2. What is printed by the following statements? Show the exact location of any blanks.

```
        REAL  DIST, VEL
        DIST = 15.68323
        VEL = 0.0270043
        PRINT 5, DIST
      5 FORMAT (1X,'DISTANCE = ',F7.4)
        PRINT 6, VEL
      6 FORMAT (1X,'VELOCITY = ',E10.2)
```

2-5 COMPLETE PROGRAMS

Only one additional statement is required to write complete FORTRAN programs. This statement, the END statement, identifies the physical end of our FORTRAN program for the compiler. The compiler stops translating statements when it reaches the END statement. Every FORTRAN program must end with the END statement, whose general form is

> **END**

Two other simple statements often appear in FORTRAN programs; they are optional, but are useful in documenting a program. The PROGRAM statement clearly identifies the beginning of a program and assigns the program name. The general form of this statement is

> **PROGRAM**   *program name*

Like a variable name, the program name can be one to six characters, begins with a letter, and contains only letters and digits. Some example PROGRAM statements are

    PROGRAM   TEST

    PROGRAM   COMPUT

    PROGRAM   SORT2

You may not use a variable in your program that has the same name as the program name.

The other optional, though useful, statement is the STOP statement, which signals the computer to terminate execution of the program. The END statement also serves this purpose but can only appear once, at the physical end of the program. The STOP statement can appear anywhere in the program that makes sense, and it can appear as often as necessary. For example, certain data values may not be valid, and we may want to stop executing the program if they occur. The general form of the STOP statement is

A program may use both a STOP and an END at the end of the program, although the STOP is not necessary if it is followed immediately by the END.

EXAMPLE 2-14 Complete Program to Convert Kilowatt-Hours to Joules

Write a program to convert an amount in kWh (kilowatt-hours) to joules. The amount in kWh is to be entered from the terminal. The output should be the number read in kWh and the converted value in joules. (Use the following conversion factor: joules = 3.6E+06 × kWh)

Solution

The steps in solving this problem are straightforward, but we still follow the algorithm development phases given in Chapter 1. We first decompose the problem solution into a series of steps, yielding the following:

DECOMPOSITION

Read amount in kilowatt-hours.
Convert amount to joules.
Print both amounts.

These steps are now written in more English-like phrases and some detail of the computation is included. We discuss the decomposition and pseudocode steps in detail in Chapter 3.

REFINEMENT IN PSEUDOCODE

CONVRT: Read kilowatt-hours.
$\qquad$ joules ← 3.6E+06 × kilowatt-hours.
$\qquad$ Print kilowatt-hours, joules.

FORTRAN PROGRAM

```
*-------------------------------------------------------*
      PROGRAM CONVRT
*
*  This program converts kilowatt-hours to joules.
*
      REAL  KWH, JOULES
*
      PRINT*, 'ENTER ENERGY IN KILOWATT-HOURS'
      READ*, KWH
      JOULES = 3.6E+06*KWH
      PRINT 5, KWH, JOULES
    5 FORMAT (1X,F6.2,' KILOWATT-HOURS = ',E9.2,' JOULES')
      END
*-------------------------------------------------------*
```

The following computer output illustrates a sample run of the program:

```
ENTER ENERGY IN KILOWATT-HOURS
5.5
    5.50 KILOWATT-HOURS = 0.20E+08 JOULES
```

Even though this program is simple, it illustrates some of the structure and style we will use in our programs throughout the text.

1. We will mark the beginning and end of each program with a comment line containing a series of dashes.
2. A brief discussion of the purpose of the program will follow the PROGRAM statement.
3. This discussion will be followed by specification statements to define the type of all variables used in the program. Even variables whose type matches the implicit type of their names will be included for documentation.
4. Any statement number will be right-justified within the group of columns 1 through 5.

In the program in Example 2–14, we printed a message to the user that specified the input that the program was expecting. After converting the value in kilowatt-hours to joules, we printed the value of kilowatt-hours along with the converted value in joules. This interaction between the program and the user resembles a conversation and is called *conversational computing*. Conversational computing is an effective technique and will be used in many of our example programs. Note that conversational computing is useful in time-sharing systems because both the input and the output information are displayed on the same screen. Conversational computing is not applicable to a batch system because the input information must be included along with the program.

2–6 APPLICATION—BACTERIA GROWTH (Biology)

A biology laboratory experiment involves the analysis of a strain of bacteria. Because the growth of bacteria in the colony can be modeled with an exponential equation, you are going to write a computer program to predict how many bacteria will be in the colony after a specified amount of time. Suppose that, for this type of bacteria, the equation to predict growth is

$$y_{new} = y_{old}e^{1.386t}$$

where y_{new} is the new number of bacteria in the colony, y_{old} is the initial number of bacteria in the colony, and t is the elapsed time in hours. Thus, when $t = 0$, we have

$$y_{new} = y_{old}e^{1.386 \cdot 0} = y_{old}$$

PROBLEM STATEMENT

Using the equation

$$y_{new} = y_{old}e^{1.386t}$$

predict the number of bacteria (y_{new}) in a bacteria colony given the initial number in the colony (y_{old}) and the time elapsed (t) in hours.

INPUT/OUTPUT DESCRIPTION

The input will be two values: the initial number of bacteria and the time elapsed. The output will be the number of bacteria in the colony after the elapsed time.

HAND EXAMPLE

You will need your calculator for these calculations. For $t = 1$ hour and $y_{old} = 1$ bacterium, the new colony contains

$$y_{new} = 1 * e^{1.386 \cdot 1} = 4.00$$

After 6 hours, the size of the colony is

$$y_{new} = 1 * e^{1.386 \cdot 6} = 4088.77$$

If we start with 2 bacteria, after 6 hours the size of the colony is

$$y_{new} = 2 * e^{1.386 \cdot 6} = 8177.54$$

ALGORITHM DEVELOPMENT

DECOMPOSITION

Read y_{old}, t.
Compute y_{new}.
Print y_{old}, t, y_{new}.

REFINEMENT IN PSEUDOCODE

GROWTH: Read y_{old}, t
    $y_{new} \leftarrow y_{old}e^{1.386t}$
    Print y_{old}, t, y_{new}

FORTRAN Program

```
*--------------------------------------------------------------*
      PROGRAM   GROWTH
*
*  This program predicts bacteria growth.
*
      REAL  YOLD, YNEW, TIME
*
      PRINT*, 'ENTER INITIAL POPULATION'
      READ*, YOLD
      PRINT*, 'ENTER TIME ELAPSED IN HOURS'
      READ*, TIME
      YNEW = YOLD*EXP(1.386*TIME)
      PRINT 10, YOLD
   10 FORMAT (1X,'INITIAL POPULATION = ',F9.4)
      PRINT 20, TIME
   20 FORMAT (1X,'TIME ELAPSED (HOURS) = ',F9.4)
      PRINT 30, YNEW
   30 FORMAT (1X,'PREDICTED POPULATION = ',F9.4)
      END
*--------------------------------------------------------------*
```

TESTING

The program output using data from one of our longhand examples is

```
ENTER INITIAL POPULATION
1.0
ENTER TIME ELAPSED IN HOURS
6.0
INITIAL POPULATION =     1.0000
TIME ELAPSED (HOURS) =     6.0000
PREDICTED POPULATION = 4088.7722
```

You should try using other values in the program to see if the results appear reasonable. Very large values of TIME will result in an overflow error. Negative values of TIME represent population decreases; but if the population falls below 1, the model is no longer applicable.

2–7   APPLICATION — CARBON DATING
(Archeology)

Carbon dating is a method for estimating the age of organic substances such as shells, seeds, and wooden artifacts. The technique compares the amount of carbon 14, a radioactive carbon, contained in the remains of the substance with the amount of carbon 14 that would have been in the object's environment at the time it was alive. The age of the cave paintings in Lascaux, France, has been estimated at 15,500 years using this technique.

Assume that you are working as an assistant to an archeologist on Saturdays. Artifacts from a recent excavation have been sent to a laboratory for carbon analysis. The lab will determine the proportion of carbon that remains in the artifact. The archeologist has shown you the following equation that gives the estimated age of the artifact in years:

$$age = \frac{-\log_e(\text{carbon 14 proportion remaining})}{0.0001216}$$

Recall that $\log_e X$ is the natural logarithm of the value X.

The archeologist would like you to write a FORTRAN program that will read the proportion of carbon 14 remaining in an artifact and then compute and print its estimated age.

PROBLEM STATEMENT

Write a program to read the proportion of carbon 14 remaining in an artifact, then compute and print its estimated age.

INPUT/OUTPUT DESCRIPTION

The input will be a real number that represents the proportion of carbon left in the artifact. The output will be a number that estimates in years the age of the artifact.

HAND EXAMPLE

Suppose that no carbon 14 has decayed; then the carbon proportion is 1.0, and the estimated age is

$$age = \frac{-\log_e(1.0)}{0.0001216} = \frac{0}{0.0001216} = 0$$

This age makes sense because the artifact must be relatively young if no carbon 14 decay has occurred.

Let's assume now that one-half of the carbon has decayed. Thus, we will use 0.5 as the proportion of carbon left and see how this affects the formula:

$$age = \frac{-\log_e(0.5)}{0.0001216} = 5700.2 \text{ years}$$

From a reference book we learn that the half-life of carbon 14 is 5700 years, so our equation works pretty well!

ALGORITHM DEVELOPMENT

DECOMPOSITION

Read proportion of carbon remaining.
Compute estimated age.
Print estimated age.

REFINEMENT IN PSEUDOCODE

AGE: Read proportion of carbon remaining

$$age \leftarrow \frac{-\log_e(\text{proportion of carbon remaining})}{0.0001216}$$

Print estimated age

To compute the estimated age, we need to compute a natural logarithm. Using Table 2–4, we find that the intrinsic function LOG performs this operation. LOG is a generic function; thus it will return a real value if its argument is real.

FORTRAN PROGRAM

```
*-------------------------------------------------------------*
      PROGRAM   DATE
*
*   This program estimates the age of an artifact from
*   the proportion of carbon remaining in the artifact.
*
      REAL   CARBON, AGE
*
      PRINT*, 'ENTER PROPORTION REMAINING FOR CARBON DATING'
      READ*, CARBON
      AGE = (-LOG(CARBON))/0.0001216
      PRINT 5, AGE
    5 FORMAT (1X,'ESTIMATED AGE OF ARTIFACT IS ',F6.1, ' YEARS')
      END
*-------------------------------------------------------------*
```

TESTING

Test your program with the examples we used in the longhand examples. A typical screen display should be

```
ENTER PROPORTION REMAINING FOR CARBON DATING
0.5
ESTIMATED AGE OF ARTIFACT IS 5700.2 YEARS
```

2-8 APPLICATION — RAILROAD TRACK DESIGN (Transportation Engineering)

When a train travels over a straight section of track, it exerts a downward force on the rails; but when it rounds a level curve, it also exerts a horizontal force outward on the rails. Both of these forces must be considered when designing the track. The downward force is equivalent to the weight of the train. The horizontal force, called centrifugal force, is a function of the weight of the train, the speed of the train as it rounds the curve, and the radius of the curve. The equation to compute the horizontal force, in pounds, is

$$\text{FORCE} = \frac{\text{WEIGHT} \times 2000}{32} \times \frac{(\text{MPH} \times 1.4667)^2}{\text{RADIUS}}$$

where WEIGHT is the weight of the train in tons, MPH is the speed of the train in miles per hour, and RADIUS is the radius of the curve in feet.

Write a FORTRAN program to read values for WEIGHT, MPH, and RADIUS. Compute and print the corresponding horizontal force generated.

PROBLEM STATEMENT

Using the equation

$$\text{FORCE} = \frac{\text{WEIGHT} \times 2000}{32} \times \frac{(\text{MPH} \times 1.4667)^2}{\text{RADIUS}}$$

determine the force generated for specific values of WEIGHT, MPH, and RADIUS.

INPUT/OUTPUT DESCRIPTION

The input will be three real numbers that represent the weight of the train in tons, the speed of the train in miles per hour, and the radius of the curve in feet. The output will be the horizontal force generated.

HAND EXAMPLE

Assume that the weight of the train is 405.7 tons, its speed is 30.5 miles per hour, and the radius of the curve is 2005.33 feet. Substituting these values into the equation gives

$$\text{FORCE} = \frac{405.7 \times 2000}{32} \times \frac{(30.5 \times 1.4667)^2}{2005.33}$$

This computation yields a horizontal force of 25,303.55 pounds.

ALGORITHM DEVELOPMENT

We begin the algorithm development by listing the steps necessary to reach the solution. Again, our problem solution is straightforward and the decomposition is the following:

DECOMPOSITION

Read train weight, train speed, and curve radius.
Compute horizontal force.
Print horizontal force.

We add detail in the decomposition step.

REFINEMENT IN PSEUDOCODE

TRAIN: Read train weight, train speed, and radius of curve

$$FORCE \leftarrow \frac{WEIGHT \times 2000}{32} \times \frac{(MPH \times 1.4667)^2}{RADIUS}$$

Print the horizontal force

In the FORTRAN program that follows, note the use of parentheses in the computation statement.

FORTRAN PROGRAM

```
*-------------------------------------------------------------*
      PROGRAM  TRAIN
*
*  This program computes the horizontal force
*  generated by a train on a level curve.
*
      REAL  WEIGHT, MPH, RADIUS, FORCE
*
      PRINT*, 'ENTER WEIGHT OF TRAIN IN TONS'
      READ*, WEIGHT
      PRINT*, 'ENTER SPEED OF TRAIN IN MILES PER HOUR'
      READ*, MPH
      PRINT*, 'ENTER RADIUS OF CURVE IN FEET'
      READ*, RADIUS
*
      FORCE = (WEIGHT*2000.0/32.0)*((MPH*1.4667)**2/RADIUS)
*
      PRINT 10, WEIGHT
   10 FORMAT (1X,'TRAIN WEIGHT - ',F8.2,' TONS')
      PRINT 20, MPH
   20 FORMAT (1X,'TRAIN SPEED - ',F8.2,' MPH')
      PRINT 30, RADIUS
   30 FORMAT (1X,'CURVE RADIUS - ',F8.2,' FEET')
      PRINT*
      PRINT 40, FORCE
   40 FORMAT (1X,'RESULTING HORIZONTAL FORCE - ',
     +          F8.2,' POUNDS')
      END
*-------------------------------------------------------------*
```

Also note that the FORMAT statement with reference number 40 was continued on a second line. The plus sign in column 6 specifies to the compiler that this is a continuation line.

TESTING

If the program is tested with the data that we used in the longhand example, the output is

```
ENTER WEIGHT OF TRAIN IN TONS
405.7
ENTER SPEED OF TRAIN IN MILES PER HOUR
30.5
ENTER RADIUS OF CURVE IN FEET
2005.33
TRAIN WEIGHT -   405.70 TONS
TRAIN SPEED -     30.50 MPH
CURVE RADIUS - 2005.33 FEET

RESULTING HORIZONTAL FORCE - 25303.55 POUNDS
```

2-9   APPLICATION — EQUIPMENT RELIABILITY (Electrical Engineering)

If you have a personal computer, or if you have a friend who has one, open the back of the computer system and look at the computer board(s) that contain its circuitry. Each board contains a large number of components. You might wonder how computers can be so reliable when so many different pieces could malfunction. Much of their reliability is due to the quality control maintained during their manufacture. However, before the design of a computer or any complicated piece of instrumentation is actually implemented, the reliability of the device is analyzed. In this section we will look at one way of estimating the reliability of a piece of instrumentation that may have large numbers of the same component in it. In order to perform the computations, we must know the reliability of a single component. This number is generally available from the manufacturer. For example, a company may sell transistors that are guaranteed to be reliable 98 percent of the time. This information tells us how reliable one transistor is, but it does not tell us how reliable a piece of instrumentation may be if it contains 5000 of these transistors.

Equations for analyzing reliability come from the area of mathematics called statistics and probability. However, in order to select the correct equation, we must know something about the design. For example, consider the following diagrams:

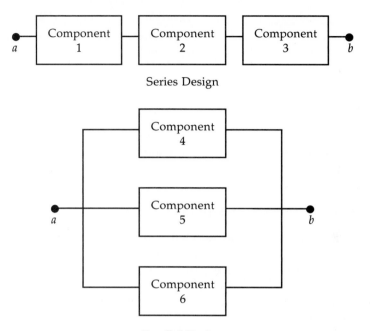

Series Design

Parallel Design

The design on the top contains three components connected serially, or in series. In order for information to flow from point *a* to point *b*, all three components must work properly. The design on the bottom contains three components connected in parallel. In order for information to flow from point *a* to point *b*, only one of the three components must work properly. If all the individual components have the same reliability, we would expect that the parallel configuration would have better overall performance. This can also be verified with mathematical equations.

In this section we are going to estimate the reliability of a piece of equipment relative to a specific component that is used in many places in the design. We are going to compute the percentage of the time that all the components will be working properly, so we are looking at a series-type design. This situation can be described using a Bernoulli equation. With the equation we can compute the probability that all the components will work properly. This probability can be expressed as the percentage of time that there will be no component failures. If this percentage is not high, we may not want to perform critical operations with the instrumentation or we may want to request that the instrumentation be redesigned.

Assume that p is the percentage of time that a single component will be good and n is the total number of components in the piece of equipment.

Then the reliability, or percentage of the time that no component will fail, is given by the Bernoulli equation below:

$$percentage = (p/100.0)^n \cdot 100.0$$

Using the Bernoulli equation, write a program that will read the reliability of a single component and the number of components in a design. Compute the percentage of time that all the components will work properly using the Bernoulli equation.

PROBLEM STATEMENT

Write a program that will compute the reliability of a piece of instrumentation relative to a specific component, using the approximation given by the Bernoulli equation.

INPUT/OUTPUT DESCRIPTION

The input will be two values; the reliability of a single component and the number of components in the instrumentation. The output will be the overall reliability of the instrumentation relative to the specific component.

HAND EXAMPLE

Suppose we are evaluating a piece of instrumentation that contains 20 transistors. Each transistor has a reliability of 96 percent. We are interested in the reliability of the instrument with no transistor failures. The calculation is performed as shown below:

$$n = 20$$
$$p = 96.0$$
$$percentage = (96.0/100.0)^{20} \cdot 100.0$$
$$= 44.2$$

where percentage is the percentage of the time that there will be no transistor failures. This number is probably lower than you expected. Even with 99 percent reliability of an individual component, the reliability of 20 of them at one time is 81.8 percent. Clearly, most instrumentation must have ways of improving reliability over that given by Bernoulli trials. Designs that use parallel features have greatly increased reliability, and different equations are used for the reliability computations.

ALGORITHM DEVELOPMENT

The algorithm for this problem is straightforward. After reading values for p and n, we are ready to compute the reliability.

DECOMPOSITION

Read reliability of component and number of components.
Compute reliability of group of components.
Print reliability.

We now refine the steps in the decomposition into pseudocode.

REFINEMENT IN PSEUDOCODE

RELY: Read P, N
        PERC $\leftarrow$ $(P/100.0)^n \cdot 100.0$
        Print PERC

In the FORTRAN program that follows, note the use of parentheses in the computation statement to make it easier to read.

FORTRAN Program

```
*----------------------------------------------------------------*
      PROGRAM  RELY
*
*  This program computes the reliability of
*  instrumentation using a Bernoulli equation.
*
      INTEGER N
      REAL P, PERC
*
      PRINT*, 'ENTER RELIABILITY OF SINGLE COMPONENT'
      PRINT*, '(USE PERCENTAGE BETWEEN 0.0 AND 100.0)'
      READ*, P
      PRINT*, 'ENTER NUMBER OF COMPONENTS IN EQUIPMENT'
      READ*, N
*
      PERC = (P/100.0)**N*100.0
*
      PRINT*, 'PERCENT OF THE TIME THAT THE EQUIPMENT'
      PRINT 5, PERC
    5 FORMAT (1X,'SHOULD WORK WITHOUT FAILURE IS ',
     +        F6.2,' %')
      END
*----------------------------------------------------------------*
```

TESTING

If we test this program with 20 components, each of which has a reliability of 96 percent, the output is:

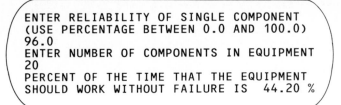

```
ENTER RELIABILITY OF SINGLE COMPONENT
(USE PERCENTAGE BETWEEN 0.0 AND 100.0)
96.0
ENTER NUMBER OF COMPONENTS IN EQUIPMENT
20
PERCENT OF THE TIME THAT THE EQUIPMENT
SHOULD WORK WITHOUT FAILURE IS   44.20 %
```

If we test this program with 20 components, each of which has a reliability of 99 percent, the output is:

```
ENTER RELIABILITY OF SINGLE COMPONENT
(USE PERCENTAGE BETWEEN 0.0 AND 100.0)
99.0
ENTER NUMBER OF COMPONENTS IN EQUIPMENT
20
PERCENT OF THE TIME THAT THE EQUIPMENT
SHOULD WORK WITHOUT FAILURE IS   81.79 %
```

SUMMARY

In this chapter we learned how to define variables and constants in FORTRAN. We discussed the arithmetic operations and intrinsic functions that allow us to compute new values using these variables and constants. Some of the considerations that are unique to computer computations were discussed with specific examples: magnitude limitations, truncation, mixed-mode operations, underflow, and overflow. Statements for reading information from the terminal and for printing answers were covered. Several complete example programs were developed.

DEBUGGING AIDS

If a program is not working correctly, you should *echo* the values that you read in the program — that is, immediately after reading them, print them out to be sure that the values you want to give the variables are being used. A common mistake is to enter the data values in the wrong order. For example, instead of entering the initial number of bacteria followed by the elapsed time, you enter the elapsed time followed by the initial number of bacteria.

If the input portion of your program is working correctly, check your assignment statements.

1. If the assignment statement is long, break it into several smaller statements.
2. Double check the placement of parentheses. Add parentheses if you are not sure what order the computer will use to compute the operations involved.

Be sure that you always have the same number of left parentheses as right parentheses.

3. Review each variable name on the right-hand side of the assignment statement to be sure you have spelled it exactly as previously used. (Did you use VEL when you should have used VELCTY?)

4. Make sure all variables on the right-hand side of the assignment statement have been previously initialized.

5. Be sure that arguments of functions are in the correct units (for example, trigonometric functions use angles in radians, not in degrees).

If you still are not getting correct answers, check the variable names in your output statements. Do you have the correct names listed?

If these steps do not help you isolate your error, ask your instructor or a classsmate to check the program. If no one is available to check your program and you cannot find the error, start over on a clean sheet of paper. Sometimes it is hard to spot your own errors because you know what you want the statements to do and you read that into the statements when searching for errors.

STYLE/TECHNIQUE GUIDES

A program should be written so that another person who knows FORTRAN can readily understand the statements and interpret the procedures — This is especially important because the person updating the program may not always be the same person who originally wrote it. To write a clearly understood program is challenging and necessitates building good habits while you are learning a language. The following guides will help you develop a style and technique that will enable you to meet these requirements.

1. Use variable names that indicate something about the values being stored in the variable. For instance, represent velocity by VELCTY instead of V, or X, or something obscure.

2. Use a consistent number of significant digits in constants. Do not use 3.14 as a value for pi in the beginning of your program and later use 3.141593. Assure this consistency by defining a variable to store the value of these constants. Use the variable instead of the constant value in subsequent statements.

3. Break long expressions into smaller expressions and recombine them in another statement. A complicated fraction can be computed by first calculating a numerator, then calculating a denominator, then dividing in a separate statement.

4. Insert extra parentheses for readability. Inserting extra pairs of parentheses is never wrong as long as they are properly located. Extra parentheses often make arithmetic expressions much more readable.

5. Use the intrinsic functions where possible.

6. Develop the habit of echo-printing values that you have read.

7. Print the physical units that correspond to the numerical values being printed; this information is vital for proper interpretation of results.

8. Do not mix modes except for exponents. Use the intrinsic functions REAL and INT to avoid mixing types by explicit conversion.

KEY WORDS

argument	intrinsic function
arithmetic expression	left-justified
assignment statement	list-directed I/O
buffer	literal
carriage control	magnitude limitation
comment line	mixed-mode operation
constant	nested function
continuation line	nonexecutable statement
conversational computing	overflow
echo	real value
executable statement	right-justified
explicit typing	rounding
exponential notation	scientific notation
formatted I/O	specification statement
generic function	statement label
implicit typing	truncation
initialize	underflow
integer value	variable
intermediate result	

PROBLEMS

We begin our problem set with modifications to programs given earlier in this chapter. Give the decomposition, refined pseudocode, and FORTRAN program for each problem.

Problems 1–5 modify the energy conversion program CONVRT, given on page 46.

1. Modify the energy conversion program so that it converts joules to kilowatt-hours.

2. Modify the energy conversion program so that it converts British thermal units to joules. (1 Btu = 1056 joules)

3. Modify the energy conversion program so that it converts calories to joules. (1 calorie = 4.19 joules)

4. Modify the energy conversion program so that it converts joules to British thermal units and to calories.

5. Modify the energy conversion program so that it converts kilowatt-hours to calories.

Problems 6–10 modify the bacteria growth program, GROWTH, given on page 49.

6. Modify the bacteria growth program so that the time elapsed is entered in minutes even though the equation still requires a time in hours.

7. Modify the bacteria growth program so that the time elapsed is entered in days even though the equation still requires a time in hours.

8. Modify the bacteria growth program so that an initial population is read from the terminal. The program should compute and print the percent increase in population as time increases from 2 hours to 3 hours.

9. Modify the bacteria growth program so that the program reads two time values from the terminal, where the first time is less than the second time. Compute and print the amount of growth between the two times, assuming an initial population value of 1.

10. Modify the bacteria growth program so that the program reads two time values from the terminal, with no restrictions on which time is larger. Compute and print the amount of growth between the two times, assuming an initial population value of 1. (*Hint:* Review the absolute value function.)

Problems 11–15 modify the carbon-dating program DATE, given on page 51.

11. Modify the carbon-dating program so that it truncates the age to the nearest year.

12. Modify the carbon-dating program so that it rounds the age to the nearest year. (*Hint:* Review the NINT function.)

13. Modify the carbon-dating program so that it gives the age in centuries instead of in years. Use two decimal places in the output age.

14. Modify the carbon-dating program so that it gives the age in centuries instead of in years. Truncate the resulting age to the nearest century.

15. Modify the carbon-dating program so that it gives the age in centuries instead of in years. Round the resulting age to the nearest century.

Problems 16–20 modify the railroad track analysis program TRAIN, given on page 53.

16. Modify the railroad track analysis program so that the weight of the train is entered in pounds instead of in tons.

17. Modify the railroad track analysis program so that the radius of the curve is entered in yards instead of in feet.

18. Modify the railroad track analysis program so that the horizontal force printed is truncated to the nearest pound.

19. Modify the railroad track analysis program so that the horizontal force printed is rounded to the nearest pound.

20. Modify the railroad track analysis program so that the speed is entered in kilometers per hour instead of in miles per hour. (Recall that 1 mile is equal to 1.609 kilometers.)

Problems 21–25 modify the equipment reliability program RELY, given on page 57. In the modifications, if P1 is the reliability of component 1, and P2 is the reliability of component 2, then the reliability of the components connected in series is:

$$\text{percentage} = (P1/100.0) \cdot (P2/100.0) \cdot 100.0$$

The reliability of two components connected in parallel is:

$$\text{percentage} = (P1/100.0 + P2/100.0 - (P1/100.0) \cdot (P2/100.0)) \cdot 100.0$$

21. Modify the reliability program so that it reads the reliabilities of two components and then computes the reliability of the two components connected in series, as shown in the following diagram:

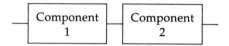

22. Modify the reliability program so that it reads the reliabilities of two components and then computes the reliability of the two components connected in parallel, as shown in the following diagram:

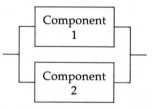

23. Modify the reliability program so that it reads the reliabilities of three components and then computes the reliability of the components connected as shown in the following diagram:

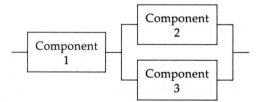

24. Modify the reliability program so that it reads the reliabilities of four compo-

nents and then computes the reliability of the components connected as shown in the following diagram:

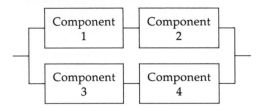

25. Modify the reliability program so that it reads the reliabilities of four components and then computes the reliability of the components connected as shown in the following diagram:

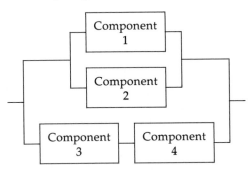

Develop programs for problems 26–39. Use the five-phase design process.

26. Write a program to read the length and width of a rectangle and compute and print its perimeter and area.

27. Write a program to read the coordinates of two points (X1,Y1), (X2,Y2). Compute the slope of the straight line between these two points where

$$\text{SLOPE} = \frac{Y2 - Y1}{X2 - X1}$$

Print the points and the slope of the line between the points.

28. Write a program to read the diameter of a circle. Compute the radius, circumference, and area of the circle. Print these new values in the following form:

```
PROPERTIES OF A CIRCLE WITH DIAMETER XXXX.XXX
(1)   RADIUS = XXXX.XXX
(2)   CIRCUMFERENCE = XXXX.XXX
(3)   AREA = XXXX.XXX
```

29. Write a program to read a measurement in meters. Print the value followed by the units, METERS. Convert the measurement to kilometers and print the value on the next line, again with the correct units. Convert the measurement to miles and print the value on the third line, with correct units. (Use 1 mile = 1.609 kilometers.)

30. A research scientist performed nutrition tests using three animals. Data on each animal includes an identification number, the weight of the animal at the beginning of the experiment, and the weight of the animal at the end of the experiment. Write a program to read this data and print a report. The report is to include the original information plus the percentage increase in weight for each animal.

31. Write a program to read three resistance values (R1, R2, R3) and compute their combined resistance (RC) for the parallel arrangement shown. Print the values of R1, R2, R3, and RC.

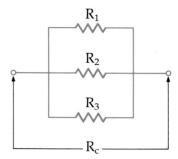

$$RC = \cfrac{1}{\cfrac{1}{R1} + \cfrac{1}{R2} + \cfrac{1}{R3}}$$

32. The distance between points with coordinates (XA,YA) and (XB,YB) is given by

$$DISTANCE = \sqrt{(XA - XB)^2 + (YA - YB)^2}$$

You are given the coordinates of three points:

point 1: (X1,Y1)
point 2: (X2,Y2)
point 3: (X3,Y3)

Write a program to read the coordinates. Next calculate and print the distance DIST12 between points 1 and 2, the distance DIST13 between points 1 and 3, and the distance DIST23 between points 2 and 3.

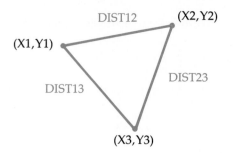

33. Write a program to read the following information from the terminal:

Year
Number of people in the civilian labor force
Number of people in the military labor force

Compute the percentage of the labor force that is civilian and the percentage that is military. Print the following information:

```
LABOR FORCE    - YEAR XXXX
NUMBER OF WORKERS (THOUSANDS) AND PERCENTAGE OF WORKERS
CIVILIAN          XXX.XXX                  XXX.XXX
MILITARY          XXX.XXX                  XXX.XXX
TOTAL             XXX.XXX                  XXX.XXX
```

34. The approximate time for electrons to travel from the cathode to the anode of a rectifier tube is given by

$$\text{TIME} = \sqrt{\frac{2 \cdot M}{Q \cdot V}} \cdot R1 \cdot Z \cdot \left(1 + \frac{Z}{3} + \frac{Z^2}{10} + \frac{Z^3}{42} + \frac{Z^4}{216}\right)$$

where Q = charge of the electron (1.60206E−19 coulombs)
M = mass of the electron (9.1083E−31 kilograms)
V = accelerating voltage in volts
$R1$ = radius of the inner tube (cathode)
$R2$ = radius of the outer tube (anode)
Z = natural logarithm of $R2/R1$

Define the values of Q and M in the constant section of your program. Read values for V, $R1$, and $R2$, then calculate Z and TIME. Print the values of V, $R1$, $R2$, and TIME.

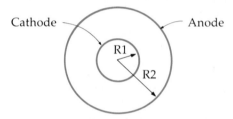

Cathode   Anode

R1

R2

Rectifier Tube

35. Write a program to compute the volume of the shell of a hollow ball. Assume that the values for the radius and for the thickness of the ball are to be read. The volume of a sphere is related to the radius r by

$$\text{VOLUME} = \frac{4}{3} \cdot \text{pi} \cdot r^3$$

36. The Gaussian density function is commonly used in engineering statistics. This function is defined in the equation that follows:

$$Y = \frac{1}{\sqrt{2 \cdot \text{pi}}} \cdot e^{-0.5 \cdot X^2}$$

Write a program to read a value of X and compute the corresponding value of Y. Print the values in the following form:

```
THE STANDARD NORMAL DENSITY FUNCTION EVALUATED
AT XXX.XX GIVES A VALUE OF XX.XXXXX
```

37. A Gaussian density function is defined in problem 36. Write a program to compute and print the change in y between x=0.0 and x=1.0. Also compute and print the change in y between x = 1.0 and 2.0 and between x = 2.0 and 3.0. Use the following output form:

```
    STANDARD GAUSSIAN DENSITY FUNCTION

    X: 0.0 TO 1.0        CHANGE IN Y:   XXX.XX
    X: 1.0 TO 2.0        CHANGE IN Y:   XXX.XX
    X: 2.0 TO 3.0        CHANGE IN Y:   XXX.XX
```

38. Write a program to read the x and y coordinates of three points from the terminal. Then compute the area of the triangle formed from these points using the following equation:

$$AREA = 0.5|X_1Y_2 - X_2Y_1 + X_2Y_3 - X_3Y_2 + X_3Y_1 - X_1Y_3|$$

Print the coordinates and the area in the following form:

```
    TRIANGLE VERTICES:
    (1)    XXX.X,  XXX.X
    (2)    XXX.X,  XXX.X
    (3)    XXX.X,  XXX.X

    TRIANGE AREA:
    XXX.XX
```

(Be sure to give a descriptive message to the user to describe the form and order for the input values.)

39. The radioactive decay of thorium is given by the equation

$$N = N_0 \cdot e^{\left[-0.693 \frac{t}{1.65 \times 10^{16}}\right]}$$

where N_0 represents the initial amount of thorium and t represents the time elapsed. When t = 0, N is equal to N_0, and no decay has occurred. As t increases, the amount of thorium is decreased. Read values for N_0 and t from the terminal, and then compute and print the amount of thorium left after the specified time has elapsed. Use the following output form:

```
    INITIAL VALUE OF THORIUM:   XXX.XXX
    TIME ELAPSED:               XXX.XXX
    REMAINING THORIUM:          XXX.XXX
```

FORTRAN STATEMENT SUMMARY

Assignment Statement:

$$variable = expression$$

Examples:

```
PI = 3.141593

AREA = SIDE*SIDE

ROOT = SQRT(X)
```

Discussion:
The left-hand side of the assignment statement must be a variable name. The right-hand side can be any form of an expression, from a simple constant to a complex arithmetic expression involving other variables and intrinsic functions.

END Statement:

```
END
```

Discussion:
This statement must be the last statement in a FORTRAN program. It is a signal to the compiler that there are no further statements to translate. Program execution stops when it reaches the END statement.

FORMAT Statement:

k **FORMAT** *(format specifications)*

Examples:

```
 5 FORMAT (1X,'TEMPERATURE DATA FROM EXPERIMENT 1')

10 FORMAT (1X,'THE VALUE OF X IS ',F7.3)

15 FORMAT (1X,I3,2X,F7.1)
```

Discussion:
The FORMAT statement must always have a statement label, which is referenced in a formatted I/O statement, such as a PRINT statement. The FORMAT statement specifies the exact form of the input or output that is being requested. For output, the specifications include the vertical spacing (how many lines to skip) and the horizontal spacing (how many spaces to skip between values).

INTEGER Statement:

$$\texttt{INTEGER} \quad variable\ list$$

Examples:

```
INTEGER   SUM
INTEGER   ID, TOTAL, X
```

Discussion:
The INTEGER statement explicitly lists all variables that will store integer values. Listing a variable name in an INTEGER statement overrides its implicit typing.

PRINT* Statement:

$$\texttt{PRINT*,} \quad expression\ list$$

Examples:

```
PRINT*, 'DISTANCE VERSUS VELOCITY MEASUREMENTS'
PRINT*, 'SLOPE = ', SLOPE
PRINT*, X, Y, X + Y
```

Discussion:
The PRINT* statement is a list-directed output statement. The value of any literals, variables, constants, or expressions in its expression list will be printed in the order in which they are listed. The form of numeric output is pre-determined by the compiler.

PRINT k Statement:

$$\texttt{PRINT}\ k,\ expression\ list$$

Examples:

```
PRINT 5, ALPHA, BETA
PRINT 50, SLOPE
PRINT 25
```

Discussion:
The PRINT k statement is a formatted output statement. The value of any variables or expressions in its expression list will be printed in the order in which they are listed according to the specifications in the FORMAT statement with label k.

PROGRAM Statement:

$$PROGRAM \quad program \ name$$

Examples:

$$PROGRAM \quad CALC$$

$$PROGRAM \quad REPORT$$

Discussion:
The PROGRAM statement is optional, but it must be the first statement in a program if it is used. It assigns a name to the program. This name must be unique and cannot be used for a variable in the program.

READ* Statement:

$$READ*, \quad variable \ list$$

Examples:

$$READ*, \quad TIME$$

$$READ*, \quad DIST, \ VELCTY$$

Discussion:
The READ* statement is a list-directed input statement that reads values for the variables in its list. The values are stored in the order in which the variables are listed. Data values must be separated by blanks or commas, and as many lines as are needed will be read. Each READ* statement will begin searching for values with a new line.

REAL Statement:

$$REAL \quad variable \ list$$

Examples:

$$REAL \quad FORCE$$

$$REAL \quad TEMP, \ PRESS, \ VOL$$

Discussion:
The REAL statement explicitly lists all variables that are to store real values. Listing a variable name in a REAL statement overrides its implicit typing.

STOP Statement:

$$STOP$$

Discussion:
The STOP statement is an optional statement that stops the execution of a program. Programs may have more than one STOP statement. The END statement also serves to stop program execution if it is executed.

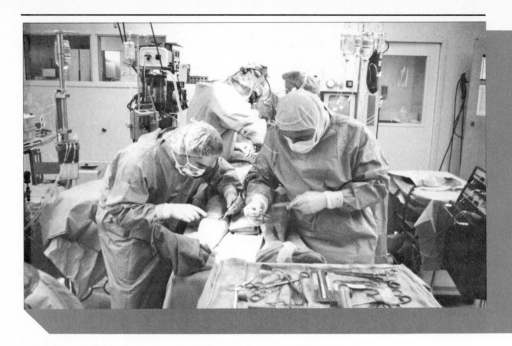

APPLICATION — Suture Packaging (Biomedical Engineering)

Sutures are strands or fibers used to sew living tissue together after an injury or an operation. Packages of sutures must be sealed carefully before they are shipped to hospitals so that contaminants cannot enter the packages. The object that seals the package is referred to as a sealing die. Generally, sealing dies are heated with an electric heater. For the sealing process to be a success, the sealing die is maintained at an established temperature and must contact the package with a predetermined pressure for an established time period. The time period in which the sealing die contacts the package is called dwell. An engineering assistant in a packaging company might be asked to write a program to analyze the data collected during the sealing of several batches of sutures. The information available would be the temperature, pressure, and dwell time for each batch, along with the acceptable range of these parameters. Write a program to generate a report analyzing the data for batches that were rejected because the packages were not sealed properly. (See Section 3–5 for the solution.)

Photo courtesy of Northridge Hospital Medical Center.

3

CONTROL STRUCTURES

Introduction

Summary

INTRODUCTION

In Chapter 2 we wrote complete FORTRAN programs, but the steps were all executed sequentially. The programs were composed of reading data, computing new data, and printing the new data. We now introduce FORTRAN statements that allow us to control the sequence of the steps being executed. This control is achieved through statements that allow us to select different paths through our programs and statements that allow us to repeat certain parts of our programs.

3–1 ALGORITHM STRUCTURE

In Chapter 1 we presented a five-step design process for problem solving:

1. State the problem clearly.
2. Describe the input and the output.
3. Work a sample problem by hand.
4. Develop an algorithm to solve the problem.
5. Test the algorithm carefully.

To describe algorithms consistently, we use a set of standard forms, or structures. When an algorithm is described in these standard structures, it is a *structured algorithm*. When the algorithm is converted into computer instructions, the corresponding program is a *structured program*.

Each structure for building algorithms can be described in an English-like notation called *pseudocode*, which we will soon discuss in detail. Because pseudocode is not really computer code, it is language independent — pseudocode only depends on the steps needed to solve a problem, not on the computer language being used. *Flowcharts* also describe the steps in algorithms. We use both techniques in this text so that you can choose the form that is most convenient for you. Neither pseudocode nor flowcharts are intended to be a formal way of describing the algorithm; they are informal ways of easily describing the steps in the algorithm without worrying about the syntax of a specific computer language. After we present the structures that we will be using and some examples of their corresponding pseudocode and flowcharts, we will develop problem solutions using both techniques so that you can compare them side-by-side.

The steps included in algorithms can be divided into three general structures:

1. Sequence: Contains steps that are performed sequentially. All of the programs in Chapter 2 were sequential.
2. Selection: Asks a question or tests a condition to determine which steps are to be performed next. For example, a step of this structure might be "if the data value is positive, add it to the sum; otherwise, print an error message."

3. Repetition: Allows us to use loops, which are sets of steps in an algorithm that are repeated. One type of loop, the *WHILE loop*, repeats the steps as long as a certain condition is true. Another type of loop, the *counting loop*, repeats the steps a specified number of times.

Other special structures are sometimes included in a list of algorithm structures. Generally, these other structures are special forms of the three structures already presented.

SEQUENCE

The sequence structure is a series of steps in an algorithm listed one after another. These steps are primarily computations, input, and output. We now compare pseudocode and flowcharts for these three operations.

Computations In pseudocode, computations are indicated by arrows, as in

$$average \leftarrow total/count$$

We read this pseudocode statement as "average is replaced by total divided by count" or "total is divided by count, giving average." In a flowchart, the computation is enclosed in a rectangle. The flowchart statement for the preceding computation is

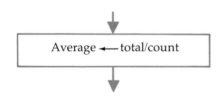

Input Input statements in pseudocode are specified by the word "Read" followed by the variables that are to be read. For example, to read a temperature value and a humidity value, we could use the following pseudocode:

Read temperature, humidity

(At this point do not worry about whether or not the names you have chosen are valid FORTRAN names).

The flowchart symbol for input is a parallelogram. The preceding pseudocode can be specified by the following flowchart statement:

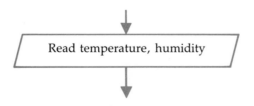

Output Output statements are specified in pseudocode by the word "Print" followed by a list of variable names and constants. The following pseudocode statement prints a literal and the value of an average:

Print 'THE AVERAGE IS ', average

The flowchart symbol for output is the same as for input. Thus, the preceding statement in flowchart form would be

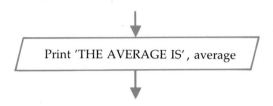

SELECTION

The selection structure is used to choose between sets of steps. It is most commonly described in terms of an IF structure that may itself have several forms. We will use three forms of the IF structure for selection. The simple IF form tests a *condition;* if the condition is true then a certain step or series of steps is performed. For example, suppose the algorithm that we are developing must count the number of students who are on the honor roll and print their student ID numbers. One step in our algorithm might be "if the grade point average (GPA) is greater than 3.0, then print the ID and add 1 to the number of students on the honor roll." This step is shown in both pseudocode and flowchart forms. Note the use of indenting in the pseudocode.

If GPA > 3.0 then
Print ID
honor roll ← honor roll + 1

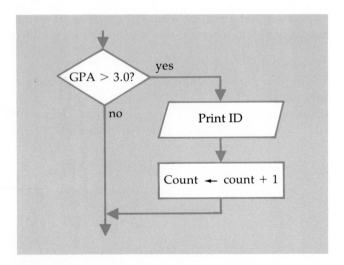

Another form of the IF structure is the IF-ELSE form. This form specifies one series of steps to be executed if a condition is true and an alternate series if the condition is false. For example, suppose that we want to modify the honor roll example to print the ID of each student; however, if the student is on the honor roll, we want to increment our honor roll count and also print the GPA beside the student's ID. We could describe this step with the following pseudocode and flowchart:

If GPA > 3.0 then
    Print ID, GPA
    honor roll ← honor roll + 1
Else
    Print ID

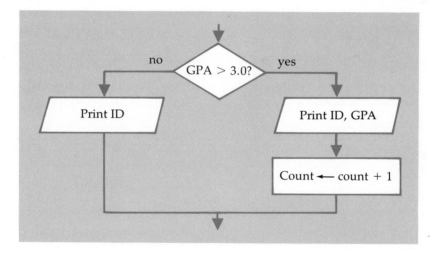

The last form of the IF structure allows us to test for multiple conditions. This IF-ELSEIF form can be illustrated by extending the honor roll example. Assume that the president's honor roll requires a GPA of greater than 3.5 and that the dean's honor roll requires a GPA of greater than 3.0. We want to count the number of students on each honor roll. Students on the president's honor roll are not to be included on the dean's honor roll. Print each student's ID and GPA if above 3.0; also include an asterisk beside the GPA if it is above 3.5. The following pseudocode and flowchart describe this set of steps:

```
If GPA > 3.5 then
    Print ID, GPA, '*'
    president's count ← president's count + 1
Else If GPA > 3.0 then
    Print ID, GPA
    dean's count ← dean's count + 1
Else
    Print ID
```

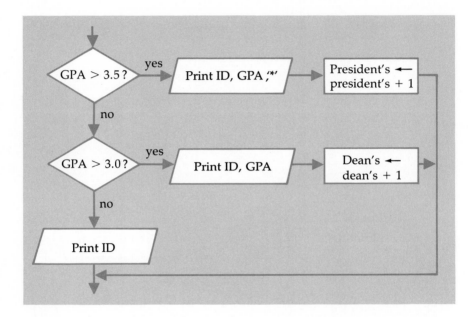

REPETITION

A WHILE loop identifies a series of steps that are to be repeated if a certain condition is true. This series is composed of sequential, selection, or other repetition steps. Suppose that we wish to continue reading data values and adding them to a sum as long as that sum is less than 1000. These steps are described in the following pseudocode and flowchart:

```
While sum < 1000 do
    Read data value
    sum ← sum + data value
```

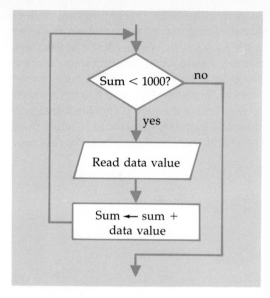

Again, note that the indenting in the pseudocode specifies the steps that are included in the WHILE loop. If we wish to print the value of the sum after exiting the WHILE loop, we can use the following pseudocode and flowchart:

While sum < 1000 do
   Read data value
   sum ← sum + data value
Print sum

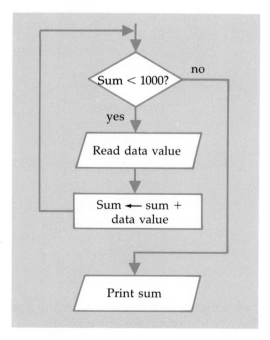

Counting loops, or *iterative loops*, repeat steps a specific number of times. For example, suppose we are going to read ten values from the terminal and perform some calculations with each value. We can describe the steps in a counting loop that is repeated ten times. However, a counting loop can be considered a special form of a WHILE loop in which a counter has been introduced. The counter represents the number of times that the loop has been executed. The counter is usually initialized to zero before the loop is executed. Inside the loop, the counter is incremented by one. The loop is then executed "while the value of the counter is less than ten." The pseudocode and flowchart for this counting loop example are

count ← 0
While count < 10 do
   (processing of data)
   count ← count + 1

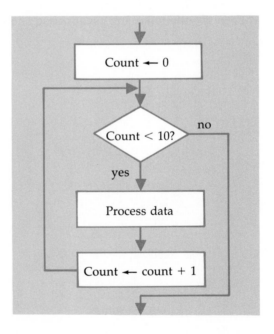

By developing pseudocode and flowcharts for the three main structures discussed, we can describe algorithms for any problem.

EXAMPLE 3-1   Average of a Set of Data Values

In Chapter 1 we illustrated top-down design in algorithm development with a program to compute the average of a set of data values. Let's look at that problem again and develop a flowchart for the solution. Assume that we are reading data values from the terminal. A value of zero indicates that we have reached the end of the data values.

Solution

The first step in algorithm development is to decompose the problem into a series of sequential steps. To compute an average, we need to sum and count the values. Thus, our decomposition is

DECOMPOSITION

Read data values and keep a sum and count.
Divide the sum by the number of data values to get the average.
Print the average.

The decomposition provides a top-level picture of the solution in general terms.

We now take each of the sequential steps in the decomposition and refine it using the structures that we have just discussed: sequential steps, selection steps, and repetition steps. The first step in the decomposition is "read data values and keep a sum and count." This step can be refined by recognizing that it is composed of setting a count and a sum to zero (sequential steps) followed by a loop to read the values and update the count and sum (repetition step). The loop should be structured into a WHILE loop, so we must determine the condition necessary to keep us in the loop. The problem statement tells us to assume that the data values have all been read when a zero is entered; thus, we want to stay in the loop "while the data value is not a zero." We need to read a data value before entering the WHILE loop. We then continue to read values inside the loop. After completing the WHILE loop, we need the sequential steps to compute the average and print it. We can now put this refinement into a flowchart. Note that we use an oval symbol to indicate the start and end of the flowchart for a complete problem.

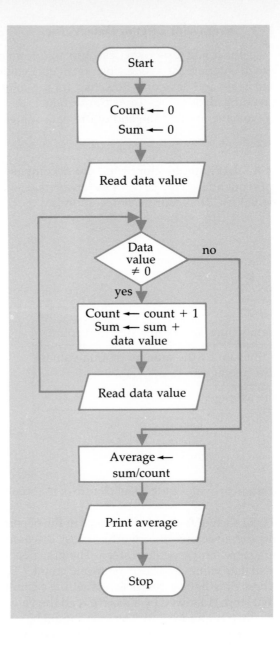

EXAMPLE 3-2   Experimental Data Analysis

Develop an algorithm to analyze a set of experimental data values, determine the minimum and the maximum values, and compute the range of the data values. Assume that a zero data value indicates that all the data values have been read.

Solution

Because this is a new algorithm, we start with a simple set of data in a hand-worked example. Assume that the following lab worksheet contains data from a recent chemistry experiment:

LAB MEASUREMENTS   9/30/89

40.56
55.92
66.31
58.35
62.88
41.99
49.70
53.21

Let's begin with the steps to find the maximum value. We look at the first value, compare it to the second value, and denote the larger of the two as the "maximum so far." Now we look at the third value and compare it to our "maximum so far." If the "maximum so far" is larger, we go to the fourth value; but if the third value is larger than our "maximum so far," we update the value in our "maximum so far." Continuing this process with the entire list of data results in labeling the maximum value as the "maximum so far." A similar process finds the minimum value. For the preceding data, our results are

maximum value = 66.31
minimum value = 40.56

Now we can compute the range of values by subtracting the minimum value from the maximum value:

range of values = 66.31 − 40.56 = 25.75

Having worked out a simple problem by hand, we are ready to begin our algorithm development. We start with decomposition of the problem; this is a good example of the "divide and conquer" concept discussed in Chapter 1.

> Read data values and determine maximum and minimum values.
>
> Subtract minimum value from maximum value to get range.
>
> Print maximum, minimum, range.

For this example, we refine the solution with pseudocode. We take each step of the decomposition and decide which structures (sequential, selection, and repetition) define the step in greater detail. Clearly, our first decomposition step requires the greatest refinement because it includes sequential steps (initializing our maximum and minimum values) plus the repetition step (the loop to read values and update our maximum and minimum values if necessary). The maximum and minimum values are commonly initialized to the first data value so we only need to read one data value outside the loop to initialize them. We then read the second data value and enter the WHILE loop. "While the data value is not zero," we update the maximum and minimum values if necessary. Note that we do not need a count of the data values or a sum for this problem. Let's write these refined steps in pseudocode.

REFINEMENT IN PSEUDOCODE

```
ANALYSIS: Read data value
          maximum ← data value
          minimum ← data value
          Read data value
          While data value is not zero do
             If data value > maximum then
                maximum ← data value
             If data value < minimum then
                minimum ← data value
             Read data value
          range ← maximum − minimum
          Print 'MAXIMUM DATA VALUE = ', maximum
          Print 'MINIMUM DATA VALUE = ', minimum
          Print 'RANGE OF VALUES = ', range
```

This was a simple algorithm; only one refinement was needed. Additional refinements are often necessary for more complex problems.

In the next two sections, we present the FORTRAN statements for the IF structures and the WHILE loop. We then return to the two algorithms we have just developed and translate them into complete FORTRAN 77 programs.

3-2 IF STRUCTURES

In Section 3-1 we presented the pseudocode and flowcharts for three IF structures. In this section we present the corresponding FORTRAN statements. All forms of the IF structure use a condition to determine which path to take in the structure. Therefore, before we discuss the forms of these statements, we want to discuss logical expressions that are used as the conditions to be tested.

LOGICAL EXPRESSIONS

A *logical expression* is analogous to an arithmetic expression but is always evaluated to either true or false, instead of a number. Logical expressions can be formed using *relational operators*, which are listed:

RELATIONAL OPERATOR	INTERPRETATION
.EQ.	Is equal to
.NE.	Is not equal to
.LT.	Is less than
.LE.	Is less than or equal to
.GT.	Is greater than
.GE.	Is greater than or equal to

Numeric variables can be used on both sides of the relation operators to yield a logical expression whose value is either true or false. For example, consider the logical expression A.EQ.B where A and B are real values. If the value of A is equal to the value of B, then the logical expression A.EQ.B is true. Otherwise, the expression is false. Similarly, if the value of X is 4.5, then the expression X.GT.3.0 is true.

We can also combine two logical expressions into a *compound logical expression* with the *logical operators* .OR. and .AND.. When two logical expressions are joined by .OR., the entire expression is true if either or both expressions are true; it is false only when both expressions are false. When two logical expressions are joined by .AND., the entire expression is true only if both expressions are true. These logical operators are used only between complete logical expressions. For example, A.LT.B.OR.A.LT.C is a valid compound logical expression because .OR. joins A.LT.B and A.LT.C. However, A.LT.B.OR.C is an invalid compound expression because C is a numeric variable, not a complete logical expression.

Logical expressions can also be preceded by the logical operator NOT. This operator changes the value of the expression to the opposite value; hence, if A.GT.B is true, then .NOT.A.GT.B is false.

A logical expression may contain several logical operators, as in

```
.NOT.(A.LT.15.4).OR.KT.EQ.ISUM
```

The *hierarchy*, from highest to lowest, is .NOT., .AND., and .OR.. In the preceding statement, the logical expression A.LT.15.4 would be evaluated, and its value, true or false, would then be reversed. This resultant value would be used, along with the value of KT.EQ.ISUM, with the logical operator .OR.. For example, if A is 5.0, KT is 5, and ISUM is 5, then the left-hand expression is false and the right-hand expression is true; but these expressions are connected by .OR., thus the entire expression is true.

Another type of variable, a *logical variable*, is also useful in writing the conditions that allow us to choose different paths and to repeat parts of our programs. A logical variable can have one of two values: true or false. A logical variable must be defined with a specification statement whose form is

```
LOGICAL    variable list
```

Logical constants are .TRUE. and .FALSE.. Therefore, the statements necessary to define a logical variable and give it a value of false are

```
LOGICAL   DONE
DONE = .FALSE.
```

Logical variables are generally used to make our programs more readable; thus, they are not usually part of the input or output. In several examples in this chapter, we will compare solutions using logical variables to ones without logical variables.

IF STATEMENT

The IF form of the IF structure can be implemented in two ways: One statement handles the situation where only one step is performed when a condition is true; the other statement handles the situation where several steps must be performed when the condition is true. The general form of the IF statement with one step to perform is

```
IF (condition) executable statement
```

Execution consists of the following steps:

1. If the condition is true, we execute the statement that is on the same line as the condition and then go to the next statement in the program.
2. If the condition is false, we jump immediately to the next statement in the program.

A typical IF statement is

```
IF (A.LT.B) SUM = SUM + A
```

If the value of A is less than the value of B, then the value of A is added to SUM. If the value of A is greater than or equal to B, then control passes to whatever statement follows the IF statement in the program. Other examples of IF statements are

```
IF (TIME.GT.1.5) READ*, DISTNC

IF (DEN.LE.0.0) PRINT*, DEN

IF (-4.NE.NUM) NUM = NUM + 1
```

The executable statement that follows the condition is typically a computation or an input/output statement — it cannot be another IF statement.

In many instances we would like to perform more than one statement if a condition is true. The form of the IF statement that allows us to perform any number of statements if a condition is true uses the words THEN and ENDIF to identify these steps. The general form is

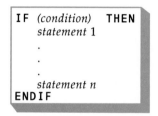

Execution consists of the following steps:

1. If the condition is true, we execute statements 1 through n and then go to the statement following ENDIF.
2. If the condition is false, we jump immediately to the statement following ENDIF.

Although not required, the statements to be performed when the condition is true should be indented to indicate that they are a group of statements within the IF statement.

EXAMPLE 3-3 Zero Divide

Assume that you have calculated the numerator NUM (explicitly typed REAL) and the denominator DEN of a fraction. Before dividing the two values, you want to see if DEN is zero. If DEN is zero, you want to print an error message and stop the program; if DEN is not zero, you want to compute the result and print it. Write the statements to perform these steps.

Solution

```
IF (DEN.EQ.0.0) THEN
    PRINT*, 'DENOMINATOR IS ZERO'
    STOP
ENDIF
FRACTN = NUM/DEN
PRINT*, 'FRACTION = ', FRACTN
```

IF statements can also be nested; the following construction includes an IF statement within an IF statement:

```
IF (condition 1) THEN
    statement 1
          .
          .
          .
    statement n
    IF (condition 2) THEN
        statement n + 1
              .
              .
              .
        statement m
    ENDIF
    statement m + 1
          .
          .
          .
    statement p
ENDIF
statement q
```

Again, the indenting of statements within the construction is not required but makes the logic easier to follow. If condition 1 is true, we then always execute statements 1 through n and statements $m + 1$ through p. If condition 2 is also true, we then also execute statements $n + 1$ through m. If condition 1 is false, we immediately go to statement q.

Consider these statements:

```
IF (GPA.GE.3.0) THEN
    PRINT*, 'HONOR ROLL'
    IF (GPA.GT.3.5) THEN
        PRINT*, 'PRESIDENT''S LIST'
    ENDIF
ENDIF
```

If the GPA is less than 3.0, the entire construction is skipped. If the GPA is between 3.0 and 3.5, only HONOR ROLL is printed. If the GPA is greater than 3.5, then HONOR ROLL is printed, followed on the next line by PRESIDENT'S LIST.

IF-ELSE STATEMENT

The IF-ELSE statement implements another form of the IF structure and allows us to execute one set of statements if the condition is true and a different set if the condition is false. The general form of the IF-ELSE statement is on the next page. If the condition is true, then statements 1 through n are executed. If the condition is false, then statements $n + 1$ through m are executed. Any statement can also be another IF or IF-ELSE statement to provide a nested structure.

```
IF (condition) THEN
    statement 1
        .
        .
        .
    statement n
ELSE
    statement n + 1
        .
        .
        .
    statement m
ENDIF
```

Now consider this set of statements which uses a logical variable VALID with the IF structure:

```
READ*, VOLTS
IF (VOLTS.GE.-5.0.AND.VOLTS.LE.5.0) THEN
    VALID = .TRUE.
ELSE
    VALID = .FALSE.
ENDIF
IF (.NOT.VALID) PRINT*, 'ERROR IN DATA'
```

In these statements, the variable VALID is true if the value in VOLTS is between −5.0 and 5.0; otherwise VALID is false. After determining the value of VALID, it can be used in other places in the program, such as in an IF statement to print an error message if the value is not valid. The advantage of using the logical variable is that we can reference it each time that we need to know if the value is valid, instead of repeating the test to see if value in VOLTS is between −5.0 and 5.0.

EXAMPLE 3-4   Velocity Computation

Give the statements for calculating the velocity VEL of a cable car. The variable DIST contains the distance of the cable car from the nearest tower. Use this equation if the cable car is within 30 feet of the tower:

$$\text{velocity} = 2.425 + 0.00175 \text{ distance}^2 \text{ ft/sec}$$

Use this equation if the cable car is further than 30 feet from the tower:

$$\text{velocity} = 0.625 + 0.12 \text{ distance} - 0.00025 \text{ distance}^2 \text{ ft/sec}$$

Correct Solution

```
IF (DIST.LE.30.0) THEN
    VEL = 2.425 + 0.00175*DIST*DIST
ELSE
    VEL = 0.625 + 0.12*DIST - 0.00025*DIST*DIST
ENDIF
```

Incorrect Solution

```
IF (DIST.LE.30.0) VEL = 2.425 + 0.00175*DIST*DIST
VEL = 0.625 + 0.12*DIST - 0.00025*DIST*DIST
```

This incorrect solution points out a common error. Suppose DIST is greater than 30, then the first logical expression is false and we proceed to the next statement to calculate VEL—this part works fine.

Now suppose the logical expression is true—that is, DIST is less than or equal to 30. We execute the assignment statement in the IF statement, correctly calculating VEL when DIST is less than or equal to 30; but the next statement that is executed is the other assignment statement, which replaces the correct value in VEL with an incorrect value.

IF-ELSEIF STATEMENT

When we nest several levels of IF-ELSE statements, it may be difficult to determine which conditions must be true (or false) to execute a set of statements. In these cases, the IF-ELSEIF statement is often used to clarify the program logic; the general form of this statement is

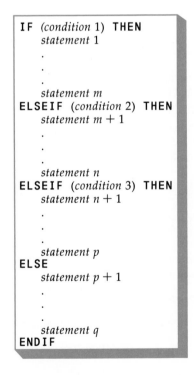

```
IF (condition 1) THEN
    statement 1
    .
    .
    .
    statement m
ELSEIF (condition 2) THEN
    statement m + 1
    .
    .
    .
    statement n
ELSEIF (condition 3) THEN
    statement n + 1
    .
    .
    .
    statement p
ELSE
    statement p + 1
    .
    .
    .
    statement q
ENDIF
```

We have shown two ELSEIF clauses; there may be more or less in an actual construction. If condition 1 is true, then only statements 1 through *m* are executed. If condition 1 is false and condition 2 is true, then only statements *m* + 1 through *n* are executed. If conditions 1 and 2 are false and condition 3 is true, then only statements $n + 1$ through p are executed. If more than one condition is true, the first condition encountered is the only one executed.

If none of the conditions are true, then statements $p + 1$ through q are executed. If there is not a final ELSE clause and none of the conditions are true, then the entire construction is skipped. The IF-ELSEIF form is also called a CASE structure because a number of cases are tested. Each case is defined by its corresponding condition.

EXAMPLE 3-5 Weight Category

An analysis of a group of weight measurements involves converting a weight value into an integer category number that is determined as follows:

CATEGORY	WEIGHT (pounds)
1	weight ≤ 50.0
2	$50.0 <$ weight ≤ 125.0
3	$125.0 <$ weight ≤ 200.0
4	$200.0 <$ weight

Write FORTRAN statements that put the correct value (1, 2, 3, or 4) into CATEGR based on the value of WEIGHT. Assume that CATEGR has been explicitly typed as an integer variable.

Solution 1

This solution uses nested IF-ELSE statements:

```
IF (WEIGHT.LE.50.0) THEN
   CATEGR = 1
ELSE
   IF (WEIGHT.LE.125.0) THEN
      CATEGR = 2
   ELSE
      IF (WEIGHT.LE.200.0) THEN
         CATEGR = 3
      ELSE
         CATEGR = 4
      ENDIF
   ENDIF
ENDIF
```

Solution 2

This solution uses the IF-ELSEIF statement:

```
IF (WEIGHT.LE.50.0) THEN
   CATEGR = 1
ELSEIF (WEIGHT.LE.125.0) THEN
   CATEGR = 2
ELSEIF (WEIGHT.LE.200.0) THEN
   CATEGR = 3
ELSE
   CATEGR = 4
ENDIF
```

As you can see, Solution 2 is more compact than Solution 1: It combines the ELSE and IF statements into the single statement ELSEIF and eliminates two of the ENDIF statements.

The order of the conditions is important in Solution 2 because the evaluation will stop as soon as a true condition has been encountered. Changing the order of the conditions and the category assignments can cause the CATEGR value to be set incorrectly.

SELF-TEST 3–1

This self-test allows you to check quickly to see if you have remembered some of the key points from Section 3–2. If you have any problems with the exercises, you should reread this section. The solutions are included at the end of the text.

For problems 1–8, use the values given to determine whether the following logical expressions are true or false.

$$A = 5.5 \quad B = 1.5 \quad I = -3 \quad DONE = .FALSE.$$

1. A.LT.10.0
2. A + B.GE.6.5
3. I.NE.0
4. B - I.GT.A
5. .NOT.(A.EQ.3*B)
6. -I.LE.I + 6
7. (A.LT.10.0).AND.(A.GT.5.0)
8. (ABS(I).GT.3).OR.DONE

For problems 9–15, give FORTRAN statements that perform the steps indicated.

9. If TIME is greater than 15.0, increment TIME by 1.0.
10. When the square root of POLY is less than 0.5, print the value of POLY.
11. If the difference between VOLT1 and VOLT2 is larger than 10.0, print the values of VOLT1 and VOLT2.
12. If the value of DEN is less than 0.005, print the message 'DENOMINATOR IS TOO SMALL.'
13. If the natural logarithm of X is greater than or equal to 3, set TIME equal to zero and increment COUNT.
14. If DIST is less than 50.0 and TIME is greater than 10.0, increment TIME by 2.0. Otherwise, increment TIME by 2.5.
15. If DIST is greater than or equal to 100.0, increment TIME by 2.0. If DIST is between 50.0 and 100.0, increment TIME by 1.0. Otherwise, increment TIME by 0.5.

3-3 WHILE LOOP STRUCTURE

The WHILE loop is an important structure for repeating a set of statements as long as a certain condition is true. In pseudocode, the WHILE loop structure is

> While condition do
>   statement 1
>   .
>   .
>   .
>   statement m
> statement p

While the condition is true, statements 1 through m are executed. After the group of statements is executed, the condition is retested. If the condition is still true, the group of statements is reexecuted. When the condition is false, execution continues with the statement following the WHILE loop (statement p in our example). The variables modified in the group of statements in the WHILE loop must involve the variables tested in the WHILE loop's condition, or the value of the condition will never change.

Standard FORTRAN 77 does not include a WHILE statement, although many compilers have implemented their own WHILE statement. We will implement the WHILE loop with the IF statement as shown below, so that our programs will be standard FORTRAN 77 and will execute on other FORTRAN 77 compilers without any conversion.

```
n  IF (condition) THEN
       statement 1
           .
           .
           .
       statement m
       GO TO n
   ENDIF
```

In this implementation we used an unconditional transfer statement whose general form is

```
GO TO n
```

where n is the statement number or label of an executable statement in the program. The execution of the GO TO statement causes the flow of program control to transfer, or *branch*, to statement n.

We are now ready to write programs for the algorithms we developed in Section 3-1.

EXAMPLE 3-6   Average of a Set of Data Values

In Example 3–1 we developed a flowchart for the algorithm to find the average of a set of data values. This flowchart is repeated here:

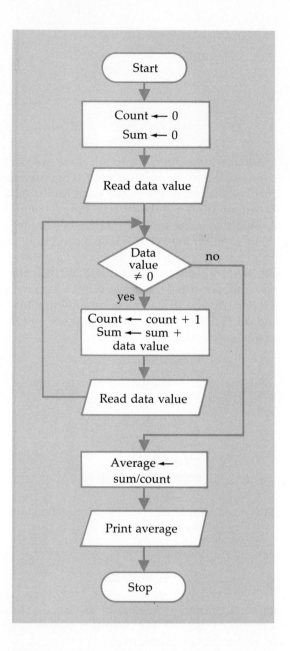

Convert this flowchart into a FORTRAN program.

Solution 1

We have covered the FORTRAN statements for the IF structures and for the WHILE loop. Using these statements, we can translate each step in the flowchart into FORTRAN.

```
*-------------------------------------------------------*
      PROGRAM  COMPUT
*
*   This program computes the average of
*   a set of experimental data values.
*
      INTEGER  COUNT
      REAL  X, SUM, AVERG
*
      SUM = 0.0
      COUNT = 0
      READ*, X
   1 IF (X.NE.0.0) THEN
         SUM = SUM + X
         COUNT = COUNT + 1
         READ*, X
         GO TO 1
      ENDIF
      AVERG = SUM/REAL(COUNT)
      PRINT 5, AVERG
   5 FORMAT (1X,'THE AVERAGE IS ',F6.2)
      END
*-------------------------------------------------------*
```

This is the program we used in Chapter 1 to illustrate the form and readability of a FORTRAN program.

Solution 2

We now present a second solution that uses a logical variable DONE to specify when we have reached the end of the data. In this solution, we initialize the logical variable to the value .FALSE.; when we find the value that indicates the end of the data, we change the value of the logical variable to .TRUE..

```
*-------------------------------------------------------*
      PROGRAM COMPUT
*
*   This program computes the average of
*   a set of experimental data values.
*
      INTEGER  COUNT
      REAL  X, SUM, AVERG
      LOGICAL  DONE
*
      DONE = .FALSE.
      SUM = 0.0
      COUNT = 0
      READ*, X
      IF (X.EQ.0.0)  DONE = .TRUE.
*
```

```
    1 IF (.NOT.DONE) THEN
        SUM = SUM + X
        COUNT = COUNT + 1
        READ*, X
        IF (X.EQ.0.0) DONE = .TRUE.
        GO TO 1
      ENDIF
*
      AVERG = SUM/REAL(COUNT)
      PRINT 5, AVERG
    5 FORMAT (1X,'THE AVERAGE IS ',F6.2)
      END
*----------------------------------------------------------*
```

EXAMPLE 3-7 Experimental Data Analysis

In Example 3–2 we developed pseudocode for the algorithm to analyze a set of experimental data values and determine the minimum and maximum values and compute the range of data values. This pseudocode is repeated again:

REFINEMENT IN PSEUDOCODE

> ANALYSIS: Read data value
> maximum ← data value
> minimum ← data value
> Read data value
> While data value is not zero do
>   If data value > maximum then
>   maximum ← data value
>   If data value < minimum then
>   minimum ← data value
>   Read data value
> range ← maximum − minimum
> Print 'MAXIMUM DATA VALUE = ', maximum
> Print 'MINIMUM DATA VALUE = ', minimum
> Print 'RANGE OF VALUES = ', range

Convert this pseudocode into a FORTRAN program.

Solution

Again, using the statements presented in this chapter for the IF structure and the WHILE loop, we can convert each step of the pseudocode into FORTRAN.

```
*----------------------------------------------------------*
      PROGRAM   ANALYZ
*
*  This program determines maximum and minimum values
*  and the range of values for a set of data values.
*
      REAL   X, MAX, MIN, RANGE
*
```

```
      READ*, X
      MAX = X
      MIN = X
      READ*, X
   1 IF (X.NE.0.0) THEN
         IF (X.GT.MAX) MAX = X
         IF (X.LT.MIN) MIN = X
         READ*, X
         GO TO 1
      ENDIF
      RANGE = MAX - MIN
      PRINT 5, MAX
   5 FORMAT (1X,'MAXIMUM DATA VALUE = ',F8.2)
      PRINT 6, MIN
   6 FORMAT (1X,'MINIMUM DATA VALUE = ',F8.2)
      PRINT 7, RANGE
   7 FORMAT (1X,'RANGE OF VALUES = ',F8.2)
      END
*--------------------------------------------------------*
```

If we use the sample data from Example 3–2, the output is

```
  MAXIMUM DATA VALUE =    66.31
  MINIMUM DATA VALUE =    40.56
  RANGE OF VALUES =    25.75
```

3–4   APPLICATION — ROCKET TRAJECTORY (Aeronautical Engineering)

A small rocket is being designed to make wind shear measurements in the vicinity of thunderstorms. Before testing begins, the designers are developing a simulation of the rocket's trajectory. They have derived the following equation that they believe will predict the performance of their test rocket, where t is the elapsed time in seconds:

$$\text{height} = 60 + 2.13t^2 - 0.0013t^4 + 0.000034t^{4.751}$$

The equation gives the height above ground level at time t. The first term (60) is the height in feet above ground level of the nose of the rocket. To check the predicted performance, the rocket is "flown" on a computer, using the preceding equation.

Develop an algorithm and use it to write a complete program to cover a maximum flight of 100 seconds. Increments in time are to be 2.0 seconds from launch through the ascending and descending portions of the trajectory until the rocket descends to within 50 feet of ground level. Below 50 feet the time increments are to be 0.05 seconds. If the rocket impacts prior to 100 seconds, the program is to stop immediately after impact. The output is to be in the following form:

```
TIME (SEC.)     HEIGHT (FT.)

0.0000          XXXX.XXXX
2.0000          XXXX.XXXX
  .
  .
  .
```

As shown in the following diagram, several possible events could occur as we simulate the flight. The height above the ground should increase for a period and then decrease until the rocket impacts. We can test for impact by testing the height for a value equal to or less than zero. It is also possible that the rocket will still be airborne after 100 seconds of flight time. Therefore, we must also test for this condition and stop the program if the value of time becomes greater than 100. In addition, we need to observe the height above ground. As the rocket approaches the ground, we want to monitor its progress more frequently; we will need to reduce our time increment from 2.0 seconds to 0.05 seconds.

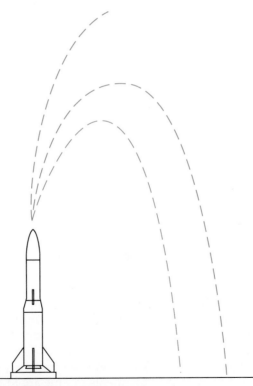

PROBLEM STATEMENT

Using the equation, compute height values and print them along with their corresponding time values. Start time at zero and increment it by 2.0 seconds until the height is less than 50 feet, then increment time by 0.05 seconds. Stop the program if the rocket impacts or if the total time exceeds 100 seconds.

$$\text{height} = 60 + 2.13t^2 - 0.0013t^4 + 0.000034t^{4.751}$$

INPUT/OUTPUT DESCRIPTION

There is no input to the program. The output is a table of time and height values in the following form:

```
TIME (SEC.)      HEIGHT (FT.)

0.0000           XXXX.XXXX
2.0000           XXXX.XXXX
  .
  .
  .
```

HAND EXAMPLE

Using a calculator, compute the first three entries in our table as shown:

```
TIME (SEC.)      HEIGHT (FT.)

0.0000           60.0000
2.0000           68.5001
4.0000           93.7719
```

We are now ready to develop the algorithm so that the computer can compute the rest of the table for us.

ALGORITHM DEVELOPMENT

The initial decomposition comprises two sequential steps, as shown:

DECOMPOSITION

Set time to zero.
Compute heights and print report.

As we begin the refinement, we find that it is easiest to do the refinement in two steps. Our initial refinement yields:

INITIAL REFINEMENT IN PSEUDOCODE

ROCKET: time ← 0
      While above ground and time ≤ 100 do
         Compute height using equation
         Print time, height
         Increment time

In our final refinement, we replace "Increment time" with the steps that take into account our height above ground. We also replace the condition "above ground" with a specific condition based on our height above ground.

ROCKET: time ← 0
          height ← 60
          While height > 0 and time ≤ 100 do
             Compute height using equation
             Print time, height
             If height < 50 then
                time ← time + 0.05
             Else
                time ← time + 2.0

Notice that the height variable was initialized to 60.0 before entering the WHILE loop. Why? Could it have been initialized to any value? Because the condition in the WHILE loop used the height variable, it had to be initialized before the condition was tested. The height must also be set to a value greater than zero or the WHILE loop would never be executed.

We can now translate our pseudocode statements into FORTRAN.

FORTRAN Program 1

```
*-----------------------------------------------------------------*
      PROGRAM  ROCKET
*
*  This program simulates a rocket flight.
*
      REAL  TIME, HEIGHT
*
      TIME = 0.0
      HEIGHT = 60.0
      PRINT 5
  5 FORMAT (1X,'TIME (SEC.)      HEIGHT (FT.)')
      PRINT*
*
  10 IF (HEIGHT.GT.0.0.AND.TIME.LE.100.0) THEN
         HEIGHT = 60.0 + 2.13*TIME**2 - 0.0013*TIME**4
     +            + 0.000034*TIME**4.751
         PRINT 15, TIME, HEIGHT
  15     FORMAT (1X,F7.4,8X,F9.4)
         IF (HEIGHT.LT.50.0) THEN
            TIME = TIME + 0.05
         ELSE
            TIME = TIME + 2.0
         ENDIF
         GO TO 10
      ENDIF
      END
*-----------------------------------------------------------------*
```

As our programs become longer, we will use comment lines with only an asterisk in column 1 to separate groups of statements that have a common function. In the preceding program, the blank comment line separated the steps that initialized variables and printed the heading from the WHILE loop.

Another solution to this problem uses the logical variables introduced in Section 3–2. In this solution, we use a logical variable called DONE. As long as neither of the conditions that indicate that we want to stop the program occurs, the value of this variable remains false. Thus, as long as .NOT.DONE is true, we want to stay in the WHILE loop.

FORTRAN Program 2

```
*------------------------------------------------------------*
      PROGRAM  FLIGHT
*
*  This program simulates a rocket flight.
*
      REAL  TIME, HEIGHT
      LOGICAL  DONE
*
      TIME = 0.0
      HEIGHT = 60.0
      DONE = .FALSE.
      PRINT 5
    5 FORMAT (1X,'TIME (SEC.)      HEIGHT (FT.)')
      PRINT*
*
   10 IF (.NOT.DONE) THEN
          HEIGHT = 60.0 + 2.13*TIME**2 - 0.0013*TIME**4
      +               + 0.000034*TIME**4.751
          PRINT 15, TIME, HEIGHT
   15     FORMAT (1X,F7.4,8X,F9.4)
          IF (HEIGHT.LT.50.0) THEN
              TIME = TIME + 0.05
          ELSE
              TIME = TIME + 2.0
          ENDIF
          DONE = HEIGHT.LE.0.0.OR.TIME.GT.100.0
          GO TO 10
      ENDIF
      END
*------------------------------------------------------------*
```

It is invalid to compare two logical variables with the relation .EQ. or .NE.. Instead, two new relations, .EQV. and .NEQV., are used to represent equivalent and not equivalent. If we wanted to compare .NOT.DONE to the value .TRUE., we could use this statement:

```
IF (.NOT.DONE.EQV..TRUE.) THEN
```

Whenever arithmetic, relational, and logical operators are in the same expression, the arithmetic operations are performed first; the relational operators are then applied to yield true or false values; and these values are evaluated with the logical operators whose precedence is .NOT., .AND., and .OR.. The relations .EQV. and .NEQV. are evaluated last.

TESTING

The first few lines and the last few lines of output are shown. The values are in agreement with the hand-worked example.

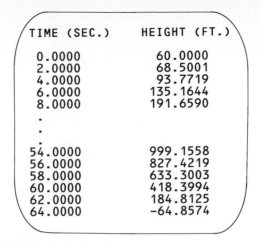

TIME (SEC.)	HEIGHT (FT.)
0.0000	60.0000
2.0000	68.5001
4.0000	93.7719
6.0000	135.1644
8.0000	191.6590
.	
.	
.	
54.0000	999.1558
56.0000	827.4219
58.0000	633.3003
60.0000	418.3994
62.0000	184.8125
64.0000	−64.8574

Can you think of ways to test different parts of the algorithm? We now know that the rocket impacts before 100 seconds of flight time; we could change the cutoff time to 50 seconds to see if this exit from the WHILE loop were working correctly. How could you modify the program to check the change in the increment of the time variable from 2.0 seconds to 0.05 seconds?

3–5 APPLICATION — SUTURE PACKAGING (Biomedical Engineering)

As we mentioned in the introductory problem for this chapter, sutures are strands or fibers used to sew living tissue together after an injury or an operation. Packages of sutures must be sealed carefully before they are shipped to hospitals so that contaminants cannot enter the packages. The object that seals the package is referred to as a sealing die. Generally, sealing dies are heated with an electric heater. For the sealing process to be a success, the sealing die is maintained at an established temperature and must contact the package with a predetermined pressure for an established time period. The time period in which the sealing die contacts the package is called dwell. We want to develop an algorithm and a FORTRAN program to analyze the data collected on batches of sutures that have been rejected. We assume that we will be given the temperature, pressure, and dwell time for each batch. For the sutures that have been sealed, the following acceptable range of parameters has been established:

Temperature: 150.0 – 170.0 degrees centigrade
Pressure: 60 – 70 psi (lb/sq in)
Dwell: 2.0 – 2.5 seconds

All sutures in a batch will be rejected if any of these conditions is not met.

Our program will ask the user to enter the batch code, temperature, pressure, and dwell time for each batch that has been rejected during some time period. We want to collect data on the reasons why the batches were rejected to attempt to find the underlying problem. For example, if most of the rejections were due to temperature problems, then we need to check the electric heater in the sealing die. If most of the rejections were due to pressure problems, then we need to check the pressure in the air cylinder that lowers the die to the package. Or, if most of the rejections were due to dwell time, then the control information in the sealing die may be in error. Clearly, the first step in locating the source of the problem must be to get a good analysis of the data from rejected batches of sutures. The data we will compute in this program will be the percentage of rejections due to temperature, the percentage of rejections due to pressure, and the percentage of rejections due to dwell time. If a batch was rejected for more than one reason, it should be counted in the total for each rejection category.

We now use our five-phase design process to develop an algorithm and a FORTRAN solution to this problem.

PROBLEM STATEMENT

Write a program to print a report analyzing the information for all batches of sutures that were not properly sealed, where a proper seal requires the following range of parameters in the sealing process:

Temperature: 150.0–170.0 degrees centigrade
Pressure: 60–70 psi (lb/sq in)
Dwell: 2.0–2.5 seconds

INPUT/OUTPUT DESCRIPTION

The input to the program will be four values for each batch that was rejected: the batch number, the temperature, the pressure, and the dwell time. A negative batch number indicates the end of the data. The output from the program will be a report giving the percentages of the batches rejected because of temperature problems, pressure problems, and dwell time problems.

HAND EXAMPLE

Assume the following data represents the information on the batches rejected during one day:

BATCH NUMBER	TEMPERATURE	PRESSURE	DWELL TIME
24551	145.5	62.3	2.13
24582	153.7	63.0	2.52
26553	160.3	58.9	2.51
26623	159.5	58.9	2.01
26624	160.5	61.3	1.98

In this data, batch 24551 was rejected because of temperature, batch 24582 was rejected because of dwell time, batch 26553 was rejected because of pressure and dwell time, batch 26623 was rejected due to pressure, and batch 26624 was rejected due to dwell time. The report summarizing this information is the following:

```
SUMMARY OF BATCH REJECT INFORMATION

20.0 % REJECTED DUE TO TEMPERATURE
40.0 % REJECTED DUE TO PRESSURE
60.0 % REJECTED DUE TO DWELL TIME
```

ALGORITHM DEVELOPMENT

The decomposition contains the following sequential steps:

DECOMPOSITION

Read data and collect information.
Print report.

Using the hand-worked example solution as a guide, we can develop the initial pseudocode for this problem.

INITIAL REFINEMENT IN PSEUDOCODE

```
SEALS: count ← 0
       Read batch, temperature, pressure, dwell
       While batch ≥ 0 do
            Determine reject reason and add to totals
            count ← count + 1
            Read batch, temperature, pressure, dwell
       Convert totals to percentages
       Print report
```

We still need to refine the step further to determine which parameters were not within the specified values, and then add to the corresponding totals. This involves three different tests: one for the temperature, one for the pressure, and one for the dwell time. We will call the rejection totals rejctt (for rejections due to temperature), rejctp (for rejections due to pressure), and rejctd (for rejections due to dwell time). The final refinement in pseudocode follows.

Final Refinement in Pseudocode

```
SEALS: count ← 0
         rejctt ← 0
         rejctp ← 0
         rejctd ← 0
         Read batch, temperature, pressure, dwell
         While batch ≥ 0 do
              If temperature out of bounds then
                   rejctt ← rejctt + 1
              If pressure out of bounds then
                   rejctp ← rejctp + 1
              If dwell out of bounds then
                   rejctd ← rejctd + 1
              count ← count + 1
              Read batch, temperature, pressure, dwell
         Convert reject totals to percentages
         Print report
```

We now convert the pseudocode steps to FORTRAN.

FORTRAN Program

```
*------------------------------------------------------------------*
      PROGRAM   SEALS
*
*  This program analyzes data on batches of sutures that have
*  not been properly sealed, and then prints a report.
*
      INTEGER  BATCH, COUNT, REJCTT, REJCTP, REJCTD
      REAL  TEMP, PRESSR, DWELL, PERCT, PERCP, PERCD
*
      COUNT = 0
      REJCTT = 0
      REJCTP = 0
      REJCTD = 0
*
      PRINT*, 'ENTER BATCH NUMBER, TEMPERATURE, PRESSURE, DWELL'
      PRINT*, 'FOR BATCHES THAT HAVE BEEN REJECTED'
      PRINT*, '(NEGATIVE BATCH NUMBER TO STOP)'
      READ*, BATCH, TEMP, PRESSR, DWELL
*
    5 IF (BATCH.GE.0) THEN
         IF (TEMP.LT.150.0.OR.TEMP.GT.170.0) REJCTT = REJCTT + 1
         IF (PRESSR.LT.60.0.OR.PRESSR.GT.70.0) REJCTP = REJCTP + 1
         IF (DWELL.LT.2.0.OR.DWELL.GT.2.5) REJCTD = REJCTD + 1
         COUNT = COUNT + 1
         PRINT*, 'ENTER NEXT SET OF DATA'
         READ*, BATCH, TEMP, PRESSR, DWELL
         GO TO 5
      ENDIF
      PERCT = REAL(REJCTT)/REAL(COUNT)*100.0
      PERCP = REAL(REJCTP)/REAL(COUNT)*100.0
      PERCD = REAL(REJCTD)/REAL(COUNT)*100.0
*
```

```
      PRINT*
      PRINT*, 'SUMMARY OF BATCH REJECT INFORMATION'
      PRINT*
      PRINT 10, PERCT
   10 FORMAT (1X,F6.2,' % REJECTED DUE TO TEMPERATURE')
      PRINT 15, PERCP
   15 FORMAT (1X,F6.2,' % REJECTED DUE TO PRESSURE')
      PRINT 20, PERCD
   20 FORMAT (1X,F6.2,' % REJECTED DUE TO DWELL')
      END
```
- -

TESTING

The output of this program from the data used in the hand example is:

```
ENTER BATCH NUMBER, TEMPERATURE, PRESSURE, DWELL
FOR BATCHES THAT HAVE BEEN REJECTED
(NEGATIVE BATCH NUMBER TO STOP)
24551          145.5          62.3          2.13
ENTER NEXT SET OF DATA
24582          153.7          63.0          2.52
ENTER NEXT SET OF DATA
26553          160.3          58.9          2.51
ENTER NEXT SET OF DATA
26623          159.5          58.9          2.01
ENTER NEXT SET OF DATA
26624          160.5          61.3          1.98
ENTER NEXT SET OF DATA
-1             0.0            0.0           0.0

SUMMARY OF BATCH REJECT INFORMATION

 20.0 % REJECTED DUE TO TEMPERATURE
 40.0 % REJECTED DUE TO PRESSURE
 60.0 % REJECTED DUE TO DWELL TIME
```

3-6   DO LOOP

In Section 3-3 we used the IF statement to build WHILE loops. A special form of the WHILE loop is the counting loop, or iterative loop. Implementing a counting loop generally involves initializing a counter before entering the loop, modifying the counter within the loop, and exiting the loop when the counter reaches a specified value. Counting loops are executed a specified number of times. The three steps (initialize, modify, and test) can be incorporated in a WHILE loop as we have already seen; but, they still require three different statements. A special statement, the DO statement, combines all three steps into one. Using the DO statement to construct a loop results in a construction called a DO loop.

The general form of the DO statement is

> **DO** *k index = initial, limit, increment*

The constant k is the number of the statement that represents the end of the loop; index is a variable used as the loop counter; initial represents the initial value given to the loop counter; limit represents the value used to determine when the DO loop has been completed; and increment represents the value to be added to the loop counter each time the loop is executed.

The values of initial, limit, and increment are the *parameters* of the DO loop. If the increment is omitted, an increment of 1 is assumed. When the value of the index is greater than the limit, control is passed to the statement following the end of the loop. The end of the loop is usually indicated by the CONTINUE statement, whose general form is

$$k\ \text{CONTINUE}$$

where k is the statement number referenced by the corresponding DO statement. Before we list the rules for using a DO loop, let's look at a simple example.

EXAMPLE 3–8   Integer Sum

The sum of the integers 1 through 50 is represented mathematically as

$$\sum_{i=1}^{50} i = 1 + 2 + \cdots + 49 + 50$$

Obviously, we do not want to write one long assignment statement of the form

$$SUM = 1 + 2 + 3 + \cdots + 50$$

A better solution is to build a loop that executes 50 times and adds a number to the sum each time, as shown in the following solutions.

WHILE Loop Solution

```
        INTEGER   SUM, NUMBER
        .
        .
        .
        SUM = 0
        NUMBER = 1
     10 IF (NUMBER.LE.50) THEN
            SUM = SUM + NUMBER
            NUMBER = NUMBER + 1
            GO TO 10
        ENDIF
```

DO Loop Solution

```
        INTEGER   SUM, NUMBER
        .
        .
        .
        SUM = 0
        DO 10 NUMBER=1,50
            SUM = SUM + NUMBER
     10 CONTINUE
```

The DO statement identifies statement 10 as the end of the loop. The index NUMBER is initialized to 1. The loop is repeated until the value of NUMBER is greater than 50. Because the third parameter is omitted, the index NUMBER is incremented automatically by 1 at the end of each loop. Comparing the DO loop solution with the WHILE loop solution, we see that the DO loop solution is shorter but that both compute the same value for SUM.

STRUCTURE OF A DO LOOP

We have seen a DO loop in a simple example. We now need to summarize the rules that relate to its structure.

1. The index of the DO loop must be a variable, but it may be either real or integer.
2. The parameters of the DO loop may be constants, variables, or expressions and can also be real or integer types.
3. The increment can be either positive or negative, but it cannot be zero.
4. A DO loop may end on any executable statement that is not a transfer, an IF statement, or another DO statement. The CONTINUE statement is an executable statement that was designed expressly for closing a DO loop; although other statements may be used, we strongly encourage the consistent use of CONTINUE to indicate the end of the loop.
5. We will use the following pseudocode for an iterative loop:

   For index = initial to limit by step do
       set of statements

   The "by step" clause is omitted if the increment is 1. The pseudocode for the iterative loop we used in Example 3–8 is

   For number = 1 to 50 do
       sum ← sum + number

6. The flowchart symbol for an iterative loop is

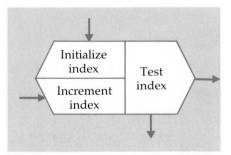

Note that the symbol is divided into three parts, each corresponding to the three steps in building an iterative loop. The flowchart for the iterative loop in Example 3−8 is

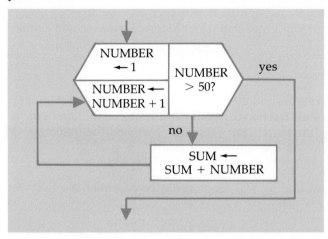

These rules define the structure of the DO loop but do not define the steps in its execution. The following discussion describes these rules.

EXECUTION OF A DO LOOP

In the following list we present a complete set of rules that relate to DO loop execution. We suggest that you read through them once and then go through the set of examples that follow the rules. Later, reread these rules. Do not worry about memorizing them; after you have gone through the set of examples, most of the rules will seem logical.

1. The test for completion is done at the beginning of the loop, as in a WHILE loop. If the initial value of the index is greater than the limit and the increment is positive, the loop will not be executed. For instance, the statement

    ### DO 10 I=5,2

    sets up a loop that ends at statement 10. The initial value of the index I is 5, which is greater than the limit 2; therefore, the statements within the loop will be skipped and control passes to the statement following statement 10.
2. The value of the index should not be modified by other statements during the execution of the loop.
3. After the loop begins execution, changing the values of the parameters will have no effect on the loop.
4. If the increment is negative, the exit from the loop will occur when the value of the index is less than the limit.
5. Although it is not recommended, you may branch out of a DO loop before it is completed. The value of the index will be the value just before the branch. (If you need to exit the DO loop before it is completed, you should restructure the loop as a WHILE loop to maintain a structured program.)

6. Upon completion of the DO loop, the index contains the last value that exceeded the limit.
7. Always enter a DO loop through the DO statement so that it will be initiated properly.
8. The number of times that a DO loop will be executed can be computed as

$$\left[\frac{\text{limit} - \text{initial}}{\text{increment}} \right] + 1$$

The brackets around the fraction represent the greatest integer value; that is, we drop any fractional portion (truncate) of the quotient. If this value is negative, the loop is not executed. If we had the following DO statement

DO 35 K=5,83,4

the corresponding DO loop would be executed the following number of times:

$$\left[\frac{83 - 5}{4} \right] + 1 = \left[\frac{78}{4} \right] + 1 = 20$$

The value of the index K would be 5, then 9, then 13, and so on until the final value of 81. The loop would not be executed with the value 85 because that value is greater than the limit, 83.

The next set of examples illustrates both the structure and the execution of the DO loop.

EXAMPLE 3-9 Polynomial Model with Integer Time

Polynomials are often used to model data and experimental results. Assume that the polynomial

$$3t^2 + 4.5$$

models the results of an experiment where t represents time in seconds. Write a complete program to evaluate this polynomial for the period of time from 1 second to 10 seconds in increments of 1 second (that is, let $t = 1, 2, 3, 4, 5, 6, 7, 8, 9,$ and 10). For each value of time, print the time and the polynomial value.

Solution

The solution to this problem requires printing the headings of the report and an iterative loop to evaluate the polynomial.

DECOMPOSITION

| Print headings. |
| Print report. |

Refining the "Print report" step into an iterative loop yields the following pseudocode.

REFINEMENT IN PSEUDOCODE

POLY1: Print headings
     For time = 1 to 10 do
       poly ← 3 · time² + 4.5
       Print time, poly

We now convert the pseudocode into a FORTRAN program.

FORTRAN PROGRAM

```
*------------------------------------------------------*
      PROGRAM  POLY1
*
*  This program prints a table of
*  values for a polynomial.
*
      INTEGER  TIME
      REAL   POLY
*
      PRINT*, 'POLYNOMIAL MODEL'
      PRINT*, 'TIME   POLYNOMIAL'
      PRINT*, '(SEC)'
      PRINT*
*
      DO 15 TIME=1,10
         POLY = 3.0*REAL(TIME)**2 + 4.5
         PRINT 10, TIME, POLY
   10    FORMAT (1X,I2,5X,F6.2)
   15 CONTINUE
      END
*------------------------------------------------------*
```

The output from this program is

```
POLYNOMIAL MODEL
TIME    POLYNOMIAL
(SEC)

  1        7.50
  2       16.50
  3       31.50
  4       52.50
  5       79.50
  6      112.50
  7      151.50
  8      196.50
  9      247.50
 10      304.50
```

EXAMPLE 3-10   Polynomial Model with Real Time

We again assume that the polynomial

$$3t^2 + 4.5$$

models an experiment where *t* represents time in seconds. Write a program to evaluate this polynomial for time beginning at zero seconds and ending at 5 seconds in increments of 0.5 seconds.

Solution

The solution to this problem requires printing the headings of the report and an iterative loop to evaluate the polynomial.

DECOMPOSITION

Print headings.
Print report.

Refining the "Print report" step into an iterative loop yields the following flowchart:

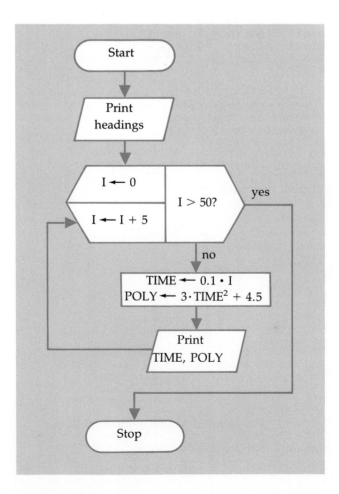

Converting the flowchart to FORTRAN gives the following program:

FORTRAN PROGRAM

```
*-------------------------------------------------------*
      PROGRAM  POLY2
*
*   This program prints a table of
*   values for a polynomial.
*
      INTEGER  I
      REAL  TIME, POLY
*
      PRINT*, 'POLYNOMIAL MODEL'
      PRINT*, 'TIME    POLYNOMIAL'
      PRINT*, '(SEC)'
      PRINT*
*
      DO 15 I=0,50,5
         TIME = 0.1*REAL(I)
         POLY = 3.0*TIME*TIME + 4.5
         PRINT 10, TIME, POLY
   10    FORMAT (1X,F4.1,5X,F5.2)
   15 CONTINUE
      END
*-------------------------------------------------------*
```

Note that the value of TIME is computed from an integer that varies from 0 to 50 in steps of 5. Another possibility would have been to use the following DO statement:

$$\text{DO 15 TIME=0.0,5.0,0.5}$$

However, it is wise to avoid DO statements such as this one with real parameters because these statements do not always execute exactly the way we expect because of truncation within the computer. For example, suppose that the value for 0.5 is stored as a value slightly less than 0.5 in our computer system. Each time we add 0.5 to the index, we are adding less than we intend, and the values are not those we intend; in this case, the value of TIME for the last time that we want to execute the loop would be less than 5.0 instead of exactly 5.0.

The output from this program is

```
POLYNOMIAL MODEL
TIME    POLYNOMIAL
(SEC)

0.0        4.50
0.5        5.25
1.0        7.50
1.5       11.25
2.0       16.50
2.5       23.25
3.0       31.50
3.5       41.25
4.0       52.50
4.5       65.25
5.0       79.50
```

EXAMPLE 3–11 Polynomial Model with Variable Time

Assume that we want to evaluate the same polynomial

$$3t^2 + 4.5$$

beginning at t equal to zero, in increments of 0.25, for a variable number of seconds. Write a program to read an integer NSEC that represents the number of seconds to be used for evaluating the polynomial. Print the corresponding table.

Solution

The solution to this problem requires reading the number of seconds that the report is supposed to cover, printing the headings of the report, and an iterative loop to evaluate the polynomial.

DECOMPOSITION

Read number of seconds.
Print headings.
Print report.

Refining the "Print report" step into an iterative loop yields the following pseudocode:

REFINEMENT IN PSEUDOCODE

```
POLY1: Read nsec
       Print headings
       For i = 0 to 100 · nsec by 25 do
           time ← 0.01 · i
           poly ← 3 · time · time + 4.5
           Print time, poly
```

We now convert the pseudocode into a FORTRAN program.

```
*-------------------------------------------------------------*
      PROGRAM   POLY3
*
*  This program prints a table of
*  values for a polynomial.
*
      INTEGER  I, NSEC
      REAL   TIME, POLY
*
      PRINT*, 'ENTER NUMBER OF SECONDS FOR TABLE'
      READ*, NSEC
      PRINT*
      PRINT*, 'POLYNOMIAL MODEL'
      PRINT*, 'TIME    POLYNOMIAL'
      PRINT*, '(SEC)'
      PRINT*
*
      DO 15 I=0,100*NSEC,25
         TIME = 0.01*REAL(I)
         POLY = 3.0*TIME*TIME + 4.5
         PRINT 10, TIME, POLY
   10    FORMAT (1X,F4.2,5X,F7.4)
   15 CONTINUE
      END
*-------------------------------------------------------------*
```

If we enter the value 4 for the number of seconds, the output from this program is

```
ENTER NUMBER OF SECONDS FOR TABLE
4

POLYNOMIAL MODEL
TIME    POLYNOMIAL
(SEC)

0.00     4.5000
0.25     4.6875
0.50     5.2500
0.75     6.1875
1.00     7.5000
1.25     9.1875
1.50    11.2500
1.75    13.6875
2.00    16.5000
2.25    19.6875
2.50    23.2500
2.75    27.1875
3.00    31.5000
3.25    36.1875
3.50    41.2500
3.75    46.6875
4.00    52.5000
```

We are now ready to develop problem solutions that use the DO statement to implement iterative loops.

This self-test allows you to check quickly to see if you have remembered some of the key points from Section 3–5. If you have any problems with the exercises, you should reread this section. The solutions are included at the end of the text.

In problems 1–6, determine the number of times that the statements in the DO loop will be executed.

1. `DO 10 NUM=3,20`
2. `DO 10 COUNT=-2,14`
3. `DO 10 K=-2,-10,-1`
4. `DO 10 TIME=10,0,-1`
5. `DO 10 TIME=10,5`
6. `DO 10 INDEX=314,-52`

For problems 7–11, give the value in COUNT after each of the following loops is executed. Assume that COUNT is initialized to zero before starting each problem.

```
 7.    DO 5 I=1,10
          COUNT = COUNT + 1
       5 CONTINUE
 8.    DO 5 K=1,10
          COUNT = COUNT + K
       5 CONTINUE
 9.    DO 5 INDEX=-2,2
          COUNT = COUNT + INDEX
       5 CONTINUE
10.    DO 5 NUM=5,0,-1
          COUNT = COUNT - NUM
       5 CONTINUE
11.    DO 5 M=5,5
          COUNT = COUNT*M
       5 CONTINUE
```

3-7   APPLICATION — TIMBER REGROWTH
(Environmental Engineering)

A problem in timber management is to determine how much of an area to leave uncut so that the harvested area is reforested in a certain period of time. It is assumed that reforestation takes place at a known rate per year, depending on climate and soil conditions. A reforestation equation expresses this growth as a function of the amount of timber standing and the reforestation rate. For example, if 100 acres are left standing after harvesting and the reforestation rate is 0.05, then $100 + 0.05*100$, or 105 acres, are forested at the end of the first year. At the end of the second year, the number of acres forested is $105 + 0.05*105$, or 110.25 acres.

Write a program to read the identification number of an area, the total number of acres in the area, the number of acres that are uncut, and the reforestation rate. Print a report that tabulates for 20 years the number of acres reforested and the total number of acres forested at the end of each year.

PROBLEM STATEMENT

Compute the number of acres forested at the end of each year for 20 years for a given area.

INPUT/OUTPUT DESCRIPTION

The input information consists of the identification number for the area of land, the total acres, the number of acres with trees, and the reforestation rate. The output is a table with a row of data for each of 20 years. Each row of information contains the number of acres reforested during that year and the total number of acres forested at the end of the year.

HAND EXAMPLE

Assume that there are 14,000 acres total with 2500 acres uncut. If the reforestation rate is 0.02, we can compute a few entries as shown:

Year 1 $2500*0.02 = 50$ acres of new growth
original 2500 acres + 50 new acres =   *2550 acres forested*

Year 2 $2550*0.02 = 51$ acres of new growth
original 2550 acres + 51 new acres =   *2601 acres forested*

Year 3 $2601*0.02 = 52.02$ acres of new growth
original 2601 acres + 52.02 new acres = *2653.02 acres forested*

ALGORITHM DEVELOPMENT

The overall structure is an iterative loop that is executed 20 times, once for each year. Inside the loop we need to compute the number of acres reforested during that year and add that number to the acres forested at the beginning of the year; this will compute the total number of acres forested at the end of the year. The output statement should be inside the loop because we want to print the number of acres forested at the end of each year.

DECOMPOSITION

Read initial information.
Print headings.
Print report.

INITIAL REFINEMENT IN PSEUDOCODE

TIMBER: Read initial information
       Print headings
       For year = 1 to 20 do
          Compute reforested amount
          Add reforested amount to uncut amount
          Print reforested amount, uncut amount

Clearly an error condition exists if the uncut area exceeds the total area. We will test for this condition and exit after printing an error message if it occurs. It is possible to imagine soil conditions that would have a zero or negative reforestation rate so we will not perform any error checking on the rate. However, all the values read will be printed, or echoed, so that the user can recognize an error in an input value. We now add these refinements to our initial pseudocode.

FINAL REFINEMENT IN PSEUDOCODE

TIMBER: Read identification, total, uncut, rate
       Print identification, total, uncut, rate
       If uncut > total then
          Print error message
       Else
          Print headings
          For year = 1 to 20 do
             refor ← uncut*rate
             uncut ← uncut + refor
             Print year, refor, uncut

From the pseudocode, the overall structure of the program is evident. The outer structure is an IF-ELSE structure, with a DO loop in the ELSE portion. We can now convert the pseudocode into FORTRAN.

FORTRAN Program

```
*------------------------------------------------------------*
      PROGRAM  TIMBER
*
*  This program computes a reforestation summary
*  for an area that has not been completely harvested.
*
      INTEGER  ID, YEAR
      REAL   TOTAL, UNCUT, RATE, REFOR
*
      PRINT*, 'ENTER LAND IDENTIFICATION (INTEGER)'
      READ*, ID
      PRINT*, 'ENTER TOTAL NUMBER OF ACRES'
      READ*, TOTAL
      PRINT*, 'ENTER NUMBER OF ACRES UNCUT'
      READ*, UNCUT
      PRINT*, 'ENTER REFORESTATION RATE'
      READ*, RATE
*
      IF (UNCUT.GT.TOTAL) THEN
          PRINT*, 'UNCUT AREA LARGER THAN ENTIRE AREA'
      ELSE
          PRINT*
          PRINT*, 'REFORESTATION SUMMARY'
          PRINT*
          PRINT 5, ID
    5     FORMAT (1X,'IDENTIFICATION NUMBER ',I5)
          PRINT 10, TOTAL
   10     FORMAT (1X,'TOTAL ACRES = ',F10.2)
          PRINT 20, UNCUT
   20     FORMAT (1X,'UNCUT ACRES = ',F10.2)
          PRINT 30, RATE
   30     FORMAT (1X,'REFORESTATION RATE = ',F5.3)
          PRINT*
          PRINT*, 'YEAR  REFORESTED   TOTAL REFORESTED'
          DO 50 YEAR=1,20
              REFOR = UNCUT*RATE
              UNCUT = UNCUT + REFOR
              PRINT 40, YEAR, REFOR, UNCUT
   40         FORMAT (1X,I3,F11.3,F17.3)
   50     CONTINUE
      ENDIF
      END
*------------------------------------------------------------*
```

Using the test data from the hand-worked example, a typical interaction is

```
ENTER LAND IDENTIFICATION (INTEGER)
?25563
ENTER TOTAL NUMBER OF ACRES
?14000.0
ENTER NUMBER OF ACRES UNCUT
?2500.0
ENTER REFORESTATION RATE
?0.02


REFORESTATION SUMMARY

IDENTIFICATION NUMBER 25563
TOTAL ACRES =    14000.00
UNCUT ACRES =     2500.00
REFORESTATION RATE = 0.020


YEAR   REFORESTED   TOTAL REFORESTED
 1       50.000        2550.000
 2       51.000        2601.000
 3       52.020        2653.020
 4       53.060        2706.080
 5       54.122        2760.202
 6       55.204        2815.406
 7       56.308        2871.714
 8       57.434        2929.148
 9       58.583        2987.732
10       59.755        3047.486
11       60.950        3108.436
12       62.169        3170.605
13       63.412        3234.017
14       64.680        3298.697
15       65.974        3364.671
16       67.293        3431.964
17       68.639        3500.604
18       70.012        3570.616
19       71.412        3642.028
20       72.841        3714.869
```

The numbers match the ones we computed by hand. Try an example to test the error condition by using an uncut area larger than the total area. What happens if the reforestation rate is 0.00, or −0.02? Should there be an upper limit on the reforestation rate? This information is not given in the original problem so we probably should not set one arbitrarily. What happens if you enter 14,000.0 instead of 14000.0? It might be a good idea to remind the program user not to use commas in numbers. How would you do this?

3-8 APPLICATION—CABLE CAR VELOCITY
(Mechanical Engineering)

This problem involves a 1000-foot cable that is stretched between two towers, with a supporting tower midway between the two end towers. The velocity of the cable car depends on its position on the cable. When the cable car is within 30 feet of a tower, its velocity is

$$\text{velocity} = 2.425 + 0.00175d^2 \text{ ft/sec}$$

where d is the distance in feet from the cable car to the nearest tower. If the cable car is not within 30 feet of a tower, its velocity is

$$\text{velocity} = 0.625 + 0.12d - 0.00025d^2 \text{ ft/sec}$$

Print a table starting with the cable car at the first tower and moving to the last tower in increments of 10 feet. At each increment of 10 feet, print the number of the nearest tower (1 = first, 2 = middle, 3 = end), the distance from the first tower, and the velocity of the cable car.

PROBLEM STATEMENT

Write a program to print a table containing distances and velocities of a cable car as it moves from the first tower to the last tower in increments of 10 feet.

INPUT/OUTPUT DESCRIPTION

There is no input to the program. The output is a table containing distances and velocities.

HAND EXAMPLE

As we begin thinking about this problem, it is helpful to draw a rough diagram of the tower configuration:

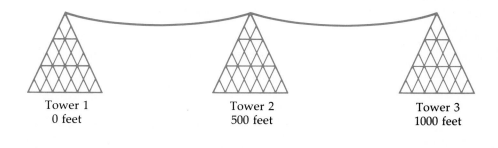

Tower 1   Tower 2   Tower 3
0 feet   500 feet   1000 feet

The cable car will be closest to Tower 1 if the total distance of the cable car from Tower 1 is 0 to 250 feet. When the total distance is greater than 250 feet but less than 750 feet, the cable car is closest to Tower 2. When the total distance is greater than or equal to 750 feet, the cable car is closest to Tower 3. (Note that when the total distance is 250 feet, we could choose Tower 1 or 2. A similar situation occurs when the total distance is 750 feet.)

Furthermore, the distance to the nearest tower is the total distance if the total distance is less than or equal to 250 feet. When the total distance is between 250 feet and 750 feet, the distance to the nearest tower is the absolute value of the total distance minus 500 feet. We use the absolute value here so that the distance is always positive. Finally, the distance to the nearest tower is 1000 feet minus the total distance when the total distance is greater than 750 feet. Pick a few values of the total distance and use these formulas to convince yourself that they are correct.

Total Distance	Distance to Nearest Tower
200	200
300	$|300 - 500| = 200$
650	$|650 - 500| = 150$
850	$1000 - 850 = 150$

ALGORITHM DEVELOPMENT

Because there is no program input, the decomposition is

DECOMPOSITION

Print headings.
Compute velocities and print report.

Using the hand-worked example solution as a guide, we can flowchart the steps needed to determine each set of entries in the table.

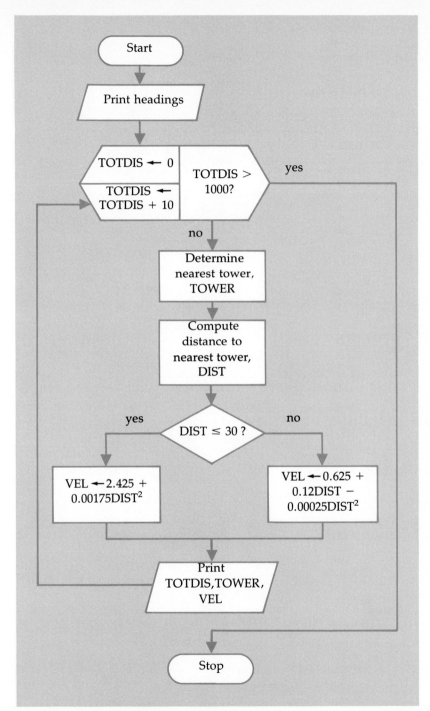

We still need to refine further two steps in the flowchart: "Determine nearest tower" and "Compute distance to nearest tower." Relying on the steps developed in our hand-worked example, we develop this refined flowchart:

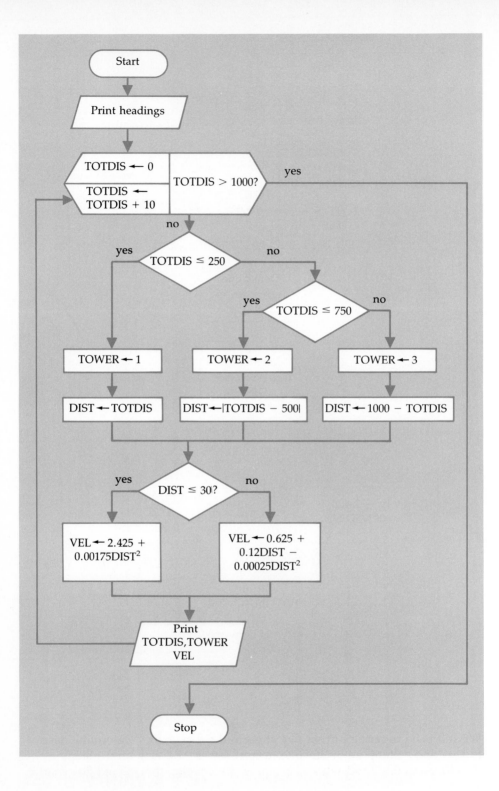

Note the use of blank comment lines to separate sets of steps in the FORTRAN solution.

FORTRAN Program

```
*----------------------------------------------------------------*
      PROGRAM  CABLE
*
*  This program computes the velocity of a cable car
*  on a thousand-foot cable with three towers.
*
      INTEGER  TOTDIS, DIST, TOWER
      REAL  VEL
*
      PRINT 1
    1 FORMAT (1X,9X,'CABLE CAR REPORT')
      PRINT*
      PRINT 2
    2 FORMAT (1X,'DISTANCE  NEAREST TOWER  VELOCITY')
      PRINT 3
    3 FORMAT (1X,'  (FT)',19X,'(FT/SEC)')
      PRINT*
*
      DO 50 TOTDIS=0,1000,10
         IF (TOTDIS.LE.250) THEN
            TOWER = 1
            DIST = TOTDIST
         ELSEIF (TOTDIS.LE.750) THEN
            TOWER = 2
            DIST = ABS(TOTDIS - 500)
         ELSE
            TOWER = 3
            DIST = 1000 - TOTDIS
         ENDIF
         IF (DIST.LE.30) THEN
            VEL = 2.425 + 0.00175*DIST*DIST
         ELSE
            VEL = 0.625 + 0.12*DIST - 0.00025*DIST*DIST
         ENDIF
         PRINT 30, TOTDIS, TOWER, VEL
   30    FORMAT (1X,I4,11X,I1,9X,F7.2)
   50 CONTINUE
      END
*----------------------------------------------------------------*
```

A portion of the output from this program is

```
                  CABLE CAR REPORT

        DISTANCE   NEAREST TOWER   VELOCITY
          (FT)                     (FT/SEC)

            0            1           2.42
           10            1           2.60
           20            1           3.13
            .            .             .
            .            .             .
            .            .             .
          980            3           3.13
          990            3           2.60
         1000            3           2.42
```

3-9 NESTED DO LOOPS

DO loops may be independent of each other, or they may be nested within other DO loops. If loops are nested, they must use different indexes or loop counters. When one loop is nested within another, the inside loop is completely executed each pass through the outer loop. To illustrate, consider the following program:

```
*-----------------------------------------------------------------*
*     PROGRAM  NEST
*
*  This program prints the indexes in nested DO loops.
*
      INTEGER  I, J
*
      PRINT*, ' I   J'
      PRINT*
      DO 20 I=1,5
         DO 10 J=3,1,-1
            PRINT 5, I, J
   5        FORMAT (1X,I3,1X,I3)
  10     CONTINUE
         PRINT*, 'END OF PASS'
  20 CONTINUE
      END
*-----------------------------------------------------------------*
```

The output from this program is

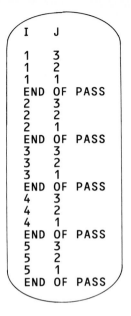

```
I    J
1    3
1    2
1    1
END  OF  PASS
2    3
2    2
2    1
END  OF  PASS
3    3
3    2
3    1
END  OF  PASS
4    3
4    2
4    1
END  OF  PASS
5    3
5    2
5    1
END  OF  PASS
```

The first time through the outer loop, I is initialized to the value 1. We thus begin executing the inner loop: The variable J is initialized to the value 3. After executing the PRINT 5 statement, we reach the end of the inner loop and J is decremented by 1 to the value 2. Because 2 is still larger than the final value of 1, we repeat the loop. J is redecremented by 1 to the value 1, and the loop is repeated again. When J is decremented again, it is less than the final value of 1, so we have completed the inner loop and the message 'END OF PASS' is printed. I is incremented to 2, and we rebegin the inner loop. This process is repeated until I is greater than 5.

EXAMPLE 3-12   Experimental Sums

Write a complete program to read 20 data values. Compute the sum of the first 5 values, the next 5 values, and so on. Print the four sums. Assume that the values are real.

Solution

Although we will read a total of 20 data values, we need only 5 values at a time; thus, an outer loop is needed to read 4 sets of data. Each set of data is 5 values; thus, the inner loop reads the 5 values. It is important to initialize to zero the variable being used to store the sum before the inner loop is begun. We then add 5 values, print the sum, and set the sum back to zero before we read the next 5 values.

The decomposition is a single step in this problem; all the other steps are performed inside the overall loop.

> Print report.

The refinement in pseudocode illustrates the structure of this algorithm, which is a loop within a loop.

REFINEMENT IN PSEUDOCODE

> SUMS: For i = 1 to 4 do
>   sum ← 0
>   For j = 1 to 5 do
>   Read value
>   sum ← sum + value
>   Print sum

We can now translate the pseudocode into FORTRAN.

FORTRAN PROGRAM

```
*------------------------------------------------------------*
      PROGRAM  SUMS
*
*   This program reads 20 values and prints
*   the sum of each group of 5 values.
*
      INTEGER  I, J
      REAL  VALUE, SUM
*
      DO 5 I=1,4
         SUM = 0.0
         DO 1 J=1,5
            READ*, VALUE
            SUM = SUM + VALUE
    1    CONTINUE
         PRINT 3, I, SUM
    3    FORMAT (1X,'SUM ',I1,' = ',F6.2)
    5 CONTINUE
      END
*------------------------------------------------------------*
```

Here is a sample of the type of output that would be printed from this program:

```
SUM 1 =    23.44
SUM 2 =    10.23
SUM 3 =    -5.69
SUM 4 =     1.01
```

EXAMPLE 3-13   Factorial Computation

Write a complete program to compute the factorial of an integer. A few factorials and their corresponding values are shown (an exclamation point following a number symbolizes a factorial):

$0! = 1$
$1! = 1$
$2! = 2*1$
$3! = 3*2*1$
$4! = 4*3*2*1$
$5! = 5*4*3*2*1$

Compute and print the factorial for four different values that are read from the terminal.

Solution

Because the factorial of a negative number is not defined, we should include an error check in our algorithm for this condition. In computing a factorial, we use a DO loop to perform the successive multiplications. Because the overall structure of this problem solution is a loop, the decomposition is again a single step.

DECOMPOSITION

Print report.

As you read the following pseudocode refinement, notice that the overall structure of the algorithm is a counting loop. Within the counting loop is an input statement and an IF-ELSE structure. Within the ELSE portion is another counting loop.

REFINEMENT IN PSEUDOCODE

```
FACT: For i = 1 to 4 do
         Read n
         If n < 0 then
             Print error message
         Else
             nfact ← 1
             If n > 1 then
                 For k = 1 to n do
                     nfact ← nfact*k
             Print n, nfact
```

Converting the refined pseudocode into FORTRAN gives the following program:

FORTRAN Program

```
*-----------------------------------------------------------*
      PROGRAM  FACT
*
*  This program computes the factorial
*  of four values read from the terminal.
*
      INTEGER  N, NFACT, I, K
*
      DO 10 I=1,4
         PRINT*, 'ENTER N'
         READ*, N
         IF (N.LT.0) THEN
            PRINT 2, N
  2         FORMAT (1X,'INVALID N = ',I8)
         ELSE
            NFACT = 1
            IF (N.GT.1) THEN
               DO 4 K=1,N
               NFACT = NFACT*K
  4            CONTINUE
            ENDIF
            PRINT 6, N, NFACT
  6         FORMAT (1X,I4,'! = ',I8)
         ENDIF
 10   CONTINUE
      END
*-----------------------------------------------------------*
```

The output from a sample run of this program is

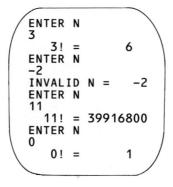

```
ENTER N
3
     3! =        6
ENTER N
-2
INVALID N =    -2
ENTER N
11
    11! = 39916800
ENTER N
0
     0! =        1
```

This self-test allows you to check quickly to see if you have remembered some of the key points from Section 3-8. If you have any problems with the exercises, you should reread this section. The solutions are included at the end of the text.

For problems 1-3, give the value in COUNT after each of the following loops is executed. Assume that COUNT is initialized to zero before starting each problem.

```
1.      DO 10 I=1,5
            DO 5 K=2,0,-1
                COUNT = 100
     5      CONTINUE
    10 CONTINUE
2.      DO 10 I=5,8
            DO 5 K=-2,1
                COUNT = COUNT + 1
     5      CONTINUE
    10 CONTINUE
3.      DO 10 I=2,0,-1
            DO 5 K=2,0,-1
                COUNT = COUNT + 1
     5      CONTINUE
            COUNT = COUNT + 1
    10 CONTINUE
```

SUMMARY

This chapter greatly expanded the types of problems we can solve in FORTRAN with use of IF statements: We can now control the order in which statements are executed. An important property of these statements is that they are entered only at the top of the structure and that they have only one exit; with only one entrance and one exit, this type of flow promotes the writing of simpler programs. We also learned to use both WHILE loops and DO loops to implement repetition steps — most of the programs in the rest of the text will use either one or the other of these loop structures.

DEBUGGING AIDS

The most helpful debugging tool is the PRINT* statement. Just knowing that your program is working incorrectly does not tell you where to begin looking for errors. If you have the computer print the values of key variables at different points in your program, however, it becomes easier to isolate the parts of the program that are not working correctly. The location of these *checkpoints*, or places to write the values of key variables, depends on the program; some of the obvious places are after reading new values for variables and after completing loops and computations.

It is also a good idea to number the checkpoints and then print the check-point number along with the other values. For instance, if you print the values of X and Y at several checkpoints, it may not be obvious which set of X and Y values have been printed. However, the following output is clear:

CHECKPOINT 3: X = 14.76   Y = -3.82

If you have narrowed the problem to an IF statement, then first check the condition. Did you use .LT. when you needed .LE.? Be careful when using NOT in an expression because the relationships can get complex. For example, .NOT.((A.EQ.1.0).OR.(B.EQ.2.0)) is also equal to (A.NE.1.0).AND.(B.NE.2.0).

Another possible error with IF statements can be traced to values being close to, but not exactly equal to, the desired value. For instance, suppose that the result of a mathematical computation should have a real value of 5.0. Because computers have limitations on the number of digits of accuracy, the result might be 4.999 or 5.001; if you check only for 5.0, you may not realize that you really have the correct value. One way to address this problem is to use the IF statement to look for values close to 5.0. For instance, if

$$|X - 5.0| < .001$$

then X is between 4.999 and 5.001. If this is close enough for the problem being solved, then replace the statement

IF (X.EQ.5.0) SUM = SUM + 1

with this statement

IF (ABS(X-5.0).LE.0.001) SUM = SUM + 1

If you believe that a programming error is within a WHILE loop, print the values of key variables at the beginning of the loop; this information will be printed each time the loop is executed, so you should be able to locate the trouble spot.

Most errors in a DO loop involve the loop parameters. When a program error seems to involve a DO loop, print the value of the index or count variable immediately within the loop. After executing the loop with this output state-ment, you can answer the following questions:

1. Did the index start with the correct value?
2. Did the index increment by the proper amount?
3. Did the index have the correct value during the last execution of the loop?

If the answer to any of these questions is no, check the DO statement itself; you probably have an error in the variables or expressions that you specified.

If the error is not in your original specification of the DO statement, print the values of the index at both the beginning and the end of the loop statements. After executing the loop with these two output statements, you will be able to determine if the value of the index is changed by the statements inside the loop. If the index is modified, you have either used the index inadvertently, which can be corrected, or you should replace the DO loop with a WHILE loop.

Another common error associated with DO loops occurs when a similar variable name is used instead of the index. For instance, if the index of the DO loop is INDEX, use INDEX and not I inside the loop when you intend to use the index value.

STYLE/TECHNIQUE GUIDES

The larger a program grows in size, the more apparent becomes the programmer's style — not only does bad style/technique become more obvious, it also becomes harder to correct. Practicing good style/technique in your small programs builds habits that will carry over into all your programming.

One of the best guides to good style is to use the WHILE loop and the DO loop consistently. With a little practice, you will find that all loops fit easily into one of these two forms. As we pointed out in the summary, these types of loops have only one entrance and one exit — enhancing readability and adding simplicity to your program.

Another characteristic of good style is the use of indenting to emphasize the statements in IF structures and loops. You can convince yourself of the importance of indenting if you try to follow a program written by someone else who has not indented statements within control structures. If loops are nested, indent each nested loop from the previous one.

Use the CONTINUE statement consistently to define the end of each DO loop. Although other statements are valid, the CONTINUE statement becomes an important part of the structure definition. Do not close more than one loop with the same CONTINUE statement.

Comment lines are yet another sign of good style; however, the use of comment lines can become excessive. Use only as many lines as are needed to show the program's organization and enhance its readability. Comment lines should be easy to distinguish from FORTRAN statements. We use blank lines before and after our comments and also use lowercase letters within the comment itself. You should always use initial comments to describe the purpose of the program. If needed, comments may be used throughout the program to identify processes, values, variables, and so on. You will also find that blank comment lines can be effective in separating different steps within a program — this technique is often used in our example programs.

A program that exhibits good style will save time in the long run because it is easier to debug. Programmers who may need to modify your programs in future projects will also appreciate your good style. Changing a few lines of FORTRAN code to achieve this will be time well spent.

KEY WORDS

branch	limit value
compound logical expression	logical expression
condition	logical operator
control structure	logical value
counting loop	loop
DO loop	nested loop
flowchart	parameter
IF-ELSEIF structure	pseudocode
IF-ELSE structure	relational operator
IF structure	repetition
increment value	selection
index	sequence
initial value	structured programming
iterative loop	WHILE loop

PROBLEMS

We begin our problem set with modifications to programs given earlier in this chapter. Give the decomposition, refined pseudocode or flowchart, and FORTRAN program for each problem.

Problems 1–5 modify the rocket trajectory program ROCKET, given on page 98.

1. Modify the rocket trajectory program so that it stops if the rocket impacts or if the total time exceeds 50 seconds.

2. Modify the rocket trajectory program so that it starts time at zero seconds and increments it by 1 second until the height is less than 50 feet; then increment time by 0.25 seconds.

3. Modify the rocket trajectory program so that it starts time at zero seconds and increments it by 0.5 seconds until the height is less than 80 feet; then increment time by 0.25 seconds.

4. Modify the rocket trajectory program so that it reads two values, INCR1 and INCR2. Start time at zero seconds and increment it by INCR1 seconds until the distance is less than 50 feet; then increment time by INCR2 seconds.

5. Modify the rocket trajectory program so that it does not print a table but instead prints two values. The first value is the time at which the rocket begins falling back to the ground and the second value is the time at which the rocket impacts. Start time at zero and increment it by 0.01 seconds.

Problems 6–10 modify the suture packaging program SEALS, given on page 103.

6. Modify the suture packaging program so that it also writes the total number of batches rejected.

7. Modify the suture packaging program so that it also writes the number of batches in each rejection category.

8. Modify the suture packaging program so that it prints an error message if the information is entered for a batch that should not have been rejected. Do not count this batch in the overall count of rejected batches.

9. Modify the suture packaging program so that it also counts and writes the total number of batches with ranges out of bounds on more than one of the parameters.

10. Modify the suture packaging program so that it counts and prints the total number of batches with ranges out of bounds on all three parameters.

Problems 11–15 modify the timber management program TIMBER, given on page 117.

11. Modify the timber management program so that a value N is read from the terminal, where N represents the number of years that are to be used in printing the table.

12. Modify the timber management program so that it computes information for 20 years but only prints information for every other year (second year, fourth year, and so on).

13. Modify the timber management program so that a value M is read from the terminal, where M represents the number of years that should be between lines in the output table. (Problem 12 is a special case where M = 2.)

14. Modify the timber management program so that instead of printing data for 20 years, it prints yearly information until at least 10 percent of the cut area has been reforested.

15. Modify the timber management program so that it prints only the final line of data after 20 years and then allows the user to input a different reforestation rate. The program should then print the final line of data after 20 years with this new reforestation rate and again allow the user to input a different reforestation rate. The program should end when a reforestation rate of 0.00 is entered. Thus, the user can compare results of several reforestation rates over the same 20 years.

Problems 16–20 modify the cable car program CABLE, given on page 123.

16. Modify the cable car velocity program so that it uses a WHILE loop instead of a DO loop.

17. Modify the cable car velocity program so that it reads the distance increment from a data line.

18. Modify the cable car velocity program so that the report includes a fourth column that gives the distance of the cable car from the nearest tower.

19. Modify the cable car velocity program so that the distance increment is 10 feet unless the cable car is less than 20 feet from a tower, in which case the distance increment should be 5 feet.

20. Modify the cable car velocity program so that there are two supporting towers between the first and last towers: The first supporting tower is 300 feet from the first tower and the second supporting tower is 300 feet from the last tower.

For problems 21–24, write complete FORTRAN programs to print tables showing the values of the input variables and the function shown using DO loops to control the loops.

21. Print a table of values for K where

$$K = 3M$$

for values of $M = 1, 2, 3, 4$.

22. Print a table of values for K where

$$K = I^2 + 2I + 2$$

for values of $I = 0, 1, 2, \ldots, 20$.

23. Print a table of values for Y where

$$Y = \frac{X^2 - 9}{X^2 + 2}$$

for values of $X = 1.5, 2.0, 2.5, \ldots, 9$.

24. Print a table of values for F where

$$F = \frac{X^2 - Y^2}{2XY}$$

for values of $X = 1, 2, \ldots, 9$, and for values of $Y = 0.5, 0.75, 1.0, \ldots, 2.5$.

Develop new programs in problems 25–33. Use the five-phase design process.

25. Write a program to print a table of consecutive even integers and their square values, beginning with 2, until the value of I is greater than 200. Use the following output format:

```
I  AND  I*I

2          4
4          16
.
.
.
```

26. Write a program to read a value FINAL. Print a table that contains values of X and $X*X$, starting with X equal to zero and incrementing by 0.5, until X is greater than FINAL. Use the following output format:

```
       X                      X
                               2

      0.0                    0.00
      0.5                    0.25
       .                       
       .                       
       .                       
```

27. Write a program that will read circuit inspection data from the terminal. Each line should contain a circuit ID number and the number of inspections successfully completed. If the number of inspections successfully completed is between 0 and 11, the inspection is in-progress; if the number of inspections successfully completed is 12, the inspection is complete and the circuit passes inspection; and if the number of inspections is -1, the inspection is complete but the circuit has failed inspection. Thus, the classification of a circuit is based on the following table:

CLASSIFICATION	TESTS COMPLETED
In-Progress	$0-11$
Passed	12
Failed	-1

The program should print a report similar to the following, with a line of output for each circuit:

```
INSPECTION REPORT

CIRCUIT ID AND CLASSIFICATION
XXXXX    -      XXXXXXXXXXX
  .
  .
  .
```

An ID of 999 will indicate the end of the data.

28. Modify problem 27 so that a final summary report follows the inspection report and has the following form:

```
INSPECTION SUMMARY

IN-PROGRESS        XXXX
PASSED             XXXX
FAILED             XXXX

TOTAL CIRCUITS          XXXXX
```

29. A rocket is being designed to test a retrorocket that is intended to permit softer landings. The designers have derived the following equations that they believe will predict the performance of the test rocket, where t represents the elapsed time in seconds:

$$\text{ACCELERATION} = 4.25 - 0.015t^2$$
$$\text{VELOCITY} = 4.25t - .005t^3$$
$$\text{DISTANCE} = 90 + 2.125t^2 - .00125t^4$$

The distance equation gives the height above ground level at time t. Thus, the first term (90) is the height in feet above ground level of the nose of the rocket at launch. To check the predicted performance, the rocket will be "flown" on a computer, using the derived equations. Write a program to print the time, height, velocity, and acceleration for the rocket from a time of zero seconds through 50 seconds, in increments of 1 second. Use the following report form:

```
                   ROCKET FLIGHT SIMULATION

      TIME        ACCELERATION      VELOCITY       DISTANCE
      (SEC)       (FT/SEC*SEC)      (FT/SEC)       (FT)

      XXX.XX        XXXX.XX         XXXX.XX        XXXX.XX
        .
        .
        .
```

30. A biologist, after discovering the omega germ, has spent 5 years determining the characteristics of the new virus. She has found that the germ has a constant growth rate. If 10 cells are present with a growth factor of 0.1, the next generation will have $10 + 10(0.1) = 11$ cells. Write a program that will compute and print a report with the following format:

```
                      OMEGA GERM GROWTH

                   NUMBER OF CELLS      PETRI DISH      GROWTH
   CULTURE NUMBER     INITIALLY       DIAMETER (CM)     RATE

       XXXX              XXXX              XXX          XX.XX

   GENERATION   NUMBER OF CELLS   % AREA OF PETRI DISH COVERED

        1           XXXX.X                 XXX.XX
        .
        .
        .
        5
```

Ten cells occupy 1 square millimeter. Use the following input data for four cultures:

CULTURE NUMBER	NUMBER OF CELLS INITIALLY	PETRI DISH DIAMETER	GROWTH RATE
1984	100	10 cm	0.50
1776	1300	5 cm	0.16
1812	600	15 cm	0.55
1056	700	8 cm	0.80

31. The square of the sine function can be represented by the following:

$$\sin^2 X = X^2 - \frac{2^3 X^4}{4!} + \frac{2^5 X^6}{6!} - \cdots = \sum_{n=1}^{\infty} \frac{(-1)^{n+1} 2^{2n-1} X^{2n}}{(2n)!}$$

Write a program to evaluate this series for an input value X, printing the results after 2, 4, 6, 8, . . . , 14 terms and comparing each sum to the true solution. Note that the term for $n = 1$ is $X*X$, and that all consecutive terms can be obtained by multiplying the previous term by

$$\frac{-(2X)^2}{2n(2n-1)}$$

The output should have the following form:

COMPARISON OF VALUES OF SINE SQUARED

NUMBER OF TERMS	SERIES SUMMATION	INTRINSIC FUNCTION	ABSOLUTE DIFFERENCE
2	XX.XXXX	XX.XXXX	XX.XXXX
4	XX.XXXX	XX.XXXX	XX.XXXX
.			
.			
14			

32. When N is an integer greater than or equal to zero, the expression N! (called N factorial) represents the product of all integers from 1 through N. We define 0! to be equal to 1. The following are a few factorials and their corresponding values:

$$0! = 1$$
$$1! = 1$$
$$2! = 1 \cdot 2 = 2$$
$$3! = 1 \cdot 2 \cdot 3 = 6$$

An approximation to N! can be computed using Stirling's formula

$$N! = \sqrt{2\pi N} \left(\frac{N}{e}\right)^N$$

where $e = 2.718282$. Write a program that reads a value of N from the terminal and then computes an approximation of N! using Stirling's formula. Print the following message before you read the value of N:

ENTER N WHERE N IS BETWEEN 1 AND 10

Limiting the size of N is necessary to ensure that the value of N! will fit within our limits of integers on most computers. The output of the program should be in this form:

XX! IS APPROXIMATELY XXXXXXX

(continued)

Continue reading values of N and computing an approximation to $N!$ until a negative value is read. If a value greater than 10 is read, print a message that the input is out of the specified range and ask the user to enter a new value.

33. The current-voltage relationship in an ideal *p-n* junction diode is described by the equation

$$I = I_s(\exp{(QV/kT)} - 1)$$

where I = current through diode, amps
    V = voltage across diode, volts
    I_s = saturation current, amps
    Q = electron charge, 1.6E−19 coulomb
    k = Boltzmann's constant, 1.38E−23 joule/degree K
    T = junction temperature, K

Write a program that calculates I as V varies from −.250 V to 0.500 V in increments of 0.125 V, for junction temperatures of 32, 100, and 212 degrees Fahrenheit. (Use the following equation to convert degrees Fahrenheit to degrees Kelvin: K = (F − 32) · (5/9) + 273.16.) Saturation current is 1 microamp in all three cases. Your output should be in the following form:

```
JUNCTION TEMPERATURE = XXX.XX F = XXX.XX K

VOLTAGE ACROSS DIODE            CURRENT THROUGH DIODE
      -0.250 V                     ±0.XXXXE±XX  A
      -0.125 V                     ±0.XXXXE±XX  A
         .
         .
         .
       0.500 V                     ±0.XXXXE±XX  A
```

FORTRAN STATEMENT SUMMARY

CONTINUE Statement:

$$k \ \texttt{CONTINUE}$$

Example:

$$\texttt{10 CONTINUE}$$

Discussion:
The CONTINUE statement is used to define the end of a DO loop. The statement number of the CONTINUE statement is also referenced in the DO statement.

DO Statement:

$$\texttt{DO} \ k \ \textit{index=initial,limit,increment}$$

Examples:

$$\texttt{DO 10 I=1,20}$$

$$\texttt{DO 20 TIME=1,200,5}$$

$$\texttt{DO 30 K=10,0,-1}$$

$$\texttt{DO 40 K=1,NUMBER}$$

Discussion:
The DO statement defines an iterative loop where k is the statement number of the statement that represents the end of the loop; index is a variable used as the loop counter; initial represents the initial value given to the loop counter; limit represents the value used to determine when the DO loop has been completed; and increment represents the value to be added to the loop counter each time that the loop is executed. If the increment is omitted, an increment of 1 is assumed.

GO TO Statement:

$$\texttt{GO TO} \ n$$

Example:

$$\texttt{GO TO 25}$$

Discussion:
The GO TO statement is an unconditional branch to the executable statement with label n. It should only be used to implement the WHILE loop.

IF Statement:

$$IF \ (condition) \ statement$$

Examples:

```
IF (A.GT.15.5) COUNT = COUNT + 1

IF (X.LE.0.0) PRINT*, 'DATA ERROR'
```

Discussion:
The IF statement is used to execute a single statement if the condition is true. The statement on the same line as the condition may not be another IF statement.

IF-THEN Statement:

```
IF (condition) THEN
     set of statements
ENDIF
```

Example:

```
IF (MIN.GE.60.0) THEN
   HOURS = HOURS + 1
   MIN = MIN - 60.0
   PRINT 5, HOURS
5     FORMAT (1X,I6,' HOURS')
ENDIF
```

Discussion:
If the condition is true, then all the statements between the THEN and the corresponding ENDIF statement are executed. This statement differs from the IF statement in that it can execute more than one statement if the condition is true.

IF-ELSE Statement:

```
IF (condition) THEN
     set of statements
ELSE
     set of statements
ENDIF
```

Example:

```
IF (TIME.GE.LAUNCH) THEN
   VELCTY=ACCEL*TIME
ELSE
   VELCTY=0.0
ENDIF
```

Discussion:
The IF-ELSE statement allows you to execute one set of statements if the condition is true and a different set of statements if the condition is false.

IF-ELSEIF Statement:

```
        IF (condition 1) THEN
            set of statements
        ELSEIF (condition 2) THEN
            set of statements
        ELSE
            set of statements
        ENDIF
```

Example:

```
        IF (TEMP.GE.65.0.AND.TEMP.LE.70.0) THEN
            PRINT 5
  5         FORMAT (1X, 'NORMAL TEMPERATURE')
        ELSEIF (TEMP.LT.65.0) THEN
            PRINT 6
  6         FORMAT (1X,'LOW TEMPERATURE')
        ELSE
            PRINT 7
  7         FORMAT (1X,'HIGH TEMPERATURE')
        ENDIF
```

Discussion:
The IF-ELSEIF statement includes several conditions. The conditions are tested in the order in which they appear in the statement. When a true condition is encountered, the set of statements following that condition is executed; control then passes to the statement following the ENDIF. If none of the conditions are true, the set of statements following the ELSE statement is executed. The ELSE portion of the IF-ELSEIF statement is optional.

LOGICAL Statement:

```
        LOGICAL   variable list
```

Examples:

```
        LOGICAL   DONE

        LOGICAL   SORTED, ERROR
```

Discussion:
The LOGICAL statement explicitly lists all variables that are to store logical variables. These variables may have values of either true or false.

APPLICATION — Critical Path Analysis (Manufacturing Engineering)

The timely use of resources is important to the success of any engineering project. It is often achieved by the use of a critical path analysis of a project. One method for this analysis starts by breaking a project into sequential events, then breaking each event into various tasks. Although one event must be completed before the next one is started, various tasks within an event can occur simultaneously. The time it takes to complete an event therefore depends on the number of days required to finish its longest task. Similarly, the total time it takes to finish a project is the sum of time it takes to finish each event.

Assume that the critical path information for a major construction project has been stored in a data file in the computer. You have been asked to analyze this information so that your company can develop a bid on the project. (See Section 4–2 for the solution.)

4

DATA FILES AND MORE I/O

INTRODUCTION

Engineers and scientists must often analyze large amounts of data. It is not reasonable to enter all this data into the computer by hand each time it is needed. We can enter the data once into a data file; then each time that data is needed, we can read it from the data file. Instead of printing the data in a report, we can write it into a data file; other programs then can use the data and it is still available if we decide to print it. In this chapter, we learn how to build and use data files. We also present more I/O features that are available in FORTRAN.

4–1   DATA FILES

Up to this point, we have entered all our data using READ* statements. When our program execution reached a READ* statement, we entered the data at the terminal, usually following a request for information. Every time we reran the program, we reentered the data.

An alternate way to enter data is with a *data file*. Data files are built separately, much as you enter your programs (which are really program files). You can use your computer system's editing capabilities to build, correct, and update the data file. Each line of the file (also called a *record*) corresponds to a line of data, which you enter by hand.

You must enter some special statements in your programs to use data files: We present them in this section, along with discussions of how to detect when you have reached the end of your data file when you did not know how many entries it contained. We also show you how to write information into a data file from your program instead of displaying it on the terminal screen or printing it with a line printer.

To use data files with our programs, we must use some new statements and some extensions of old statements. Each of these statements references the filename of the file that we want to use in our program. You assign a filename when a file is built. If you build a data file with your computer system's editor, you assign the filename before you begin entering the data.

To use data files, we must use new forms of input and output statements. The list-directed input statement that reads information from a data file uses the following general form:

READ *(unit number,*) variable list*

The list-directed output statement that writes information into a data file uses the following general form:

WRITE *(unit number,*) expression list*

The formatted output statement that writes information into a data file uses the following general form:

> **WRITE** *(unit number,k) expression list*

where *k* is the statement number of the corresponding FORMAT statement. In all of these general forms, the unit number is used to specify the number of the file that we wish to read or the number of the file into which we wish to write data. Because a program may use several different data files, this unit number identifies the file that is to be used with a specific statement. The asterisk following the unit number specifies that you are using list-directed input or output.

Most computer systems are attached to several input or output devices. Each device is assigned a unit number. For example, if a laser printer has been assigned unit number 8, then the following statement would direct that the values of X and Y be printed on the laser printer:

```
WRITE (8,*) X, Y
```

Many systems assign the standard input device (typically the terminal keyboard) to unit number 5 and the standard output device (typically the terminal screen) to unit number 6 — these devices are used when your program executes READ* or PRINT* statements. Avoid using preassigned unit numbers with your data files; if your computer system assigns unit number 5 and 6 as previously defined, do not use these with your data files. Confusion could result if your program assigned a data file to unit 6, and the program then executed a PRINT* statement.

The statement that assigns a unit number to a data file is the OPEN statement. Its general form is

> **OPEN (UNIT=***integer expression***, FILE=***filename***, STATUS=***literal***)**

The integer expression designates the unit number to be used in READ or WRITE statements. The filename refers to the name given to the file when it was built. The STATUS literal tells the computer whether we are opening an input file to be used with READ statements or an output file to be used with WRITE statements. If the file is an input file, it already has data in it and is specified with STATUS='OLD'; if the file is an output file, it does not contain data yet and is specified with STATUS='NEW'.

The OPEN statement must precede any READ or WRITE statements that use the file. The OPEN statement should be executed only once; therefore, it should not be inside a loop. Some systems require a REWIND statement after opening an input file to position the file at its beginning. The REWIND statement and additional information on building and accessing data files are presented in Chapter 9.

We now look at several examples to illustrate these statements.

EXAMPLE 4-1 Parallel Resistance

A data file RES3 contains three data lines, each containing a resistance value from a resistor in an instrumentation circuit. Write a complete program to read the three real resistances and compute their combined resistance *(RC)* for a parallel arrangement, as shown:

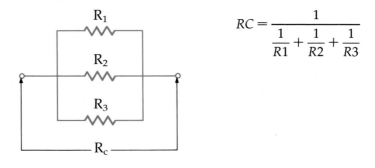

$$RC = \cfrac{1}{\dfrac{1}{R1} + \dfrac{1}{R2} + \dfrac{1}{R3}}$$

Print the value of *RC*. The resistance is measured in ohms.

Solution

The decomposition of this problem solution is

DECOMPOSITION

Read R1, R2, R3.
Compute RC.
Print RC.

Adding detail to the computation step gives the following refinement in pseudocode.

REFINEMENT IN PSEUDOCODE

RESIS1: Read R1, R2, R3
　　　　Print R1, R2, R3
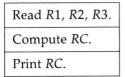
$$RC \leftarrow \cfrac{1}{\dfrac{1}{R1} + \dfrac{1}{R2} + \dfrac{1}{R3}}$$
　　　　Print RC

As we convert these steps into FORTRAN, we must remember that the data is being read from a data file RES3 that has already been built. The name of the file is determined when the file is built, but we may choose any unit number to refer to the file as long as the number is not preassigned by our computer system.

FORTRAN Program

```
*------------------------------------------------------------*
*       PROGRAM   RESIS1
*
*   This program reads a data file with three resistance
*   values and computes their equivalent parallel value.
*
        REAL   R1, R2, R3, RC
*
        OPEN (UNIT=10,FILE='RES3',STATUS='OLD')
        READ (10,*) R1, R2, R3
        PRINT 5, R1, R2, R3
    5 FORMAT (1X,'INPUT VALUES ARE: ',F7.2,2X,F7.2,2X,F7.2)
        RC = 1.0/(1.0/R1 + 1.0/R2 + 1.0/R3)
        PRINT 10, RC
   10 FORMAT (1X,'COMBINED PARALLEL RESISTANCE = ',
      +          F7.1,' OHMS')
        END
*------------------------------------------------------------*
```

Data File RES3

```
                          1000.0
                          1100.0
                          2000.0
```

Using data file RES3, the output of this program is

```
INPUT VALUES ARE: 1000.00  1100.00  2000.00
COMBINED PARALLEL RESISTANCE =   415.1 OHMS
```

Example 4–1 used a small data file, but the advantages of a data file become obvious with large amounts of data. Once the data file is built, no matter how many times you run a program that uses the file, you do not have to reenter the data. It is easy to change and update a data file with the editing capabilities available on terminal systems. In addition, data files can be shared by various programs, reducing data redundancy and minimizing the memory requirements.

Data files can be built by a FORTRAN program with WRITE statements; instead of using the terminal screen or line printer as an output device, we can write the information into a data file. This is often done when plotting data; the data to be plotted is first written into a data file, and the plotter then uses the data file.

EXAMPLE 4–2   Parallel Resistance with Output File

Modify the program in Example 4–1 such that the combined resistance (RC) is printed and also stored in a file called RESC.

Solution

Because this solution is so similar to that of Example 4–1, we include only the modified FORTRAN program and the input and output from a sample test run.

FORTRAN Program

```
*---------------------------------------------------------*
      PROGRAM  RESIS2
*
*  This program reads a data file with three resistance
*  values and computes their equivalent parallel value,
*  which is printed and stored in a data file.
*
      REAL  R1, R2, R3, RC
*
      OPEN (UNIT=10,FILE='RES3',STATUS='OLD')
      OPEN (UNIT=11,FILE='RESC',STATUS='NEW')
*
      READ (10,*) R1, R2, R3
      PRINT 5, R1, R2, R3
    5 FORMAT (1X,'INPUT VALUES ARE: ',F7.2,2X,F7.2,2X,F7.2)
      RC = 1.0/(1.0/R1 + 1.0/R2 + 1.0/R3)
      PRINT 10, RC
   10 FORMAT (1X,'COMBINED PARALLEL RESISTANCE = ',
     +         F7.1,' OHMS')
      WRITE (11,*) RC
      END
*---------------------------------------------------------*
```

Data File RES3

```
                    1000.0
                    1100.0
                    2000.0
```

Using data file RES3, the screen and corresponding data file output from this program are

```
INPUT VALUES ARE: 1000.00   1100.00   2000.00
COMBINED PARALLEL RESISTANCE =    415.1 OHMS
```

Data File RESC

```
                    415.1
```

TRAILER AND SENTINEL SIGNALS

Many applications require the computer to read a number of data values, such as test scores or experimental results. The DO loop can accomplish these tasks if you know exactly how many data values are in the file. For instance, if 50 data values are to be read, we can use a DO loop of this form:

```
DO 10 COUNT=1,50
   READ (15,*) X
    .
    .
    .
10 CONTINUE
```

If the number of data values to be read is available in another variable, we can use a DO loop of this form:

```
      DO 10 COUNT=1,NUM
         READ (15,*) X
            .
            .
            .
      10 CONTINUE
```

However, you may not always know exactly how many data values need to be read prior to executing your program; you must be careful in handling these situations because if you execute a READ statement for which there is no data line, an execution error will occur and program execution will stop. There are two techniques for handling an unspecified number of input data values: one uses a *trailer*, or *sentinel*, signal and the other uses an end-of-file option in the READ statement.

The first technique uses special data values called trailer, or sentinel, signals to indicate the end of the data. For example, a valid identification number for a student record may be three digits, ranging from 000 to 500. If we were reading student records, we could use an identification number of 999 as a trailer signal. As we read each data line, we test the identification number for the value 999; when we find 999, we then exit the loop. This process can be structured easily in a WHILE loop; but because the condition uses a value from the data, we must read one student record before entering the WHILE loop, as shown:

```
         READ (15,*) ID, GPA
      5 IF (ID.NE.999) THEN
            .
            .
            .
         READ (15,*) ID, GPA
            GO TO 5
      ENDIF
```

If we need to know the number of data values read, a counter can be used in the WHILE loop. Be sure not to count the trailer value as a valid data value. This technique should look familiar because we have already used it in some of our example programs.

EXAMPLE 4–3   Test Scores with Trailer Signal

A group of integer test scores have been entered into a data file TESTS1, one score per line. The last line contains a negative value to signal the end of the test scores. Write a complete program to read the data, compute the test average, and print the number of tests and the test average.

Solution

The decomposition of this problem is

DECOMPOSITION

Read and total test scores.
Compute average.
Print average.

In the refinement of this decomposition, we include the WHILE loop, which reads and totals the test scores until we read a negative value.

Refinement in Pseudocode

```
AVERG1: number ← 0
        total ← 0
        Read test
        While test ≥ 0 do
            number ← number + 1
            total ← total + test
            Read test
        average ← total/number
        Print number, average
```

As we convert the pseudocode into FORTRAN statements, remember that we are reading the test scores from a data file — thus we need to use the OPEN statement and the new form of the READ statement.

FORTRAN Program

```
*-----------------------------------------------------------*
      PROGRAM  AVERG1
*
*  This program computes the average of a group of test
*  scores that are followed by a negative value.
*
      INTEGER  TEST, TOTAL, NUMBER
      REAL   AVERG
*
      OPEN (UNIT=12,FILE='TESTS1',STATUS='OLD')
      NUMBER = 0
      TOTAL = 0
      READ (12,*) TEST
    5 IF (TEST.GE.0) THEN
          NUMBER = NUMBER + 1
          TOTAL = TOTAL + TEST
          READ (12,*) TEST
          GO TO 5
      ENDIF
      AVERG = REAL(TOTAL)/REAL(NUMBER)
      PRINT 10, NUMBER, AVERG
   10 FORMAT (1X,'THE AVERAGE OF ',I4,
     +         ' TEST SCORES IS ',F5.1)
      END
*-----------------------------------------------------------*
```

A sample data file and the corresponding output from this program are

Data File TESTS1

```
                            85
                            92
                            100
                            87
                            75
                            73
                            81
                            -1
```

```
 ╭──────────────────────────────────────────────╮
  THE  AVERAGE  OF     7 TEST SCORES IS   84.7
 ╰──────────────────────────────────────────────╯
```

END OPTION

If a set of data does not have a trailer signal at the end, and if we do not know the number of data lines in the file, we must use a different technique with the WHILE loop. In pseudocode, we want to perform these steps:

> While more data do
> Read variables
> Process variables

To implement this in FORTRAN, we use an option available with the READ statement that tests for the end of the data. A list-directed READ statement that uses this option has the following general form:

> READ (*unit number,* ***,END=***n*) *variable list*

As long as there is data to read in the data file, this statement executes exactly like this:

> READ (*unit number,******) *variable list*

However, if the last line of the data file has already been read and we execute the READ statement again, instead of getting an execution error, control is passed to the statement referenced in the END option, statement *n*. If the READ statement were executed a second time after the end of the data, an execution error would occur.

A READ statement with the END option is actually a special form of the WHILE loop. When using it in your programs, use the same indenting style as used in the WHILE loop. A GO TO statement is also needed to complete the WHILE loop, as shown:

```
 8 READ (13,*,END=10) A, B
      .
      .
      .
      GO TO 8
10 .
      .
      .
```

This is a special implementation of the WHILE loop that is used when you do not know the number of data lines to be read and there is no trailer signal at the end of the file. Remember, if you have a trailer value, test for that value to exit the loop instead of using the END option.

The two techniques presented in this section should not be used together; they are techniques for handling two different data situations.

EXAMPLE 4-4   Test Scores without Trailer Signal

A group of integer test scores has been entered into a data file TESTS2, one score per line, with no trailer line. Write a complete program to read the data, compute the test average, and print the number of tests and the test average.

Solution

The decomposition of the problem is the same as in Example 4-3.

DECOMPOSITION

Read and total test scores.
Compute average.
Print average.

As we refine the solution, we indicate which technique we will use for detecting the end of the file. Because there is no trailer signal, we do not need to read the first data line outside the loop. The condition in the WHILE loop determines whether or not there is more data to read. If there is not more data, we exit the WHILE loop.

REFINEMENT IN PSEUDOCODE

```
AVERG2: number ← 0
        total ← 0
        While more tests do
          Read test
          number ← number + 1
          total ← total + test
        average ← total/number
        Print number, average
```

In converting the pseudocode to FORTRAN, note that the READ statement with the END option replaces both the WHILE statement and the standard READ statement.

FORTRAN PROGRAM

```
*-------------------------------------------------------*
      PROGRAM  AVERG2
*
*  This program computes the average of a group of test
*  scores that do not have a trailer line in the file.
*
      INTEGER  TEST, TOTAL, NUMBER
      REAL  AVERG
*
```

```
      OPEN (UNIT=8,FILE='TESTS2',STATUS='OLD')
      NUMBER = 0
      TOTAL = 0
  5 READ (8,*,END=10) TEST
        NUMBER = NUMBER + 1
        TOTAL = TOTAL + TEST
        GO TO 5
 10 AVERG = REAL(TOTAL)/REAL(NUMBER)
    PRINT 15, NUMBER, AVERG
 15 FORMAT (1X,'THE AVERAGE OF ',I4,
    +         ' TEST SCORES IS ',F5.1)
      END
*-----------------------------------------------------------*
```

A sample data file and the corresponding output from this program are

DATA FILE TESTS2

```
              85
              92
             100
              87
              75
              73
              81
```

```
   THE AVERAGE OF      7 TEST SCORES IS   84.7
```

4−2 APPLICATION — CRITICAL PATH ANALYSIS (Manufacturing Engineering)

A critical path analysis is a technique used to determine the time schedule for a project. This information is important in the planning stages before a project is begun, and it is also useful to evaluate the progress of a project that is partially completed. One method for this analysis starts by breaking a project into sequential events, then breaking each event into various tasks. Although one event must be completed before the next one is started, various tasks within an event can occur simultaneously. The time it takes to complete an event, therefore, depends on the number of days required to finish its longest task. Similarly, the total time it takes to finish a project is the sum of time it takes to finish each event.

Assume that the critical path information for a major construction project has been stored in a data file in the computer. You have been asked to analyze this information so that your company can develop a bid on the project. Specifically, the management would like a summary report that lists each event along with the number of days for the shortest task in that event and the number of days for the longest task in that event. In addition they would like the total project length computed in days and converted to weeks (five days per week).

The data file named PROJECT contains three integers per line. The first number is the event number, the second number is the task number, and the third number is the number of days required to complete the task. The data has been stored such that all the task data for event 1 is followed by all the task data for event 2, and so on. The task data for a particular event is also in order. You do not know ahead of time how many entries are in the file, but there is an upper limit of 98 total events, so a trailer signal is used to indicate the last line in the data file. The last line will contain a value of 99 for the event number and zeros for the corresponding task and days.

PROBLEM STATEMENT

Write a program to determine and print a project completion timetable.

INPUT/OUTPUT DESCRIPTION

The input to the program is a data file that contains the critical path information for the events in the project. The information in the file is in order by events, with the event number starting at 1. Within an event, the task information is also in order. Each line of the file contains the event number, task number, and corresponding number of days necessary to complete the task. There is a maximum of 98 events, and the last line in the file will be indicated by a trailer signal with a value of 99 for the event number. The output is to be a summary report with the following format:

```
PROJECT COMPLETION TIMETABLE

EVENT NUMBER        MINIMUM DAYS        MAXIMUM DAYS
X                   X                   X
.
.
.


TOTAL PROJECT LENGTH = XX DAYS
                     = XX WEEKS X DAYS
```

HAND EXAMPLE

Use the following set of project data for the hand example:

Event Number	Task Number	Days
1	1	5
1	2	4
2	1	3
2	2	7
2	3	4
3	1	6
99	0	0

The corresponding report based on this data is shown next:

```
PROJECT COMPLETION TIMETABLE

EVENT NUMBER        MINIMUM DAYS        MAXIMUM DAYS
1                   4                   5
2                   3                   7
3                   6                   6

TOTAL PROJECT LENGTH = 18 DAYS
                     =  3 WEEKS 3 DAYS
```

ALGORITHM DEVELOPMENT

The decomposition of this problem solution is:

DECOMPOSITION

Read project event data and print event information
Print summary information

To develop an algorithm, we look at the way we compiled the data in the hand example. Because all the data for the first event is together, we scan down the list of data for event 1 and keep track of the minimum number of days and maximum number of days. When we reach the first task for event 2, we print the information related to event 1 and then repeat the process for event 2. We continue until we reach event 99, which is a signal that we do not have any more data. We print the information for the last event and then print the summary information using a total in which we accumulated the total maximum number of days for all the events.

INITIAL REFINEMENT IN PSEUDOCODE

PATH: total ← 0
      Read event, task, days
      number ← event
      min ← days
      max ← days
      While not done do
          If same event then
            Update min and max
          Else
            Print number, min, max
            total ← total + max
            number ← event
            min ← days
            max ← days
          Read event, task, days
      Print number, min, max for last event
      Print total

As we refine the pseudocode, we need to be more specific about how we determine if we are done. We also need to add more details to the update for the minimum and maximum days for an event. Finally, when we print the total, we also need to compute and print the number of weeks.

FINAL REFINEMENT IN PSEUDOCODE

```
PATH: total ← 0
      Read event, task, days
      number ← event
      min ← days
      max ← days
      If event = 99 then
         done ← true
      Else
         done ← false
      While not done do
         If event = number then
            If days < min then
               min ← days
            If days > max then
               max ← days
         Else
            Print number, min, max
            total ← total + max
            number ← event
            min ← days
            max ← days
         Read event, task, days
         If event = 99 then
            done ← true
      Print number, min, max for last event
      weeks ← total/5
      plus ←total − weeks*5
      Print total, weeks, plus
```

Note that we will need to do the computation for WEEKS so that the result is an integer instead of a real value. As we convert the final pseudocode into FORTRAN, we must remember to open the data file and use the new form of the READ statement.

FORTRAN Program

```
*----------------------------------------------------------------*
      PROGRAM   PATH
*  This program determines the critical path
*  information for a project.
*
      INTEGER   EVENT, TASK, DAYS, TOTAL, NUMBER, MIN, MAX,
     +          WEEKS, PLUS
      LOGICAL   DONE
*
      OPEN (UNIT=8,FILE='PROJECT',STATUS='OLD')
      TOTAL = 0
      PRINT*, 'PROJECT COMPLETION TIMETABLE'
      PRINT*
      PRINT*, 'EVENT NUMBER     MINIMUM TIME     MAXIMUM TIME'
*
      READ (8,*) EVENT, TASK, DAYS
      NUMBER = EVENT
      MIN = DAYS
      MAX = DAYS
      IF (EVENT.EQ.99) THEN
         DONE = .TRUE.
      ELSE
         DONE = .FALSE.
      ENDIF
*
    5 IF (.NOT.DONE) THEN
         IF (EVENT.EQ.NUMBER) THEN
            IF (DAYS.LT.MIN) THEN
               MIN = DAYS
            ELSEIF   (DAYS.GT.MAX) THEN
               MAX = DAYS
            ENDIF
         ELSE
            PRINT 10, NUMBER, MIN, MAX
   10       FORMAT (1X,I2,14X,I3,13X,I3)
            TOTAL = TOTAL + MAX
            NUMBER = EVENT
            MIN = DAYS
            MAX = DAYS
         ENDIF
         READ (8,*) EVENT, TASK, DAYS
         IF (EVENT.EQ.99) DONE = .TRUE.
         GO TO 5
      ENDIF
      PRINT 10, NUMBER, MIN, MAX
      TOTAL = TOTAL + MAX
*
      WEEKS = TOTAL/5
      PLUS = TOTAL - WEEKS*5
      PRINT*
      PRINT 15, TOTAL
   15 FORMAT (1X,'TOTAL PROJECT LENGTH = ',I3,' DAYS')
      PRINT 20, WEEKS, PLUS
   20 FORMAT (1X,'                        = ',I3,' WEEKS',
     +          I2,' DAYS')
      END
*----------------------------------------------------------------*
```

Note that the days remaining after subtracting the number of days in the full weeks could have been computed using the MOD function, as shown here:

$$PLUS = MOD(TOTAL,5)$$

TESTING

If we use the sample set of data from the hand example with this program, the following report is printed:

```
PROJECTION COMPLETION TIMETABLE

EVENT NUMBER      MINIMUM DAYS      MAXIMUM DAYS
1                 4                 5
2                 3                 7
3                 6                 6

TOTAL PROJECT LENGTH = 18 DAYS
                     = 3 WEEKS 3 DAYS
```

4–3   APPLICATION—POPULATION STUDY (Sociology)

The population of Shakespeare, New Mexico (1880–1980) has been stored in a data file called PEOPLE. Each line of the data file contains a year and the corresponding population. The data lines are in ascending order by year. Write a program to read the data and determine the two consecutive years in which the percentage increase in population was the greatest.

PROBLEM STATEMENT

Find the two consecutive years in which the percentage increase in population was the greatest for Shakespeare, New Mexico.

INPUT/OUTPUT DESCRIPTION

The input is a data file with 101 lines. Each line contains a year and corresponding population. The data is in ascending order by year. The output is the two consecutive years with the largest percentage increase in population.

HAND EXAMPLE

First, we look at some typical data and compute the percentage increase in the data each year to be sure that we understand the computations involved.

Year	Population	Percentage Increase
1950	82	
1951	56	32% $[(56 - 82)/82 \cdot 100]$
1952	71	27% $[(71 - 56)/56 \cdot 100]$
1953	86	21% $[(86 - 71)/71 \cdot 100]$
1954	102	19% $[(102 - 86)/86 \cdot 100]$

During the years listed, the largest percentage increase was from 1951 to 1952. Note that this was not the largest increase in actual population. The largest increase in actual population occurred from 1953 to 1954.

ALGORITHM DEVELOPMENT

The decomposition of the steps in this algorithm can be described as

DECOMPOSITION

Read data and determine years with largest percentage increase.
Print result.

To compute the change in population from one year to the next, we need the previous year (old value) and the following year (new value). Thus, as we refine the decomposition, we need to read the first value (old value) outside our loop so that we can read the following year (new value) and compute the change within the loop. We execute the steps within this loop 100 times.

INITIAL REFINEMENT IN PSEUDOCODE

```
CENSUS: Read first set of data
        year of increase ← first year
        For year=1 to 100 do
            Read next set of data
            Compute percentage increase in population
            If new increase > previous best then
                year of increase ← current year
        Print year of increase and its previous year
```

Because we need not only the information on the current line but also the information on the previous data line to compute the population increase, we use the following variables:

YRNEW	The year just read from a data line
YROLD	The year from the previous data line
POPNEW	The population just read from a data line
POPOLD	The population from the previous data line
PERC	The current percentage increase in population
GPIYR	The year in which there was the greatest percentage increase
GPI	The percentage that represents the greatest percentage increase

Note that in the final pseudocode we are initially setting the first pair of years as the ones with the greatest percentage increase. Each time through the loop, we compare this increase with the current increase; if the current increase is higher, this value is placed in the variable GPI (greatest percent increase), and the year is placed in GPIYR.

FINAL REFINEMENT IN PSEUDOCODE

CENSUS: Read yrold, popold
       For $i = 1$ to 100 do
          Read yrnew, popnew
          perc ← (popnew − popold) · 100/popold
          If $i = 1$ or perc > gpi then
             gpi ← perc
             gpiyr ← yrnew
          yrold ← ynew
          popold ← popnew
        yr1 ← gpiyr − 1
        yr2 ← gpiyr
        Print yr1, yr2

We now convert our final pseudocode into FORTRAN. Because our data is being read from a data file, we must remember to open the data file and use the new form of the READ statement.

FORTRAN Program

```
*------------------------------------------------------------*
      PROGRAM  CENSUS
*
*  This program reads 101 population values and determines
*  the years of greatest percentage increase in population.
*
      INTEGER  YROLD, YRNEW, POPOLD, POPNEW,
     +         GPIYR, YR1, YR2, I
      REAL  PERC, GPI
*
      OPEN (UNIT=15,FILE='PEOPLE',STATUS='OLD')
      GPI = 0.0
      READ (15,*) YROLD, POPOLD
      DO 50 I=1,100
         READ (15,*) YRNEW, POPNEW
         PERC = (POPNEW - POPOLD)*100.0/POPOLD
         IF (I.EQ.1.OR.PERC.GT.GPI) THEN
            GPI = PERC
            GPIYR = YRNEW
         ENDIF
         YROLD = YRNEW
         POPOLD = POPNEW
   50 CONTINUE
      YR1 = GPIYR - 1
      YR2 = GPIYR
      PRINT 55, YR1, YR2
   55 FORMAT (1X,'GREATEST PERCENT INCREASE OCCURRED',
     +         ' BETWEEN ',I4,' AND ',I4)
      END
*------------------------------------------------------------*
```

TESTING

A sample output from this program is

```
GREATEST PERCENT INCREASE OCCURRED BETWEEN 1890 AND 1891
```

If you want to test this program with a smaller data file, you can easily change the final value in the DO loop statement to a smaller number. For example, if you build a test file with 10 sets of data, change the DO loop statement to

DO 50 I=1,9

In this program we updated the greatest percentage increase when (I.EQ.1.OR.PERC.GT.GPI). Why is it necessary to include the expression I.EQ.1? For most data sets, the logical expression I.EQ.1 is not necessary because as soon as a percentage increase greater than zero is encountered, it replaces the values of zero used to initialize GPI. However, suppose all increases are negative; without the compound logical expression, our final result would be incorrect.

4-4 FORMATTED INPUT

To specify the columns to be used in reading data from a data line, we use a formatted READ statement. The general form of a formatted READ statement is

READ *k, variable list*

The variable list determines the order in which new values are stored, and *k* is a format reference number that refers to the FORMAT statement that will describe the positions to be read. A typical READ/FORMAT combination is

```
      READ 2, DIST, VEL
    2 FORMAT (F4.1,3X,F4.2)
```

If the FORMAT statement is being used to read information from a data file, a typical READ/FORMAT combination is

```
      READ (10,5) X,Y
    5 FORMAT (F5.1,2X,F6.1)
```

The form of the FORMAT appears the same as that used with PRINT statements; even the specifications look familiar. There are, however, differences between the specifications used for reading data values and those used for writing data values. Also, no carriage control is needed with READ statements. Each READ statement begins reading at column 1 of a new data line. The new values must agree in type (integer or real) with the variables in the list.

We now look at each specification individually, as we did for the PRINT statement specifications.

X SPECIFICATION

The X specification will skip positions on the data line. Its general form is nX, where n represents the number of positions to skip; thus, we can skip over unnecessary values.

I SPECIFICATION

The I specification is required when reading a value into an integer variable. The form of this specification is Iw where w represents the number of positions to use on the data line. Any blanks in the w positions will be interpreted as zeros. Any characters besides numbers, plus or minus signs, and blanks will cause an execution error. Thus, 5.0 cannot be read with an I3 specification; but, $_{bb}5$ will be read correctly with an I3 specification.

EXAMPLE 4-5   MEAN and NORM

Read the values of the variables MEAN and NORM from a data line. MEAN is in columns 1-4 and NORM is in columns 10-11.

Correct Solution

FORTRAN STATEMENTS

```
          READ 1, MEAN, NORM
        1 FORMAT (I4,5X,I2)
```

DATA LINE

$$b^{123}bbbbb^{10}$$

COMPUTER MEMORY

MEAN $\boxed{123}$

NORM $\boxed{10}$

The first four columns, $_b$123, are used to assign a value to MEAN. The first blank is interpreted as a zero; thus 0123 is stored in MEAN. We then skip the next five columns. From columns 10-11, we pick up the value 10 for NORM.

Incorrect Solution

FORTRAN STATEMENTS

```
          READ 2, MEAN, NORM
        2 FORMAT (1X,I4,5X,I2)
```

DATA LINE

$$b^{123}bbbbb^{10}b$$

COMPUTER MEMORY

MEAN $\boxed{1230}$

NORM $\boxed{0}$

If carriage control is used with READ statements, incorrect values may be stored in memory. Using the preceding format, we skip the first columns and use the next four columns for determining the value of MEAN. These columns contain 123$_b$, which is interpreted as 1230. We then skip five columns, and use the next two columns for determining the value of NORM. The contents 0$_b$ will be interpreted as 0.

F SPECIFICATION

The F specification can be used to read a value for a real variable. The form of this specification is Fw.d, where w represents the total number of positions to use on the data line and d represents the number of decimal positions. As with the I specification, any blanks in the w positions will be interpreted as zeros. If there is a decimal point included in the w positions, the value will be stored as it was entered, regardless of what value has been given to d. Thus, if a real value DIST is read with a F4.1 specification, and the four characters are 1.26, the value of DIST is 1.26. If there is no decimal point within the specified positions, the value of d is used to position a decimal place before storing the value. Thus, if the characters 1246 are read with an F4.1 specification, the value stored is 124.6, a value with one decimal position. Note that printing this value would require an F5.1 specification; the same specification will therefore not always work for both input and output.

EXAMPLE 4-6 TIME and TEMP

Read two variables, TIME and TEMP. TIME will be in columns 10–13, with two decimal positions, and TEMP will be in columns 16–18, with one decimal position.

Solution

FORTRAN STATEMENTS

```
        READ 200, TIME, TEMP
    200 FORMAT (9X,F4.2,2X,F3.1)
```

DATA LINE

$$\text{bbbbbbbbb}^{4.66}{}_{bb}{}^{125}$$

COMPUTER MEMORY

TIME $\boxed{4.66}$

TEMP $\boxed{12.5}$

Because there was no decimal point in the TEMP field, which was read with F3.1, one was positioned in the three numbers so that one position was a decimal position.

When running a program in a batch-processing system (as opposed to a time-sharing system), your computer and compiler will require additional information. This *job control information* is unique to your computer system; it consists of information such as your name, the compiler you are using, and other additional data about your program. Your instructor or the computer center documentation will provide you with the job control requirments for your computer system.

The placement of the control lines and a program to calculate the slope of the line between two points are given in Figure 4–1.

```
      JOB CONTROL
      INFORMATION  {   (system dependent)

                     *------------------------------------------------*
                     *         PROGRAM   SLOPE1
                     *
                     *   This program computes the slope of a
                     *   straight line through two points.
                     *
                     *         REAL   X1, Y1, X2, Y2, SLOPE
                     *
      FORTRAN              READ 10, X1, Y1, X2, Y2
      PROGRAM        10 FORMAT (F4.1,F4.1,F4.1,F4.1)
                           SLOPE = (Y2 - Y1)/(X2 - X1)
                           PRINT 20, X1, Y1, X2, Y2, SLOPE
                        20 FORMAT (1X,'THE SLOPE OF THE LINE ',
                        +          'THROUGH (',F4.1,',',F4.1,
                        +          ') AND (',F4.1,',',F4.1,
                        +          ') IS',F4.1)
                           END
                     *------------------------------------------------*

      JOB CONTROL
      INFORMATION  {   (system dependent)

      DATA         {   ᵦ5.5ᵦ3.1ᵦ0.5-1.6

      JOB CONTROL
      INFORMATION  {   (system dependent)
```

FIGURE 4-1 Job control information placement and FORTRAN program with data.

The output from the program in Figure 4-1 is

```
          1111111111222222222233333333334444444444555555555566666
12345678901234567890123456789012345678901234567890123456789012345678901234
```

```
THE SLOPE OF THE LINE THROUGH ( 5.5, 3.1) AND ( 0.5,-1.6) IS 0.9
```

E SPECIFICATION

The E specification is used in a READ/FORMAT combination when a variable is entered in an E format, or exponential form. The general form is Ew.d, where w represents the total number of positions that are being considered, and d represents the number of decimal positions when the value is expressed in exponential form. If a decimal point is included, its placement will override the value of d. If no decimal point is included, one is located, according to d, before storing the value. It is not necessary that the width be at least seven positions greater than the number of decimal positions (as is necessary for output with an E format).

For READ statements, the E format will accept many forms of input. The following list shows some of the different ways in which the value 1.26 can be entered in a field read with E9.2. Note that the data can even be in an F specification form.

DATA LINE	VALUE STORED
0.126E_b01	1.26
1.26_bE_b00	1.26
1.26_{bbbbb}	1.26
12.60E-01	1.26
_{bbb}.126E1	1.26
_{bbbbb}126	1.26

Remember that the system will use two positions for the exponent if they are available. Thus $_{bbb}$.126E1 will be interpreted as 1.26, but $_{bb}$.126E1$_b$ will be interpreted as $_{bb}$.126E10, or 0.126X 10**10.

EXAMPLE 4–7 Job Number and Computer Time

Read two values. The first value, in columns 2–6, represents an integer job number assigned to a computer run. The second value, in columns 10–16, represents the number of computer seconds used to run the program. This computer time will be entered in an exponential form, with two decimal places.

Solution

FORTRAN STATEMENTS

```
       READ 10, NUM, CTIME
    10 FORMAT (1X,I5,3X,E7.2)
```

DATA LINE

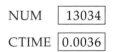

COMPUTER MEMORY

NUM	13034
CTIME	0.0036

EXAMPLE 4–8 Nutrition Research Results

A research scientist performed nutrition tests using three animals. Data on each animal includes an identification number, the weight of the animal at the beginning of the experiment, and the weight of the animal at the end of the experiment. This data is stored in a data file called TEST1, and the data values for each animal are on a separate line: the integer identification number in columns 1–5, the initial weight in columns 10–14, and the final weight in columns 15–18. Both weights have one decimal position. Write a complete program to read this information and print a report. The report is to include both the original information and the percentage increase in weight for each test animal.

Solution

The decomposition is only a single step.

DECOMPOSITION

> Generate report.

In the refinement, we break the report generation step into a loop that reads the data for each animal, then computes and prints the corresponding data line.

REFINEMENT IN PSEUDOCODE

```
RESRCH: Print headers
        For i = 1 to 3 do
            Read ID, initial weight, final weight
            percent increase ← (final − initial)/initial · 100
            Print ID, initial, final, percent increase
```

Converting the pseudocode into a FORTRAN program gives the following:

FORTRAN PROGRAM

```
*--------------------------------------------------------------*
      PROGRAM  RESRCH
*
*  This program prints a report on the results of
*  an experiment involving three test animals.
*
      INTEGER  I, ID
      REAL  IWT, FWT, PERC
*
      PRINT 5
    5 FORMAT (1X,'TEST RESULTS')
      PRINT*
      PRINT 10
   10 FORMAT ('NUMBER   INITIAL WT   FINAL WT   ',
     +        'PERCENTAGE INCREASE')
*
      OPEN (UNIT=10,FILE='TEST1',STATUS='OLD')
      DO 25 I=1,3
          READ (10,15) ID,IWT,FWT
   15     FORMAT (I5,4X,F5.1,F5.1)
          PERC = (FWT - IWT)/IWT*100.0
          PRINT 20, ID,IWT,FWT
   20     FORMAT (1X,I4,5X,F5.1,6X,F5.1,6X,F10.5)
   25 CONTINUE
      END
*--------------------------------------------------------------*
```

A sample data file and its corresponding output are

DATA FILE

$$bbb^{10}bbbbbb^{5.3}bb^{6.2}$$
$$bbb^{11}bbbbbb^{5.2}bb^{5.2}$$
$$bbb^{12}bbbbbb^{5.3}bb^{5.1}$$

COMPUTER OUTPUT

```
TEST RESULTS

NUMBER   INITIAL WT   FINAL WT   PERCENTAGE INCREASE
  10         5.3         6.2            16.98112
  11         5.2         5.2             0.00000
  12         5.3         5.1            -3.77359
```

4-5 ADDITIONAL FORMAT FEATURES

In this section we present several useful features of FORMAT statements. We illustrate each feature with an example.

REPETITION

If we have two identical specifications in a row, we can use a constant in front of the specification (or sets of specifications) to indicate repetition. For instance, I2,I2,I2 can be replaced by 3I2. Often our FORMAT statements can be made shorter with repetition constants. The following pairs of FORMAT statements illustrate the use of repetition constants:

```
10 FORMAT (3X,I2,3X,I2)
10 FORMAT (2(3X,I2))

20 FORMAT (1X,F4.1,F4.1,1X,I3,1X,I3,1X,I3)
20 FORMAT (1X,2F4.1,3(1X,I3))
```

SLASH

The FORMAT statement may also contain the character slash (/). Commas around the slash in a FORMAT are optional. If the slash is in a READ statement, a new data line is read when the slash is encountered. The slash also can be used with PRINT statements. It is important, however, to interpret the slash as a signal that says "print the current buffer and start a new one"—the carriage control character following the slash will determine whether the spacing between lines is single spacing, double spacing, or some other spacing.

EXAMPLE 4-9 Real Values

Read the values HT1 and HT2 from one data line, TIME from a second line, and VEL from a third data line. Each number is entered in four columns, with one decimal position. There are no extra columns between HT1 and HT2.

Solution 1

FORTRAN Statements

```
        READ 15, HT1, HT2, TIME, VEL
    15 FORMAT (2F4.1/F4.1/F4.1)
```

Data Lines

```
        16.518.2
        00.5
        -4.6
```

Computer Memory

HT1 | 16.5 |

HT2 | 18.2 |

TIME | 0.5 |

VEL | −4.6 |

Solution 2

In this solution, we do not use the slash. Notice the extra READ statements that are required.

FORTRAN Statements

```
        READ 15, HT1,HT2
    15 FORMAT (2F4.1)
        READ 16, TIME
        READ 16, VEL
    16 FORMAT (F4.1)
```

Data Lines

```
        16.518.2
        00.5
        -4.6
```

Computer Memory

HT1 | 16.5 |

HT2 | 18.2 |

TIME | 0.5 |

VEL | −4.6 |

EXAMPLE 4-10   Title and Heading

Print the heading TEST RESULTS followed by column headings TIME and HEIGHT. Separate the column headings by five columns and center the heading over the columns.

Solution 1

FORTRAN STATEMENTS

```
    PRINT 5
  5 FORMAT (1X,2X,'TEST RESULTS'/1X,'TIME      HEIGHT')
```

BUFFER CONTENTS

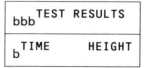

COMPUTER OUTPUT

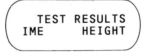

When the slash is encountered, we "print the current buffer." The carriage control character is a space; thus, the first line is printed after spacing to the next line. We then "start a new buffer." The 1X specification puts a blank in the first position in the buffer. When we reach the end of the FORMAT, this line will be single spaced from the first line. If the 1X had been omitted and our system used carriage control, the character T would have been used for carriage control; this is an undefined carriage control character, which also causes single spacing. However, the computer output would be

```
     TEST RESULTS
     IME       HEIGHT
```

Solution 2

In this solution, we use the slash to leave a blank line between the main header and the column headings.

FORTRAN STATEMENTS

```
    PRINT 5
  5 FORMAT (1X,2X,'TEST RESULTS'//1X,'TIME      HEIGHT')
```

BUFFER CONTENTS

| bbb TEST RESULTS |
| bbbbbbbbbbbbbbbb |
| b TIME   HEIGHT |

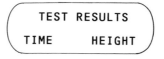

The first slash encountered prints the first buffer and starts a new buffer. Another slash is encountered, which causes the buffer filled with blanks to be printed and starts a new buffer. This buffer is filled and the end of the FORMAT is reached, causing this last buffer to be printed.

TAB SPECIFICATION

The tab specification Tn allows you to shift directly to a specified position, n, in the input or output buffer. The following pairs of FORMAT statements function exactly the same:

```
500 FORMAT (58X,'EXPERIMENT NO. 1')
500 FORMAT (T59,'EXPERIMENT NO. 1')

550 FORMAT (1X,'SALES',10X,'PROFIT',10X,'LOSS')
550 FORMAT (1X,'SALES',T17,'PROFIT',T33,'LOSS')

600 FORMAT (F6.1,15X,I7)
600 FORMAT (F6.1,T22,I7)
```

The TLn and TRn specifications tab left or right for n positions from the current position. The following formats are therefore equivalent:

```
85 FORMAT (1X,25X,'HEIGHT',5X,'WEIGHT')
85 FORMAT (T27,'HEIGHT',TR5,'WEIGHT')
```

The tab specifications are especially useful in aligning column headings and data.

NUMBER OF SPECIFICATIONS

Suppose there are more FORMAT specifications than variables on a READ or PRINT list, as shown:

```
READ 1, SPEED,DIST
1 FORMAT (4F5.2)
```

In these cases, the computer uses as much of the specification list as it needs and ignores the rest. In our example, SPEED and DIST would be matched to the first two specifications; the last two specifications would be ignored. This rule occasionally allows us to use the same FORMAT with several statements.

Suppose there are fewer FORMAT specifications than variables on a READ or PRINT list, as shown:

```
PRINT 20, TEMP, VOL
20 FORMAT (1X,F6.2)
```

In these cases, we match variables and specifications until we reach the end of the FORMAT. Then, two events occur:

1. With a READ statement, we go to the next data line; with a PRINT statement, we print the current buffer and start a new one.
2. We back up in the FORMAT specification list with both READ and PRINT statements until we reach a left parenthesis, and we again begin matching the remaining variables to the specifications at that point. If a repetition constant is in front of this left parenthesis, it applies to the FORMAT specifications being reused.

In the previous statements, TEMP would be matched to the F6.2 specification. Because there is no specification for VOL, we do the following:

1. Print the value of TEMP after single spacing.
2. Back up to the beginning of the FORMAT specification list (first left parenthesis) and match the F6.2 to the value of VOL. We then reach the end of the list and single space to print the value of VOL. TEMP and VOL are thus printed on separate lines.

SELF-TEST 4–1

This self-test allows you to check quickly to see if you have remembered some of the key points from Section 4–5. If you have any problems with the exercises, you should reread this section. The solutions are included at the end of the text.

For problems 1–2, show the values that will be stored in the variables after execution of the following READ statements.

1.   `READ 15, ID, HT, WIDTH`
      `15 FORMAT (I4,2X,2F4.1)`

   Data Line:
   1456$_{bb}$14.6$_{bb}$.7

2.   `READ 7, ID, HT, WIDTH`
      `7 FORMAT (I2,F4.1,2X,F4.2)`

   Data Line:
   $_{bb}$13.7$_{bb}$.865

In problems 3–6, tell how many data lines are required for the following READ statements to work correctly. Indicate which variables are on each line and which columns must be used.

```
3.    READ 4, TIME, DIST, VEL, ACCEL
    4 FORMAT (4F6.3)
4.    READ 14, TIME, DIST, VEL, ACCEL
   14 FORMAT (F6.2)
5.    READ 2, TIME, DIST, VEL, ACCEL
    2 FORMAT (F3.2/F4.1)
6.    READ 3, TIME, DIST
      READ 3, VEL, ACCEL
    3 FORMAT (4F6.3)
```

In problems 7–9, show the output from the following PRINT statements. Be sure to indicate the vertical as well as the horizontal spacing. Use the following variables and corresponding values:

```
    TIME = 4.55,    RESP1 = 0.00074,    RESP2 = 56.83
```

```
7.    PRINT 5, TIME, RESP1, RESP2
    5 FORMAT (1X,F6.2,5X,2F7.4)
8.    PRINT 4, TIME, RESP1, TIME, RESP2
    4 FORMAT (1X,'TIME = ',F5.2,2X,'RESPONSE 1 = ',F8.5/
    +         1X,'TIME = ',F5.2,2X,'RESPONSE 2 = ',F8.5)
9.    PRINT 1, TIME, RESP1, RESP2
    1 FORMAT (1X,'EXPERIMENT RESULTS'//1X,'TIME',2X,
    +         'RESPONSE 1',2X,'RESPONSE 2'/
    +         1X,F4.2,2E12.3)
```

4-6 APPLICATION—QUALITY CONTROL
(Manufacturing Engineering)

In a manufacturing or assembly plant, quality control receives close attention. One of the key responsibilities of a quality-control engineer is to collect accurate data on the quality of the product being manufactured. This data can be used to identify problem areas in the assembly line or in the materials being used in the product.

   In this section, we use information collected over a 1-month period that specifies both the type of defect and the number of defects detected in the assembly of the computer board for a personal computer. These defects have been divided into three categories: broken wires, defective integrated circuit chips (ICs), and defective non-IC components (such as resistors and capacitors). The data has been stored in a file called REPORT. The first line in the data file contains the number of boards assembled in the period of time represented by the data in the file. Each line following contains a board identification number followed by three integers that represent the number of broken wires, defective ICs, and defective non-ICs, respectively, on the board.

At least one of these numbers is greater than zero because the file contains only information on boards with defects.

Our program is to read this set of information and compute the total number of defects in each category and the number of boards with defects. We are also to print the board identification numbers for boards that have three or more defects. This information will allow the quality-control engineer to identify trouble areas by using the identification numbers to determine the date of assembly and the lot of materials used in those computer boards.

PROBLEM STATEMENT

Print a report analyzing the defects in a set of computer boards.

INPUT/OUTPUT DESCRIPTION

The input to the program is to be entered from a data file. The first line in the file contains the total number of boards assembled. Each line following contains a board identification number and three integers representing the three types of defects that may occur in the board: broken wires, defective ICs, and defective non-ICs. The end of the data is indicated by a 99999 in board identification. The output is a report with the following information:

```
          MONTHLY QUALITY ANALYSIS REPORT

  IDENTIFICATION NUMBERS OF BOARDS WITH THREE OR MORE DEFECTS:

      XXX

  TOTAL NUMBER OF BOARDS ASSEMBLED = XXXX

  TOTAL BOARDS WITH DEFECTS = XXXX

      XXXX BOARDS WITH BROKEN WIRES
      XXXX BOARDS WITH DEFECTIVE IC COMPONENTS
      XXXX BOARDS WITH DEFECTIVE NON-IC COMPONENTS

  DEFECT ANALYSIS

      XXX.X% OF DEFECTS ARE BROKEN WIRES
      XXX.X% OF DEFECTS ARE DEFECTIVE IC COMPONENTS
      XXX.X% OF DEFECTS ARE DEFECTIVE NON-IC COMPONENTS
```

HAND EXAMPLE

Assuming that a total of 528 computer boards were assembled during the month, consider the following set of defect data:

IDENTIFICATION	DEFECTS IN THE THREE CATEGORIES
528	
145	0 0 1
188	1 1 0
410	0 1 0
312	2 0 0
366	0 0 1
368	0 0 1
279	1 1 2
407	1 0 0
99999	0 0 0

The analysis of the sample data yields the following quality analysis report:

```
            MONTHLY QUALITY ANALYSIS REPORT

IDENTIFICATION NUMBERS OF BOARDS WITH THREE OR MORE DEFECTS:

    279

TOTAL NUMBER OF BOARDS ASSEMBLED =   528

TOTAL BOARDS WITH DEFECTS =      8

        4 BOARDS WITH BROKEN WIRES
        3 BOARDS WITH DEFECTIVE IC COMPONENTS
        4 BOARDS WITH DEFECTIVE NON-IC COMPONENTS

DEFECT ANALYSIS

        38.5% OF DEFECTS ARE BROKEN WIRES
        23.1% OF DEFECTS ARE DEFECTIVE IC COMPONENTS
        38.5% OF DEFECTS ARE DEFECTIVE NON-IC COMPONENTS
```

ALGORITHM DEVELOPMENT

Most of the information in the report is based on totals that we need to determine as the data is entered. For example, we need the following:

Total number of boards assembled

Total number of boards with defects

Total number of boards with broken wires

Total number of boards with defective ICs

Total number of boards with defective non-IC components

Total number of broken wires

Total number of defective ICs

Total number of defective non-IC components

Recall that we also want to print the identification number of any board that has three or more defects. Because we do not know in advance how many of these boards there are, we cannot easily keep the identification numbers in memory; therefore, we print the identification numbers as soon as we read them. The WHILE loop for reading this data is executed "while ID is not 99999," so we need to read the first set of defect data before we test this WHILE condition.

Putting these ideas into our decomposition step yields

DECOMPOSITION

Read data and compute totals and print ID for boards with three or more defects.
Compute data for defect summary.
Print report.

Adding more detail to these steps, our refinement in pseudocode becomes

REFINEMENT IN PSEUDOCODE

QUALTY: Initialize all totals to zero
        Read number of boards assembled
        Read ID, defects
        While ID not equal to 99999 do
           If number of defects ≥ 3 print ID
           Increment appropriate totals
           Read ID, defects
        Compute additional totals and percentages
        Print report

We are now ready to convert the steps in pseudocode into FORTRAN statements. We again list the totals that we need, along with the FORTRAN names that we are using for them.

BOARDS	Total number of boards assembled
BDDEF	Total number of boards with defects
BDWIRE	Total number of boards with broken wires
BDIC	Total number of boards with defective ICs
BDNON	Total number of boards with defective non-ICs
WIRE	Total number of broken wires
IC	Total number of defective ICs
NON	Total number of defective non-IC components

FORTRAN Program

```
*---------------------------------------------------------------*
      PROGRAM  QUALTY
*
*  This program uses defect data to print
*  a Quality Analysis Report.
*
      INTEGER  BOARDS, BDDEF, BDWIRE, BDIC, BDNON, WIRE,
     +         IC, NON, ID, NWIRE, NIC, NNON, DEFECT
      REAL  PERCW, PERCIC, PERCNO
*
      BDDEF = 0
      BDWIRE = 0
      BDIC = 0
      BDNON = 0
      WIRE = 0
      IC = 0
      NON = 0
      OPEN (UNIT=10,FILE='REPORT',STATUS='OLD')
      READ (10,*) BOARDS
*
      PRINT*, '            MONTHLY QUALITY ANALYSIS REPORT'
      PRINT*
      PRINT*, 'IDENTIFICATION NUMBERS OF BOARDS WITH ',
     +        'THREE OR MORE DEFECTS:'
      PRINT*
*
      READ (10,*) ID, NWIRE, NIC, NNON
   10 IF (ID.NE.99999) THEN
         IF (NWIRE + NIC + NNON.GE.3) PRINT 15, ID
   15    FORMAT (1X,I8)
         BDDEF = BDDEF + 1
         IF (NWIRE.GT.0) BDWIRE = BDWIRE + 1
         IF (NIC.GT.0) BDIC = BDIC + 1
         IF (NNON.GT.0) BDNON = BDNON + 1
         WIRE = WIRE + NWIRE
         IC = IC + NIC
         NON = NON + NNON
         READ (10,*) ID, NWIRE, NIC, NNON
         GO TO 10
      ENDIF
*
      PRINT 20, BOARDS, BDDEF, BDWIRE, BDIC, BDNON
   20 FORMAT (/,1X,'TOTAL NUMBER OF BOARDS ASSEMBLED = ',I4,//,
     +         1X,'TOTAL  BOARDS WITH DEFECTS = ',I4,//,
     +         1X,5X,I4,'  BOARDS WITH BROKEN WIRES',/,
     +         1X,5X,I4,'  BOARDS WITH DEFECTIVE IC COMPONENTS',/,
     +         1X,5X,I4,'  BOARDS WITH DEFECTIVE NON-IC COMPONENTS')
      DEFECT = WIRE + IC   + NON
      PERCW = REAL(WIRE)*100.0/REAL(DEFECT)
      PERCIC = REAL(IC)*100.00/REAL(DEFECT)
      PERCNO = REAL(NON)*100.0/REAL(DEFECT)
      PRINT 30, PERCW, PERCIC, PERCNO
   30 FORMAT (/,1X,'DEFECT ANALYSIS',//,
     +         1X,5X,F5.1,'% OF DEFECTS ARE BROKEN WIRES',/,
     +         1X,5X,F5.1,'% OF DEFECTS ARE DEFECTIVE ',
     +                    'IC COMPONENTS',/,
     +         1X,5X,F5.1,'% OF DEFECTS ARE DEFECTIVE ',
     +                    'NON-IC COMPONENTS')
      END
*---------------------------------------------------------------*
```

Several of the literals in our FORMAT statements were too long to fit on one line and had to be separated into two lines. Instead of continuing the literal to column 72, it is more readable if we split the line between words.

TESTING

If we use our sample data from the program, our output is

```
              MONTHLY QUALITY ANALYSIS REPORT

IDENTIFICATION NUMBERS OF BOARDS WITH THREE OR MORE DEFECTS:

     279

TOTAL NUMBER OF BOARDS ASSEMBLED =   528

TOTAL BOARDS WITH DEFECTS =      8

        4 BOARDS WITH BROKEN WIRES
        3 BOARDS WITH DEFECTIVE IC COMPONENTS
        4 BOARDS WITH DEFECTIVE NON-IC COMPONENTS

DEFECT ANALYSIS

        38.5% OF DEFECTS ARE BROKEN WIRES
        23.1% OF DEFECTS ARE DEFECTIVE IC COMPONENTS
        38.5% OF DEFECTS ARE DEFECTIVE NON-IC COMPONENTS
```

Once our program is working correctly with a typical set of data, we should design data sets that test special conditions. For example, we should test this program with data that does not include one of the defects; if we eliminate all the IC defects in our sample set, the preceding program produces the following report:

```
              MONTHLY QUALITY ANALYSIS REPORT

IDENTIFICATION NUMBERS OF BOARDS WITH THREE OR MORE DEFECTS:

     279

TOTAL NUMBER OF BOARDS ASSEMBLED = 528

TOTAL BOARDS WITH DEFECTS =      7

        4 BOARDS WITH BROKEN WIRES
        0 BOARDS WITH DEFECTIVE IC COMPONENTS
        4 BOARDS WITH DEFECTIVE NON-IC COMPONENTS

DEFECT ANALYSIS

        50.0% OF DEFECTS ARE BROKEN WIRES
         0.0% OF DEFECTS ARE DEFECTIVE IC COMPONENTS
        50.0% OF DEFECTS ARE DEFECTIVE NON-IC COMPONENTS
```

When entering the data in the file REPORT, is it necessary to include three zeros after the identification number 99999? Yes, it is necessary because the corresponding READ statement lists four variables; otherwise, an execution error will occur.

SUMMARY

This chapter presented a number of I/O features available in FORTRAN. The most important feature is the data file. Data files are necessary in engineering and science applications because they often use large amounts of data. We will use data files frequently throughout this text so that you can become comfortable with them.

We also presented details on formatted input and output. The only way to become proficient with formatting is to use it frequently. We suggest that you use list-directed input and output in your testing and debugging phases. Once you get correct answers, use formatted output statements to give a neat and attractive form to your answers.

DEBUGGING AIDS

The following steps will help you correct input and output statements that are not working properly.

1. Check to be sure you have given values to all variables in an output list.
2. Echo values that you read; that is, immediately after reading a value, print it for a comparison check.
3. If any of your output values contains asterisks instead of numbers, enlarge the width of the corresponding specifications or use an E format.
4. Be sure that the order of variables in the input or output list matches the order you used when writing the format.
5. Check every line of output to ensure that you have correctly specified carriage control unless you are using list-directed output. Look for incorrect spacing between lines or missing first letters or numbers in the output.
6. Be sure that you have as many FORMAT specifications as variable names in the READ or PRINT list. In general, do not try to share FORMAT statements.
7. Be sure you do not have the characters I and 1 or the characters O (letter) and 0 (number) interchanged.
8. Be sure that you have not exceeded column 72 on long statements.
9. Do not combine too many lines of output in a single output statement.
10. Use unformatted statements to print values first. After you determine that the values are correct, change to formatted statements, if needed.

11. Check input formats to ensure that you have not included carriage control.

12. Be careful splitting a literal specification when continuing a long format to the next line. Break the literal into two literals so that unexpected blanks do not appear; for example, consider the following FORMAT statement:

```
10 FORMAT (1X,'EXPERIMENTAL RESULTS
+              FROM PROJECT #1')
```

Any blanks between the word RESULTS and column 72 of the first line and between the continuation character + and the word FROM will be inserted in the literal. Thus, the heading would appear something like:

```
EXPERIMENTAL RESULTS                    FROM PROJECT #1
```

A better solution is to split the literal into two literals, which is illustrated in the following FORMAT and its corresponding output:

```
10 FORMAT (1X,'EXPERIMENTAL RESULTS ',
+              'FROM PROJECT #1')
```

```
EXPERIMENTAL RESULTS FROM PROJECT #1
```

STYLE/TECHNIQUE GUIDES

1. Develop the habit of echo printing values that you have read.

2. Print the physical units that correspond to the numeric values being printed — this information is vital for proper interpretation of results.

3. Be consistent about your placement of FORMAT statements. Either put the FORMAT immediately after the statement that uses it, or put the FORMAT just before the END statement in your program.

4. Label FORMAT statements so that the numbers are in ascending order and they fit into the order of other statements in your program. Do not, however, number statements sequentially — you may need to insert additional statements later.

5. Make your carriage control evident. For instance, use (1X,F4.1) instead of (F5.1).

6. Label values printed. Use (1X,'X=',F3.1) instead of (1X,F3.1).

7. Use an E format to print values for which you cannot approximate the size. After seeing the answer, you can change the E specification to an F specification that will accommodate the value, if you wish.

8. Do not print more significant digits than you have. For instance, if you compute sums with values that have one decimal position, do not print the result with three decimal positions.

9. Generally, it is best to use the same number of specifications in the FORMAT as there are variable names in the variable list.

10. Do not use extremely long FORMAT statements; use additional statements with separate FORMAT statements.

11. Remember that the slash character must always be followed by carriage control in output statements.

KEY WORDS

data file	record
END option	sentinel signal
job control information	trailer signal

PROBLEMS

We begin our problem set with modifications to programs developed earlier in this chapter. Give the decomposition, refined pseudocode or flowchart, and FORTRAN program for each problem.

Problems 1–5 modify the critical path analysis program PATH, given on page 157.

1. Modify the critical path analysis program so that it prints the event number and task number for the task that requires the maximum amount of time.

2. Modify the critical path analysis program so that it prints the event number for the event that requires the maximum amount of time.

3. Modify the critical path analysis program so that it prints the average amount of time required for the tasks.

4. Modify the critical path analysis program so that it prints the event and task number for all tasks requiring more than five days.

5. Modify the critical path analysis program so that it prints a list of the events and the number of tasks in each event.

Problems 6–10 modify the population growth program CENSUS, given on page 161.

6. Modify the population growth program so that it finds the two consecutive years in which the percentage increase in population was the smallest.

7. Modify the population growth program so that it finds and prints the year and the corresponding population that was the smallest population value. Print all years with this minimum population.

8. Modify the population growth program so that it computes the average increase in population per year for the total period of time represented by the data in the data file.

9. Modify the population growth program so that it finds the two consecutive years in which the actual increase in population was the largest.

10. Modify the population growth program so that it prints the population values for the two consecutive years in which the actual increase in population was the smallest.

Problems 11–15 modify the quality control program QUALITY, given on page 177.

11. Modify the quality control program so that it prints an error message if the identification number is greater than 5000.

12. Modify the quality control program so that it prints the percentage of boards with defects.

13. Modify the quality control program so that it prints the total number of defects.

14. Modify the quality control program so that it prints the identification numbers of boards with a defect in two or more of the categories.

15. Modify the quality control program so that it determines and prints the number of boards with one defect, the number of boards with two defects, the number of boards with three defects, and the number of boards with more than three defects.

In problems 16–30 develop programs using the five-phase design process.

16. As a practicing engineer, you have been collecting data on the performance of a new solar device. You have been measuring the sun's intensity and the voltage produced by a photovoltaic cell exposed to the sun. These measurements have been taken every 30 minutes during daylight hours for 2 months. Because the sun sets at a different time each day, the number of measurements taken each day may vary.

Each line of valid data contains the sun's intensity (integer), the time (24-hour form where 1430 represents 2:30 PM), and the voltage (real). A trailer signal contains 9999 for the sun's intensity. Write a complete program to read this data and compute and print the total number of measurements, the average intensity of the sun, and the average voltage value.

17. Write a program for a nutrition study that will read the value of N from the first line in a data file called WEIGHTS. If N is zero or negative, stop the program; otherwise, use N to specify the number of data lines remaining in the data file, where each data line contains an identification number (integer), the initial weight, and the final weight of a participant in the study. Print a table containing this original data and the percentage increase in weight for each participant. Number the lines. Use the following report form:

NUTRITION STUDY

	ID	INITIAL WT	FINAL WT	PERCENT INCREASE
1.	XXX	XXX.X	XXX.X	XXX.XX
2.	XXX	XXX.X	XXX.X	XXX.XX
	.	.	.	.
	.	.	.	.
	.	.	.	.
N.	XXX	XXX.X	XXX.X	XXX.XX

18. Write a program for analyzing pressure data. Read 20 lines of data with three integer numbers per line from a data file called RESULTS. Each line represents pressure measurements made in three different chambers. Find the maximum pressure in each chamber and print the following:

```
MAXIMUM PRESSURE IN CHAMBER 1 = XXXX
MAXIMUM PRESSURE IN CHAMBER 2 = XXXX
MAXIMUM PRESSURE IN CHAMBER 3 = XXXX
```

19. Twenty-four temperature measurements for two compounds have been taken at 20-minute intervals over a period of time. Each pair of temperatures is entered in a data file TEMP in the order in which the measurements were made. Write a program to read the data and print it in the following manner:

TEMPERATURE MEASUREMENTS

TIME ELAPSED HOURS	AND MINUTES	COMPOUND 1	COMPOUND 2
0	0	XXXXX	XXXXX
0	20	XXXXX	XXXXX
0	40	XXXXX	XXXXX
1	00	XXXXX	XXXXX
1	20	XXXXX	XXXXX
1	40	XXXXX	XXXXX
2	0	XXXXX	XXXXX
.	.	.	.
.	.	.	.
.	.	.	.
7	40	XXXXX	XXXXX

20. Modify problem 19 so that the following output lines are printed after the temperature measurements:

```
MINIMUM TEMPERATURE AND TIME ELAPSED (HOURS AND MINUTES)
        COMPOUND 1         XXXXX              XX        XX
        COMPOUND 2         XXXXX              XX        XX
```

21. Write a program to compute fuel cost information for an automobile. The input data is stored in a data file called MILES. The first line in the file contains the initial mileage (odometer reading). Each following data line contains information collected as the automobile was refueled and includes the new mileage reading, the cost of the fuel, and the number of gallons of fuel. The last line of the file contains a negative value and two zeros, instead of the refueling information. The output of the program should compute the

cost per mile and the number of miles per gallon for each line of input data. Use the report format shown:

```
                 FUEL COST INFORMATION

MILES        GALLONS      COST     COST/MILE    MILES/GALLON
XXX.X         XX.X       XX.XX       X.XX          XX.X
 .
 .
 .
```

22. Add the following summary information at the end of the report printed in problem 21:

```
              SUMMARY INFORMATION

        TOTAL MILES               XXXX.X
        TOTAL COST               XXXXX.XX
        TOTAL GALLONS             XXXX.X
        AVERAGE COST/MILE          X.XX
        AVERAGE MILES/GALLON       XX.X
```

23. Oil exploration and recovery is an important concern of large petroleum companies. Profitable oil recovery requires careful testing by drilling seismic holes and blasting with specific amounts of dynamite. For optimum seismic readings, a specific ratio between the amount of dynamite and the depth of the hole is required. Assume that each stick of dynamite is $2\frac{1}{2}$ feet long, and weighs 5 pounds. The ideal powder charge requires a ratio of 1:3 for the dynamite to depth-of-hole ratio. Thus, a 60-foot hole would require 20 feet of dynamite, which is equal to 8 sticks, or 40 pounds. The actual powder charge is not always equal to the ideal powder charge because the ideal powder charge may not be in 5-pound increments; in these cases, the actual powder charge should be rounded down to the nearest 5-pound increment. (You cannot cut or break the dynamite into shorter lengths for field operations.)

    The following example should clarify this process:

    Hole depth = 85 feet
    Ideal charge = 85/3 = 28.33333 feet
    $\qquad\qquad\quad$ = 11.33333 sticks
    $\qquad\qquad\quad$ = 56.66666 pounds
    Actual charge = 55 pounds
    $\qquad\qquad\quad$ = 11 sticks

    Information on the depths of the holes to be tested each day is stored in a data file called DRILL. The first line contains the number of sites to be tested that day. Each following line contains integer information for a specified site that gives the site identification number and the depth of the hole in feet. Write a complete program to read this information and print the following report:

SITE ID	DEPTH (FT)	IDEAL POWDER CHARGE (LBS)	ACTUAL POWDER CHARGE (LBS)	STICKS
-------	-----	------------	------------	------
12980	85	56.6666	55	11
.	.	.	.	.
.	.	.	.	.
.	.	.	.	.

(*Hint:* The MOD function would be useful in this program.)

24. Modify the program in problem 23 so that a final summary report follows the drilling report and has the form

    TOTAL POWDER USED = XXXXX LBS   (XXXX STICKS)
    TOTAL DRILLING FOOTAGE = XXXXXX FT

25. Modify the program in problem 24 so that it takes into consideration a special situation: If the depth of the hole is less than 30 feet, the hole is too shallow for blasting. Instead of printing the charge values for such a hole, print the site identification number, the depth, and the message HOLE TOO SHALLOW FOR BLASTING. The summary report printed at the end of the report should not include data for these shallow holes. Add a line to the summary report that contains the number of holes too shallow for blasting.

26. Beam analysis is an important part of the structural analysis conducted before construction of a building begins. A frequently used type of beam is a cantilever beam, which is fixed on one end and free on the other. The amount of deflection when a load is applied to this type of beam can be computed with the following equation:

$$\text{DEFLECTION} = \frac{(L)(a^2)}{2(E)(I)} \cdot \left(\text{length} - \frac{a}{3.0}\right)$$

where L = applied load in pounds
   a = length from fixed end to applied load in feet
   E = elasticity of material (wood, steel, . . .)
   I = moment of inertia of the beam, which can be computed with the following equation:

$$I = \frac{(\text{base})(\text{height})^3}{12}$$

Assume that we have information on five different beams in a data file BEAM. The data for each beam is given in the following five real values, which are stored in one data line in the proper units for the equations above:

                    Beam length
                    Beam base
                    Beam height
                    Elasticity constant
                    Applied load

Write a program to read the information for each beam and print a report that places the applied load at 1-foot intervals starting at one foot from the fixed end and moving down the length of the beam. The output for a beam should contain the following information:

```
BEAM NO. 1     TOTAL LENGTH = XXX.XX FT

     DISTANCE OF LOAD FROM FIXED END          DEFLECTION
                1.0                             XXX.XX
                2.0                             XXX.XX
                 .                                 .
                 .                                 .
                 .                                 .
```

27. Modify the program in problem 26 so that the deflections for each beam are printed only as long as they are less than 5 percent of the beam length. When the beam deflection is greater than or equal to 5 percent, the program should stop computing values for that beam and go on to the next. If the deflection distance of 5 percent is never reached, the program should print an appropriate message. The header line for each beam should also contain the 5 percent length computation. An example of this output is

```
BEAM NO. 1     TOTAL LENGTH = 10.00 FT
               5% OF LENGTH =  0.50 FT

     DISTANCE FROM FIXED END            DEFLECTION
              1.00                         0.15
              2.00                         0.38
              3.00                         0.48

BEAM NO. 2     TOTAL LENGTH =  3.00 FT
               5% OF LENGTH =  0.15 FT

     DISTANCE FROM FIXED END            DEFLECTION
              1.00                         0.04
              2.00                         0.09
              3.00                         0.12

          DEFLECTION OF 5% OF LENGTH NOT REACHED
```

28. Assume that a data file called DATAXY contains a set of data coordinates that are to be used by several different programs. The first line of the file contains the number of data coordinates in the file, and each of the rest of the lines contain the x and y coordinates for one of the data points. Some of the programs need to use the coordinates in polar form instead of rectangular form. Rather than have each program that needs polar coordinates convert the data, we will generate a second data file that has each point in polar form, which is a radius and an angle in radians. Then, no matter how many programs use the data, it only has to be converted to polar coordinates once, and each program can then reference the appropriate file. Write a program to generate a new file called POLAR that contains coordinates in polar form instead of rectangular form. The following equations convert a coordinate in

rectangular form to polar form:

$$r = \sqrt{x^2 + y^2}$$
$$\text{theta} = \tan^{-1}(y/x)$$

(Be sure that the first line of the new data file specifies the number of data coordinates.)

29. Rewrite the program from problem 28, assuming that the original file is POLAR and that it contains data coordinates in polar form. The new output file should be called DATAXY and should contain data coordinates in rectangular form. The equations for converting polar coordinates to rectangular coordinates are

$$x = r\cos(\text{theta})$$
$$y = r\sin(\text{theta})$$

30. Rewrite the program from problem 28 such that it creates a new data file called DATA. The first line of data should still contain the number of coordinates in the data file. Each following line of the data file should contain four values. The first two values represent the rectangular coordinates (x and y), and the next two values represent the corresponding polar coordinates (r and theta) for the data point.

FORTRAN STATEMENT SUMMARY

OPEN Statement:

OPEN (UNIT=*integer expression*, FILE=*filename*, STATUS=*literal*)

Examples:

OPEN (UNIT=15,FILE='EXAMS',STATUS='OLD')

OPEN (UNIT=10,FILE='ACCEL',STATUS='NEW')

Discussion:
The OPEN statement is used to designate that a particular data file will be used for all input or output statements that refer to the unit number in the OPEN statement. If the file is an input file, then its status is 'OLD'; if the file is an output file, then its status is 'NEW'.

READ * Statement:

READ (*unit number,* *,END=n*) *variable list*

Examples:

READ (10,*) X, Y

READ (15,*,END=50) TIME, TEMP

Discussion:
This form of the READ statement is used with data files. The specific data file is referenced by the unit number, which must correspond to a unit number assigned to a file by an OPEN statement. The asterisk specifies that the statement is a list-directed input statement. The END clause is optional and will cause control to be passed to the statement with statement number n if the READ statement is executed after the last line of data has been read.

READ k Statement:

READ (*unit number,k,*END=n) *variable list*

Examples:

READ (15,5) X, Y, Z

READ (15,20,END=50) TIME, DIST

Discussion:
This form of the READ statement is used with data files. The specific data file is referenced by the unit number, which must correspond to a unit number assigned to a file by an OPEN statement. The format statement to be used in reading the data is referenced by the second number in the parentheses. The END clause is optional and will cause control to be passed to the statement with statement number n if the READ statement is executed after the last line of data has been read.

WRITE * Statement:

WRITE (*unit number,**) *variable list*

Examples:

WRITE (13,*) A, B, C

WRITE (10,*) X

Discussion:

This WRITE statement is a list-directed output statement that writes information into a data file specified by the unit number. The unit number must correspond to the unit number of a file that has been assigned in an OPEN statement.

WRITE *k* Statement:

WRITE (*unit number,k*) *variable list*

Examples:

WRITE (10,5) A, B, C

WRITE (15,15) X

Discussion:

This WRITE statement is a formatted output statement that writes information into a data file specified by the unit number. The unit number must correspond to the unit number of a file that has been assigned in an OPEN statement. The format statement is referenced by the second number in the parentheses.

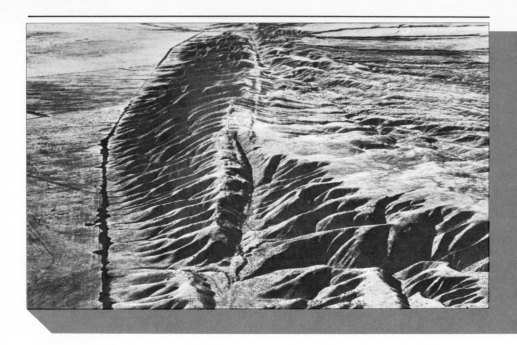

APPLICATION — Earthquake Measurements (Civil Engineering)

Engineers and scientists are hopeful that one day they will be able to predict accurately the size and location of major earthquakes. Data from seismometers, instruments that record the earth's motion, is collected from locations around the world. By studying this data that is collected before, during, and after earthquakes, scientists hope to identify changes that will aid in this prediction process.

Write a program that will sort the data collected from one seismometer during recent earthquakes so that the order of the data is from smallest earthquake to largest earthquake. (See Section 5–5 for the solution.)

Photo courtesy of U. S. Dept. of Interior.

5

ARRAY PROCESSING

INTRODUCTION

This chapter develops a method for storing groups of values without explicitly giving each value a different name — each group (called an array) has a common name but individual values have a unique index or subscript. This technique allows us to analyze the data using loops, where the common name remains the same but the index or subscript becomes a variable that changes with each pass through the loop. Because the data values are stored in separate memory locations, we can also access the data as often as needed without rereading it. An array is used to store the earthquake data in the chapter opener application because we need to have all the data available in order to sort it.

5–1   ONE-DIMENSIONAL ARRAYS

An *array* is a group of storage locations that have the same name. Individual members of an array are called *elements* and are distinguished by using the common name followed by a *subscript* or an index in parentheses. Subscripts are represented by consecutive integers, usually beginning with the integer 1. A one-dimensional array can be visualized as either one column of data or one row of data. The storage locations and associated names for a one-dimensional integer array J of 5 elements and a one-dimensional real array DIST with 4 elements are shown:

J(1)	2
J(2)	−5
J(3)	14
J(4)	80
J(5)	−12

1.2	−0.8	36.9	−0.07

DIST(1)   DIST(2)   DIST(3)   DIST(4)

STORAGE AND INITIALIZATION

The DIMENSION statement, a nonexecutable statement, is used to reserve memory space or storage for an array. In its general form, a list of array names and their corresponding sizes follows the word DIMENSION, as shown:

```
DIMENSION   array1(size), array2(size), . . .
```

Array sizes must be specified with constants, not variables. A DIMENSION statement that reserves storage for the two arrays previously mentioned is

```
DIMENSION   J(5), DIST(4)
```

The number in parentheses after the array name gives the total number of values that can be stored in that array. Two separate DIMENSION statements, with one array listed in each statement, would also be valid but not preferable because it would require an extra statement. All DIMENSION statements must be placed before any executable statements in your program because they are specification statements.

The type of values stored in an array can be specified implicitly through the choice of array name or explicitly with a REAL, INTEGER, or LOGICAL statement. The following statement specifies that AREA is an array of 15 elements that contains integer values

```
INTEGER   AREA(15)
```

The typing of an array, whether implicit or explicit, applies to all elements of the array; hence, an array cannot contain both real values and integer values. Explicitly typed array names do not appear in DIMENSION statements because the array size has also been specified in the type statement. Because explicit typing is desirable, we will use explicit typing statements instead of DIMENSION statements for defining the arrays in our examples.

The range of subscripts associated with an array can be specified with a beginning subscript number and an ending subscript number. Both numbers must be integers separated by a colon and must follow the array name in the DIMENSION statement or the type statement. The following statements reserve storage for a real array TAX whose elements are TAX(0), TAX(1), TAX(2), TAX(3), TAX(4), and TAX(5); and an integer array INCOME whose elements are INCOME(-3), INCOME(-2), INCOME(-1), INCOME(0), INCOME(1), IN-COME(2), and INCOME(3):

```
REAL   TAX(0:5)
```

```
INTEGER   INCOME(-3:3)
```

Also note that the following declarations are equivalent:

```
INTEGER   AREA(1:15)
```

```
INTEGER   AREA(15)
```

Unless otherwise stated, we will assume in our text that all array subscripts begin with the integer 1. However, there are situations in which the range of the subscripts logically starts with an integer other than 1; for instance, in Section 4–3 (Application — Population Study), we discussed a set of population values from the years 1880–1980. If this data were to be stored in an array, it might be convenient to use the year to specify the corresponding population. We could specify such an array with the following statement:

```
INTEGER   POPUL(1880:1890)
```

Then, if we wish to refer to the population for 1885, we use the reference POPUL(1885).

Values are assigned to array elements in the same way that values are assigned to regular variables. The following are valid assignment statements:

```
J(1) = 0
```

```
J(5) = NUM*COUNT
```

```
DIST(2) = 46.2 + SIN(X)
```

It is not valid to use an array name without a subscript in an assignment statement.

It is also extremely helpful to use variables and expressions, instead of constants, as subscripts. The following loop initializes all elements of the array J to the value 10. Observe that the variable I is used as a subscript and also as the DO loop index:

```
    DO 20 I=1,5
        J(I) = 10
 20 CONTINUE
```

The next loop initializes the array J to the values shown:

```
    DO 30 I=1,5
        J(I) = I
 30 CONTINUE
```

1	2	3	4	5

J(1) J(2) J(3) J(4) J(5)

The values of the array DIST are initialized to real values with this set of statements:

```
    DO 5 K=1,4
        DIST(K) = REAL(K)*1.5
  5 CONTINUE
```

1.5	3.0	4.5	6.0

DIST(1) DIST(2) DIST(3) DIST(4)

The previous examples illustrate that a subscript can be an integer constant or an integer variable. Subscripts can also be integer expressions, as indicated in the following statements:

```
J(2*I) = 3

R(J) = R(J-1)

B = TR(2*I) + TR(2*I+1)
```

Whenever an expression is used as a subscript, be sure the value of the expression is between the starting and ending subscript value. If a subscript is outside the proper range, the program will not work correctly. With some compilers, a logic error message is given if a subscript is out of bounds, other compilers use an incorrect value for the invalid array reference, causing serious errors that are difficult to detect.

INPUT AND OUTPUT

To read data into an array from a terminal or from a data file, we use the READ statement. If we wish to read an entire array, we can use the name of the array without subscripts. We can also specify specific elements in a READ statement. If the array A contains 3 elements, then the following two READ statements are equivalent; if the array A contains 8 elements, then the first READ statement reads values for all 8 elements and the second READ statement reads values for only the first 3 elements:

```
READ*, A

READ*, A(1), A(2), A(3)
```

Array values may also be read using an *implied DO loop*. Implied DO loops use the indexing feature of the DO statement and may be used only in input and output statements and in the DATA statement presented in Section 5−2. For example, if we wish to read the first 10 elements of the array R, we can use the following implied DO loop in the READ statement:

```
READ*, (R(I), I=1,10)
```

Further examples illustrate the use of these techniques for reading data into an array.

EXAMPLE 5−1 Temperature Measurements

A set of 50 temperature measurements has been entered into a data file, 1 value per line. The file is accessed with unit number 9. Give a set of statements to read this data into an array:

TEMP(1) ← Line 1 of data file
TEMP(2) ← Line 2 of data file
.
.
.
TEMP(50) ← Line 50 of data file

Solution 1

The READ statement in this solution reads 1 value, but it is in a loop that is executed 50 times and reads the entire array:

```
REAL   TEMP(50)
         .
         .
         .
DO 10 I=1,50
      READ (9,*) TEMP(I)
10 CONTINUE
```

Solution 2

The READ statement in this solution contains no subscript; thus, it reads the entire array:

```
REAL   TEMP(50)
         .
         .
         .
READ (9,*) TEMP
```

Solution 3

The READ statement in this solution contains an implied loop and is equivalent to a READ statement that listed TEMP(1), TEMP(2), . . . , TEMP(50):

```
REAL   TEMP(50)
       .
       .
       .
READ (9,*) (TEMP(I), I=1,50)
```

Note that Solution 2 and Solution 3 are exactly the same as far as the computer is concerned; they both represent one READ statement with 50 variables. Solution 1 is the same as 50 READ statements with 1 variable per READ statement. If the data file contains 50 lines, each with 1 temperature measurement, all three solutions store the same data in the array TEMP.

However, suppose that each of the 50 lines in the data file has two numbers: a temperature measurement and a humidity measurement. Solution 1 will read a new data line for each temperature measurement because it is the equivalent of 50 READ statements. But, because Solutions 2 and 3 are the equivalent of one READ statement with 50 variables listed, they will go to a new line only when they run out of data. Thus, the data is stored as shown:

TEMP(1) ← First temperature
TEMP(2) ← First humidity
TEMP(3) ← Second temperature
TEMP(4) ← Second humidity

.
.
.

This is a subtle, but important, distinction: The computer does not recognize that an error has occurred in the last example shown. It has data for the array and continues processing, assuming it has the correct data.

EXAMPLE 5-2 Rainfall Data

A set of 28 daily rainfall measurements is stored in a data file, with 1 week of data per line. The unit number is again assumed to be 9. Give statements to read this data into an array called RAIN:

RAIN(1)	RAIN(2)	. . .	RAIN(7) ← Line 1 of data file
RAIN(8)	RAIN(9)	. . .	RAIN(14) ← Line 2 of data file
RAIN(15)	RAIN(16)	. . .	RAIN(21) ← Line 3 of data file
RAIN(22)	RAIN(23)	. . .	RAIN(28) ← Line 4 of data file

Correct Solution

The READ statement in this solution contains no subscript and thus reads the entire array. Because each line contains 7 data values, 4 lines of data are required:

```
REAL   RAIN(28)
   .
   .
   .
READ (9,*) RAIN
```

Incorrect Solution

The READ statement in this solution reads 1 value, and the READ statement is in a loop executed 28 times; thus, 28 lines of data are required. Because the data file contains only 4 lines of data, an execution error occurs:

```
REAL   RAIN(28)
   .
   .
   .
DO 10 I=1,28
      READ (9,*) RAIN(I)
10 CONTINUE
```

Techniques to print values in an array are similar to those used to read values into an array. The following examples illustrate the use of DO loops and implied loops for arrays in PRINT statements.

EXAMPLE 5-3 Mass Measurements

A group of 30 mass measurements are stored in a real array MASS. Print the values in the following tabulation:

```
MASS( 1) = XXX.X   KG
MASS( 2) = XXX.X   KG
   .
   .
   .
MASS(30) = XXX.X   KG
```

Solution

For each output line, we need to reference 1 value in the array. The values of the subscript can be generated with a DO statement that has an index of 1 – 30. The output form of this solution is important; go through it carefully to be sure you understand the placement of the literals in the FORMAT statement:

```
REAL   MASS(30)
   .
   .
   .
DO 20 I=1,30
      PRINT 15, I, MASS(I)
15    FORMAT (1X,'MASS(',I2,') = ',F5.1,'  KG')
20 CONTINUE
```

EXAMPLE 5-4 Distance, Velocity, Acceleration

Arrays DIS, VEL, and ACC each contain 50 values: The first value in each array represents the distance, velocity, and acceleration, respectively, of a test rocket at time equal to 1 second. The second set of values represents data for time equal to 2 seconds, and so on. Print the data in the following tabulation:

```
TIME    DISTANCE    VELOCITY    ACCELERATION
(SEC)   (M)         (M/SEC)     (M/(SEC*SEC))
  1     XXX.XX      XXX.XX      XXX.XX
  .        .           .           .
  .        .           .           .
  .        .           .           .
 50     XXX.XX      XXX.XX      XXX.XX
```

Correct Solution

The index of the DO loop is used as a subscript for each array reference. This solution is the equivalent of 50 PRINT statements, each with 4 output variables:

```
      REAL  DIS(50), VEL(50), ACC(50)
         .
         .
         .
      PRINT 5
    5 FORMAT (1X,'TIME    DISTANCE    VELOCITY',
     +             '    ACCELERATION')
      PRINT 6
    6 FORMAT (1X,'(SEC)   (M)         (M/SEC) ',
     +             '   (M/(SEC*SEC))')
      DO 10 I=1,50
         PRINT 7, I, DIS(I), VEL(I), ACC(I)
    7    FORMAT (1X,I3,4X,F6.2,5X,F6.2,5X,F6.2)
   10 CONTINUE
```

Incorrect Solution

This solution is incorrect because each time through the loop, we are printing the index I, the entire DIS array (50 values), the entire VEL array (50 values), and the entire ACC array (50 values)—thus, each time through the loop, we print 151 values.

```
      REAL  DIS(50), VEL(50), ACC(50)
         .
         .
         .
      PRINT 5
    5 FORMAT (1X,'TIME    DISTANCE    VELOCITY',
     +             '    ACCELERATION')
      PRINT 6
    6 FORMAT (1X,'(SEC)   (M)         (M/SEC) ',
     +             '   (M/(SEC*SEC))')
      DO 10 I=1,50
         PRINT 7, I, DIS, VEL, ACC
    7    FORMAT (1X,I3,4X,F6.2,5X,F6.2,5X,F6.2)
   10 CONTINUE
```

This self-test allows you to check quickly to see if you have remembered some of the key points from Section 5-1. If you have any problems with the exercises, you should reread this section. The solutions are included at the end of the text.

Problems 1-3 contain statements that initialize and print one-dimensional arrays. Show the output from each set of statements. Assume that each set of statements is independent of the others.

```
1.      INTEGER  I, M(10)
        DO 5 I=1,10
           M(I) = I + 1
      5 CONTINUE
        PRINT*, 'ARRAY VALUES:'
        DO 15 I=1,10
           PRINT 10, M(I)
     10    FORMAT (1X,I4)
     15 CONTINUE

2.      INTEGER  K, LIST(8)
        DO 5 K=1,8
           LIST(9-K) = K
      5 CONTINUE
        PRINT 10, (LIST(K), K=1,5)
     10 FORMAT (1X,5I5)

3.      INTEGER  J
        REAL  TIME(20)
        DO 5 J=1,20
           TIME(J) = REAL(J-1)*0.5
      5 CONTINUE
        DO 15 J=1,20,4
           PRINT 10, J, TIME(J)
     10    FORMAT (1X,'TIME ',I2,' = ',F5.2)
     15 CONTINUE
```

5-2   DATA STATEMENT

The DATA statement is a specification statement and is therefore nonexecutable; it is useful in initializing both simple variables and arrays. The general form of the DATA statement is

> **DATA**   *list of variable names /list of constants/*

An example of a DATA statement to initialize simple variables is

```
DATA  SUM, VEL, VOLT, LENGTH /0.0, 32.75, -2.5, 10/
```

The number of data values must match the number of variable names. The data values should also be of the correct type so that the computer does not have to convert them. The preceding DATA statement initializes the following variables:

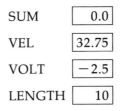

SUM	0.0
VEL	32.75
VOLT	−2.5
LENGTH	10

Because the DATA statement is a specification statement, it should precede any executable statements; it is therefore located near the beginning of your program, along with the REAL, INTEGER, LOGICAL, and DIMENSION statements. It follows these other statements because the specification of the types of variables or the declaration of an array should precede values given to the corresponding memory locations.

Caution should be exercised when using the DATA statement because it initializes values only at the beginning of program execution; this means that the DATA statement cannot be used in a loop to reinitialize variables. If it is necessary to reinitialize variables, you must use assignment statements.

If a number of values are to be repeated in the list of values, a constant followed by an asterisk indicates a repetition. The following statement initializes all 4 variables to zero:

```
DATA   A, B, C, D /4*0.0/
```

The next two statements initialize the variables I, J, and K to 1, and X, Y, and Z to −0.5. Notice the change in the order of the variable names between the two statements:

```
DATA   I, J, K, X, Y, Z /3*1, 3*-0.5/
```

or

```
DATA   I, X, J, Y, K, Z /3*(1, -0.5)/
```

A DATA statement can also be used to initialize one or more elements of an array:

```
INTEGER   J(5)
REAL    TIME(4)
DATA    J, TIME /5*0, 1.0, 2.0, 3.0, 4.0/
```

J | 0 | 0 | 0 | 0 | 0 |

TIME | 1.0 | 2.0 | 3.0 | 4.0 |

or

```
REAL    HOURS(5)
DATA    HOURS(1) /60.0/
```

HOURS $\boxed{60.0}\boxed{?}\boxed{?}\boxed{?}\boxed{?}$

The question marks indicate that some array elements were not initialized by the DATA statement. A syntax error would have occurred if the subscript were left off the array reference HOURS(1) because the number of variables would then not match the number of data values; that is, HOURS represents 5 variables, but HOURS(1) represents only 1 variable.

An implied loop can also be used in a DATA statement to initialize all or part of an array, as in

```
INTEGER  YEAR(100)
DATA   (YEAR(I), I=1,50) /50*0/
```

The first 50 elements of the array are initialized to zero and the last 50 are not initialized. You must therefore make no assumptions about the contents of the last 50 values in the array.

5–3   APPLICATION—NATIONAL PARK SNOWFALL (Meteorology)

The daily snowfall for the month of January has been stored in a data file called JAN. Each data line contains 1 week of snowfall amounts recorded in inches. Line 1 contains the data for the first week in January; line 2 contains the data for the second week in January; and so on. Determine the average daily snowfall and the number of days with above-average snowfall for January.

PROBLEM STATEMENT

Compute the average snowfall for January and the number of days with above-average snowfall.

INPUT/OUTPUT DESCRIPTION

The input data is contained in a file called JAN that contains the snowfall for each day in January. The output is the average daily snowfall and the number of days with above-average snowfall.

HAND EXAMPLE

For a hand-worked example, we use 1 week's data instead of 1 month's data. The values are:

Day 1	4.2 inches
Day 2	3.1 inches
Day 3	1.5 inches
Day 4	0.2 inches
Day 5	0.0 inches
Day 6	0.0 inches
Day 7	1.8 inches

To determine the average value, we total the amounts and then divide by 7, which yields 10.8/7, or 1.54 inches. We now compare this value to the original data values and find that 3 days had snowfalls above the average. Notice that we had to use the data values twice—thus, we must use an array. The array allows us to read all the data to compute the total and still have all the values accessible for comparing them to the average.

ALGORITHM DEVELOPMENT

After completion of the hand-worked example, the initial decomposition is straightforward.

DECOMPOSITION

Read snowfall data.
Compute average snowfall.
Determine the number of days with above-average snowfall.
Print average, number of days.

In the refinement, we need two loops: one to total the data and the other to compare the data to the average. Note that the loops are independent. We must complete the first loop and calculate the average before we can compare the individual values to the average. Often, we can read a data value and add it to a total in the same loop, as shown:

```
      DO 10 I=1,31
         READ (10,*) SNOW(I)
         TOTAL = TOTAL + SNOW(I)
   10 CONTINUE
```

However, the preceding loop requires that the data be stored 1 value per line in the data file. Since our data file contains 1 week of data per data line, we must read the complete set of data before we can compute the total.

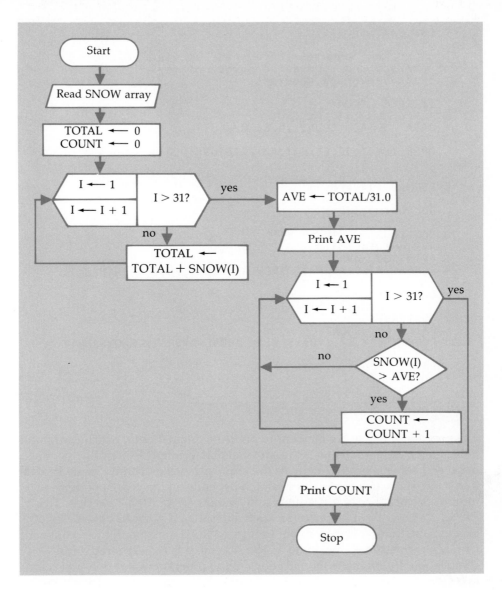

```
*----------------------------------------------------------------*
      PROGRAM  SNOFAL
*
* This program computes the average snowfall
* for January and counts the number of days
* with above-average snowfall.
*
      INTEGER  COUNT
      REAL   SNOW(31), TOTAL, AVE
      DATA   TOTAL, COUNT /0.0, 0/
*
      OPEN (UNIT=10,FILE='JAN',STATUS='OLD')
      READ (10,*) SNOW
      PRINT 5, SNOW
    5 FORMAT (1X,4F8.1)
*
      DO 10 I=1,31
         TOTAL = TOTAL + SNOW(I)
   10 CONTINUE
      AVE = TOTAL/31.0
      PRINT 20, AVE
   20 FORMAT (1X,'AVERAGE SNOWFALL IS ',F5.2,' INCHES')
*
      DO 30 I=1,31
         IF (SNOW(I).GT.AVE) COUNT = COUNT + 1
   30 CONTINUE
      PRINT 40, COUNT
   40 FORMAT (1X,I2,' DAYS WITH ABOVE-AVERAGE SNOWFALL')
*
      END
*----------------------------------------------------------------*
```

TESTING

The program includes a statement to print the original data, which is useful in debugging a program. How is the snowfall data printed? Is it 1 value per line or several values per line? Because the entire array is listed in a single PRINT statement, the number of values printed depends on the corresponding format specification; in this example, the values are printed 4 per line. This PRINT statement can be removed easily after the program has been carefully tested. Sometimes it is convenient to turn a PRINT statement into a comment by placing an asterisk in column 1: The statement is then ignored during compilation. If you make modifications to the program or if it does not seem to be working properly, it is easy to remove the asterisk and reactivate the PRINT statement in the program. The computer output that follows does not include the output from this PRINT statement, but it does show the last two lines of output:

DATA VALUES

```
4.2  3.1  1.5  0.2  0.0  0.0  1.8
1.1  0.9  0.0  0.0  0.0  0.2  0.0
0.9  1.4  1.2  0.3  0.0  0.0  0.0
0.0  0.0  1.5  1.2  0.4  1.6  0.7
0.3  0.0  0.0
```

```
AVERAGE SNOWFALL IS  0.73 INCHES
12 DAYS WITH ABOVE-AVERAGE SNOWFALL
```

5-4   SORTING ALGORITHMS

In this section we develop algorithms to sort a one-dimensional array or list in *ascending*, or low-to-high, order. (With minor alterations, the algorithm can be changed to one that sorts into *descending*, high-to-low, order. We will also see in Chapter 8 that these sort algorithms can be used to alphabetize character data.) The topic of sorting techniques is the subject of entire textbooks and courses; therefore this text will not attempt to present all the important aspects of sorting. Instead, we present three common sorting techniques and develop pseudocode and FORTRAN solutions for all three so that you can compare the different techniques.

Selection Sort   This is a simple sort that is based on finding the minimum value and placing it first in the list, finding the next smallest value and placing it second in the list, and so on.

Bubble Sort   This is a simple sort that is based on interchanging adjacent values in the array until all the values are in the proper position. This sort is sometimes called a multipass sort.

Insertion Sort   This sort begins at the top of the list, comparing adjacent elements. If an element is out of order, it is continually exchanged with the value above it in the list until it is in its proper place. The sort then continues with the next element out of order.

No one sort algorithm is the best to use for all situations. In order to choose a good algorithm, you need to know something about the expected order of the data. For example, if your data is already very close to being in the correct order, both the insertion sort and the version of the bubble sort presented in this section are good choices. If your data is in a random order, or close to the opposite order desired, then the insertion sort or the selection sort are good choices. None of these sorts is efficient if you are sorting a very large set of data. You should consult texts which cover other types of sorts in order to choose a good sort algorithm for a large set of data.

In the three sort algorithms presented in this section we will use only one array. If you need to keep the original order of the data as well as the sorted data, copy the original data into a second array and sort it. Since the actual number of values in the array may be less than the maximum number of values that could be stored in it, we will assume that the variable COUNT specifies the actual number of data values to be sorted.

SELECTION SORT

We begin the discussion of the *selection sort* with a hand example. Consider the list of data values below:

Original List

4.1
7.3
1.7
5.2
1.3

In this algorithm, we first find the minimum value. Scanning down the list, we find that the last value, 1.3, is the minimum. We now want to put the value 1.3 in the first position of the array, but we do not want to lose the value 4.1 that is currently in the first position. Therefore, we will exchange the values.

The switch of two values requires three steps, not two as you might imagine. Consider these statements:

$$X(I) = X(J)$$
$$X(J) = X(I)$$

Suppose X(I) contained the value 3.0 and X(J) contained the value -1.0. The first statement will change the contents of X(I) from the value 3.0 to the value -1.0. The second statement will move the value in X(I) to X(J), so that both locations contain -1.0. These steps are shown next, along with the changes in the corresponding memory locations:

	X(I)	X(J)
	3.0	-1.0
X(I) = X(J)	-1.0	-1.0
X(J) = X(I)	-1.0	-1.0

A correct way to switch the two values is shown here, along with the changes in the corresponding memory locations:

	X(I)	X(J)	HOLD
	3.0	-1.0	?
HOLD = X(I)	3.0	-1.0	3.0
X(I) = X(J)	-1.0	-1.0	3.0
X(J) = HOLD	-1.0	3.0	3.0

Once we have switched the first value in the array with the value that has the minimum value, we search the values in the array from the second value to the last value for the minimum in that list. We then switch the second value with the minimum. We continue this until we are looking at the next-to-last and last values. If they are out of order, we switch them. At this point, the entire array will be sorted into an ascending order, as shown in the diagram below:

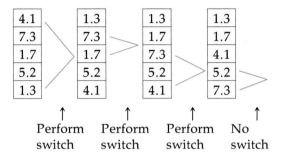

| | Perform switch | Perform switch | Perform switch | No switch |

We now develop the pseudocode and FORTRAN statements for this selection sort.

DECOMPOSITION

Sort list of data values into ascending order.

In the refinement below, notice that we do not keep track of the minimum value itself; instead, we are interested in keeping track of the subscript or location of the minimum value. We need the subscript in order to be able to switch positions with another element in the array. Since the portion of the array that we search for the next minimum gets smaller, we use two variables, FIRST and LAST, to keep track of this array portion. FIRST will start at 2 and increment by one each time we do a switch. LAST will always be equal to COUNT since we search to the bottom of the list of valid values each time.

PSEUDOCODE FOR SELECTION SORT

(Assumes: the values are already stored in the array X; and a variable COUNT specifies the number of valid data values in the array.)

```
last ← count
For j = 1 to count − 1 do
    ptr ← j
    first ← j + 1
    For k = first to last do
        If x(k) < x(ptr) then
            ptr ← k
    Switch values in x(j) and x(ptr)
```

The only step that needs more detail is the step to switch values, because we must specify the three different moves that are necessary. We can add this additional detail as we convert the pseudocode to FORTRAN.

```
          .
          .
          .
     LAST = COUNT
     DO 10 J=1,COUNT-1
        PTR = J
        FIRST = J + 1
        DO 5 K=FIRST,LAST
           IF (X(K).LT.X(PTR)) PTR = K
  5     CONTINUE
        HOLD = X(J)
        X(J) = X(PTR)
        X(PTR) = HOLD
 10 CONTINUE
```

BUBBLE SORT

The basic step to the *bubble sort* algorithm is a single pass through the array, comparing adjacent elements. If a pair of adjacent elements is in the correct order (that is, the first value less than or equal to the second value), we go to the next pair. If the pair is out of order, we switch the values and then go to the next pair.

The single pass through the array can be performed in a counting loop with index J. Each pair of adjacent values will be referred to by the subscripts J and J + 1. If the number of valid data elements in the array is stored in COUNT, we will make COUNT − 1 comparisons of adjacent values in a single pass through the array.

A single pass through a one-dimensional array, switching adjacent elements that are out of order, is not guaranteed to sort the values. Consider a single pass through the following array:

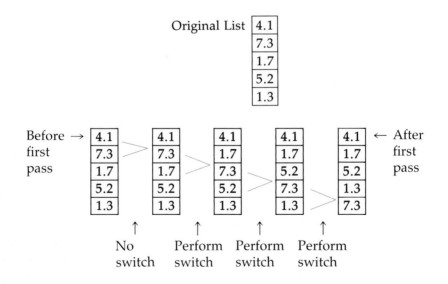

It will take two more complete passes before the array is sorted into ascending order, as shown in the following diagram:

After first pass	
	4.1
	1.7
	5.2
	1.3
	7.3

After second pass	
	1.7
	4.1
	1.3
	5.2
	7.3

After third pass	
	1.7
	1.3
	4.1
	5.2
	7.3

After fourth pass	
	1.3
	1.7
	4.1
	5.1
	7.3

A maximum of COUNT passes may be necessary to sort an array with this technique. If no switches are made during a single pass through the array, however, it is in ascending order. Thus, our algorithm for sorting a one-dimensional array will be to perform single passes through the array making switches until no elements are out of order. In developing the pseudocode we use a logical variable SORTED that is initialized to true at the beginning of each pass through the data array. If any adjacent values are out of order, we switch the values and then change the value of SORTED to false because at least one pair of values was out of order on the pass. At the end of a pass through the data, if the value of SORTED is still true, the array is in ascending order.

We will make one more addition to the algorithm. Observe that during the first pass through the array we switch any adjacent pairs that are out of order. Although this does not necessarily sort the entire array, it is guaranteed to move the largest value to the bottom of the list. During the second pass, the next-largest value will be moved to the next-to-the-last position. Therefore, when we make each pass through the array, we must start at the first position, but we do not need to check values all the way to the end. In fact, with each pass we can reduce the number of positions that we check by one.

We now develop the pseudocode and FORTRAN statements for this bubble sort.

DECOMPOSITION

> Sort list of data values into ascending order.

Pseudocode for Bubble Sort

(Assumes: the values are already stored in the array X; and a variable COUNT specifies the number of valid data values in the array.)

sorted ← false
first ← 1
last ← count − 1
While not sorted do
    sorted ← true
    For j = first to last do
        If x(j) > x(j + 1) then
            Switch values
            sorted ← false
    last ← last − 1

The only step that needs more detail is the step to switch values, because we need to specify the three different moves that are necessary. These moves are specified in the following FORTRAN statements.

FORTRAN Statements

```
      .
      .
      .
      SORTED = .FALSE.
      FIRST = 1
      LAST = COUNT - 1
    5 IF (.NOT.SORTED) THEN
          SORTED = .TRUE.
          DO 10 J=FIRST,LAST
              IF (X(J).GT.X(J+1)) THEN
                  HOLD = X(J)
                  X(J) = X(J+1)
                  X(J+1) = HOLD
                  SORTED = .FALSE.
              ENDIF
   10     CONTINUE
          LAST = LAST - 1
          GO TO 5
      ENDIF
```

INSERTION SORT

The *insertion sort* starts at the beginning of the list, comparing adjacent elements. If an element is out of order, we switch it with the previous element and check to see if it is now in its proper place. If not, we switch it with the new previous element, and again check. We continue moving the element up in the array until it is in its proper position. We then return to the position in the list where we located the element out of order and pick up at that point, comparing the next pair of adjacent elements. When we reach the end of the list, it will be in order because each element that we found out of order was inserted in its proper position before we continued. The following diagram shows these steps with our sample array.

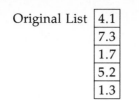

Original List

4.1
7.3
1.7
5.2
1.3

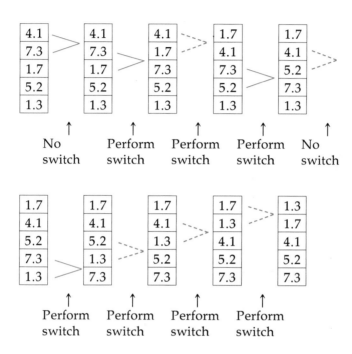

4.1		4.1		4.1		1.7		1.7
7.3		7.3		1.7		4.1		4.1
1.7		1.7		7.3		7.3		5.2
5.2		5.2		5.2		5.2		7.3
1.3		1.3		1.3		1.3		1.3

↑   ↑   ↑   ↑   ↑

No switch   Perform switch   Perform switch   Perform switch   No switch

1.7		1.7		1.7		1.7		1.3
4.1		4.1		4.1		1.3		1.7
5.2		5.2		1.3		4.1		4.1
7.3		1.3		5.2		5.2		5.2
1.3		7.3		7.3		7.3		7.3

↑   ↑   ↑   ↑

Perform switch   Perform switch   Perform switch   Perform switch

We now develop the pseudocode and FORTRAN statements for this insertion sort.

DECOMPOSITION

> Sort list of data values into ascending order.

In the following refinement, notice that we use the subscript j of the counting loop to point to our position before we begin backing up in the array to find the proper position for the element out of order. After putting the element in the correct spot, we can jump back to the next pair of elements in the list that we need to compare, since the value of the subscript j has not been changed.

Pseudocode for Insertion Sort

(Assumes: the values are already stored in the array X; and a variable COUNT specifies the number of valid data values in the array.)

For j = 1 to count − 1 do
  If x(j) > x(j + 1) then
    done ← false
    k ← j
    While not done do
      Switch x(k) with x(k + 1)
      If (k = 1) or (x(k) ≥ x(k − 1)) then
        done ← true
      Else
        k ← k − 1

Again, the step to switch values will need the three moves necessary to interchange the values of x(k) and x(k+1). The corresponding FORTRAN statements are then the following:

FORTRAN Statements

```
      .
      .
      .
      DO 10 J=1,COUNT-1
          IF (X(J).GT.X(J+1)) THEN
              DONE = .FALSE.
              K = J
    5         IF (.NOT.DONE) THEN
                  HOLD = X(K)
                  X(K) = X(K+1)
                  X(K+1) = HOLD
                  IF (K.EQ.1) THEN
                      DONE = .TRUE.
                  ELSEIF (X(K).GT.X(K-1)) THEN
                      DONE = .TRUE.
                  ELSE
                      K = K - 1
                  ENDIF
                  GO TO 5
              ENDIF
          ENDIF
   10 CONTINUE
```

The final condition was separated into two separate conditions in the FORTRAN statements because it would be invalid to examine X(K − 1) if K has the value 1.

SELF-TEST 5-2

This self-test allows you to check quickly to see if you have
remembered certain key points from Section 5-4. If you have any
problems with the exercises, you should reread this section. The
solutions are included at the end of the text. Consider the following
list with six elements in it:

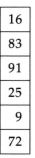

| 16 |
| 83 |
| 91 |
| 25 |
| 9 |
| 72 |

1. Show the sequence of changes that occur in the list if it is
   sorted using the selection sort algorithm.
2. Show the sequence of changes that occur in the list if it is sorted
   using the bubble sort algorithm.
3. Show the sequence of changes that occur in the list if it is
   sorted using the insertion sort algorithm.

5-5   APPLICATION—EARTHQUAKE
MEASUREMENTS (Civil Engineering)

In this application we analyze data that might be collected in a field laboratory
that monitors seismic (earthquake) activity. This data is collected by
instruments called seismometers that are located around the world. Suppose
that a location in California has been the site of earthquake activity for a
number of years. The magnitude of each event has been recorded using the
Richter scale. This data is stored in a data file MOTION in the chronological
order in which the earthquakes occurred. Write a program to read this
information, sort it into ascending order based on magnitude, and print the
data in this new order.

The initial line of the data file contains a five-digit integer that represents
the location number for the laboratory. When new earthquakes occur, the
information is added to the end of the file. Therefore, you do not know ahead
of time how many data values are in the file. You can, however, assume an
upper limit of 200 data values.

PROBLEM STATEMENT

Sort a group of earthquake measurements into ascending order and print the values in the new order.

INPUT/OUTPUT DESCRIPTION

The earthquake measurements are stored in a data file, 1 value per line. The first line of the data file contains a location number. The number of entries in the file is not known ahead of time. The output is to be a listing of the same set of data sorted into an ascending order.

HAND EXAMPLE

Using the following example test file data, we sort the data into ascending order and print it.

DATA FILE MOTION

```
17758
2.5810
1.5000
1.6200
3.7800
4.2500
1.7330
```

SORTED OUTPUT LIST

```
1.5000
1.6200
1.7330
2.5810
3.7800
4.2500
```

ALGORITHM DEVELOPMENT

In Section 5–4 we presented three different sort techniques. Any of the three techniques could be used in this example; we have selected the first sort algorithm, the selection sort. You may want to review the selection sort algorithm before continuing with this development.

The decomposition of this problem solution breaks into the following steps:

DECOMPOSITION

| Read location number. |
| Print location number. |
| Read quake values. |
| Sort quake values. |
| Print quake values. |

Initial Refinement in Pseudocode

EARTH: Read location number
     Print location number
     $i \leftarrow 1$
     While more quake data do
      Read quake(i)
      $i \leftarrow i + 1$
     $n \leftarrow i - 1$
     Sort quake array
     Print quake array

We now refine the sort step using the selection sort algorithm. The steps are copied here from the previous section, with the appropriate change in variable names.

Final Refinement in Pseudocode

EARTH: Read location number
     Print location number
     $i \leftarrow 1$
     While more quake data do
      READ quake(i)
      $i \leftarrow i + 1$
     $n \leftarrow i - 1$
     last $\leftarrow$ n
     For j = 1 to n $-$ 1 do
      ptr $\leftarrow$ j
      first $\leftarrow$ j + 1
      For k = first to last do
        If x(k) $<$ x(ptr) then
          ptr $\leftarrow$ k
      Switch values in x(j) and x(ptr)
     Print quake array

The only step that needs more detail is the step to switch values, because we must specify the three different moves that are necessary. We can add this additional detail as we convert the pseudocode to FORTRAN.

```
*-----------------------------------------------------------*
      PROGRAM  EARTH
*
*  This program will read a file of earthquake data
*  and sort and print it in ascending order.
*
      INTEGER  LOCATE, I, N, J, PTR, LAST, FIRST, K
      REAL  QUAKE(200), HOLD
*
      OPEN (UNIT=9,FILE='MOTION',STATUS='OLD')
      READ (9,*) LOCATE
      PRINT 5, LOCATE
    5 FORMAT (1X,'LOCATION NUMBER: ',I5)
*
      I = 1
   10 READ (9,*,END=20) QUAKE(I)
         I = I + 1
         GO TO 10
*
   20 N = I - 1
      LAST = N
      DO 40 J=1,N-1
         PTR = J
         FIRST = J + 1
         DO 30 K = FIRST, LAST
            IF (QUAKE(K).LT.QUAKE(PTR)) PTR = K
   30    CONTINUE
         HOLD = QUAKE(J)
         QUAKE(J) = QUAKE(PTR)
         QUAKE(PTR) = HOLD
   40 CONTINUE
*
      DO 60 I=1,N
         PRINT 50, I, QUAKE(I)
   50    FORMAT (1X,I3,'.',3X,F6.4)
   60 CONTINUE
*
      END
*-----------------------------------------------------------*
```

TESTING

As our programs become longer, testing becomes more of a challenge; a good procedure is to test the program in pieces. An easy way to accomplish this is to insert PRINT statements followed by a STOP statement after the portion of the program that you want to check. When you are convinced that this portion is working, remove the PRINT statements and the STOP statement and modify them to check the next portion. For example, to test the input portion of the program just developed, insert the following statements after statement 20:

```
      PRINT 22, LOCATE, N
   22 FORMAT (1X,'LOCATION = ',I5,'; N = ',I4)
      PRINT 23
   23 FORMAT (1X,'QUAKE DATA:')
      PRINT 24, (QUAKE (I), I=1,N)
   24 FORMAT (1X,5F5.2)
      STOP
```

To test the sort portion, use a small data set so that you are not overwhelmed with data. Insert the PRINT statements previously used to print the QUAKE array just after statement 40; this will print the data values after each pass through the array, just as we did in the hand-worked example. If there are problems, move the PRINT statements inside the DO loop, just before statement 40, which will allow you to see the results of each comparison. Notice how these pieces that we test individually correspond to the overall steps in the initial decomposition.

When you have the algorithm working, be sure to use a variety of test data sets. Use sets that are already in order and sets that are in reverse order, in addition to sequences in random order. The output from a sample set of data would be in this form:

Data File MOTION

```
17758
2.5810
1.5000
1.6200
3.7800
4.2500
1.7330
```

Computer Output

```
LOCATION NUMBER: 17758
  1.    1.5000
  2.    1.6200
  3.    1.7330
  4.    2.5810
  5.    3.7800
  6.    4.2500
```

After sorting the array QUAKE, we changed the order of the values from one that was sequential in time to one that is in ascending order. In so doing, we lost the original order within our program. The data file is still in the original order, but our program has the data only in ascending order. If the program also needed the original data, we could copy the original data into a second array after it was read, but before it was sorted. Then, after sorting, we would have two arrays of data—one in the original order and one in ascending order.

5-6 TWO-DIMENSIONAL ARRAYS

If we visualize a one-dimensional array as a single column of data, we can visualize a two-dimensional array as a group of columns, as illustrated:

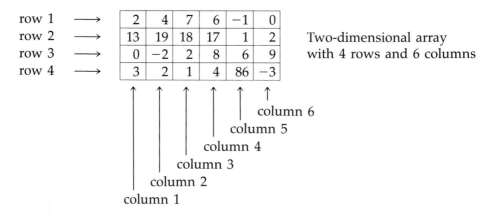

The diagram depicts an integer array with 24 elements. As in one-dimensional arrays, each of the 24 elements has the same array name. However, one subscript is not sufficient to specify an element in a two-dimensional array; for instance, if the array's name is M, it is not clear whether M(3) should be the third element in the first row or the third element in the first column. To avoid ambiguity, elements in a two-dimensional array are referenced with two subscripts: The first subscript references the row and the second subscript references the column. Thus, M(2,3) refers to the number in the second row, third column. In our diagram, M(2,3) contains the value 18.

STORAGE AND INITIALIZATION

Two-dimensional arrays must be specified with a DIMENSION statement or a type statement — but not both. The following type statements reserve storage for a one-dimensional real array B of 10 elements, a two-dimensional real array C with 3 rows and 5 columns, a two-dimensional real array NUM with 5 rows and 2 columns, and a two-dimensional integer array J with 7 rows and 4 columns:

```
REAL  B(10), C(3,5), NUM(5,2)
INTEGER  J(7,4)
```

This next statement reserves storage for a two-dimensional array with three rows and three columns:

```
REAL  R(0:2,-1:1)
```

Two-dimensional arrays can be initialized with assignment statements, with input statements, and with the DATA statement. A two-dimensional array name can be used without subscripts in input statements, DATA statements, and output statements; if the name of the array is used in one of these statements without subscripts, the array is accessed in column order. We will always explicitly use subscripts with two-dimensional arrays in order to be clear whether we are referencing the array elements in row order or in column order. It is common notation to use I for the row subscript and J for the column subscript.

EXAMPLE 5-5 Array Initialization, AREA

Define an array AREA with 5 rows and 4 columns. Fill it with the values shown:

1.0	1.0	2.0	2.0
1.0	1.0	2.0	2.0
1.0	1.0	2.0	2.0
1.0	1.0	2.0	2.0
1.0	1.0	2.0	2.0

Solution 1

```
          REAL   AREA(5,4)
          .
          .
          .
          DO 10 I=1,5
              AREA(I,1) = 1.0
              AREA(I,2) = 1.0
              AREA(I,3) = 2.0
              AREA(I,4) = 2.0
       10 CONTINUE
```

Solution 2

```
     REAL   AREA(5,4)
     DATA   ((AREA(I,J),I=1,5),J=1,4) /10*1.0,  10*2.0/
```

EXAMPLE 5-6 Array Initialization, SUM

Define and fill the integer array SUM as shown:

1	1	1
2	2	2
3	3	3
4	4	4

Solution 1

If we observe that each element of the array contains its corresponding row number, then the following solution can be used:

```
          INTEGER  SUM(4,3)
          .
          .
          .
          DO 10 I=1,4
              DO 5 J=1,3
                  SUM(I,J) = I
        5     CONTINUE
       10 CONTINUE
```

Solution 2

The following DATA statements also initialize the array correctly:

```
INTEGER  SUM(4,3)
DATA  ((SUM(I,J),I=1,4),J=1,3)   /3*(1, 2, 3, 4)/
```

or

```
INTEGER  SUM(4,3)
DATA  ((SUM(I,J),J=1,3),I=1,4)   /3*1, 3*2, 3*3, 3*4/
```

EXAMPLE 5-7   Identity Matrix

A *matrix* is another name for a two-dimensional array. When using matrix operations to solve engineering and science problems, we frequently use a matrix called an *identity matrix*. This matrix has the same number of rows as columns, so it is also called a *square matrix*. The identity matrix contains all 0's except for the main diagonal elements, which are 1's. (The main diagonal is composed of elements that have the same value for row number and for column number.) An identity matrix with 5 rows and 5 columns is shown.

1.0	0.0	0.0	0.0	0.0
0.0	1.0	0.0	0.0	0.0
0.0	0.0	1.0	0.0	0.0
0.0	0.0	0.0	1.0	0.0
0.0	0.0	0.0	0.0	1.0

Define and fill an array with these values.

Solution

Because the value 1.0 appears at different positions in each row of the array, we cannot use the same type of solution we used in Example 5–6. If we list the elements that contain the value 1.0, we find that they are positions (1,1), (2,2), (3,3), (4,4), and (5,5); thus, the row and the column number are the same value. Recognizing this pattern, we can initialize the array as follows:

```
            REAL   IDEN(5,5)
            .
            .
            .
            DO 10 I=1,5
               DO 5 J=1,5
                  IF (I.EQ.J) THEN
                     IDEN(I,J) = 1.0
                  ELSE
                     IDEN(I,J) = 0.0
                  ENDIF
         5     CONTINUE
        10 CONTINUE
```

INPUT AND OUTPUT

The main difference between using values from a one-dimensional array and using values from a two-dimensional array is that the latter requires two subscripts. Most loops used in the reading or printing of two-dimensional arrays are therefore nested loops.

EXAMPLE 5-8 Medical Data

The analysis of a medical experiment requires the use of a set of data containing the weight of 100 participants at the beginning and at the end of an experiment. The integer data values have been stored in a data file and are accessed using unit number 13. Each line in the file contains the initial weight and the final weight of a participant. Give statements to define a two-dimensional array to store the data and to read the information from the file into the array.

Solution 1

```
      INTEGER  WEIGHT(100,2)
      .
      .
      .
      DO 10 I=1,100
         READ (13,*) WEIGHT(I,1), WEIGHT(I,2)
   10 CONTINUE
```

Solution 2

```
   INTEGER  WEIGHT(100,2)
   .
   .
   .
   READ (13,*) (WEIGHT(I,1), WEIGHT(I,2), I=1,100)
```

EXAMPLE 5-9 Terminal Inventory

A large technical firm keeps an inventory of the locations of its computer terminals in a data file. Assume that this data has already been read into a two-dimensional array. There are 4 types of terminals, represented by the 4 columns, and 20 laboratories using the terminals, represented by the 20 rows of the array. Print the data in a form similar to the following:

```
   TERMINAL INVENTORY
   - - - - - - - - - - - - - - - - - - - - - - - -
   TYPE        1    2    3    4
   - - - - - - - - - - - - - - - - - - - - - - - -
   LAB   1    XX   XX   XX   XX
   LAB   2    XX   XX   XX   XX
     .
     .
     .
   LAB  20    XX   XX   XX   XX
```

Solution

This solution uses the index of a DO loop as the row subscript. The index of an implied loop in the PRINT statement supplies the column subscript. Thus, each time the PRINT statement is executed, one row of data is printed.

```
        INTEGER   INVEN(20,4)
        .
        .
        .
        PRINT 5
      5 FORMAT (1X,'TERMINAL INVENTORY')
        PRINT 10
     10 FORMAT (1X,'- - - - - - - - - - - - - - - - - - - - - - - - - -')
        PRINT 15
     15 FORMAT (1X,'TYPE          1    2    3    4')
        PRINT 20
     20 FORMAT (1X,'- - - - - - - - - - - - - - - - - - - - - - - - - -')
        DO 200 I=1,20
            PRINT 30, I, (INVEN(I,J), J=1,4)
     30     FORMAT (1X,'LAB',I4,3X,I2,3X,I2,3X,I2,3X,I2)
    200 CONTINUE
```

SELF-TEST 5-3

This self-test allows you to check quickly to see if you have remembered some of the key points from Section 5-6. If you have any problems with the exercises, you should reread this section. The solutions are included at the end of the text.

Problems 1-3 contain statements that initialize and print two-dimensional arrays. Draw the array and indicate the contents of each position in the array. Then, show the output from each set of statements. Assume that each set of statements is independent of the others.

```
1.      INTEGER   I,  J,  CH(5,4)
        DO  10 I=1,5
            DO 5 J=1,4
                CH(I,J)  =  I*J
      5     CONTINUE
     10 CONTINUE
        PRINT 15,  (CH(3,J),J=1,4)
     15 FORMAT (1X,I5)

2.      INTEGER   I,  J,  K(3,3)
        DO 20 I=1,3
            K(I,1)  =  5
            K(I,2)  =  -5
            K(I,3)  =  0
     20 CONTINUE
        PRINT 30 (K(3,J),  J=1,3)
     30 FORMAT (1X,I4)
```

```
3.      INTEGER  I, J
        REAL  DIST(4,3), SUM
        SUM = 10.0
        DO 10 J=1,3
            DO 5 I=1,4
                SUM = SUM + 1.5
                DIST(I,J) = SUM
    5       CONTINUE
   10 CONTINUE
        DO 20 I=1,2
            PRINT 15, (DIST(I,J), J=1,3)
   15       FORMAT (1X,3F5.1)
   20 CONTINUE
```

5-7 APPLICATION—POWER PLANT DATA ANALYSIS (Power Engineering)

The following table of data represents typical power outputs in megawatts from a power plant over a period of 8 weeks. Each row represents 1 week's data; each column represents data taken on the same day of the week. The data is stored 1 row per data line in a data file called PLANT.

	Day 1	Day 2	Day 3	Day 4	Day 5	Day 6	Day 7
Week 1	207	301	222	302	22	167	125
Week 2	367	60	120	111	301	400	434
Week 3	211	72	441	102	21	203	317
Week 4	401	340	161	297	441	117	206
Week 5	448	111	370	220	264	444	207
Week 6	21	313	204	222	446	401	337
Week 7	213	208	444	321	320	335	313
Week 8	162	137	265	44	370	315	322

A program is needed to read the data, analyze it, and print the results in the following composite report:

```
                COMPOSITE INFORMATION
AVERAGE DAILY POWER OUTPUT = XXX.X MEGAWATTS
NUMBER OF DAYS WITH GREATER THAN AVERAGE POWER OUTPUT = XX
DAY(S) WITH MINIMUM POWER OUTPUT:
        WEEK X   DAY X
              .
              .
              .
```

PROBLEM STATEMENT

Analyze a set of data from a power plant to determine its average daily power output, the number of days with greater-than-average output, and the day or days that had minimum power output.

INPUT/OUTPUT DESCRIPTION

The input is a data file with 1 week's data per line, in an integer form. The file contains data for 8 weeks. The output is to be a report as shown:

```
              COMPOSITE INFORMATION
AVERAGE DAILY POWER OUTPUT = XXX.X MEGAWATTS
NUMBER OF DAYS WITH GREATER THAN AVERAGE POWER OUTPUT = XX
DAY(S) WITH MINIMUM POWER OUTPUT:
          WEEK X    DAY X
             .
             .
             .
```

HAND EXAMPLE

For the hand-worked example, we use a smaller set of data, but one that still maintains the two-dimensional array form. Consider this set of data:

	Day 1	Day 2
Week 1	311	405
Week 2	210	264
Week 3	361	210

First, we must sum all the values and divide by 6 to determine the average, which yields 1761/6, or 293.5 megawatts. Second, we compare each value to the average to determine how many values were greater than the average. In our small set of data, 3 values were greater than the average. Third, we must determine the number of days with minimum power output, which involves two steps: going through the data again to determine the minimum value; and going back through the data to find the day or days with the minimum power value, then printing its/their position(s) in the array. Using the small set of data, we find that the minimum value is 210, and it occurred on two days. Thus, the output from our hand-worked example is

```
              COMPOSITE INFORMATION
AVERAGE DAILY POWER OUTPUT = 293.5 MEGAWATTS
NUMBER OF DAYS WITH GREATER THAN AVERAGE POWER OUTPUT = 3
DAY(S) WITH MINIMUM POWER OUTPUT:
              WEEK 2    DAY 1
              WEEK 3    DAY 2
```

ALGORITHM DEVELOPMENT

Before we decompose the problem solution, it is important to spend some time considering the best way to store the data that we need for the program. Unfortunately, once we become comfortable with arrays, we tend to overuse them. Using an array complicates our programs because of the subscript handling. We should always ask ourselves, "Should we really use an array for this data?"

If the individual data values will be needed more than once, an array is probably required. An array is also necessary if the data is not in the order needed. In general, arrays are helpful when we must read all the data before we can go back and begin processing it. However, if an average of a group of data values is all that is to be computed, we probably do not need an array; as we read the values, we can add them to a total, and read the next value into the same memory location as the previous value. The individual values are not needed again because all the information required is now in the total.

Now, let us look at our specific problem and determine whether or not we need to use an array. First, we need to compute an average daily power output. Then, we need to count the number of days with output greater than average, which requires that we compare each output value to the average. For this application, we need to store all the data in an array, and a two-dimensional array is the best choice of data structure.

When we performed the solution by hand, we made several passes through the data to obtain different pieces of information. As we begin to develop the computer solution, we would like to minimize the number of passes through the data. We can compute the sum of the data points in the same loop in which we determine the minimum data value. However, we must make a separate pass through the data to determine how many values are greater than the average. Because the number of days with greater-than-average output is printed before we print the specific day or days that has/have minimum output, we need separate loops for these operations. For this solution, we need three loops (passes) through the array.

DECOMPOSITION

Read data.
Compute information.
Print information.

Initial Refinement in Pseudocode

PWRPLT: Read data
      Compute average power and minimum power
      Print average power
      Count days with above-average power
      Print count of days
      Print days with minimum power

Final Refinement in Pseudocode

PWRPLT: Read data
      Compute average and minimum value
      Print heading, average
      count ← 0
      For each data value do
        If data value > average then
          count ← count + 1
      Print count
      For each data value do
        If data value = minimum then
          Print row position, column position

FORTRAN Program

```
*-------------------------------------------------------------*
      PROGRAM  PWRPLT
*
*  This program computes and prints a composite report
*  summarizing eight weeks of power plant data.
*
      INTEGER  POWER(8,7), MIN, TOTAL, COUNT, I, J
      REAL    AVE
      DATA    TOTAL, COUNT /0, 0/
*
      OPEN (UNIT=12,FILE='PLANT',STATUS='OLD')
      DO 5 I=1,8
         READ (12,*) (POWER(I,J), J=1,7)
    5 CONTINUE
*
      MIN = POWER(1,1)
      DO 15 I=1,8
         DO 10 J=1,7
            TOTAL = TOTAL + POWER(I,J)
            IF (POWER(I,J).LT.MIN) MIN = POWER(I,J)
   10    CONTINUE
   15 CONTINUE
      AVE = REAL(TOTAL)/56.0
*
      DO 25 I=1,8
         DO 20 J=1,7
            IF (POWER(I,J).GT.AVE) COUNT = COUNT + 1
   20    CONTINUE
   25 CONTINUE
*
```

```
      PRINT 30
   30 FORMAT (1X,15X,'COMPOSITE INFORMATION')
      PRINT 35, AVE
   35 FORMAT (1X,'AVERAGE DAILY POWER OUTPUT = ',F5.1,
     +          ' MEGAWATTS')
      PRINT 40, COUNT
   40 FORMAT (1X,'NUMBER OF DAYS WITH GREATER THAN ',
     +          'AVERAGE POWER OUTPUT = ',I2)
      PRINT 45
   45 FORMAT (1X,'DAY(S) WITH MINIMUM POWER OUTPUT:')
      DO 60 I=1,8
         DO 55 J=1,7
            IF (POWER(I,J).EQ.MIN) PRINT 50, I, J
   50       FORMAT (1X,12X,'WEEK ',I2,'   DAY ',I2)
   55    CONTINUE
   60 CONTINUE
*
      END
*----------------------------------------------------------------*
```

TESTING

This program should be tested in stages; again, the decomposition gives a
good idea of the overall steps involved and can thus be used to identify the
steps that should be tested individually. Remember that one of the most
useful tools for debugging is the PRINT statement — use it to print the values
of key variables in loops that may contain errors.

The output from this program using the data file given at the beginning
of this section is

```
                 COMPOSITE INFORMATION
AVERAGE DAILY POWER OUTPUT = 254.4 MEGAWATTS
NUMBER OF DAYS WITH GREATER THAN AVERAGE POWER OUTPUT = 29
DAY(S) WITH MINIMUM POWER OUTPUT:
               WEEK  3   DAY   5
               WEEK  6   DAY   1
```

5-8 APPLICATION — TERRAIN NAVIGATION
(Aeronautical Engineering)

The study of terrain navigation has become popular with the advent of
remotely-piloted vehicles such as planes, missiles, and tanks. The systems
that guide these vehicles must be tested over a variety of land formations and
topologies. Elevation information for large grids of land is available in
computer databases. One way of measuring the "difficulty" of a land grid
with respect to terrain navigation is to determine the number of peaks in the
grid (a peak is a point that has lower elevations all around it).

The program we develop in this application will read the elevation information for a set of grids. Then, for each grid, we will determine the number of peaks in that grid according to our definition.

We assume that the file that contains the elevation information is called ELEVTN. The first line for each grid contains an identification number. The second line contains the number of points along the side of the grid and the number of points along the top of the grid. The elevation data for that grid then begins on the next line, with the data for the top row first, then the second row, and so on. If the data for the first row does not fit on one line, as many lines as are needed will be used. However, each new row of data will begin on a new line. The last line in the data file contains an identification number of 99999. You can assume that the maximum size grid will be 100 points by 100 points. For each grid, print the identification number, the total number of points in the grid, and the number of peaks in the grid.

PROBLEM STATEMENT

Determine the number of peaks in a grid of elevation values, where we assume that a peak is defined by a point that is higher than all four of its surrounding points.

INPUT/OUTPUT DESCRIPTION

The input is a data file called ELEVTN that contains information on a number of grids. Each set of information contains the grid identification, the number of points along the side of the grid, the number of points along the top of the grid, and the elevations points in row order. The output is to be a report that lists each grid identification number, the total number of points in the grid, and the number of peaks within the grid.

HAND EXAMPLE

Assume that the following data represents the elevations for a grid that has 6 points along the side and 8 points along the top. We have circled peaks within the data.

```
92547
6   8
25    59    63    23    21    34    21    50
32    45    43    30   (37)   32    30    27
34    38    38    39    36    28    28    35
40   (45)   42   (48)   32    30    27    25
39    39    40    42    48   (49)   25    30
31    31    31    32    32    33    44    35
99999
```

The output for this grid is

IDENTIFICATION	NUMBER OF POINTS	NUMBER OF PEAKS
92547	48	4

You probably realized that the search for peaks need only consider interior points in the grid. A point along the edge cannot be counted as a peak because we do not know the elevation on one of its sides. If we are considering a point at location MAP(I,J), then the four adjacent points are at positions MAP(I − 1,J), MAP(I + 1,J), MAP(I,J − 1), and MAP(I,J + 1), as shown:

	MAP(I-1,J)	
MAP(I,J-1)	MAP(I,J)	MAP(I,J+1)
	MAP(I+1,J)	

Thus, for MAP(I,J) to be a peak, the following must be true:

```
MAP(I,J-1) < MAP(I,J)
MAP(I,J+1) < MAP(I,J)
MAP(I-1,J) < MAP(I,J)
MAP(I+1,J) < MAP(I,J)
```

If all of these conditions are met for a point MAP(I,J), it represents a peak.

DECOMPOSITION

Print heading.
Read map information and generate report.

REFINEMENT IN PSEUDOCODE

NAVIG: Print heading
       Read ID
       While ID not = 99999 do
          Read NROW, NCOL
          Read array MAP
          count ← 0
          For each interior point do
             If interior point is higher than all four
               adjacent points then increment count
          Print ID, number of peaks
          Read ID

FORTRAN Program

```
*----------------------------------------------------------------*
      PROGRAM   NAVIG
*
*  This program reads the elevation data for a set of land
*  grids and determines the number of peaks in each grid.
*
      INTEGER  MAP(100,100), I, J, ID, NROWS, NCOLS, COUNT
*
      PRINT 5
   5 FORMAT (1X,'SUMMARY OF LAND GRID ANALYSIS')
      PRINT 10
  10 FORMAT (1X,'IDENTIFICATION   NUMBER OF POINTS   ',
     +          'NUMBER OF PEAKS')
*
      OPEN (UNIT=15,FILE='ELEVTN',STATUS='OLD')
      READ (15,*) ID
  15 IF (ID.NE.99999) THEN
          READ (15,*) NROWS, NCOLS
          DO 20 I=1,NROWS
              READ (15,*) (MAP(I,J), J=1,NCOLS)
  20      CONTINUE
          COUNT = 0
          DO 30 I=2,NROWS-1
              DO 25 J=2,NCOLS-1
                  IF ((MAP(I-1,J).LT.MAP(I,J)).AND.
     +                (MAP(I+1,J).LT.MAP(I,J)).AND.
     +                (MAP(I,J-1).LT.MAP(I,J)).AND.
     +                (MAP(I,J+1).LT.MAP(I,J))) THEN
                      COUNT = COUNT + 1
                  ENDIF
  25          CONTINUE
  30      CONTINUE
          PRINT 35, ID, NROWS*NCOLS, COUNT
  35      FORMAT (1X,I7,10X,I7,10X,I7)
          READ (15,*) ID
          GO TO 15
      ENDIF
*
      END
*----------------------------------------------------------------*
```

TESTING

Using the data from the hand-worked example, our output is

```
SUMMARY OF LAND GRID ANALYSIS
IDENTIFICATION    NUMBER OF POINTS    NUMBER OF PEAKS
    92547              48                  4
```

As you try to think of any special cases that might cause problems for this program, you can probably think of some unique grid shapes, such as grids with 1 or 2 rows or 1 or 2 columns. If we look at our program, we see that the DO loops used in counting peaks are

```
DO 30 I=2,NROWS-1
  DO 25 J=2,NCOLS-1
```

If we substitute 2 for NROWS and NCOLS, we have the following loops:

```
DO 30 I=2,1
   DO 25 J=2,1
```

These loops would not be executed, and because the number of peaks was initialized to zero, the number of peaks would remain at zero. Thus, the program can handle these unique grid cases correctly. If the values of NROWS and NCOLS were less than 1 or greater than 100, then the program would not work correctly. It might be a good idea to test NROWS and NCOLS after they are read and print an appropriate error message if they are out of bounds.

Note: This program will locate individual peaks; but, it will not locate a ridge where two or more adjacent peaks are at the same elevation. Our algorithm would need to be modified if we were interested in this type of formation.

5-9 MULTIDIMENSIONAL ARRAYS

FORTRAN allows as many as seven dimensions for arrays. We can easily visualize a three-dimensional array, such as a cube. We are also familiar with using three coordinates, X, Y, and Z, to locate points. This idea extends into subscripts. The following three-dimensional array could be defined with this statement:

```
REAL   T(3,4,4)
```

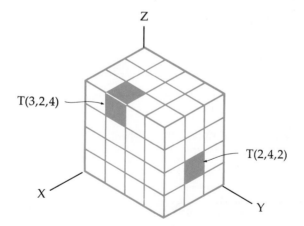

If we use the three-dimensional array name without subscripts, we access the array with the first subscript changing fastest, the second subscript changing second fastest, and the third subscript changing the slowest. Thus, using the array T from the previous diagram, these two statements are equivalent:

```
READ *, T

READ *, (((T(I,J,K), I=1,3), J=1,4), K=1,4)
```

It should be evident that three levels of nesting in DO loops are often needed to access a three-dimensional array.

Most applications do not use arrays with more than three dimensions, probably because visualizing more than three dimensions seems too abstract. However, here is a simple scheme that may help you to picture even a seven-dimensional array.

Four-Dimensional Array Picture a row of three-dimensional arrays. The first subscript specifies a unique three-dimensional array. The other three subscripts specify a unique position in that array.

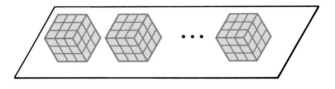

Five-Dimensional Array Picture a block or grid of three-dimensional arrays. The first two subscripts specify a unique three-dimensional array. The other three subscripts specify a unique position in that array.

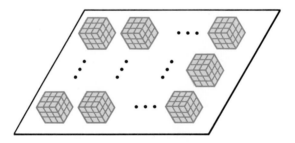

Six-Dimensional Array Picture a row of blocks or grids. One subscript specifies the grid. The other five subscripts specify the unique position in the grid.

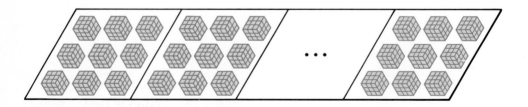

Seven-Dimensional Array Picture a grid of grids or a grid of blocks. Two subscripts specify the grid. The other five subscripts specify the unique position in the grid.

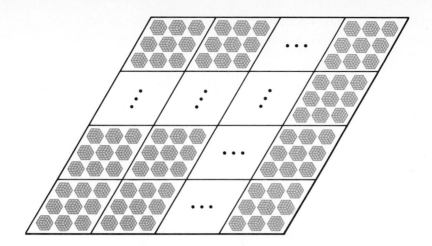

Now that you can visualize multidimensional arrays, a natural question is "What dimension array do I use for solving a problem?" There is no single answer. A problem that can be solved with a two-dimensional array of 4 rows and 3 columns can also be solved with four one-dimensional arrays of 3 elements each. Usually, the data fits one array form better than another; you should choose the form that is the easiest for you to work with in your program. For example, if you have census data from 10 countries over the period 1950–1980, you would probably use an array with 10 rows and 31 columns, or 31 rows and 10 columns. If the data represents the populations of 5 cities from each of 10 countries for the period 1950–1980, a three-dimensional array would be most appropriate: The three subscripts would represent year, country, and city.

SUMMARY

In this chapter we learned how to use an array — a group of storage locations that all have a common name but are distinguished by one or more subscripts. Arrays are one of the most powerful elements in FORTRAN because they allow us to keep large amounts of data easily accessible to our programs. The remaining chapters in this text rely heavily on arrays for storing and manipulating data. Also presented were three sort algorithms.

DEBUGGING AIDS

Because arrays are so convenient for handling large amounts of data, a natural tendency is to overuse them — and, unfortunately, arrays can also introduce new errors. As you debug programs that use arrays, consider the decision to use each array: Ask yourself, "Will I need this data more than once?" and "Must this data be stored before I can use it?" If the answers to both questions are "No," you should eliminate the array and replace it with simple variables. You will also probably be eliminating some loops and statements involving subscripts; these changes may not only reduce the number of errors in your program but will also reduce its overall complexity.

If arrays are necessary, then consider each of the following items if your program is working incorrectly:

Size — The array specification must specify the maximum number of elements that is to be stored in the array. Although you do not have to use all the elements of an array, you can never use more elements than originally specified.

Subscript — Check each subscript to be sure that it represents an integer that falls within the proper range of values. Particularly check for subscript values that are one value too small or one value too large.

DO Loop — If you are using the index of a DO loop as a subscript, be sure you have used the same variable identifier in your statements. That is, if the DO loop index is K, did you use I instead of K as a subscript?

Reverse Subscripts — When you are working with multidimensional arrays, be sure you have the subscripts in the proper order. Do you want B(K,L) or B(L,K)?

STYLE/TECHNIQUE GUIDES

As mentioned in "Debugging Aids," be sure that you really need an array before implementing an algorithm with an array. If you need arrays to solve your problem, take some time to decide the optimum size. Depending on the application, you may find that a two-dimensional array with 10 rows and 2 columns is more direct and understandable than two separate arrays of 10 elements each. Choose the array structure that best suits the data.

Be consistent in your choice of subscript names. Common practice is to use the variable I for the first subscript, J for the second subscript, and K for the third subscript. If you follow the same pattern or a similar pattern, it is much easier to decide the nesting of loops and the values of DO loop indexes that are also used as subscripts.

KEY WORDS

array	multidimensional array
ascending order	multipass sort
bubble sort	one-dimensional array
descending order	selection sort
element	sort
implied DO loop	subscript
insertion sort	two-dimensional array

PROBLEMS

We begin our problem set with modifications to programs developed in this chapter. Give the decomposition, refined pseudocode or flowchart, and FOR-TRAN program for each problem.

Problems 1–5 modify the average snowfall program SNOFAL, given on page 204.

1. Modify the average snowfall program so that it prints the number of days in the month with no snowfall.
2. Modify the average snowfall program so that it prints the maximum snowfall and the day(s) on which it occurred.
3. Modify the average snowfall program so that it prints the minimum snowfall and the number of days on which it occurred.
4. Modify the average snowfall program so that it prints the longest number of consecutive days for which there was no snowfall.
5. Modify the average snowfall program so that it prints the longest number of consecutive days for which there was measurable snowfall.

Problems 6–10 modify the earthquake measurement program EARTH, given on page 216.

6. Modify the earthquake measurement program so that it sorts the data values into descending order.
7. Modify the earthquake measurement program so that it prints the average earthquake value.
8. Modify the earthquake measurement program so that it prints the maximum earthquake value.
9. Modify the earthquake measurement program so that it prints the median earthquake value.
10. Modify the earthquake measurement program so that it computes and prints the number of earthquake values that are in the same position in the list both before and after the ascending sort.

Problems 11–15 modify the power plant data analysis program PWRPLT, given on page 226.

11. Modify the power plant data analysis program so that it prints the minimum power output, in addition to printing the days on which it occurred.
12. Modify the power plant data analysis program so that it prints both the minimum and the maximum power outputs.
13. Modify the power plant data analysis program so that it reads a value N that determines the number of weeks that will be used for the report. Assume that N will never be more than 20.
14. Modify the power plant data analysis program so that it prints a count of the

number of days with the minimum power output instead of printing the specific days.

15. Modify the power plant data analysis program so that it prints the average daily power output for each week of data.

Problems 16–20 modify the terrain navigation program NAVIG, given on page 230.

16. Modify the terrain navigation program so that it prints a count of the number of land grids analyzed.

17. Modify the terrain navigation program so that it prints the location (row and column subscripts) of the peaks in each land grid.

18. Modify the terrain navigation program so that it computes and prints the percentage of points in each grid that are peaks.

19. Modify the terrain navigation program so that it prints the maximum and minimum elevations for each land grid.

20. Modify the terrain navigation program so that it computes and prints the average elevation for each land grid.

For problems 21–24, assume that K, a one-dimensional array of 50 integer values, has already been filled with data.

21. Give FORTRAN statements to find and print the maximum value of K in the following form:

```
MAXIMUM VALUE IS XXXXX
```

22. Give FORTRAN statements to find and print the minimum value of K and its position or positions in the array in the following form:

```
MINIMUM VALUE OF K IS
K(XX) = XXXXX
```

23. Give FORTRAN statements to count the number of positive values, zero values, and negative values in K. The output form should be

```
XXX POSITIVE VALUES
XXX ZERO VALUES
XXX NEGATIVE VALUES
```

24. Give FORTRAN statements to replace each value of K with its absolute value; then print the array K with two values per line.

Develop these programs and program segments. Use the five-phase design process for all complete programs.

25. An array TIME contains 30 integers. Give statements that will print every other value, beginning with the second value, in this form:

```
TIME( 2) CONTAINS XXXX SECONDS
TIME( 4) CONTAINS XXXX SECONDS
        .
        .
        .
TIME(30) CONTAINS XXXX SECONDS
```

26. An array WIND of 70 integer values represents the average daily wind velocities in Chicago over a 10-week period. Assume the array with 10 rows and 7 columns has been filled. Give FORTRAN statements to print the data so that each week is on a separate line. Use a heading as shown:

```
CHICAGO WIND VELOCITY (MILES/HOUR)
  XXX    XXX    XXX    XXX    XXX    XXX    XXX
```

27. Give FORTRAN statements to print the last 10 elements of a real array M of size N. For instance, if M contains 25 elements, the output form is

```
M( 16) = XXX.X
M( 17) = XXX.X
   .
   .
   .
M( 25) = XXX.X
```

28. Give FORTRAN statements to interchange the first and one-hundredth elements, the second and ninety-ninth elements, and so on, of the array NUM that contains 100 integer values. See the diagram that follows:

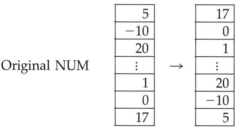

(*Hint:* You will need a temporary storage when you switch values.)

29. An array TREMOR contains integer counts of the number of daily earth tremors detected for 100 days following a major earthquake. Give the FORTRAN statements necessary to find the average of the first 50 days and the second 50 days. Print the following:

```
                     AVERAGES
    FIRST 50 TREMORS       SECOND 50 TREMORS
         XXX.XX                 XXX.XX
```

30. Write a complete program that will read as many as 20 integers from a file NUMBER, one integer per line. The last line will contain 9999. Write the data in the reverse order from which it was read; thus, the value 9999 will be the first value printed.

31. When a plot is made from experimental data, sometimes the scatter of the data points is such that it is difficult to select a "best representative line" for

the plot. In such a case, the data can be adjusted to reduce the scatter by using a "moving average" mathematical method of finding the average of three points in succession and replacing the middle value with this average.

Write a complete program to read an array Y of 20 real values from a file EXPR where the values are entered one per line. Build an array Z of 20 values where Z is the array of adjusted values. That is, Z(2) is the average of Y(1), Y(2), and Y(3); Z(3) is the average of Y(2), Y(3), and Y(4); and so on. Notice that the first and last values of Y cannot be adjusted and should be moved to Z without being changed. Do not destroy the original values in Y. Print the original and the adjusted values next to each other in a table.

32. A truck leasing company owns 12 delivery vans which are leased to several operators. Maintenance hours for each truck are allocated using a maintenance rate multiplied by the total number of hours accumulated by the entire fleet. The maintenance rate for each truck is determined from its percentage of the total fleet hours, and the following table:

PERCENT OF HOURS	MAINTENANCE RATE
0.00 – 9.99	0.02
10.00 – 24.99	0.04
25.00 – 100.00	0.06

A vehicle identification number and the monthly hours of use are entered in a data file HOURS. Write a complete program to read the data, convert each truck's hours to a percentage of the total fleet hours, and compute its maintenance hours using the maintenance rate. Round the calculated maintenance hours to the nearest hour, and ensure that each truck is allotted a minimum of one hour of maintenance each month. Print the following report:

```
MONTHLY MAINTENANCE REPORT
ID              HOURS           PERCENT         MAINTENANCE HOURS
XXX             XXXX            XXX.X           XXX
 .
 .
 .
TOTALS          XXXXX           XXX.X           XXXX
```

Test your program with the following input data:

ID	HOURS
002	61
009	83
012	101
016	55
025	410
036	97
037	66
040	70
043	122
044	136
045	23
046	142

33. Write a complete program that will read a two-dimensional array called RAIN containing 12 rows (one for each month) and 5 columns (one for each year 1978–1982). Each row of real values is entered on a data line in a file WATER. Determine and print the following table of information:

```
AVERAGE YEARLY RAINFALL
1978 - XXX.XX
1979 - XXX.XX
1980 - XXX.XX
1981 - XXX.XX
1982 - XXX.XX

MAXIMUM RAINFALL
MONTH XX   YEAR XXXX

MINIMUM RAINFALL
MONTH XX   YEAR XXXX
```

34. Assume that the reservations for an airplane flight have been stored in a file called FLIGHT. The plane contains 38 rows with 6 seats in each row. The seats in each row are numbered 1–6 as follows:

1 Window seat, left side

2 Center seat, left side

3 Aisle seat, left side

4 Aisle seat, right side

5 Center seat, right side

6 Window seat, right side

The file FLIGHT contains 38 lines of information corresponding to the 38 rows. Each line contains 6 values corresponding to the 6 seats. The value for any seat is either 0 or 1, representing either an empty or an occupied seat.

Write a complete program to read the FLIGHT information into a two-dimensional array called SEAT. Find and print all pairs of adjacent seats that are empty. Adjacent aisle seats should not be printed. If all three seats on one side of the plane are empty, then two pairs of adjacent seats should be printed. Print this information in the following manner:

```
AVAILABLE SEAT PAIRS
     ROW      SEATS
     XX       X,X
      .
      .
      .
     XX       X,X
```

If no pairs of seats are available, print an appropriate message.

35. The horsepower needed to pump water through a nuclear plant's cooling system is a function of the length of the pipe and the volume flowrate of the water. The following table shows the horsepower required for six different flowrates through five different cooling loops.

| | Flowrate | | | | | |
	1	2	3	4	5	6
1	2.1	4.0	8.7	15.2	21.0	34.8
2	2.7	4.2	9.1	18.0	30.0	41.5
Loop 3	4.0	12.9	27.3	52.6	94.4	131.8
4	3.3	10.0	22.7	44.7	80.9	11.2
5	1.8	4.1	8.5	15.3	27.2	46.4

Write a program that uses a DATA statement to initialize an array called POWER for storing the data above for the various combinations of flowrates and pipeline loops. The array's columns represent the six different flowrates in gallons per second and the rows represent the five cooling loops. The horsepower needed to pump J gallons per second through cooling loop I is stored in POWER(I,J). For example, POWER(3,2) contains 12.9, so the horsepower required to pump two gallons per second through cooling loop 3 is 12.9.

The program should ask the user to enter the flowrate in gallons per second for each loop. After rounding the flowrate to the nearest integer, find the corresponding horsepower needed for that cooling loop. If the flowrate is over 6.5 gallons per second or less than 0.5 gallons per second, print an error message. Print the horsepower needed for each loop, and the total horsepower needed for the entire cooling system.

36. Engineering data files often contain the dates on which information was recorded along with the information itself. If the data file is large, the date is often stored in a Julian date form, which is the year followed by the number of the day in the year (1 to 365) since the Julian date will need only five digits, while a Gregorian date (month-day-year) requires six digits. For example, 010982 is a Gregorian date that converts to 82009 in Julian form. Write a complete program to convert a Gregorian date to a Julian date. Be sure to take leap years into account. (*Hint:* Use an array to store the number of days in each month.)

37. In problem 36 we saw that engineering data files sometimes contain Julian dates to minimize storage. However, when the information in the files is printed in reports we want to convert the Julian dates to the more common Gregorian dates. Write a complete program to convert a Julian date to a Gregorian date.

38. A communication system often uses multiple lines, or channels, for sending information. Assume that a communication system has five channels for sending information. There is always a background noise signal on the channel, and the average noise value is monitored because it can indicate the quality of the channel for transmitting information. Assume that background noise for the five channels has been collected in a data file. The data file contains 200 lines of information, with five numbers per line that represent the noise level of the five channels at a specific time. Write a program to read the information into a two-dimensional array. Then compute and print the average noise value for each channel, and the percent of time that the noise is above average for each channel.

FORTRAN STATEMENT SUMMARY

DATA Statement:

DATA   *list of variable names /list of values/*

Example:

DATA   X, Y, COUNTR /1.0, 15.78, 0.0/

Discussion:

The DATA statement is used to initialize variables at the beginning of your program. It is a specification statement and thus should be positioned before any executable statements.

DIMENSION Statement:

DIMENSION   *array1(size), array2(size), . . .*

Example:

DIMENSION   LIST(50), GRID(5,8)

Discussion:

The DIMENSION statement is used to define arrays and their corresponding sizes. Elements in an array are referenced using a common name plus a subscript that specifies a unique element of the array. When arrays are defined with the DIMENSION statement, the array type is implicitly specified depending on the first letter of the array name. Because this statement is a specification statement, it should be positioned before any executable statements.

APPLICATION — Traffic Flow (Transportation Engineering)

The design of transportation systems becomes increasingly important as our population and urban areas increase. Their design must incorporate not only current needs but also projected needs. The data for determining needs and projections includes simple information such as the traffic flow in the current transportation system. Write a program to analyze traffic flow information and determine the average number of cars that pass through an intersection per minute. (See Section 6–7 for the solution.)

6

IMPLEMENTING TOP-DOWN DESIGN WITH FUNCTIONS

INTRODUCTION

As our programs become longer and more complicated, we find it harder to maintain program readability and simplicity. We also find that we frequently need to perform the same set of operations at more than one location in our programs. These problems can be solved with *subprograms*, which are groups of statements that are defined separately and then referenced when we need them in our programs. FORTRAN has two types of subprograms: functions and subroutines. In this chapter we review the intrinsic function (such as the square root function and the logarithm function) and learn how to write our own functions to perform computations unique to our applications. The function is quite useful in solving engineering and science problems because many of our solutions involve arithmetic computations.

6–1 INTRINSIC FUNCTIONS

A *function* computes a single value, such as the square root of a number or the average of an array. You have already used functions in the form of intrinsic functions such as SQRT and SIN. These *intrinsic functions* are in the compiler and are accessible directly from your program. The intrinsic functions (or *library functions*) available in FORTRAN 77 are listed in Appendix A. You should read through the list so that you are aware of the types of operations that can be performed with intrinsic functions. When you need to use one of these operations, you can refer to Appendix A for details on how to use that specific function.

Although we introduced intrinsic functions in Chapter 2, we can summarize the main components of these functions:

1. The function name and its input values (or *arguments*) collectively represent a single value.
2. A function can never be used on the left-hand side of an equal sign in an assignment statement.
3. The name of the intrinsic function typically determines the type of output from the function (for example, if the name begins with one of the letters I through N, its value is an integer).
4. The arguments of a function are generally of the same type as the function itself. For a few exceptions, refer to the list of intrinsic functions in Appendix A.
5. The arguments of a function must be enclosed in parentheses.
6. The arguments of a function may be constants, variables, expressions, or other functions.

Generic functions accept arguments of any allowable type and return a value of the same type as the argument. Thus, the generic function ABS will return an integer absolute value if its argument is an integer; but, it will return a real absolute value if its argument is real. The table in Appendix A identifies generic functions.

EXAMPLE 6-1   Odd and Even Values

Read an integer and then print the word ODD or EVEN, depending on the value read.

Solution

In this solution we use the intrinsic function MOD. This function has two integer arguments, I and J. The function returns the integer remainder in the division of I by J. This operation is also called modulo division — hence, the function is called a MOD function. Some example values for I, J, and MOD(I,J) are

I	J	MOD(I,J)
3	2	1
4	2	0
6	4	2
10	4	2
88	3	1

If a number K is even, it is a multiple of 2, and MOD(K,2) is zero. If K is odd, then MOD(K,2) is 1. The statements that determine if an integer is odd or even using this function are

```
      PRINT*, 'ENTER AN INTEGER'
      READ*, K
      IF (MOD(K,2).EQ.0) THEN
          PRINT 5, K
    5     FORMAT (1X,I5,' IS EVEN')
      ELSE
          PRINT 6, K
    6     FORMAT (1X,I5,' IS ODD')
      ENDIF
```

The MOD function can also be used to determine if a number is a multiple of another number. For instance, if MOD(M,5) is zero, then M is a multiple of 5.

6-2   STATEMENT FUNCTIONS

Engineering and science applications often require a function that is not included in the intrinsic function list. If the computation is needed frequently or requires several steps, we should implement it as a function instead of listing all the computations each time we need them. FORTRAN allows us to write our own functions in two ways: as a statement function or as a function subprogram. If the computation can be written in a single assignment statement we can use the statement function which will be discussed in this section; otherwise we must use the function subprogram that will be discussed in sections 6-4 and 6-5.

The *statement function* is a function defined at the beginning of your program, along with your type statements and array definitions. It is a nonexecutable statement; thus, it should precede any executable statement. The definition of the statement function contains the name of the function, followed by its arguments in parentheses, on the left-hand side of an equal sign; the expression for computing the function value is on the right-hand side of an equal sign. The general form for this statement is

function name (argument list) = expression

The function name can be included in a type statement; otherwise, implicit typing will determine the function type.

Example 6–2 illustrates the use of the statement function in a complete program.

EXAMPLE 6–2   Triangle Area

The area of a triangle can be computed from the lengths of two sides and the angle between them:

$$\text{AREA} = 0.5*\text{SIDE1}*\text{SIDE2}*\text{SIN(ANGLE)}$$

Write a program that reads the lengths of the three sides of a triangle and the angles opposite each side.

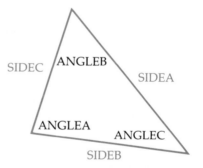

Compute and print the area of the triangle using one pair of sides and its corresponding angle. Then compute and print the area using another pair of sides and its corresponding angle. Finally, compute and print the area using the last pair of sides and its corresponding angle. Use a statement function to compute these areas.

Solution

The solution to this problem contains three steps: read the sides and the angles, compute the area in three ways, and print the areas.

DECOMPOSITION

Read the sides and angles of a triangle.
Compute the area in three ways.
Print the three areas.

REFINEMENT IN PSEUDOCODE

TRIANG: Read sides *a, b, c* and angles *a, b, c*
Compute area using side *b*, side *c*, and angle *a*
Compute area using side *a*, side *c*, and angle *b*
Compute area using side *a*, side *b*, and angle *c*
Print three areas

FORTRAN PROGRAM

```
*-------------------------------------------------------*
      PROGRAM  TRIANG
*
*   This program reads the lengths of the sides of a triangle
*   along with the corresponding angles in radians. It then
*   computes and prints the area of the triangle using three
*   different sets of information.
*
      REAL   SIDEA, SIDEB, SIDEC, A, B, C, AREA,
     +       AREAA, AREAB, AREAC, SIDE1, SIDE2, ANGLE
      AREA(SIDE1,SIDE2,ANGLE) = 0.5*SIDE1*SIDE2*SIN(ANGLE)
*
      PRINT*, 'ENTER THE LENGTHS OF THE THREE SIDES OF A'
      PRINT*, 'TRIANGLE IN THE FOLLOWING ORDER:'
      PRINT*, 'SIDE A    SIDE B    SIDE C'
      READ*, SIDEA, SIDEB, SIDEC
      PRINT*
      PRINT*, 'ENTER THE ANGLE OPPOSITE SIDE A,'
      PRINT*, 'THEN THE ANGLE OPPOSITE SIDE B,'
      PRINT*, 'AND THEN THE ANGLE OPPOSITE SIDE C.'
      PRINT*, '(IN RADIANS)'
      READ*, A, B, C
      PRINT*
*
      AREAA = AREA(SIDEB,SIDEC,A)
      AREAB = AREA(SIDEC,SIDEA,B)
      AREAC = AREA(SIDEA,SIDEB,C)
      PRINT*, 'THE THREE AREA COMPUTATIONS YIELD:'
      PRINT 5, AREAA, AREAB, AREAC
    5 FORMAT (1X,F6.2,3X,F6.2,3X,F6.2)
*
      END
*-------------------------------------------------------*
```

The following output represents a typical user interaction with this program:

```
ENTER THE LENGTHS OF THE THREE SIDES OF A
TRIANGLE IN THE FOLLOWING ORDER:
SIDE A     SIDE B     SIDE C
1.0   1.0   1.414

ENTER THE ANGLE OPPOSITE SIDE A,
THEN THE ANGLE OPPOSITE SIDE B,
AND THEN THE ANGLE OPPOSITE SIDE C.
(IN RADIANS)
0.785 0.785 1.571

THE THREE AREA COMPUTATIONS YIELD:
   0.50       0.50       0.50
```

Note that the arguments in the statement function definition are SIDE1, SIDE2, and ANGLE. These arguments do not represent variables used in our program; they tell the compiler that the statement function has three real arguments. When we referenced the function AREA to compute AREAA, note that the variable SIDEB corresponded to the argument SIDE1, the variable SIDEC corresponded to the argument SIDE2, and the variable C corresponded to the argument ANGLE. When we referenced the function AREA to compute AREAB and AREAC, different variables corresponded to the arguments SIDE1, SIDE2, and ANGLE.

Suppose that you forgot to define the statement function AREA. The first statement in your program that uses the function is

```
AREAA = AREA(SIDEB,SIDEC,A)
```

Many compilers assume that AREA is an array that you forgot to define, and they print an error message related to undefined arrays, instead of undefined statement functions. As a result, you may look in the wrong place in your program to correct this error. When you use statement functions, be aware that the compiler may confuse an undefined statement function with an undefined array; similarly, the compiler may diagnose an undefined array as an undefined statement function.

If you want to enter the angles in degrees, you can convert the degrees to radians in an assignment statement such as

```
A = A*(PI/180.0)
```

You can also perform the degree-to-radian conversion within the statement function, as shown:

```
AREA(SIDE1,SIDE2,ANGLE) = 0.5*SIDE1*SIDE2*
+                        SIN(ANGLE*3.14159/180.0)
```

The constant (3.14159/180.0) could be replaced by 0.0175, but leaving it as a division documents the computation for anyone else looking at the program.

SELF-TEST 6–1

This self-test allows you to check quickly to see if you have remembered some of the key points from Section 6–3. If you have any problems with the exercises, you should reread this section. The solutions are included at the end of the text.

For each of the following, give the statement function required to perform the computation.

1. Area of a circle: $A = \pi r^2$

2. Radians from degrees: $\text{radians} = \dfrac{180}{\pi} \cdot \text{degrees}$

3. Degrees from radians: $\text{degrees} = \dfrac{\pi}{180} \cdot \text{radians}$

4. Kinetic energy T: $T = \dfrac{mw^2a^2s}{4}$

5. Radius of a circle: $r = \sqrt{x^2 + y^2}$

6–3   APPLICATION—TEMPERATURE CONVERSIONS (Chemistry)

In this application, we develop a program to print a temperature conversion table. To be flexible, we will let the program user specify the type of conversion (Fahrenheit to Centigrade or Centigrade to Fahrenheit), the starting temperature, the change in temperature for each line, and the ending temperature. The output headings should reflect the correct temperature units. The two equations that we need are

$$\text{CENTIGRADE} = (\text{FAHRENHEIT} - 32) \cdot (5/9)$$
$$\text{FAHRENHEIT} = \text{CENTIGRADE} \cdot (9/5) + 32$$

Each of these computations requires only a single statement; thus, we can implement them as statement functions.

PROBLEM STATEMENT

Write a program that prints a conversion table for temperatures in Fahrenheit and Centigrade degrees.

INPUT/OUTPUT DESCRIPTION

The input to the program includes the temperature unit for the input values, the initial temperature value, the change in temperature from one line to the next, and the final temperature value. The output is a temperature conversion table.

HAND EXAMPLE

Assume that we want to convert degrees Fahrenheit to degrees Centigrade. Start the table at zero degrees, increment each line by 10 degrees, and stop when the last line in the table is 50 degrees. Using the preceding equation for converting Fahrenheit to Centigrade, we obtain the following table:

```
            TEMPERATURE CONVERSION TABLE
      DEGREES, FAHRENHEIT       DEGREES, CENTIGRADE
          0.00                      -17.78
         10.00                      -12.22
         20.00                       -6.67
         30.00                       -1.11
         40.00                        4.44
         50.00                       10.00
```

ALGORITHM DEVELOPMENT

The overall steps required for this algorithm are shown in the decomposition.

DECOMPOSITION

Read input specifications.
Print table.

As we refine these steps, we see that reading the input specifications is a series of sequential steps that print messages to the user requesting the necessary data and then reading the data. Printing the table involves a WHILE loop that is repeated until we have printed all the lines requested in the table. If we use NEXT to represent the next temperature to be converted, we want to remain in the WHILE loop "while NEXT is less than or equal to the final temperature value." These steps are detailed in the following flowchart:

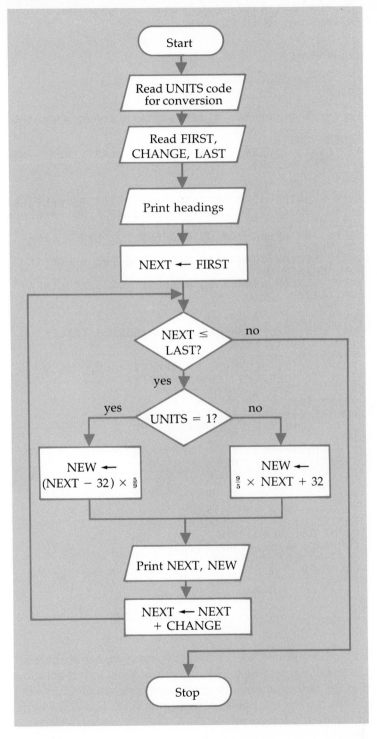

The flowchart is detailed enough to translate the steps into FORTRAN. Note the emphasis in the program on clearly specifying to the user exactly what form to use for entering data.

FORTRAN Program 1

```
*----------------------------------------------------------*
      PROGRAM  TABLE1
*
*  This program generates a temperature conversion table.
*
      INTEGER  UNITS
      REAL  CENT, FAHREN, FIRST, CHANGE, LAST, NEXT, NEW, TEMP
      CENT(TEMP) = (TEMP - 32.0)*0.5555556
      FAHREN(TEMP) = 1.8*TEMP + 32.0
*
      PRINT*, 'ENTER 1 TO CONVERT FAHRENHEIT TO CENTIGRADE'
      PRINT*, 'ENTER 2 TO CONVERT CENTIGRADE TO FAHRENHEIT'
      READ*, UNITS
      PRINT*, 'ENTER NUMBER OF DEGREES FOR FIRST LINE'
      READ*, FIRST
      PRINT*, 'ENTER CHANGE IN DEGREES BETWEEN LINES'
      READ*, CHANGE
      PRINT*, 'ENTER NUMBER OF DEGREES FOR LAST LINE'
      READ*, LAST
*
      PRINT 5
   5  FORMAT (1X,10X,'TEMPERATURE CONVERSION TABLE')
      IF (UNITS.EQ.1) THEN
         PRINT 10
  10     FORMAT (1X,'DEGREES, FAHRENHEIT',6X,
     +            'DEGREES, CENTIGRADE')
      ELSE
         PRINT 15
  15     FORMAT (1X,'DEGREES, CENTIGRADE',6X,
     +            'DEGREES, FAHRENHEIT')
      ENDIF
      NEXT = FIRST
  20  IF (NEXT.LE.LAST) THEN
         IF (UNITS.EQ.1) THEN
            NEW = CENT(NEXT)
         ELSE
            NEW = FAHREN(NEXT)
         ENDIF
         PRINT 25, NEXT, NEW
  25     FORMAT (1X,F9.2,18X,F9.2)
         NEXT = NEXT + CHANGE
         GO TO 20
      ENDIF
*
      END
*----------------------------------------------------------*
```

Although this solution works correctly and is readable, there are often many ways to solve the same problem. For example, in this solution, we observe that the two equations for converting temperatures are similar. The following steps rewrite the two equations into linear equations with different slopes and different y-intercepts:

$$\text{Centigrade} = (\text{Fahrenheit} - 32) \cdot (5/9)$$
$$= \text{Fahrenheit} \cdot (5/9) - 32 \cdot (5/9)$$
$$= 0.5555556 \cdot \text{Fahrenheit} - 17.77778$$
$$\text{Fahrenheit} = \text{Centigrade} \cdot (9/5) + 32$$
$$= 1.8 \cdot \text{Centigrade} + 32$$

If NEXT contains the temperature that we are going to convert, and NEW is to contain this new value, then both equations can be written in this form:

NEW = SLOPE*NEXT + INTERC

Thus, instead of using two statement functions, we can use one statement function with three arguments as shown in the following program.

FORTRAN Program 2

```
*---------------------------------------------------------------*
      PROGRAM   TABLE2
*
* This program generates a temperature conversion table.
*
      INTEGER  UNITS
      REAL  CONV, FIRST, CHANGE, LAST, NEXT, NEW,
     +      SLOPE, INTERC, TEMP, A, B
      CONV(TEMP,A,B) = A*TEMP + B
*
      PRINT*, 'ENTER 1 TO CONVERT FAHRENHEIT TO CENTIGRADE'
      PRINT*, 'ENTER 2 TO CONVERT CENTIGRADE TO FAHRENHEIT'
      READ*, UNITS
      PRINT*, 'ENTER NUMBER OF DEGREES FOR FIRST LINE'
      READ*, FIRST
      PRINT*, 'ENTER CHANGE IN DEGREES BETWEEN LINES'
      READ*, CHANGE
      PRINT*, 'ENTER NUMBER OF DEGREES FOR LAST LINE'
      READ*, LAST
*
      PRINT 5
    5 FORMAT (1X,10X,'TEMPERATURE CONVERSION TABLE')
      IF (UNITS.EQ.1) THEN
          PRINT 10
   10     FORMAT (1X,'DEGREES, FAHRENHEIT',6X,
     +            'DEGREES, CENTIGRADE')
          SLOPE = 0.5555556
          INTERC = -17.77778
      ELSE
          PRINT 15
   15     FORMAT (1X,'DEGREES, CENTIGRADE',6X,
     +            'DEGREES, FAHRENHEIT')
          SLOPE = 1.8
          INTERC = 32.0
      ENDIF
      NEXT = FIRST
   20 IF (NEXT.LE.LAST) THEN
          NEW = CONV(NEXT,SLOPE,INTERC)
          PRINT 25, NEXT, NEW
   25     FORMAT (1X,F9.2,18X,F9.2)
          NEXT = NEXT + CHANGE
          GO TO 20
      ENDIF
*
      END
*---------------------------------------------------------------*
```

If we test either of the programs with our hand-worked example data, the following output is

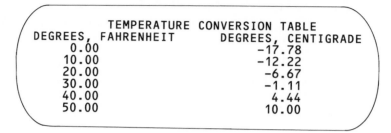

```
              TEMPERATURE  CONVERSION  TABLE
     DEGREES,  FAHRENHEIT         DEGREES,  CENTIGRADE
          0.00                        -17.78
         10.00                        -12.22
         20.00                         -6.67
         30.00                         -1.11
         40.00                          4.44
         50.00                         10.00
```

In this application we did not error check the input values. What would happen if the last temperature value entered was less than the first temperature value entered? The first time that the WHILE condition was executed, it would be false; thus, the WHILE loop would never be executed. The program would end without an error, but only the headings would be printed.

What would happen if the starting temperature and the change were such that the next temperature was never equal to the last temperature? For example, suppose FIRST was specified to be 0.0, CHANGE was specified to be 2.0, and LAST was specified to be 9.0. Output lines would be printed for values 0.0, 2.0, 4.0, 6.0, and 8.0. When the temperature was incremented to 10.0, it would exceed the last value, and we would exit the WHILE loop.

6–4 TOP-DOWN DESIGN AND STRUCTURE CHARTS

In previous chapters we stressed the importance of using top-down design techniques in algorithms and programs. The WHILE loop, DO loop, and IF structures are essential ingredients in structured programming. Another key element in simplifying program logic is the use of modules. These modules, called functions and subroutines in FORTRAN, allow us to write programs composed of nearly independent segments or routines. In fact, when we decompose the problem solution into a series of sequentially executed steps, we are decomposing the problem into steps that could be structured very easily into functions and subroutines. The following are some important advantages to breaking programs into modules:

1. You can write and test each module separately from the rest of the program.
2. Debugging is easier because you are working with smaller sections of the program.

3. Modules can be used in other programs without rewriting or retesting.
4. Programs are more readable and thus more easily understood because of the modular structure.
5. Several programmers can work on different modules of a large program relatively independent of one another.
6. Individual parts of the program become shorter and therefore simpler.
7. A module can be used several times by the same program.

Since modules are so important in writing readable, well-structured programs, we are going to present functions in this chapter and subroutines in the next chapter. The similarities and differences in the two types of modules are easier to see if we study them one at a time.

We have used the decomposition diagram to show the sequential steps necessary to solve a problem. Another type of diagram, the *structure chart*, is also very useful as we decompose our problem solution into smaller problems. While the decomposition diagram outlines the sequential operations needed, the structure chart outlines the modules but does not indicate the order in which they are to be executed.

The diagram below contains a structure chart for a program similar to one that we will be developing in Section 6–6. In the program we are reading oil well production data from a data file. For each oil well we read the daily production in barrels, compute a daily average for the week, and print this information in the report. In addition, we keep summary information for all the wells and print it at the end of the report. A report heading module is used at the beginning of each page to print the header information. The modules shown in this structure chart include both functions and subroutines.

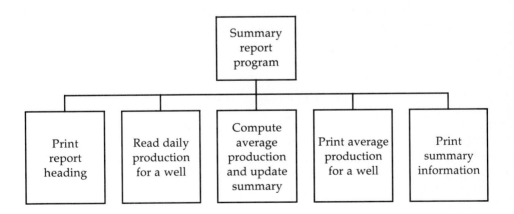

It is important to distinguish between a decomposition diagram and the structure chart. The decomposition diagram for this program shows the sequential order of the steps of the solution.

Print heading.
Read data, accumulate totals, and print report.
Print summary information.

Note that the decomposition does not identify any of the steps as modules. The structure chart, on the other hand, clearly defines the module definitions for the program but does not show the order in which the modules are used. Thus, both charts are useful in describing the algorithm that is being developed for the problem solution because they represent different information about the solution.

The steps to compute an intrinsic function are actually within the compiler and the steps to compute a statement function are within the program itself. Only user-written functions will contain statements that are in a separate module and thus only user-written functions and subroutines will appear in a structure chart.

6–5 FUNCTION SUBPROGRAMS

Because intrinsic functions are contained in a library available to the compiler, you may find that a function in one computer manufacturer's compiler may not be available in another's. For example, a function to generate random numbers is frequently used in computer simulations; but, not all systems include a function to generate random numbers. You may also find that you would like to use a function that is not available in any compiler. These problems can be solved by writing your own function.

A function subprogram, which is a program itself, is separate from the *main program.* It begins with a nonexecutable statement that identifies the function with a name and an argument list, as shown in the general form

FUNCTION *name (argument list)*

Because a function is separate from the main program, it must end with an END statement. The function must also contain a RETURN statement, which returns control to the statement that referenced the function. The general form of the RETURN statement is

RETURN

The rules for choosing a function name are the same as those for choosing a program name. In addition, the first letter of the function name specifies the type of value returned unless it is included in an explicit type specification. The following statements illustrate a simple example with a structure chart, a main program, and the function subprogram:

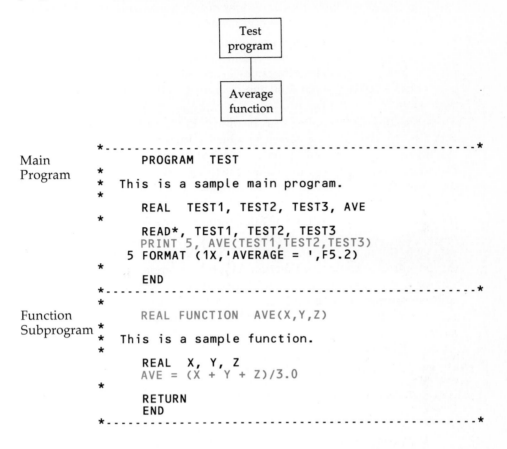

```
*-------------------------------------------------------*
        PROGRAM   TEST
*
*  This is a sample main program.
*
        REAL   TEST1, TEST2, TEST3, AVE
*
        READ*, TEST1, TEST2, TEST3
        PRINT 5, AVE(TEST1,TEST2,TEST3)
      5 FORMAT (1X,'AVERAGE = ',F5.2)
*
        END
*-------------------------------------------------------*
*
        REAL FUNCTION  AVE(X,Y,Z)
*
*  This is a sample function.
*
        REAL   X, Y, Z
        AVE = (X + Y + Z)/3.0
*
        RETURN
        END
*-------------------------------------------------------*
```

The labels on the left: "Main Program" beside the first block, "Function Subprogram" beside the second block.

Several rules must be observed in writing a function subprogram.

1. The function arguments referenced in the main program must match in type, number, and order, the arguments used in the function statement. In the preceding example, TEST1 corresponds to X, TEST2 corresponds to Y, and TEST3 corresponds to Z.
2. If one of the arguments is an array, its dimensions must be specified in both the main program and in the function subprogram.
3. The value to be returned to the main program is stored in the function name using an assignment statement.
4. When the function is ready to return control to the statement that referenced it, a RETURN statement is used. A function may contain more than one RETURN statement.
5. A function can contain references to other functions, but it cannot contain a reference to itself.

6. A function subprogram is usually placed immediately after the main program, but it also may appear before the main program; in either case, the function is compiled as a separate program. If you have more than one function, the order of the functions does not matter as long as each function is completely separate from the other functions.

7. A main program and its subprograms can be stored in the same program file or in separate files. If they are stored in separate files, it is necessary to link them before the main program can be executed. The statements required to perform the linking depend on the operating system being used (system dependent).

8. The same statement numbers may be used in both a function and in the main program. No confusion occurs as to which statement is referenced because the function and the main program are completely separate. Similarly, a function and a main program can use the same variable name, such as SUM, to store different sums as long as the variable SUM is not an argument to the function.

9. If you wish to define the type of value returned by a function explicitly, the name of the function must appear in a type statement in the main program as well as in the function statement itself. The following statements illustrate the definition of an integer function AVE that computes an integer average. Compare this main program and function to the previous example that computes a real average.

```
*-----------------------------------------------------------*
      PROGRAM   TEST
*
*   This is a sample main program.
*
      INTEGER   TEST1, TEST2, TEST3, AVE
*
      READ*, TEST1, TEST2, TEST3
      PRINT 5, AVE(TEST1,TEST2,TEST3)
    5 FORMAT (1X,'AVERAGE =',I5)
      END
*-----------------------------------------------------------*
*
      INTEGER FUNCTION   AVE(I,J,K)
*
*   This is a sample function.
*
      INTEGER   I, J, K
*
      AVE = (I + J + K)/3
      RETURN
      END
*-----------------------------------------------------------*
```

For documentation purposes, our examples explicitly type all function subprograms.

10. Do not try to change the values of the function arguments while inside the function. Some compilers return the new values to the main program; others do not. If you need to return more than the function value itself, use a subroutine (discussed in Chapter 7) instead of a function.

We now present a series of examples to illustrate the use of these rules in writing and using your own functions.

EXAMPLE 6-3   Sales Bonus

A local company has a number of computer programs that are used in maintaining its accounts and preparing payrolls. Several of the programs need to compute the bonus earned by salespeople who work for the company. Instead of recomputing the sales bonus in each program, subprograms are used. This bonus is computed from the total sales of the salesperson, using the following table:

TOTAL SALES	BONUS PERCENT
sales $<$ $1000	1%
$1000 $\leq$ sales $<$ $2000	2%
$2000 $\leq$ sales $<$ $2500	3%
$2500 $\leq$ sales	5%

The function is to be called BONUS and has one argument, the total sales for the salesperson.

Solution 1

Because a function subprogram is a program separate from the main program, you should approach function design and implementation much as you would a complete program. Follow the same guidelines for developing a decomposition diagram, then refine it using pseudocode or flowcharts until it is detailed enough to convert into FORTRAN. Because the function receives values through the argument list, the pseudocode or flowchart should begin with the name of the function and the variables that are arguments to the function.

DECOMPOSITION OF BONUS(SALES)

Compute bonus based on sales.
Return.

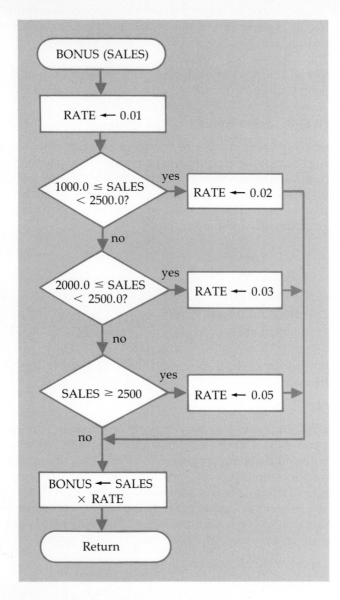

FORTRAN FUNCTION

```
*------------------------------------------------------------*
      REAL FUNCTION  BONUS(SALES)
*
*   This function computes a bonus based on sales.
*
      REAL  SALES, RATE
*
      RATE = 0.01
      IF (SALES.GE.1000.0.AND.SALES.LT.2000.0) RATE = 0.02
      IF (SALES.GE.2000.0.AND.SALES.LT.2500.0) RATE = 0.03
      IF (SALES.GE.2500.0) RATE = 0.05
      BONUS = SALES*RATE
*
      RETURN
      END
*------------------------------------------------------------*
```

A main program that uses this function might include a statement such
as the following, which reads the sales for one of the salespersons and
then prints the sales and bonus:

```
      .
      .
      .
      READ*, ID, SALES
        PRINT 5, ID, SALES, BONUS(SALES)
    5 FORMAT (1X,'SALESPERSON:',I5,3X,'SALES:',F8.2,3X,
    +          'BONUS:',F5.2)
      .
      .
      .
```

Solution 2

This solution uses the IF-ELSEIF statement. The same main program can
be used with this function.

FORTRAN FUNCTION

```
*------------------------------------------------------------*
      REAL FUNCTION  BONUS(SALES)
*
*   This function computes a bonus based on sales.
*
      REAL  SALES, RATE
*
      IF (SALES.LT.1000.0) THEN
          RATE = 0.01
      ELSEIF (SALES.LT.2000.0) THEN
          RATE = 0.02
      ELSEIF (SALES.LT.2500.0) THEN
          RATE = 0.03
      ELSE
          RATE = 0.05
      ENDIF
      BONUS = SALES*RATE
*
      RETURN
      END
*------------------------------------------------------------*
```

Incorrect Solution

The following function is similar to the function in Solution 2, but this one does not work correctly. See if you can spot the error before reading the explanation.

FORTRAN FUNCTION

```
*-----------------------------------------------------------*
      REAL FUNCTION  BONUS(SALES)
*
*  This function computes a bonus based on sales.
*
      REAL  SALES, RATE
*
      IF (SALES.GT.2500.0) THEN
         RATE = 0.05
      ELSEIF (SALES.LT.2500.0) THEN
         RATE = 0.03
      ELSEIF (SALES.LT.2000.0) THEN
         RATE = 0.02
      ELSEIF (SALES.LT.1000.0) THEN
         RATE = 0.01
      ENDIF
      BONUS = SALES*RATE
*
      RETURN
      END
*-----------------------------------------------------------*
```

The key to understanding the problem with this solution is to remember the manner in which an IF-ELSEIF statement is executed. As soon as a true condition is encountered, the appropriate steps are executed and control passes to the ENDIF at the end of the structure; even if two conditions are true, the first one encountered is the only one tested. Suppose that the SALES amount is $900. The commission rate should be 1%; however, because SALES is less than 2500.0, the rate is computed to be 3% and control is passed to the ENDIF and then to the computation for BONUS.

As stated earlier, when arrays are used as arguments in a function, they must be dimensioned in the function subprogram as well as in the main program. Generally, the array will have the same size in the function as it does in the main program; however, when the size of an array is an argument to the subprogram, we must use a technique called *variable dimensioning*. This technique allows us to specify an array of variable size in the subprogram. The argument value then sets the size of the array when the subprogram is executed. We illustrate the use of an array with a fixed size in Example 6–4 and with a variable size in Example 6–5. (Note that variable dimensioning refers to dimensioning of an array used as an argument to a subprogram. Any array that is not a subprogram argument, but that is defined and used in a subprogram, must be dimensioned in the subprogram with a constant; it is not dimensioned in the main program.)

EXAMPLE 6-4   Array Average, Fixed Array Size

Write a function that receives an array of 20 real values. Compute the average of the array and return it as the function value.

Solution

The decomposition and refinement in pseudocode for the function are given.

DECOMPOSITION OF AVE(x)

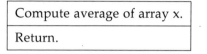

Compute average of array x.
Return.

REFINEMENT IN PSEUDOCODE

$$AVE(x): \text{sum} \leftarrow 0.0$$
$$\text{For } i = 1 \text{ to } 20$$
$$\text{sum} \leftarrow \text{sum} + x(i)$$
$$\text{ave} \leftarrow \text{sum}/20.0$$
$$\text{Return}$$

FORTRAN FUNCTION

```
*------------------------------------------------------*
      REAL FUNCTION  AVE(X)
*
*  This function computes the average
*  of a real array with twenty values.
*
      INTEGER  I
      REAL  X(20), SUM
*
      SUM = 0.0
      DO 10 I=1,20
         SUM = SUM + X(I)
   10 CONTINUE
      AVE = SUM/20.0
*
      RETURN
      END
*------------------------------------------------------*
```

A portion of a main program that might use this function is

```
          PROGRAM  GRADES
*
*  This program computes homework averages.
*
          INTEGER  ID, I
          REAL  SCORES(20), HWAVE
*
          READ*, ID
          READ*, (SCORES(I),I=1,20)
*
          HWAVE = AVE(SCORES)
             .
             .
             .
```

EXAMPLE 6-5 Median Value, Variable Array Size

The median of a list of sorted numbers is defined as the number in the middle: In the list −5, 2, 7, 36, and 42, the number 7 is the median. If the list has an even number of values, the median is defined as the average of the 2 middle values: In the list −5, 2, 7, 36, 42, and 82, the median is (7 + 36)/2, or 21.5.

Write a function called MEDIAN that has 2 parameters: a real array and an integer that specifies the number of values in the array. The function should assume that the elements of the array have already been sorted. Return the median value of the array as the function value.

Solution

The decomposition of this function is shown.

DECOMPOSITION OF MEDIAN(x,n)

Determine median of array x.
Return.

In Section 6−2, we used the MOD function to determine if an integer was odd or even. We can use the same technique to determine if the number of elements (n) in the array is odd or even. If n is odd, we must decide which subscript refers to the middle value. For example, if n = 5, we want the median to refer to the third value, which is referenced by $(n/2) + 1$. Recall that we are dividing 2 integers, and the result will be truncated to another integer. If n is even, we want to refer to the 2 middle values and compute their average. If n = 6, we want to use the third and fourth values, which can be referenced by $(n/2)$ and $(n/2) + 1$.

REFINEMENT IN PSEUDOCODE

> MEDIAN(x,n): If n is odd, then
> median ← x($n/2$ + 1)
> else
> median ← (x($n/2$) + x($n/2$ + 1))/2
> Return

As we convert the pseudocode into FORTRAN, we must remember to specify that the function MEDIAN is a real function (the default will be an integer).

FORTRAN FUNCTION

```
*-------------------------------------------------------*
      REAL FUNCTION  MEDIAN(X,N)
*
*  This function determines the median value
*  in a sorted list of real values.
*
      INTEGER  N
      REAL  X(N)
*
      IF (MOD(N,2).NE.0) THEN
          MEDIAN = X(N/2+1)
      ELSE
          MEDIAN = (X(N/2) + X(N/2+1))/2.0
      ENDIF
*
      RETURN
      END
*-------------------------------------------------------*
```

This function could be tested by a program with the following structure chart and statements:

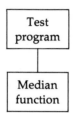

FORTRAN PROGRAM

```
*-------------------------------------------------------*
      PROGRAM  TEST
*
*  This program is written to test the median function.
*
      INTEGER  N, I
      REAL  X(10), MEDIAN
*
      PRINT*, 'ENTER NUMBER OF VALUES FOR ARRAY (<11)'
      READ*, N
      PRINT*, 'NOW ENTER SORTED ARRAY VALUES'
      READ*, (X(I), I=1,N)
      PRINT 5, MEDIAN(X,N)
    5 FORMAT (1X,'MEDIAN = ',F7.2)
*
      END
*-------------------------------------------------------*
              MEDIAN function goes here
*-------------------------------------------------------*
```

In Example 6-6, we use a two-dimensional array as an argument in a function.

EXAMPLE 6-6 Two-Dimensional Array Maximum

Write a function that will receive an array of integers with 5 rows and 7 columns. The function should return the maximum value in the array.

Solution

DECOMPOSITION OF MAXVAL(K)

Determine maximum of array k.
Return.

To find the maximum value in the array, we initialize the maximum to the first value in the array; then, we compare the rest of the elements in the array to the maximum, replacing the maximum value with any larger value that we find.

REFINEMENT IN PSEUDOCODE

$$\text{MAXVAL(k): maxval} \leftarrow k(1,1)$$
$$\text{For } i = 1,5 \text{ do}$$
$$\text{For } j = 1,7 \text{ do}$$
$$\text{If } k(i,j) > \text{maxval then}$$
$$\text{maxval} \leftarrow k(i,j)$$
$$\text{Return}$$

FORTRAN FUNCTION

```
*-------------------------------------------------------*
      INTEGER FUNCTION  MAXVAL(K)
*
*   This function determines the maximum value
*   in an integer array with 5 rows and 7 columns.
*
      INTEGER  K(5,7), I, J
*
      MAXVAL = K(1,1)
      DO 10 I=1,5
         DO 5 J=1,7
            IF (K(I,J).GT.MAXVAL) MAXVAL = K(I,J)
    5    CONTINUE
   10 CONTINUE
*
      RETURN
      END
*-------------------------------------------------------*
```

A statement that might use the function in the main program, after filling an array NUMBER that has 5 rows and 7 columns, is shown in the following group of statements:

```
      INTEGER  NUMBER(5,7), MAXVAL
         .
         .
         .
      PRINT 5, MAXVAL(NUMBER)
    5 FORMAT (1X,'MAXIMUM NUMBER IS ',I5)
```

Problems can arise when you use variable dimensioning with arrays that have more than one dimension. The following is an example: First, we modify the MAXVAL function so that the number of rows and the number of columns are variables.

FORTRAN Function

```
*------------------------------------------------------------*
      INTEGER FUNCTION  MAXVAL(K,M,N)
*
*  This function determines the maximum value
*  in an integer array with M rows and N columns.
*
      INTEGER  K(M,N), M, N, I, J
*
      MAXVAL = K(1,1)
      DO 10 I=1,M
         DO 5 J=1,N
            IF (K(I,J).GT.MAXVAL) MAXVAL = K(I,J)
    5    CONTINUE
 10 CONTINUE
*
      RETURN
      END
*------------------------------------------------------------*
```

If we modify the function reference to the one shown, the correct maximum value is printed:

```
INTEGER  NUMBER(5,7), MAXVAL
      .
      .
      .
PRINT 5, MAXVAL(NUMBER,5,7)
5 FORMAT (1X,'MAXIMUM NUMBER IS ',I5)
```

Suppose we want to determine the maximum value using only the first 2 rows and the first 2 columns of the array NUMBER, as shown in the diagram:

The following statements seem reasonable, but they are incorrect:

```
INTEGER  NUMBER(5,7), MAXVAL
      .
      .
      .
PRINT 5, MAXVAL(NUMBER,2,2)
5 FORMAT (1X,'MAXIMUM NUMBER IS ',I5)
```

These statements are incorrect because FORTRAN stores a two-dimensional array by columns. The array NUMBER is actually stored in memory as shown in the following diagram:

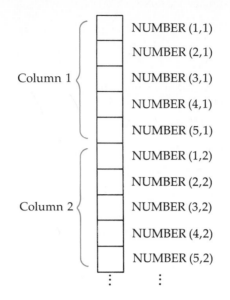

When we reference the array NUMBER in our function and specify that it has 2 rows and 2 columns, FORTRAN assumes that the values in NUMBER are stored in the following order:

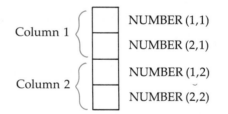

When we put the preceding two diagrams side-by-side, we can see that the array elements do not always match:

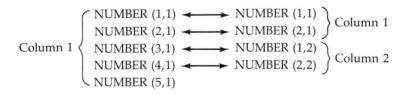

In fact, if we reference an array with 2 rows and 2 columns using the array NUMBER, the elements that we are actually going to use are outlined in the following diagram:

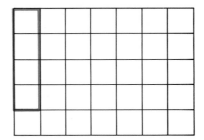

This problem does not result in a compiler error; but, the values used by the function are not those that we expect it to use, which can then present a difficult error to find in a program. In general, you should not use variable dimensions with arrays that have more than one dimension. If you have an application that requires variable dimensioning with two-dimensional arrays, include the declared sizes of the array in the argument list, along with the variable sizes to be used in the function. For example, if an array is defined to have MAXM rows and MAXN columns in the main program, use the array specification illustrated in the following function:

```
*------------------------------------------------------------*
      INTEGER FUNCTION   MAXVAL(K,M,N,MAXM,MAXN)
*
*    This function determines the maximum value in an integer
*    array with M rows and N columns (original size
*    MAXM by MAXN).
*
      INTEGER  M, N, MAXM, MAXN, K(MAXM,MAXN), I, J
*
      MAXVAL = K(1,1)
      DO 10 I=1,M
         DO 5 J=1,N
            IF (K(I,J).GT.MAXVAL) MAXVAL = K(I,J)
    5    CONTINUE
   10 CONTINUE
*
      RETURN
      END
*------------------------------------------------------------*
```

This self-test allows you to check quickly to see if you have remembered some of the key points from Section 6-5. If you have any problems with the exercises, you should reread this section. The solutions are included at the end of the text.

For the following problems, give the value of X, assuming that A = −5, B = −6.2, C = 0.1, and D = 16.2. The function TEST is given:

```
*-------------------------------------------------------*
      REAL FUNCTION  TEST(X,Y,Z)
*
*   This function returns either 0.5 or -0.5
*   depending on the values of X, Y, Z.
*
      REAL  X, Y, Z
*
      IF (X.GT.Y.OR.Y.GT.Z) THEN
          TEST = 0.5
      ELSE
          TEST = -0.5
      ENDIF
*
      RETURN
      END
*-------------------------------------------------------*
```

1. X = TEST(5.2,5.3,5.6)
2. X = TEST(B,C,A)
3. X = TEST(ABS(A),C,D)
4. X = TEST(C,C,D*D)

6-6 APPLICATION—OIL WELL PRODUCTION (Petroleum Engineering)

The daily production of oil from a group of wells is entered into a data file each week for analysis. One of the reports that uses this data file computes the average production from each well and prints a summary of the overall production from this group of wells.

Write a FORTRAN program that will read the information from the data file and generate this report. Assume that the first line of the data file contains a date (month, day, and year of the first day of the week that corresponds to the production data). Each following line in the data file contains an integer identification number for the well and 7 real numbers that represent the well's production for the week. The number of wells to be analyzed varies from week to week, so a trailer line is included at the end of the file; this trailer contains the integer 99999, followed by seven zeros. You may assume that no well will have this integer as its identification number.

The report generated should have the following format:

```
OIL WELL PRODUCTION
WEEK OF XX-XX-XX

WELL ID          AVERAGE PRODUCTION
                 (IN BARRELS)
XXXXX            XXX.XX
```

Include a final line at the end of the report that gives the total number of oil wells plus their overall average.

Use the following set of data (stored in a file called WELLS) for testing the program:

```
05 06 86
52      87      136     0       54      60      82      51
63      54      73      88      105     20      21      105
24      67      98      177     35      65      98      0
8       23      34      52      67      180     80      3
64      33      55      79      108     118     130     20
66      40      44      63      89      36      54      36
67      20      35      76      87      154     98      80
55      10      13      34      23      43      12      0
3       34      56      187     34      202     23      34
2       98      98      87      34      54      100     20
25      29      43      54      65      12      15      17
18      45      65      202     205     100     99      98
14      36      34      98      34      43      23      9
13      0       9       8       4       3       2       10
36      23      88      99      65      77      45      35
38      23      100     134     122     111     211     0
81      23      34      54      98      5       93      82
89      29      58      39      20      50      30      47
99      100     12      43      98      34      23      9
45      23      93      75      93      2       34      8
88      23      301     23      83      23      9       20
77      28      12      43      43      92      83      98
39      98      43      12      23      54      23      98
12      43      54      92      84      75      72      91
48      83      138     189     73      27      49      10
99999 0 0 0 0 0 0 0
```

PROBLEM STATEMENT

Generate a report on oil well production from daily production data. Give the average production for individual wells and the overall average.

INPUT/OUTPUT DESCRIPTION

The input is a data file with daily production data for a group of oil wells. The first line in the file contains the date of the first day in the week. Each following line contains the identification number of a well and the 7 daily production values for that well. The last line in the file contains 99999, which signals the end of the file. The output is a report in the following form:

```
              OIL WELL PRODUCTION
              WEEK OF XX-XX-XX

              WELL ID          AVERAGE PRODUCTION
                               (IN BARRELS)
              XXXXX            XXX.XX
```

HAND EXAMPLE

For the hand-worked example, we use the first 5 lines of the data file given at
the beginning of this application, along with the trailer line. Thus, our data
file is

```
05 06 86
52     87    136    0      54    60     82    51
63     54    73     88     105   20     21    105
24     67    98     177    35    65     98    0
8      23    34     52     67    180    80    3
99999 0      0      0      0     0      0     0
```

We use the date in the first line of the data file in our heading. Each
individual data line in the report contains the well identification (the first
value in each line) followed by the average. We compute the average from
the 7 daily values that follow the identification. We continue computing the
individual averages until we reach the trailer signal 99999. At this point, we
average the individual wells and print a final summary line. For this small set
of data, our output is

```
    OIL WELL PRODUCTION
    WEEK OF   5- 6-86

    WELL ID          AVERAGE PRODUCTION
                     (IN BARRELS)
       52            67.14
       63            66.57
       24            77.14
        8            62.71

    OVERALL AVERAGE FOR   4 WELLS IS   68.39
```

ALGORITHM DEVELOPMENT

Before we consider the steps in the algorithm, we should first decide the best
way to store the data. For instance, do we want to store it in a two-
dimensional array, or do we want to store the individual oil production
amounts in a one-dimensional array, or can we avoid arrays altogether?

We answer these questions by looking at the way in which we need to
use the data. To compute the individual well average, we need a sum of the
individual production amounts. Because all 7 values are entered in the same
data line, we must read them at the same time—we need an array to store
the 7 daily production amounts for an individual well. To compute the overall
average, we need a sum of the individual averages and a count of the number
of wells—we do not need to keep the individual averages from each well.

In summary, we need a one-dimensional array to store the individual production values, and we do not need a two-dimensional array to store all the data.

We now decompose the algorithm into a sequence of steps. At the same time, we need to decide which operations or steps should be written as functions. Experience is the best guide as to selecting which operations to define as functions. By studying how functions are used in the example programs, you will become more proficient at making these decisions. Remember that there are often several ways that functions can be used in a program.

We start by looking at the general decomposition and initial refinement of the algorithm.

DECOMPOSITION

Generate report.
Print summary line.

INITIAL REFINEMENT IN PSEUDOCODE

REPORT: Read date
      Read ID, oil production
      While ID not = 99999 do
        Determine individual average
        Print individual average
        Update overall average and well count
        Read next ID, oil production
      Print summary information

After completing the decomposition and the initial refinement, we can determine if any of the operations should be written as functions. Computations that are repeated in an algorithm and steps that involve long computations are good candidates for functions. Program readability suffers when the details of some of the steps become long and tedious. Even though the steps may be performed only once, placing them in a function may make the program simpler.

For the oil well production problem, a function can be used to compute the individual oil well averages. This operation is needed only once in the main loop; but, it involves several steps — the main program will be more readable if the steps are moved to a function subprogram. The function to compute the individual averages is also one that would be useful in other programs that compute averages. To be flexible, we write the function assuming that the data is in an array whose size is one of the function arguments.

REPORT: Read date
          number of wells ← 0
          total oil ← 0.0
          Read ID, oil production
          While ID not = 99999 do
             Compute individual average with function
             Print individual average
             Increment number of wells by 1
             Add individual well average to total oil
             Read next ID, production data
          Print summary information

FUNCTION PSEUDOCODE

AVE(oil, n): sum ← 0.0
          for $i = 1$ to n
            sum ← sum + oil(i)
          ave ← sum/n
          return

The structure chart for the solution is shown next, along with the FORTRAN program.

FORTRAN Program

```
*--------------------------------------------------------*
      PROGRAM  REPORT
*
*  This program generates a report from the daily
*  production information for a set of oil wells.
*
      INTEGER  MO, DA, YR, ID, N, I
      REAL  OIL(7), TOTAL, AVE, INDAVE
      DATA  N, TOTAL /0, 0.0/
*
      OPEN (UNIT=12,FILE='WELLS',STATUS='OLD')
      READ (12,*) MO, DA, YR
      PRINT*, 'OIL WELL PRODUCTION'
      PRINT 5, MO, DA, YR
    5 FORMAT (1X,'WEEK OF ',I2,'-',I2,'-',I2)
      PRINT*
      PRINT*, 'WELL ID         AVERAGE PRODUCTION'
      PRINT*, '                  (IN BARRELS)'
*
      READ (12,*) ID, (OIL(I), I=1,7)
   10 IF (ID.NE.99999) THEN
         INDAVE = AVE(OIL,7)
         PRINT 15, ID, INDAVE
   15    FORMAT (1X,I5,9X,F6.2)
         N = N + 1
         TOTAL = TOTAL + INDAVE
         READ (12,*) ID, (OIL(I), I=1,7)
         GO TO 10
      ENDIF
*
      PRINT*
      PRINT 20, N, TOTAL/REAL(N)
   20 FORMAT (1X,'OVERALL AVERAGE FOR ',I3,
     +            ' WELLS IS ',F6.2)
*
      END
*--------------------------------------------------------*
*
      REAL FUNCTION  AVE(X,N)
*
*  This function computes the average
*  of a real array with N values.
*
      INTEGER  N, I
      REAL  X(N), SUM
*
      SUM = 0.0
      DO 10 I=1,N
         SUM = SUM + X(I)
   10 CONTINUE
      AVE = SUM/REAL(N)
*
      RETURN
      END
*--------------------------------------------------------*
```

Could the variable SUM have been initialized in the function with a DATA
statement? (The answer is no. Why?)

Begin testing this program using a small data set such as the one in the hand-worked example. The output from this program using the data file given at the beginning of this application is

```
OIL WELL PRODUCTION
WEEK OF   5- 6-86

WELL ID          AVERAGE PRODUCTION
                   (IN BARRELS)
   52               67.14
   63               66.57
   24               77.14
    8               62.71
   64               77.57
   66               51.71
   67               78.57
   55               19.29
    3               81.43
    2               70.14
   25               33.57
   18              116.29
   14               39.57
   13                5.14
   36               61.71
   38              100.14
   81               55.57
   89               39.00
   99               45.57
   45               46.86
   88               68.86
   77               57.00
   39               50.14
   12               73.00
   48               81.29
OVERALL AVERAGE FOR   25 WELLS IS   61.04
```

Could the last line of the data file contain only the trailer identification value 99999 (are the seven zeros necessary in the last line of the data file)? If you try running the program without these last seven zeros, you will find that an execution error occurs because the program has run out of data. Because the identification number and the well production values are on the same line, we must read them with one READ statement. Each time the READ statement is executed, it reads 8 values before control passes to the next statement. When the READ statement reaches the last line in the data file, it needs 7 values in addition to the 99999 value before it can test for the trailer value.

6-7   APPLICATION—TRAFFIC FLOW
(Transportation Engineering)

To study traffic flow at various intersections in large cities, the cars that pass through an intersection during certain time intervals are counted. The data collected can then be analyzed to determine the changes in traffic flow as well as to identify the intersections with the most traffic. In this application, we use traffic flow data to compute the average number of cars that pass through an intersection in 1 minute.

   We assume that the data is contained in a file, and that each line of the file contains the intersection identification, the beginning time, the ending time, and the number of cars that passed during that time interval. We assume that the data is added to the file as it is collected; thus, the file is not in order by intersection. We must read all the information in the file to be sure that we have not missed any information. Because there is no special trailer line at the end of the file, we use the END option (a special form of the WHILE loop discussed in Chapter 4) to detect the last line in the file.

PROBLEM STATEMENT

Write a program that will read an intersection identification from the terminal. Compute the average number of cars that passes through the intersection per minute, using the data in a traffic flow data file named CARS.

INPUT/OUTPUT DESCRIPTION

The input to the program comes from two sources: an intersection identification is entered from the terminal and data is read from a traffic flow data file. The output is the average number of cars that passes through the intersection per minute.

HAND EXAMPLE

For our hand-worked example, we assume that the traffic flow data file contains the following information:

INTERSECTION	BEGINNING TIME	ENDING TIME	CARS
23	1330	1338	27
17	1422	1435	52
23	1407	1502	91
23	1507	1512	24

(Note that the time is stored using a 24-hour clock. The first 2 digits represent the hour, and the last 2 digits represent the number of minutes. At midnight, the time begins at 0000 for the new day. The time 0930 represents 9:30 AM and 2130 represents 9:30 PM. This representation assures that the ending time will be an integer larger than the beginning time. We will assume that a single measurement does not extend from one day into the next.)

We are now ready to compute the average number of cars per minute through an intersection. If the intersection number is 23, then the average is computed as shown:

INTERSECTION 23

First measurement	1330 to 1338 = 8 minutes, 27 cars
Next measurement	1407 to 1502 = 55 minutes, 91 cars
Next measurement	1507 to 1512 = 5 minutes, 24 cars

The average is computed by dividing the total number of cars by the total number of minutes, or

$$\frac{(27 + 91 + 24)}{(8 + 55 + 5)} = \frac{142}{68} = 2.09 \text{ cars/minute}$$

Note that the number of minutes in each observation is not simply the difference between the two times. For example, the difference between the integers 1502 and 1407 is 95; but if these integers represent time on a 24-hour clock, the difference is 55 minutes. Thus, we need to be careful about the steps we use to compute the number of minutes in an observation. Because this computation yields a single value, we use a function subprogram. The function converts the beginning and ending time measurements into minutes and then subtracts the two numbers. The MOD function is useful in changing a time based on a 24-hour clock to the number of hours and minutes. For example, consider the time 1330. The number of minutes is 30, which can be computed from the expression MOD(1330,100); the number of hours is 13, which can be computed from the expression 1330/100. (Note that the result of the integer division is 13, not 13.3.) The total number of minutes is then computed by multiplying the number of hours by 60 and adding the number of minutes, or 13 · 60 + 30. After the function converts both the beginning time and the ending time to minutes, it can return the difference of the 2 values as the number of minutes in the observation.

ALGORITHM DEVELOPMENT

The decomposition for this problem can be defined with the following steps.

DECOMPOSITION

Read intersection number.
Determine total cars and total minutes for this intersection using data file.
Compute and print average cars per minute.

Computing the number of cars and the number of minutes of observation for this intersection can be done in a loop that is executed as long as there is more data. When we exit this loop and print the average, we need to allow for the situation in which there are no observations for the desired intersection. We use these ideas in the refined pseudocode.

REFINEMENT IN PSEUDOCODE

ANALYZ: Read intersection identification
          total cars ← 0
          total minutes ← 0
          While more information in file do
            Read traffic information
            If traffic identification = intersection then
              add minutes to total minutes
              add cars to total cars
          If total minutes = 0 then
            Print 'NO OBSERVATIONS FOR THIS INTERSECTION'
          Else
            average ← total cars/total minutes
            Print average

The structure chart for the solution is shown next, along with the FORTRAN program.

```
*------------------------------------------------------------*
      PROGRAM   ANALYZ
*
*  This program reads traffic flow information from a
*  data file and computes the average number of cars
*  per minute through a specific intersection.
*
      INTEGER   ID, FILEID, BEGIN, END, FLOW,
     +          MINUTE, TOTMIN, TOTCAR
      DATA   TOTMIN, TOTCAR /0, 0/
*
      PRINT*, 'ENTER INTERSECTION IDENTIFICATION'
      READ*, ID
      OPEN (UNIT=10,FILE='CARS',STATUS='OLD')
    5 READ (10,*,END=50) FILEID, BEGIN, END, FLOW
         IF (FILEID.EQ.ID) THEN
            TOTMIN = TOTMIN + MINUTE(BEGIN,END)
            TOTCAR = TOTCAR + FLOW
         ENDIF
         GO TO 5
   50 IF (TOTMIN.EQ.0) THEN
         PRINT 55, ID
   55    FORMAT (1X,'NO OBSERVATIONS FOR INTERSECTION ',I3)
      ELSE
         PRINT 60, ID
   60    FORMAT (1X,'INTERSECTION ',I3)
         PRINT 65, REAL(TOTCAR)/REAL(TOTMIN)
   65    FORMAT (1X,'AVERAGE CARS PER MINUTE = ',F6.2)
      ENDIF
*
      END
*------------------------------------------------------------*
*
      INTEGER FUNCTION   MINUTE(BEGIN,END)
*
*  This function computes the number of minutes
*  between the beginning time and the ending time.
*
      INTEGER   BEGIN, END, BEGHR, BEGMIN, ENDHR, ENDMIN
*
      BEGHR = BEGIN/100
      BEGMIN = MOD(BEGIN,100)
      ENDHR = END/100
      ENDMIN = MOD(END,100)
      MINUTE = (ENDHR*60 + ENDMIN) - (BEGHR*60 + BEGMIN)
*
      RETURN
      END
*------------------------------------------------------------*
```

Could we have printed FILEID in place of ID in the statement that prints the intersection number? Printing FILEID instead of ID would be a logic error that might be hard to identify. FILEID contains the last intersection number in the data file; unless this last entry matches the identification that we entered with the terminal, we will print the wrong identification number with the average that was computed.

The following output is the result of three different runs of the program using the data given in the hand-worked example: We entered 23 as the desired intersection number in the first run; we entered 17 as the desired intersection number in the second run; we entered 44 as the desired intersection number in the third run.

```
INTERSECTION  23
AVERAGE CARS PER MINUTE =    2.09
```

```
INTERSECTION  17
AVERAGE CARS PER MINUTE =    4.00
```

```
NO OBSERVATIONS FOR INTERSECTION   44
```

What would happen if there were several observations for an intersection but no cars passed through the intersection during the observations? Because TOTMIN would not be zero, we do not have to worry about division by zero. TOTCAR would be zero, though, and the average value would be zero. The program would print the intersection number and follow that with an average of 0.00.

6-8 FUNCTIONS FOR SEARCH ALGORITHMS

Solutions to different problems often include some of the same steps, such as computing the average of a set of values or finding the maximum of a set of values. Once we have written a function, such as one to compute the average of the values in an array, we can often reuse a function in another program with little or no modification to the function. Another very common operation performed with arrays is searching the array for a specific value. We may want to know if a particular value is in the array, how many times it occurs in the array, or where it first occurs in the array. All these forms of searches determine a single value, and thus are good candidates for functions. In this section we will develop several functions for searching an array; then when you need to perform a search in a program, you can probably use one of these functions with little or no modification to the function.

Searching algorithms fall into two groups: those for searching an unordered list and those for searching an ordered list.

UNORDERED LIST

We first consider searching an unordered list; thus we assume the elements are not necessarily sorted into an ascending numerical order, or any other order that may aid us in searching the array. The algorithm to search an unordered array is just a simple sequential search: check the first element, check the second element, and so on. There are several ways that we could implement this function. We could develop the function as an integer function that returns the position of the desired value in the array or zero if the desired value is not in the array. We could develop the function as an integer function that returns the number of times the element occurs in the array. We could also develop the function as a logical function that returns a value of true if the element is in the array or false if the element is not in the array. All these ideas represent valid functions, and we could think of programs that would use each of these forms. Since we have already written functions that return an integer value and functions that return a real value, we will implement this function as a logical function. We will call the function FOUND in order to make references to the function read smoothly. A reference to the function FOUND, as it might appear in a main program, is shown next.

```
IF (FOUND(X,COUNT,KEY)) THEN
    PRINT*, 'ITEM IS IN STOCK'
ELSE
    PRINT*, 'ITEM IS NOT IN STOCK'
ENDIF
```

Note that the function has three arguments, the array (X), the number of valid data values in the array (COUNT), and the value for which we are searching (KEY).

EXAMPLE 6-7   Search Function for Unordered List

Write a logical function to search an unordered list for a specific value. The function should return a value of true if the specific value is found; otherwise the function should return a value of false. The function will need three arguments—the array, the number of valid data entries in the array, and the value for which we are searching. Assume that all these values are integers.

Solution

In the development of the function, we assume that the values are already stored in the array X, a variable COUNT specifies the number of valid data values in the array, and the variable KEY contains the value for which we are searching.

DECOMPOSITION OF FOUND(X,COUNT,KEY)

Search an unordered list for a specific value.

FOUND(x,count,key): If count > 0 then
        done ← false
        i ← 1
      Else
        done ← true
        found ← false
      While not done do
        If x(i) = key then
           done ← true
           found ← true
        Else
           i ← i + 1
        If i > count then
           done ← true
           found ← false
      Return

Converting this to a FORTRAN function yields the following:

FORTRAN Function

```
*--------------------------------------------------------------*
      LOGICAL FUNCTION  FOUND(X,COUNT,KEY)
*
*  This function determines whether or not
*  the key value is in an unordered array.
*
      INTEGER   X(COUNT), COUNT, KEY, I
      LOGICAL   DONE
*
      IF (COUNT.GT.0) THEN
         DONE = .FALSE.
         I = 1
      ELSE
         DONE = .TRUE.
         FOUND = .FALSE.
      ENDIF
    5 IF (.NOT.DONE) THEN
         IF (X(I).EQ.KEY) THEN
            DONE = .TRUE.
            FOUND = .TRUE.
         ELSE
            I = I + 1
         ENDIF
         IF (I.GT.COUNT) THEN
            DONE = .TRUE.
            FOUND = .FALSE.
         ENDIF
         GO TO 5
      ENDIF
      RETURN
      END
*--------------------------------------------------------------*
```

We now present a program that could be used to test the search function. The program will ask the user to enter a set of data to be stored in the array. It will then ask the user to enter a specific value to be used in searching the array. The program will use the function to do the search; the program will then print a message giving the result of the search. The structure chart for the program is shown next:

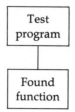

FORTRAN Main Program

```
*- - - - - - - - - - - - - - - - - - - - - - - - - - - - - - - - - - - - - - - - - -*
      PROGRAM  TEST
*
*   This program tests the search function.
*
      INTEGER   X(10), COUNT, KEY, J
      LOGICAL   FOUND
*
      PRINT*, 'ENTER COUNT (<11) OF VALUES FOR LIST'
      READ*, COUNT
      PRINT*, 'ENTER VALUES'
      READ*, (X(J),J=1,COUNT)
      PRINT*, 'ENTER VALUE FOR SEARCH'
      READ*, KEY
*
      IF (FOUND(X,COUNT,KEY)) THEN
          PRINT*, KEY,' FOUND IN THE LIST'
      ELSE
          PRINT*, KEY,' NOT FOUND IN THE LIST'
      ENDIF
      END
*- - - - - - - - - - - - - - - - - - - - - - - - - - - - - - - - - - - -*
                    FOUND function goes here
*- - - - - - - - - - - - - - - - - - - - - - - - - - - - - - - - - - - -*
```

An example of a test of the function FOUND using this program is shown below:

```
ENTER COUNT (<11) OF VALUES FOR LIST
3
ENTER VALUES
26     -3     7
ENTER VALUE FOR SEARCH
15
      15 NOT FOUND IN THE LIST
```

ORDERED LIST

We now consider searching an ordered, or sorted, list of values. Consider the list of ordered values below and assume that we are searching for the value 25:

−7
2
14
38
52
77
105

As soon as you reached the value 38, you knew that 25 was not in the list because you knew that the list was ordered. Therefore, we do not have to search the entire list, as we would have to do for an unordered list; we only need to search past the point where the key value should have been located. If the list is in ascending order we search until the current value in the array is larger than the key; if the list is in descending order we search until the current value in the array is smaller than the key value.

We present two common algorithms for searching an ordered list. The first searches sequentially until we either find the item or recognize that we have passed the position where it would have been in the list. The second algorithm first checks the middle of the array and decides if the item for which we are searching is in the first half of the array or the second half of the array. If it is in the first half, we then check the middle of the first half and decide whether the item is in the first fourth of the array or the second fourth of the array. The process of dividing the array into smaller and smaller pieces continues until we find the element or find the position where it should have been. Since this technique continually divides the part of the array that we are searching in half, it is sometimes called a *binary search.*

Example 6-8 Search Function for Ordered List

Write a logical function to sequentially search an ordered list for a specific value. The function should return a value of true if the specific value is found; otherwise the function should return a value of false. The function will need three arguments — the array, the number of valid data entries in the array, and the value for which we are searching. Assume that all these values are integers.

Solution

In the development of the function, we assume that the sorted values are already stored in the array X, a variable COUNT specifies the number of valid data values in the array, and the variable KEY contains the value for which we are searching.

Decomposition of FOUND(x,count,key)

```
Search ordered list for a specific value.
```

Pseudocode for Sequentially Searching an Ordered List

```
FOUND(x,count,key): If count > 0 then
                        done ← false
                        i ← 1
                     Else
                        done ← true
                        found ← false
                     While not done do
                        If x(i) = key then
                           done ← true
                           found ← true
                        Else if x(i) > key then
                           done ← true
                           found ← false
                        Else
                           i ← i + 1
                        If i > count then
                           done ← true
                           found ← false
                     Return
```

Converting this to a FORTRAN function yields the following:

```
*-------------------------------------------------*
      LOGICAL FUNCTION  FOUND(X,COUNT,KEY)
*
*  This function determines whether or not
*  the key value is in an ordered array
*  using a sequential search.
*
      INTEGER  X(COUNT), COUNT, KEY, I
      LOGICAL  DONE
*
      IF (COUNT.GT.0) THEN
         DONE = .FALSE.
         I = 1
      ELSE
         DONE = .TRUE.
         FOUND = .FALSE.
      ENDIF
    5 IF (.NOT.DONE) THEN
         IF (X(I).EQ.KEY) THEN
            DONE = .TRUE.
            FOUND = .TRUE.
         ELSEIF (X(I).GT.KEY) THEN
            DONE = .TRUE.
            FOUND = .FALSE.
         ELSE
            I = I + 1
         ENDIF
         IF (I.GT.COUNT) THEN
            DONE = .TRUE.
            FOUND = .FALSE.
         ENDIF
         GO TO 5
      ENDIF
      RETURN
      END
*-------------------------------------------------*
```

EXAMPLE 6-9   Binary Search Function for Ordered List

Write a logical function to implement a binary search for a specific value
using an ordered list. The function should return a value of true if the
specific value is found; otherwise the function should return a value of
false. The function will need three arguments — the array, the number of
valid data entries in the array, and the value for which we are searching.
Assume that all these values are integers.

Solution

In the development of the function, we assume that the values are
already stored in the array X, a variable COUNT specifies the number of
valid data values in the array, and the variable KEY contains the value for
which we are searching.

DECOMPOSITION OF FOUND(x,count,key)

Search an ordered list for a specific value using a binary search.

We first illustrate the binary search algorithm with the list used in the previous example in which we were searching sequentially for the value 25.

−7
2
14
38
52
77
105

There are seven values, the first referenced by a subscript value of 1 and the last referenced by a subscript value of 7. In a binary search, we compute the middle position by adding the first position number to the last position number and dividing by two. This should be done as an integer division. In our case, 7 plus 1 equals 8, and 8 divided by 2 is 4. Thus, we check the fourth position and compare its value to the value for which we are searching. The fourth value is 38, which is larger than 25, so we can narrow our search to the top half of the array. Our first position is still 1, and our last position is changed to the position above the middle position, or 3. We now divide that part of the array in half and compute the new midpoint to be (1 + 3)/2, or 2. The second value is 2, which is smaller than 25, so we can narrow our search to the second quarter of the array. Our first position is now one past the middle position, or 3, and our last position is 3. When the first and last positions are the same, we have narrowed in on the position where the value should be. Thus, we can exit the search algorithm. This specific example is illustrated in the following diagram. Follow through each step to be sure that you understand the sequence of steps needed.

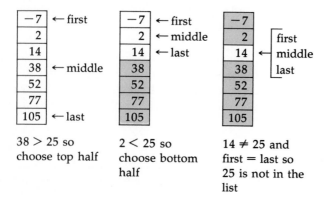

When the number of elements in the array is even, it is possible for the position of the first element to be greater than the position of the last element if the desired value is not in the list. Therefore, if the position of the first element is equal to or greater than the position of the last element, then the key value is not in the list. We now develop the detailed steps for searching an ordered list using a binary search.

Pseudocode for a Binary Search with an Ordered List

```
FOUND(x,count,key): If count ≤ 0 then
                         found ← false
                    Else
                        done ← false
                        found ← false
                        first ← 1
                        last ← count
                        While not done do
                            middle ← (first + last)/2
                            If x(middle) = key then
                                found ← true
                                done ← true
                            If not done then
                                If first ≥ last then
                                    done ← true
                                Else if x(middle) > key then
                                    last ← middle − 1
                                Else
                                    first ← middle + 1
                    Return
```

Converting this to a FORTRAN function yields the following:

```
*---------------------------------------------------------*
      LOGICAL FUNCTION   FOUND(X,COUNT,KEY)
*
*  This function determines whether or not
*  the key value is in an ordered array
*  using a binary search.
*
      INTEGER   X(COUNT), COUNT, KEY, FIRST, LAST, MIDDLE
      LOGICAL   DONE
*
      IF (COUNT.LE.0) THEN
          FOUND = .FALSE.
      ELSE
          DONE = .FALSE.
          FOUND = .FALSE.
          FIRST = 1
          LAST = COUNT
    5     IF (.NOT.DONE) THEN
              MIDDLE = (FIRST + LAST)/2
              IF (X(MIDDLE).EQ.KEY) THEN
                  FOUND = .TRUE.
                  DONE = .TRUE.
              ENDIF
              IF (.NOT.DONE) THEN
                  IF (FIRST.GE.LAST) THEN
                      DONE = .TRUE.
                  ELSEIF (X(MIDDLE.GT.KEY) THEN
                      LAST = MIDDLE - 1
                  ELSE
                      FIRST = MIDDLE + 1
                  ENDIF
              ENDIF
              GO TO 5
          ENDIF
      ENDIF
      RETURN
      END
*---------------------------------------------------------*
```

The program presented in Example 6-7 for testing the search function for an unordered list could be used to test the search functions developed in examples 6-8 and 6-9. The only change needed is an additional message to the user to specify that the data values must be in ascending order.

While both the sequential sort and the binary search correctly search for an item in an ordered list, the sequential sort is more efficient for small lists, and the binary search is more efficient for large lists.

SUMMARY

A function is a module that represents a single value. FORTRAN contains many intrinsic functions that compute values such as trigonometric functions and logarithms. We can also write our own functions. The statement function is a specification statement that defines a function within our program. A statement function can only be used when the function can be defined in a single assignment statement. A function subprogram is an independent module that is used to define functions that require more than a single assignment statement. All three forms of functions are useful in engineering and science applications because they simplify the computations in our programs. Several forms of functions for searching an array were also presented.

DEBUGGING AIDS

Testing a function should be approached much like testing a complete program. You will also need a simple program, called a *driver*, to initialize the input to the function that you are testing. This driver program should print the output of the function so that you can determine if it is returning the proper value. If it is not returning the proper value, the following list of checks may help you locate the problem:

1. Be sure that the function is returning the proper type of value. The easiest way to ensure this is to use explicit typing with the function.
2. Be sure that each path to a RETURN provides a value for the function.
3. Be sure that the variables listed in the main program match the arguments listed in the function subprogram. Check the corresponding variables for correct type and order.
4. Print the values of all variables just before using the function and just after returning from the function as you debug it.
5. Include PRINT statements in the function just as you do in a main program to help isolate trouble spots.
6. Remember that variables should not be initialized within the function with a DATA statement because these are not initialized with each use of the function. The DATA statement only initializes variables when the program is first begun.

STYLE/TECHNIQUE GUIDES

Using statement functions and function subprograms to replace computations within a main program greatly improve program structure and readability. The structure of a function subprogram should receive the same attention as the structure of a main program. If a function becomes long and difficult to read, perhaps additional functions should be used. Function subprograms can reference intrinsic functions and even other function subprograms. Once you have decided which operations will be written as functions, follow these three style suggestions:

1. Choose descriptive names for your functions.
2. Use comments in the functions as you would in the main program. In particular, use comments at the beginning of a function to describe its purpose and to define its arguments, if necessary.
3. For clarity, use the same variables in the argument list of the function as those used in the main program, if possible. If the function is needed several times with different arguments, choose completely different function variable names to avoid confusion with main program variables.

KEY WORDS

argument	main program
binary search	module
driver	search algorithm
function	statement function
generic function	structure chart
intrinsic function	subprogram
library function	variable dimensioning

PROBLEMS

We begin our problem set with modifications to programs developed earlier in this chapter. Give the decomposition, refined pseudocode or flowchart, and FORTRAN solution for each problem.

Problems 1–5 modify the temperature conversion program TABLE1, given on page 252.

1. Modify the temperature conversion program so that it reads a variable specifying the number of lines in the table instead of a number of degrees for the last line.
2. Modify the temperature conversion program so that the statement functions convert temperatures using units in Centigrade and in Kelvin. Both conversion equations can be derived from the following equation that converts degrees Kelvin to degrees Centigrade:

$$Centigrade = Kelvin - 273.15$$

3. Modify the temperature conversion program so that the statement functions convert temperatures using units in Rankin and in Fahrenheit. Both conversion equations can be derived from the following equation that converts degrees Fahrenheit to degrees Rankin:

$$Rankin = Fahrenheit + 459.67$$

4. Modify the temperature conversion program so that the statement functions convert temperatures using units in Rankin and in Kelvin. Both conversion

equations can be derived from the following equation that converts degrees Kelvin to degrees Rankin:

$$\text{Rankin} = 1.8 \times \text{Kelvin}$$

5. Modify the temperature conversion program so that it contains statement functions to convert temperatures from any of the units Fahrenheit, Centigrade, Kelvin, and Rankin, to any of the other units.

Problems 6–10 modify the oil well production program REPORT, given on page 275.

6. Modify the oil production program so that it asks the user to enter the current date and then prints this date in the upper right-hand corner of the first page of the report. Thus, the report will show the date that the report was run in addition to the date of the time period for which the data was collected.
7. Modify the oil production program so that the maximum weekly production is determined and printed after the summary line.
8. Using an additional function, modify the oil production program so that it determines the maximum daily production for each oil well. Print this value in addition to the well average.
9. Using an additional function, modify the oil production program so that it determines the total production for each oil well. Print this value in addition to the well average.
10. Modify the oil production program so that it determines the average oil production for an oil well based on non-zero production days. Thus, if a well produced 0 barrels of oil one day of the week, the average would be based on 6 days instead of 7.

Problems 11–15 modify the traffic flow program ANALYZ, given on page 280.

11. Modify the traffic flow program so that it prints the number of cars passing through the intersection and the total number of minutes of observation.
12. Modify the traffic flow program so that it computes an average of cars per minute for the combined data in the data file.
13. Modify the traffic flow program so that it will reopen the data file after computing the average for an intersection. Continue reading intersections and computing averages until an intersection number of 99999 is reached.
14. Modify the traffic flow program so that it will count the number of different intersections that are represented by the data in the data file.
15. Modify the traffic flow program so that it will allow an observation to extend past midnight. (Thus, the ending time could be smaller than the beginning time: For example, if the beginning time is 2330 and the ending time is 0030, the total time period is 60 minutes.)

For problems 16–20, write the function subprogram whose return value is described. The input to the function is an integer array K of 100 elements.

16. MAXI(K), the maximum value of the array K.

17. MINI(K), the minimum value of the array K.

18. NPOS(K), the number of values greater than or equal to zero in the array K.

19. NNEG(K), the number of values less than zero in the array K.

20. NZERO(K), the number of values equal to zero in the array K.

For problems 21–24, assume that you have a function subprogram DENOM, with input value x, to compute the following expression:

$$x^2 + \sqrt{1 + 2x + 3x^2}$$

Give the main program statements that use this function to compute and print each of the following expressions:

21. ALPHA $= \dfrac{6.9 + y}{y^2 + \sqrt{1 + 2y + 3y^2}}$

22. BETA $= \dfrac{\sin y}{y^4 + \sqrt{1 + 2y^2 + 3y^4}}$

23. GAMMA $= \dfrac{2.3z + z^4}{z^2 + \sqrt{1 + 2z + 3z^2}}$

24. DELTA $= \dfrac{1}{\sin^2 y + \sqrt{1 + 2 \sin y + 3 \sin^2 y}}$

In problems 25–30, develop these programs and functions. Use the five-phase design process.

25. Write a function whose input is a 2-digit integer. The function is to return a 2-digit number whose digits are reversed from the input number. Thus, if 17 is the input to the function, 71 is the output.

26. Write a function FACT that receives an integer value and returns the factorial of the value. Recall that the definition of a factorial is

$$0! = 1$$
$$n! = n \cdot (n - 1) \cdot (n - 2) \cdot \ldots \cdot 1$$

If $n < 0$, the function should return a value of zero.

27. Write a function TOTAL that will convert three arguments representing hours, minutes, and seconds to all seconds. For example, TOTAL(3,2,5) should return the integer value 10,925.

28. The cosine of an angle may be computed from this series, where x is measured in radians:

$$\cos x = 1 - \frac{x^2}{2!} + \frac{x^4}{4!} - \frac{x^6}{6!} + \cdots$$

Write a function COSX whose input is an angle in radians. The function should compute the first 10 terms of the series and return that approximation of the cosine. Use the factorial function developed in problem 26. (*Hint:* The alternating sign can be obtained by computing $(-1)**K$. When K is even, $(-1)**K$ is equal to $+1$; when K is odd, $(-1)**K$ is equal to -1.)

29. Rewrite the function in problem 28 such that it computes the cosine with only as many terms of the series as are necessary to ensure that the absolute value of the last term is less than 0.000001.

30. Write a main program that will produce a table with three columns. The first column (x) should contain angles from 0.0–3.1 radians in increments of 0.1 radians. The second column should contain the cosines of the angles as computed by the intrinsic function. The third column should contain the cosines as computed by the function in problem 28. Print the cosine values with an F9.7 format.

31. Engineering programs often utilize experimental data which has been collected and then stored in tabular form. The programs read the data and use it to generate plots, displays, or additional data. Examples of such data include wind tunnel force data on a new aircraft design, rocket motor thrust data, or automobile engine horsepower and torque data. The table of data below gives the thrust output of a new rocket motor as a function of time from ignition.

TIME	THRUST
0.0	0.0
1.0	630.0
2.0	915.0
5.0	870.0
8.0	860.0
12.0	885.0
13.0	890.0
15.0	895.0
20.0	888.0
22.0	860.0
23.0	872.0
26.0	810.0
30.0	730.0
32.0	574.0
33.0	217.0
34.0	0.0

Write a function called THRUST which computes the motor thrust for a rocket flight simulation program. The function should estimate the thrust for a specified time value using data from the table above. If the specified time value is not one of the times in the table then the new data value can be determined from the tabulated values by using *linear interpolation*, which is also called linear proportional scaling. For example, the estimated thrust at T = 2.2 seconds would be computed in the following manner:

$$\text{THRUST} = 915.0 + \left(\frac{2.2 - 2.0}{5.0 - 2.0}\right) \cdot (870.0 - 915.0)$$

$$= 912.0$$

Assume that the function has two arguments: the two-dimensional real array with 35 rows and two columns, and the new value of time. If the time matches a time entry in the table, then the function should return the corresponding thrust value. If the time value does not match a time entry in the table, then the function should interpolate for a corresponding thrust value. Assume that the function will not be referenced if the time is less than zero or greater than 34.0.

FORTRAN STATEMENT SUMMARY

FUNCTION Statement:

> **FUNCTION** *name (argument list)*

Examples:

> **FUNCTION   SUM(X,N)**
>
> **REAL FUNCTION   AVE(TESTS)**

Discussion:

The FUNCTION statement assigns a name to a function and lists the arguments that represent the input to the function. The value returned by the function is assigned to the name of the function. We recommend explicit typing of the function to clearly specify the type of value that is being returned by the function.

Statement Function:

> *name (argument list) = expression*

Example:

> **AREA(SIDE) = SIDE*SIDE**

Discussion:

A statement function is a function that can be computed with a single assignment statement. It is defined at the beginning of the program instead of in a separate subprogram definition.

APPLICATION — Waste Water Treatment (Chemical Engineering)

When waste water from industrial plants is released into streams the organic material in the waste water decomposes through chemical and bacterial action. Oxygen is consumed in this process as carbon dioxide and water are produced. As the oxygen is consumed the waste water is deoxygenated. At the same time oxygen is also continuously being absorbed into the stream from the air, and thus the waste water is reoxygenated. These two processes, deoxygenation and reoxygenation, take place at different rates. The rate of each depends on the oxygen level in the combined mixture of waste water and stream water. Write a program to analyze these processes using information from a data file. (See Section 7–3 for the solution.)

7

IMPLEMENTING TOP-DOWN DESIGN WITH SUBROUTINES

INTRODUCTION

FORTRAN supports two types of subprograms: functions and subroutines. In Chapter 6 we learned to write our own functions, and we saw a number of applications that used functions. In this chapter we learn to write *subroutines* and how to choose the type of subprogram that best fits a problem solution. Both functions and subroutines are used frequently in our text to illustrate their importance in making our programs simpler and more readable.

7 – 1   SUBROUTINE SUBPROGRAMS

In Chapter 6 we saw that a function subprogram is a module that computes a single value and returns that value through the function reference. FORTRAN contains a number of intrinsic functions that are available to our programs, and we can also write our own functions as either statement functions or as function subprograms. Although these functions are useful when we need to compute a single value, there are applications in which we would like to use a module to return many values or to print a message. In these instances, a subroutine is required. A subroutine differs from a function in the following ways:

1. A subroutine does not represent a value; thus, its name should be chosen for documentation purposes and not to specify a real or integer value.
2. A subroutine is referenced with an executable statement whose general form is

> **CALL**   *subroutine name (argument list)*

3. A subroutine uses the argument list not only for subprogram inputs but also for any output. To provide output to the main program, the arguments in the CALL statement must match in type, number, and order those used in the subroutine definition. The argument variable names themselves, though, do not have to match.
4. A subroutine may return one value, many values, or no value.

   Writing a subroutine is much like writing a function, except that the first line in a subroutine identifies it as a subroutine. The general form of this statement is

> **SUBROUTINE**   *name (argument list)*

   Subroutine output is returned by the arguments rather than by the name. (Remember that a function's output is returned by its name.)
   Because the subroutine is a separate program, the arguments are the only link between the main program and the subroutine. Thus, the choice of subrou-

---

tine statement numbers and variable names is independent of the choice of statement numbers and variable names used in the main program. When arrays are used as arguments, it is generally advisable to use the same array sizes in both the main program and the subroutine. Variable dimensioning can also be used in subroutines; you may want to review the discussion on variable dimensioning on page 262 in Chapter 6.

The subroutine, like the function, requires a RETURN statement to return control to the main program or to the subprogram that called it. It also requires an END statement because it is a complete program module.

EXAMPLE 7–1 Array Statistics

Information commonly needed from a set of data includes the average, the minimum value, and the maximum value. These values can be computed using three functions; however, if all three are required, it is more efficient to compute them simultaneously. Write a subroutine that is called with the statement

$$\texttt{CALL STAT(X,N,XAVE,XMIN,XMAX)}$$

where N is the number of elements in the real array X.

Solution

A subroutine, like a function, is a complete program that should be developed using the decomposition and refinement process. Because we have already developed solutions for determining averages, minimums, and maximums, these steps are straightforward. Note that we include the name of the subroutine and its parameters in the decomposition and refinement steps, just as we did with functions.

DECOMPOSITION OF STAT(X,N,XAVE,XMIN,XMAX)

Determine xmin, xmax, xsum.
Compute xave.
Return.

REFINEMENT IN PSEUDOCODE

```
STAT(x,n,xave,xmin,xmax):
    sum ← x(1)
    xmin ← x(1)
    xmax ← x(1)
    For i = 2 to n do
        sum ← sum + x(i)
        If x(i) < xmin then xmin ← x(i)
        If x(i) > xmax then xmax ← x(i)
    xave ← sum/n
    Return
```

We now present a program that reads a set of exam scores and then calls
the subroutine STAT to compute some statistics from the scores.

FORTRAN Program

```
*-----------------------------------------------------------*
      PROGRAM  SCORES
*
*  This program reads a set of test scores and
*  then computes their average, minimum, and maximum.
*
      INTEGER  N, I
      REAL   TESTS(100), AVE, MIN, MAX
*
      PRINT*, 'ENTER NUMBER OF TESTS (<101)'
      READ*, N
      PRINT*, 'ENTER TEST SCORES'
      READ*, (TESTS(I), I=1,N)
*
      CALL STAT(TESTS,N,AVE,MIN,MAX)
*
      PRINT 5, AVE
    5 FORMAT (1X,'AVERAGE TEST SCORE = ',F6.2)
      PRINT 10, MIN, MAX
   10 FORMAT (1X,'MINIMUM SCORE = ',F6.2,5X,
     +         'MAXIMUM SCORE = ',F6.2)
*
      END
*-----------------------------------------------------------*
*
      SUBROUTINE  STAT(X,N,XAVE,XMIN,XMAX)
*
*  This subroutine computes the average, minimum,
*  and maximum of a real array with N values.
*
      INTEGER  N, I
      REAL  X(N), XAVE, XMIN, XMAX, SUM
*
      SUM = X(1)
      XMIN = X(1)
      XMAX = X(1)
      DO 10 I=2,N
          SUM = SUM + X(I)
          IF (X(I).LT.XMIN) XMIN = X(I)
          IF (X(I).GT.XMAX) XMAX = X(I)
   10 CONTINUE
      XAVE = SUM/REAL(N)
*
      RETURN
      END
*-----------------------------------------------------------*
```

EXAMPLE 7–2   Sort Subroutine

In Chapter 5, we wrote a program that included the steps to sort a one-dimensional array. This operation is used so frequently that we will rewrite it in the form of a subroutine. To make it flexible, we use a variable in the argument list to specify the number of elements in the array. We suggest that you store this subroutine in your file area so that it can be accessed easily. Note that we copy the input array X into an array Y before sorting Y; this allows us to keep the original order in X and have the ascending order in Y. If you do not wish to use two arrays, use this CALL statement in the following program:

`CALL SORT(X,X,N)`

Solution

We could use any of the three sort algorithms from Chapter 5 in the subroutine. Since we used the selection sort in another program in Chapter 5, we will use the bubble sort here. The structure chart for this program is:

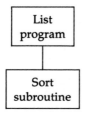

FORTRAN PROGRAM

```
*---------------------------------------------------------*
      PROGRAM  LIST
*
*  This program reads a list of real values,
*  sorts them in ascending order, and prints them.
*
      INTEGER  N, I
      REAL  X(25), Y(25)
*
      PRINT*, 'ENTER THE NUMBER OF VALUES TO SORT'
      PRINT*, '(MAXIMUM 25)'
      READ*, N
      PRINT*, 'ENTER THE VALUES'
      READ*, (X(I), I=1,N)
*
```

continued

```
          CALL SORT(X,Y,N)
*
          PRINT*, 'VALUES IN ASCENDING ORDER:'
          DO 10 I=1,N
              PRINT 5, Y(I)
    5         FORMAT (1X,F5.2)
   10 CONTINUE
*
          END
*--------------------------------------------------------*
*
          SUBROUTINE  SORT(X,Y,N)
*
*  This subroutine sorts an array X into an array Y
*  in ascending order. Both arrays have N values.
*
          INTEGER  N, I, FIRST, LAST
          REAL  X(N), Y(N), TEMP
          LOGICAL  SORTED
*
          DO 10 I=1,N
              Y(I) = X(I)
   10 CONTINUE
*
          SORTED = .FALSE.
          FIRST = 1
          LAST = N - 1
   15 IF (.NOT.SORTED) THEN
              SORTED = .TRUE.
              DO 20 I=FIRST,LAST
                  IF (Y(I).GT.Y(I+1)) THEN
                      TEMP = Y(I)
                      Y(I) = Y(I+1)
                      Y(I+1) = TEMP
                      SORTED = .FALSE.
                  ENDIF
   20         CONTINUE
              LAST = LAST - 1
              GO TO 15
          ENDIF
*
          RETURN
          END
*---------------------------------------------------------*
```

In the main program, we specified that the list of values to be sorted had a maximum of 25 values (because we dimensioned our arrays to 25 values). Thus, we can use 25 values or less, but not more than 25. The subroutine itself does not have any maximum; it can sort any number of values as long as the values are part of an array that has been properly defined in the main program.

This self-test allows you to check quickly to see if you have remembered some of the key points from Section 7–1. If you have any problems with these exercises, you should reread this section. The solutions are included at the end of the text.

Questions 1–2 refer to the following program and subroutine. The program generates an array of 10 numbers, containing the integers 1–10. The subroutine modifies these numbers.

FORTRAN Program

```
*------------------------------------------------------------*
      PROGRAM  QUIZ
*
*  This program tests your understanding of subroutines.
*
      INTEGER  K(10), I
*
      DO 10 I=1,10
         K(I) = I
   10 CONTINUE
*
      CALL MODIFY(K,10)
*
      PRINT*, 'NEW VALUES OF K ARE:'
      PRINT 15, (K(I), I=1,10)
   15 FORMAT (1X,5I5)
*
      END
*------------------------------------------------------------*
*
      SUBROUTINE  MODIFY(K,N)
*
*  This subroutine modifies elements in K.
*
      INTEGER  N, K(N), I
*
      DO 5 I=1,N
         K(I) = K(I)*2
    5 CONTINUE
*
      RETURN
      END
*------------------------------------------------------------*
```

1. What is the program output?
2. What is the program output if the reference to the subroutine is replaced with the following statement?

CALL MODIFY(K,5)

7-2 APPLICATION—SIMULATION DATA
(Computer Science/Engineering)

A routine to generate random numbers is useful in many engineering and science applications. Most game programs use randomly generated numbers to make the program appear to have a mind of its own—it chooses different actions each time the game is played. Programs that simulate something, such as tosses of a coin or the number of people at the bank window, also use random number generators.

In this application we use a random number generator to simulate (or model) noise that might occur in a piece of instrumentation, such as static. These applications of random events or random numbers use a random number generator routine. The routine that we present generates numbers between 0.0 and 1.0. The numbers are uniformly distributed across the interval between 0.0 and 1.0, which means that we are just as likely to get 0.4455 as we are to get 0.0090. This random number generator requires an argument that is a seed to the computation. When we give the routine a different seed, it returns a different random number. If we want a series of random numbers, we initialize the seed once, and we do not modify it again. The random number generator modifies the seed itself from one call of the routine to the next.

Although the routine computes and returns a single value, it also needs a seed whose value is preserved from one call to the routine to the next. Therefore, we really have two values that are being returned from the routine. You can now see why we use a subroutine instead of a function to implement this random number generator. The details of this random number generator are beyond the scope of this text. It essentially causes the computer to compute integers that are too large to store. The portion of the number that can be stored is a random sequence that is used to determine the random number. If you want more information on this algorithm, see S. D. Stearns, "A Portable Random Number Generator for Use in Signal Processing," Sandia National Laboratories Technical Report.

FORTRAN Subroutine

```
*----------------------------------------------------------------*
      SUBROUTINE  RANDOM(SEED,RANDX)
*
*   This subroutine generates random values
*   between 0.0 and 1.0 using an integer seed.
*
      INTEGER  SEED
      REAL  RANDX
*
      SEED = 2045*SEED + 1
      SEED = SEED - (SEED/1048576)*1048576
      RANDX = REAL(SEED + 1)/1048577.0
*
      RETURN
      END
*----------------------------------------------------------------*
```

The main program that follows allows you to enter a seed; the program then prints the first 10 random numbers generated with that seed. Try the program with different seeds and observe that you get different numbers. An example output is shown for a seed of 12357 so that you can check to see if your subroutine is working properly.

FORTRAN PROGRAM

```
*------------------------------------------------------------*
      PROGRAM   TEST
*
*  This program tests the random number generator.
*
      INTEGER   I, SEED
      REAL   X
*
      PRINT*, 'ENTER A POSITIVE INTEGER SEED VALUE'
      READ*, SEED
      PRINT*, 'RANDOM NUMBERS:'
      DO 10 I=1,10
         CALL RANDOM(SEED,X)
         PRINT 5, X
    5    FORMAT (1X,F8.6)
   10 CONTINUE
*
      END
*------------------------------------------------------------*
                  RANDOM subroutine goes here
*------------------------------------------------------------*
```

SAMPLE OUTPUT

```
ENTER A POSITIVE INTEGER SEED
12357
RANDOM NUMBERS:
0.099414
0.299419
0.310731
0.442812
0.548521
0.725532
0.712078
0.199705
0.395030
0.834445
```

We are now ready to discuss the application problem. We are going to develop an algorithm for a program that generates a data file that simulates a sine wave plus noise. The program uses both the intrinsic sine function and the subroutine to generate random numbers. The data file contains values of the signal

$$f(t) = 2 \sin(2 \cdot pi \cdot t) + noise$$

for $t = 0.0, 0.01, \ldots, 1.00$. Each value of the sine wave is added to a random number produced by the random number generator. Because the sine wave can vary from -2 to $+2$, and the random number generator can vary from 0 to 1, we can expect our experimental signal to vary from -2 to 3. This signal should be stored in a data file called SIGNAL, where each line of the data file should contain the value of t and the corresponding signal value.

PROBLEM STATEMENT

Generate a data file that contains samples of a sine wave $2 \sin(2 \cdot pi \cdot t)$, with uniform random noise between 0.0 and 1.0 added to it. The data points are to be evaluated with $t = 0.0, 0.01, \ldots, 1.00$.

INPUT/OUTPUT DESCRIPTION

The only input to the program is the seed to start the random number generator. The output is a data file called SIGNAL that contains 101 lines of data. Each line of data contains a value of time and the corresponding signal value.

HAND EXAMPLE

In our discussion of the random number generator, we illustrated the first 10 random numbers generated with seed 12357. Using these random numbers, the first 10 data points of the file SIGNAL are

```
f(0.00) = 2*sin(2*pi*0.00) + 0.099414 = 0.0994144
f(0.01) = 2*sin(2*pi*0.01) + 0.299419 = 0.4250000
f(0.02) = 2*sin(2*pi*0.02) + 0.310731 = 0.5613975
f(0.03) = 2*sin(2*pi*0.03) + 0.442812 = 0.8175746
f(0.04) = 2*sin(2*pi*0.04) + 0.548521 = 1.0459008
f(0.05) = 2*sin(2*pi*0.05) + 0.725532 = 1.3435660
f(0.06) = 2*sin(2*pi*0.06) + 0.712078 = 1.4483271
f(0.07) = 2*sin(2*pi*0.07) + 0.199705 = 1.0512636
f(0.08) = 2*sin(2*pi*0.08) + 0.395030 = 1.3585374
f(0.09) = 2*sin(2*pi*0.09) + 0.834445 = 1.9060986
```

ALGORITHM DEVELOPMENT

This program is straightforward. The only input is the random seed. The program then generates the signal values and writes them in a data file. We do not need arrays because each data value is needed only once.

DECOMPOSITION

| Read random number seed. |
| Generate data values and write them to the file. |

Refined Flowchart

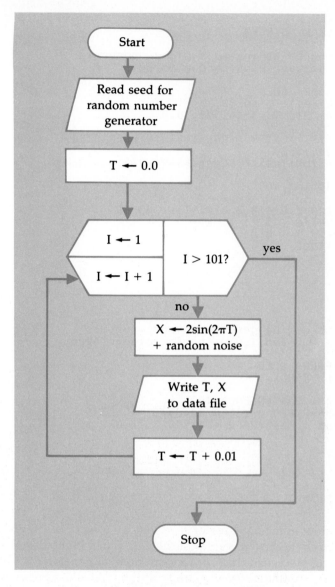

The structure chart for this program is the following:

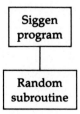

FORTRAN Program

```
*--------------------------------------------------------*
      PROGRAM  SIGGEN
*
*  This program generates a signal composed
*  of a sine wave plus random noise.
*
      INTEGER  SEED, I
      REAL  PI, T, NOISE, X
      DATA  PI, T /3.141593, 0.0/
*
      PRINT*, 'ENTER A POSITIVE INTEGER SEED'
      READ*, SEED
      OPEN (UNIT=15,FILE='SIGNAL',STATUS='NEW')
*
      DO 10 I=1,101
         CALL RANDOM(SEED,NOISE)
         X = 2.0*SIN(2.0*PI*T) + NOISE
         WRITE (15,*) T, X
         T = T + 0.01
   10 CONTINUE
*
      END
*--------------------------------------------------------*
*
      SUBROUTINE  RANDOM(SEED,RANDX)
*
*  This subroutine generates random values
*  between 0.0 and 1.0 using an integer seed.
*
      INTEGER  SEED
      REAL  RANDX
*
      SEED = 2045*SEED + 1
      SEED = SEED - (SEED/1048576)*1048576
      RANDX = REAL(SEED + 1)/1048577.0
*
      RETURN
      END
*--------------------------------------------------------*
```

TESTING

Use the random number generator seed that we used in the hand-worked example. Check the first 10 values of the data signal in the data file; if these match, we can be certain that our random number generator is working. It is difficult to test thoroughly a program with random values because we cannot expect (and should not get) the same values if we change the seed for the random number generator. However, the trend of the data should be the same. For example, in this problem, we should be able to see the sine wave in the data even though we use different random numbers for the noise. A plotting routine is helpful here. (In Chapter 8, problem 33 discusses a simple plot routine that can be used to plot data on your terminal screen.) Some plots of the data from program SIGGEN are shown. The first plot shows the sine wave with no noise; the next two plots are plots of the data file using different random seeds.

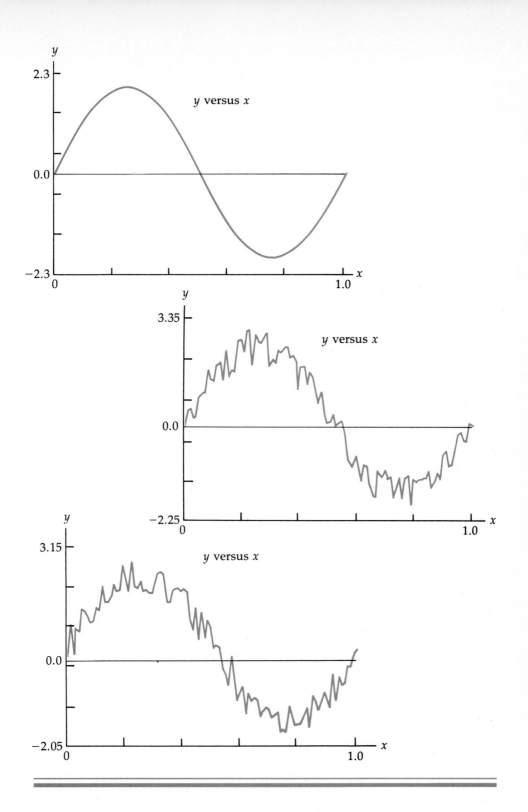

7-3 APPLICATION — WASTE WATER TREATMENT (Chemical Engineering)

Organic material in waste water from industrial plants decomposes through chemical and bacterial action. Oxygen is consumed in this process as carbon dioxide and water are produced. As the oxygen is consumed, the waste water is deoxygenated. A standard procedure for determining the rate of deoxygenation begins by diluting a waste water sample with fresh water containing a known amount of dissolved oxygen. The combined sample is then held at 20° C for 5 days and then checked for the amount of final oxygen. A biological oxygen demand (BOD) is then calculated from the initial and final oxygen levels. The biological oxygen demand for a 20 day test (at 20° C) is called the first-stage demand. It can be calculated using the five day (BOD) measurements.

Although oxygen is consumed from the stream when waste water is discharged, oxygen is also continuously being absorbed into the stream from the air. These two processes, deoxygenation and reoxygenation, take place at different rates. The rate of each depends on the oxygen level in the combined mixture of waste water and stream water. Initially, the rate of deoxygenation is rapid as there is a large amount of oxygen in the mixture. For this same reason the rate of reoxygenation is slow. As oxygen is consumed in decomposing the organic material, the oxygen level of the mixture drops. The lower oxygen level in the mixture causes the deoxygenation rate to decrease. It also causes the reoxygenation rate to increase. Hence, the dissolved oxygen level in the mixture decreases with time, reaches a minimum, and then increases. As the dissolved oxygen level decreases below the normal oxygen level of the stream, an oxygen deficit in the mixture is said to occur. The oxygen deficit of the mixture can be calculated in the following manner:

First, calculate the biological oxygen demand for the mixture of the stream and the waste water discharge:

$$bodmix = \frac{bods \cdot qs + bodd \cdot qd}{qs + qd}$$

where *bods* is the biological oxygen demand of the stream
  bodd is the biological oxygen demand of the discharge
  qs is the stream flow rate in million gallons/day
  qd is the discharge flow rate in million gallons/day

Next, estimate the first stage demand *(fsmix)* at the mixture temperature *(tmix)* in degrees centigrade, using the following formula:

$$f\,smix = \frac{bodmix}{0.68} \cdot [(0.02 \cdot tmix) + 0.6]$$

Finally, calculate the oxygen deficit as a function of time with the equation:

$$defct = \left\{ \frac{kd \cdot f\,smix}{kr - kd} \cdot [10^{-kd \cdot t} - 10^{-kr \cdot t}] \right\} + [doxygn \cdot 10^{-kr \cdot t}]$$

where kd is the coefficient of deoxygenation
$\quad kr$ is the coefficient of reoxygenation
$\quad doxygn$ is the initial oxygen deficit
$\quad t$ is the elapsed time in days

Also, kd can be estimated by:

$$kd = 0.1 \cdot 1.047^{(tmix-20)}$$

Assume that you have been hired as a private consultant to a new water analysis laboratory, Clear View Unlimited. Your contract is to write a FORTRAN program to calculate the oxygen deficit as a function of time for several streams being analyzed. The information for the streams is stored in a file called STREAMS. The value in the first data line contains the number of streams in the file. Then each subsequent data line contains the information for one stream in the following order: qd, qs, $bodd$, $bods$, $tmix$, kr, and $doxygn$. (All these data values are in the units mentioned in the earlier discussion.) Your program should calculate the oxygen deficit for each stream in the file over a time period using 0.1 day increments. It should find the maximum deficit and when it occurred for each stream. The time period for the analysis will be entered by the user when the program is run.

PROBLEM STATEMENT

Write a FORTRAN program to determine the maximum oxygen deficit for each stream in a data file over a time period using 0.1 day increments.

INPUT/OUTPUT DESCRIPTION

The stream information for the program is stored in a data file. The first line of the file specifies how many streams are to be analyzed. Then, for each stream to be analyzed, an additional line in the file gives the values for qd, qs, $bodd$, $bods$, $tmix$, kr, and $doxygn$. The user will enter the time period to use in the analysis.

HAND EXAMPLE

For a hand example, we will use the following values for the equations:

$$qd = 2.5$$
$$qs = 65.0$$
$$bodd = 0.1$$
$$bods = 15.0$$
$$tmix = 17.6$$
$$kr = 0.45$$
$$doxygn = 7.3$$

The following table lists the value for days in increments of 0.1 for one day and the corresponding deficit:

DAYS	DEFICIT
0.1	6.974
0.2	6.671
0.3	6.391
0.4	6.131
0.5	5.888
0.6	5.662
0.7	5.451
0.8	5.254
0.9	5.070
1.0	4.896

If we were analyzing this stream over one day, the maximum deficit of 6.974 occurred at day 0.1.

ALGORITHM DEVELOPMENT

The decomposition for this problem is the following:

DECOMPOSITION

Print header.
Compute and print the maximum deficit and the day that it occurred for each stream.

As we refine the steps in the decomposition, we want to consider steps that might be written as functions and subroutines. In this problem, we read a set of parameters for each stream and then use them to compute two values, the maximum deficit and the day that it occurred. Since the computations involved are rather long, a subroutine would be a good way to implement the computations of these two values. (A function is not appropriate since there are two values that need to be returned to the main program.) We now develop a flowchart for the main program and a separate flowchart for the subroutine to calculate the maximum deficit and the day that it occurred.

Flowchart for Main Program

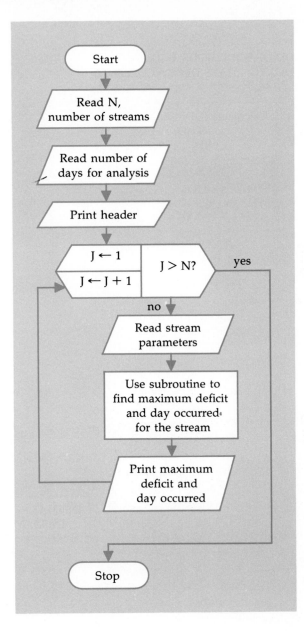

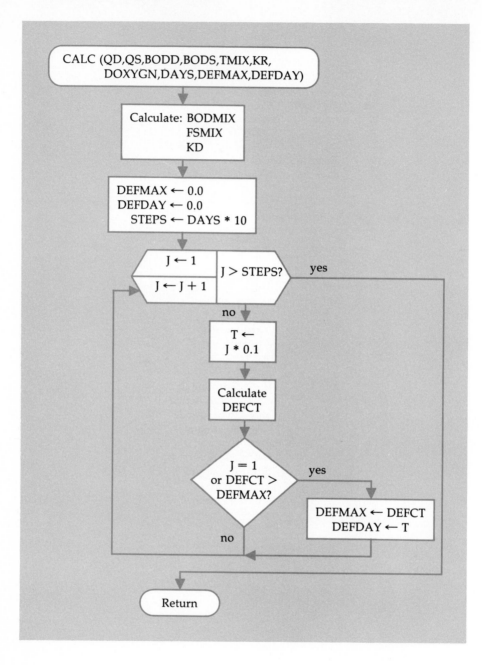

The structure chart for this solution and the corresponding FORTRAN program follow:

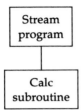

FORTRAN Program

```
*------------------------------------------------------------*
      PROGRAM   STREAM
*
*  This program computes the maximum oxygen deficit for
*  a group of waste water discharge streams.
*
      INTEGER   N, J
      REAL   DAYS, QD, QS, BODD, BODS, TMIX, KR, DOXYGN,
     +       DEFMAX, DEFDAY
*
      OPEN (UNIT=10,FILE='STREAMS',STATUS='OLD')
      PRINT*, 'ENTER TIME PERIOD FOR STREAM ANALYSIS'
      PRINT*, '(USE TIME IN TENTHS OF DAYS XX.X)'
      READ*, DAYS
      PRINT*
      PRINT*, 'OXYGEN DEFICIT ANALYSIS OF ',
     +        'WASTE WATER DISCHARGE STREAMS'
      PRINT*
*
      READ (10,*) N
      DO 30 J=1,N
         READ (10,*) QD, QS, BODD, BODS, TMIX, KR, DOXYGN
         CALL CALC(QD,QS,BODD,BODS,TMIX,KR,DOXYGN,
     +             DAYS,DEFMAX,DEFDAY)
         PRINT 10, J, DEFMAX
   10    FORMAT (1X,'STREAM ',I3,':',' MAXIMUM DEFICIT = ',F6.3)
         PRINT 20, DEFDAY
   20    FORMAT (1X,12X,'OCCURRED AT DAY ',F3.1)
         PRINT*
   30 CONTINUE
*
      END
*------------------------------------------------------------*
*
      SUBROUTINE   CALC(QD,QS,BODD,BODS,TMIX,KR,DOXYGN,
     +                  DAYS,DEFMAX,DEFDAY)
*
*  This subroutine calculates the maximum oxygen deficit for a
*  stream along with the day that it occurred.
*
      INTEGER   STEPS, J
      REAL   QD, QS, BODD, BODS, TMIX, KR, DOXYGN,
     +       FSMIX, KD, BODMIX, DEFCT,
     +       DAYS, DEFMAX, DEFDAY, T, TEMP1, TEMP2, TEMP3
*
```

continued

```
      BODMIX = ((BODS*QS) + (BODD*QD))/(QS + QD)
      FSMIX = BODMIX*(0.02*TMIX + 0.6)/0.68
      KD = 0.1*(1.047**(TMIX - 20.0))
*
      DEFMAX = 0.0
      DEFDAY = 0.0
      STEPS = INT(DAYS*10.0)
*
      DO 10 J=1,STEPS
         T = REAL(J)*0.1
         TEMP1 = (KD*FSMIX)/(KR - KD)
         TEMP2 = 10.0**(-KD*T) - 10.0**(-KR*T)
         TEMP3 = DOXYGN*(10.0**(-KR*T))
         DEFCT = (TEMP1*TEMP2) + TEMP3
         IF (J.EQ.1.OR.DEFCT.GT.DEFMAX) THEN
            DEFMAX = DEFCT
            DEFDAY = T
         ENDIF
   10 CONTINUE
*
      RETURN
      END
*-------------------------------------------------------------*
```

TESTING

A sample data file and its corresponding output are shown below:

Data File STREAMS

```
4
2.5     65.0    0.1     15.0    17.6    0.45    7.3
5.0    108.0    2.5     23.0    12.5    1.85    2.5
23.9     3.5    0.0    145.0    17.6    0.20    1.3
5.0    108.0    2.5      0.5    20.5    0.20    2.3
```

```
ENTER TIME PERIOD FOR STREAM ANALYSIS
(USE TIME IN TENTHS OF DAYS XX.X)
4.0

OXYGEN DEFICIT ANALYSIS OF WASTE WATER DISCHARGE STREAMS

STREAM    1: MAXIMUM DEFICIT = 6.974
             OCCURRED AT DAY 0.1

STREAM    2: MAXIMUM DEFICIT = 1.997
             OCCURRED AT DAY 0.1

STREAM    3: MAXIMUM DEFICIT = 6.374
             OCCURRED AT DAY 2.9

STREAM    4: MAXIMUM DEFICIT = 2.216
             OCCURRED AT DAY 0.1
```

When you are testing this program, it would be a good idea to put a PRINT statement inside the loop that is computing the deficit for each increment of a day. By checking the set of values computed each time through the DO loop in the subroutine, you can be sure that the steps to determine the maximum deficit are working properly.

7–4 SUBROUTINES FOR INSERTING AND DELETING

In the previous chapter we presented a number of common techniques that we implemented with functions. In this section we develop subroutines for inserting and deleting elements in a list. These techniques are also commonly used in engineering and scientific programs, and like the functions from Chapter 6, will be useful in a variety of programs. The common techniques discussed in the last couple of chapters are often called *software tools* because they are used so frequently. You may want to store these functions and subroutines so they will be convenient to add to programs as you need them.

We now consider the steps to insert or delete an element in an ordered list. We assume that the list is ordered in an array and that the value of a variable COUNT will specify how many of the elements in the array represent actual data values.

INSERTING IN AN ORDERED LIST

Before we develop the pseudocode for inserting a value in an ordered list of values, we look at a simple hand example:

Original List

123
247
253
496

There are four valid entries in the array, although we assume that the size of the array might be much larger. Suppose we want to insert the value 147. Think through the steps as you perform them. You scan down the array until you find a value larger than 147, you move all the rest of the array elements down one position in the array, and then insert the new value in the position left open after moving the rest of the array down. (We use the terms "up one position in the array" to mean toward the top of the array, or the top of the page. "Down one position in the array" means toward the bottom of the array, or the bottom of the page.) The number of valid elements in the array has now been increased by 1. The new contents of the array are the following:

Modified List

123
147
247
253
496

Suppose we now want to insert the value 512. As we scan down the list, we find that we reach the end and the value to be inserted is greater than the last value in the list. We add the new value at the end of the list, and increment the count.

Modified List

123
147
247
253
496
512

Are there any special cases that can occur when inserting values in an ordered list? What happens if the value to be inserted is already in the list? If the list is updating the list of valid users for a computer system, we don't want to list the identification for a person more than once, so we would not insert the value again if it were already there; on the other hand, if the list represents bank transactions on a specific account, there could be multiple transactions on the same account, so we would want to add the additional information. As another special case, suppose the count equals the defined size of the array; that is, the array is full. To know how to handle this situation requires knowing more about the problem being solved. In some cases we would want to print an error message stating that the array was full and the value could not be added; in other cases we would want to insert the new value and move the rest of the elements down in the array until we reached the end of the array — thus losing the last value in the array.

EXAMPLE 7-3　Subroutine for Inserting in an Ordered List

Write a subroutine to insert a value in an ordered list. The arguments of the subroutine include the array X, a variable COUNT that specifies the number of valid data values in the array, the variable LIMIT that contains the defined size of the array, and the variable NEW that contains the value to be inserted in the array. Write the subroutine so that it will add a new value to the array even if it is already in the array. If a new element is added to a full array, the last value in the array will be lost.

Solution

It should be clear that inserting a value in an ordered list requires a subroutine instead of a function because many values in the array may be changed by an insertion. We also need to increment the value of COUNT if the array was not full when we did the insertion. We now derive the detailed steps for the subroutine.

DECOMPOSITION OF INSERT(LIMIT,NEW,COUNT,X)

Insert new item in ordered list.

INITIAL PSEUDOCODE

```
INSERT(limit,new,count,x): If count = limit then
                                Print message that last
                                    value will be lost
                            done ← false
                            j ← 1
                            While (j ≤ count) and
                                    (not done) do
                                If x(j) < new value then
                                    j ← j + 1
                                Else
                                    done ← true
                            If j > count then
                                Update count
                                Add new value at end of list
                            Else
                                Update count
                                Insert new value at this point
                            Return
```

We still need to refine a couple of these steps. When we exit the WHILE loop, the first IF structure tests to see if J is greater than COUNT. If the condition is true, the new element goes at the end of the values. Thus, if the array is not full, we increment the count and add the new value at the end of the list of valid values; however, if the array is already full, we do nothing because the new value would belong at the end of the list of valid values, and there is no room there.

When the new value belongs within the list, we must insert it carefully. First we go to the end of the valid data and move the last value down one position. Then we can move the next-to-the-last value to the position vacated. We continue to move values down until we have moved the value in the position where the new value is to be inserted; we can then insert the new value. If the array is full when we perform the insertion, the value in the last position will be lost. The final pseudocode refinement details these steps.

FINAL REFINEMENT

```
INSERT(limit,new,count,x): If count = limit then
                              Print message that last
                                  value will be lost
                           done ← false
                           j ← 1
                           While (j ≤ count) and
                                   (not done) do
                             If x(j) < new value then
                                 j ← j + 1
                             Else
                                 done ← true
                           If j > count then
                             If count < limit then
                                 count ← count + 1
                             x(count) ← new value
                           Else
                             If count < limit then
                                 count ← count + 1
                             For k = count to j + 1 by −1 do
                                 x(k) ← x(k − 1)
                             x(j) ← new value
                           Return
```

Before we convert this to FORTRAN, consider the situation of inserting a value in an empty list, that is, a list which has no valid data values in it and thus has a count of zero. Look at the pseudocode and see if it will handle this situation. (It does, but be sure that you are convinced.) Converting this final refinement to FORTRAN yields the following:

```
*--------------------------------------------------------*
      SUBROUTINE  INSERT (LIMIT,NEW,COUNT,X)
*
*  This subroutine inserts an element in an ordered list.
*
      INTEGER  LIMIT, NEW, COUNT, X(LIMIT), J, K
      LOGICAL  DONE
*
      IF (COUNT.EQ.LIMIT) THEN
         PRINT*, 'ARRAY IS FULL'
         PRINT*, 'LAST VALUE WILL BE LOST'
      ENDIF
      DONE = .FALSE.
      J = 1
    5 IF ((J.LE.COUNT).AND.(.NOT.DONE)) THEN
         IF (X(J).LT.NEW) THEN
            J = J + 1
         ELSE
            DONE = .TRUE.
         ENDIF
         GO TO 5
      ENDIF
*
      IF (J.GT.COUNT) THEN
         IF (COUNT.LT.LIMIT) COUNT = COUNT + 1
         X(COUNT) = NEW
      ELSE
         IF (COUNT.LT.LIMIT) COUNT = COUNT + 1
         DO 10 K=COUNT,J+1,-1
            X(K) = X(K-1)
   10    CONTINUE
         X(J) = NEW
      ENDIF
*
      RETURN
      END
*--------------------------------------------------------*
```

The insertion technique is not trivial. It requires a thorough understanding of arrays and subscript handling. Go through the pseudocode and corresponding FORTRAN statements until you understand the steps. After we develop the subroutine for deleting an element from an ordered list, we present a program for testing both the insertion and the deletion subroutines.

DELETING FROM AN ORDERED LIST

After you master the insertion technique, you will find the deletion technique easier because there are many similarities. We again assume that the list is ordered in an array and that the value of a variable COUNT will specify how many of the elements in the array represent actual data values. Let's begin with a simple hand example:

Original List	123
	247
	253
	496

As before, there are four valid entries in the original array, but we still assume that the actual size of the array could be larger. Suppose we want to delete value 253. Think through the steps as you perform them: you scan down the array until you find the value, you remove the value, and you move the rest of the array values up one position in the array. The number of valid elements in the array has now been decreased by 1. The new contents of the array are the following:

Modified List	123
	247
	496

Are there any special cases that can occur when deleting values in an ordered list? What happens if the value to be deleted is not in the list? In this situation we probably want to print a message to the user. What happens if we delete the only element in the list? In this situation the count will be decremented to the value zero and we will have an empty list.

We are now ready to develop the detailed steps for deleting an item from an ordered list.

EXAMPLE 7-4   Subroutine for Deleting from an Ordered List

Write a subroutine to delete a value from an ordered list. The arguments of the subroutine include the array X, a variable COUNT that specifies the number of valid data values in the array, and the variable OLD that contains the value to be deleted from the array.

DECOMPOSITION OF DELETE(OLD,COUNT,X)

Delete item from ordered list.

DELETE(old,count,x): done ← false
    j ← 1
    While (j ≤ count) and (not done) do
        If x(j) < old then
            j ← j + 1
        Else
            done ← true
    If (j > count) or (x(j) > old) then
        Write message that value
            is not in the list
    Else
        Update count
        Delete old value from list

Will this pseudocode handle the situation in which the array is empty? Since COUNT will be equal to zero, the condition in the WHILE loop will be false the first time it is tested, because the value of J is 1. A message will be printed that the value is not in the list, which handles the situation properly.

We still need to refine a couple of the steps in the pseudocode. When we exit the WHILE loop, the IF structure tests to see if the element was actually in the loop. If we searched until we reached the end of the loop (j > count) or until we passed the position where the element should have been (x(j) > old), we write a message indicating that the element was not in the list. If the element was in the list, we need to subtract one from the count and "delete old value from list." However, we really do not explicitly delete the old value. Instead, we move the value below the old value up one position in the array, the value below that one up one position in the array, and so on until we have moved all the values below the one to be deleted up one position in the array. The final pseudocode refinement details these steps.

FINAL REFINEMENT

DELETE(old,count,x): done ← false
    j ← 1
    While (j ≤ count) and (not done) do
        If x(j) < old then
            j ← j + 1
        Else
            done ← true
    If (j > count) or (x(j) > old) then
        Write message that value
            is not in the list
    Else
        count ← count − 1
        For k = j to count do
            x(k) ← x(k + 1)

Converting this final pseudocode to FORTRAN yields the following statements:

FORTRAN SUBROUTINE

```
*-------------------------------------------------*
      SUBROUTINE  DELETE (OLD,COUNT,X)
*
*  This subroutine deletes an element from an ordered list.
*
      INTEGER  OLD, COUNT, X(COUNT), J, K
      LOGICAL  DONE
*
      DONE = .FALSE.
      J = 1
    5 IF ((J.LE.COUNT).AND.(.NOT.DONE)) THEN
         IF (X(J).LT.OLD) THEN
            J = J + 1
         ELSE
            DONE = .TRUE.
         ENDIF
         GO TO 5
      ENDIF
*
      IF ((J.GT.COUNT).OR.(X(J).GT.OLD)) THEN
         PRINT*, 'VALUE TO DELETE IS NOT IN LIST'
      ELSE
         COUNT = COUNT - 1
         DO 10 K=J,COUNT
            X(K) = X(K+1)
   10    CONTINUE
      ENDIF
*
      RETURN
      END
*-------------------------------------------------*
```

These two subroutines have been developed independently of a specific application to ensure that they will be useful in a number of applications. However, just because these routines are not part of a specific problem, we cannot skip the important step of testing them. Therefore, we will write a special program (called a driver) to test the subroutines. The driver program allows us to test modules independently of a specific program. In the driver program below, the user is asked to enter a list of ordered values. The values are stored; then the user is allowed to perform both deletions and insertions. The driver has the following structure chart:

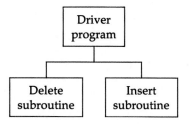

In the program, we indicate the position of the subroutines to show clearly where they would be included. The order of the routines is not important; they could be interchanged with no effect on the program.

FORTRAN Program

```
*--------------------------------------------------------------*
      PROGRAM  DRIVER
*
*  This driver tests both the insertion and deletion routines.
*
      INTEGER  X(10), COUNT, I, CODE, NEW, OLD, LIMIT
      LOGICAL  DONE
      DATA  LIMIT /10/
*
      PRINT*, 'ENTER COUNT (<11) OF VALUES FOR LIST'
      READ*, COUNT
      PRINT*, 'ENTER VALUES IN ASCENDING ORDER'
      READ*, (X(I),I=1,COUNT)
*
      DONE = .FALSE.
    5 IF (.NOT.DONE) THEN
          PRINT*, 'ENTER -1 FOR DELETE, 1 TO INSERT, ',
     +            '9 TO QUIT'
          READ*, CODE
          IF (CODE.EQ.-1) THEN
              PRINT*, 'ENTER VALUE TO DELETE'
              READ*, OLD
              CALL DELETE(OLD,COUNT,X)
          ELSEIF (CODE.EQ.1) THEN
              PRINT*, 'ENTER VALUE TO INSERT'
              READ*, NEW
              CALL INSERT(LIMIT,NEW,COUNT,X)
          ENDIF
          IF (CODE.EQ.9) THEN
              DONE = .TRUE.
          ELSE
              PRINT*, 'NEW LIST'
              DO 10 I=1,COUNT
                  PRINT*, X(I)
   10         CONTINUE
          ENDIF
          GO TO 5
      ENDIF
*
      END
*--------------------------------------------------------------*
                DELETE subroutine goes here
*--------------------------------------------------------------*
                INSERT subroutine goes here
*--------------------------------------------------------------*
```

An example of a test of the insert and delete subroutines using this driver follows:

```
ENTER COUNT (<11) OF VALUES FOR LIST
3
ENTER VALUES IN ASCENDING ORDER
5   13   17
ENTER -1 FOR DELETE, 1 TO INSERT, 9 TO QUIT
1
ENTER VALUE TO INSERT
8
NEW LIST:
        5
        8
        13
        17
ENTER -1 FOR DELETE, 1 TO INSERT, 9 TO QUIT
-1
ENTER VALUE TO DELETE
15
VALUE TO DELETE IS NOT IN LIST
NEW LIST:
        5
        8
        13
        17
ENTER -1 FOR DELETE, 1 TO INSERT, 9 TO QUIT
9
```

If you did not want to require that the user enter data that had already been sorted, you could add a sort subroutine such as the one that we developed in Example 7–2 on page 303. The new structure chart for the program would then be the one shown below:

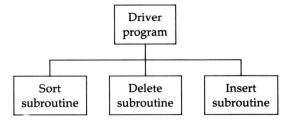

The steps in the driver program that prompt the user to enter the data would then be replaced by the following:

```
PRINT*, 'ENTER COUNT (<11) OF VALUES FOR LIST'
READ*, COUNT
PRINT*, 'ENTER VALUES'
READ*, (X(I),I=1,COUNT)
CALL SORT(X,X,COUNT)
```

This self-test allows you to check quickly to see if you have remembered some of the key points from Section 7-4. If you have any problems with this exercise, reread this section. The solutions are included at the end of the text.

Given below is a FORTRAN program that includes the INSERT subroutine developed in this section. The program reads an array of integers that are entered in a random order. Add statements to the program that will sort the array using the INSERT subroutine. Do not modify the INSERT subroutine and do not add any other modules. (*Hint:* You may want to consider calling the INSERT subroutine from a DO loop.)

FORTRAN PROGRAM

```
*-------------------------------------------------------------*
      PROGRAM  QUIZ
*
*  This program tests your understanding of the insert
*  subroutine.
*
      INTEGER  X(10), COUNT, J
*
      PRINT*, 'ENTER COUNT (<11) OF VALUES FOR LIST'
      READ*, COUNT
      PRINT*, 'ENTER VALUES IN RANDOM ORDER'
      READ*, (X(J),J=1,COUNT)
*
*  Replace this statement with statements to sort the
*  array of values using the INSERT subroutine.
*
      PRINT*, 'ORDERED LIST'
      DO 10 J=1,COUNT
         PRINT*, X(J)
  10  CONTINUE
      END
*-------------------------------------------------------------*
            INSERT subroutine from page 323 goes here
*-------------------------------------------------------------*
```

7-5 APPLICATION—COMPUTER SECURITY
(Computer Science/Engineering)

Computer security is an important issue because so much information is stored in computer systems. Some of this information is confidential. One way to maintain security is to limit access to the computer systems that store this data. A limited access system must keep a list of users that have permission to use the system. New users are added to the list as they are approved; others are deleted from the list when they no longer need access to the system. In this application we assume that such a list uses Social Security numbers for identifying users. This list is kept in ascending order in a data file. A trailer signal of 999999999 is at the end of the file. The number of users varies, but we assume that the actual number of users never exceeds 499. Thus, with the trailer signal, the list never exceeds 500 values.

As we develop a program that allows Social Security numbers to be added and deleted from this list, we must be concerned about the *user interface*—the part of the program that interfaces the user to the steps in the program itself. The user interface needs to be designed to be easy to use so that users will make fewer errors when entering the information. (Programs that are easy to use are also called *user-friendly* programs.) We will assume that the user will be entering Social Security numbers from the keyboard for additions and deletions. Since the input is probably entered from request forms, we will allow the information to be entered in any order; that is, we will not require all deletions before the insertions, and we will not assume that the Social Security numbers to be inserted or deleted are in any particular order.

Because we are inserting and deleting elements in a computer access list, it does not make sense to insert an element already in the list. Therefore, we must modify the insertion subroutine from the previous section so that a message is printed if the element is already in the list. Similarly, if the list is full we do not want to insert another element in the list because we would lose the last element in the list. Therefore, before referencing the insert subroutine we will check to see if the list is full and, if so, print a message to the user.

PROBLEM STATEMENT

Write a program to update a computer access list.

INPUT/OUTPUT DESCRIPTION

The computer access list is stored in ascending order in a data file named ACCESS that has a trailer signal of 999999999. The input to the program is a set of Social Security numbers to be added to the list or deleted from the list. The output is an updated list of information stored in a file named

NEWACCES. Error messages are also printed on the terminal screen if numbers to be added are already in the file or if numbers to be deleted are not in the file.

HAND EXAMPLE

Assume that the current access list contains the following Social Security numbers:

203294433
289129430
319330022
450123452
999999999

The updates to this list include the following insertions and deletions:

additions:	122899823
	244448353
	595959591
deletions:	289129430

After updating the list, the new computer access list is the following:

122899823
203294433
244448353
319330022
450123452
595959591
999999999

ALGORITHM DEVELOPMENT

The decomposition of this problem solution is

DECOMPOSITION

Read access list from file.
Perform insertions and deletions to list.
Write updated list to new file.

We will use the following code to determine whether the user wants to insert a number, delete a number, or quit the program:

Code Value	Operation Desired
−1	deletion
1	addition
0	quit

We now refine the decomposition steps into pseudocode.

REFINEMENT IN PSEUDOCODE

UPDATE: Read ssn list from data file
      done ← false
      While not done do
         Print message asking for code
         Read code
         If code = −1 then
            Print message asking for ssn
            Read old
            Delete old from ssn list
         Else if code = 1 then
            If count = limit then
               Print message that list is full
            Else
               Print message asking for ssn
               Read new
               Insert new in ssn list
         Else
            done ← true
      Write ssn list to new file

We now present the pseudocode for the insertion routine. (Since the deletion subroutine developed in the previous section does not require any modifications, we do not list it again.) Some modifications are needed in the insertion routine because we do not want to insert a duplicate number in the computer access list. Instead, we will print a message that the number is already in the list. If the list is full, we will not perform an insertion because we would lose a value; instead, before we reference the insertion subroutine, we will check to see if the list is full and print a message if it is full. Also, since the list includes a trailer signal of 999999999, any insertions will be before that value, so we can omit the test for inserting at the end of the list.

The pseudocode assumes that the values are already in an ascending order in the array X, a variable COUNT specifies the number of data values (including the trailer signal) in the array, a variable LIMIT contains the defined size of the array, and the variable NEW contains the value to be inserted in the array.

Pseudocode for Insertion in an Ordered List

```
INSERT(limit,new,count,x):  done ← false
                            j ← 1
                            While (not done) do
                                 If x(j) < new value then
                                       j ← j + 1
                                 Else
                                       done ← true
                            If x(j) = new then
                                 Print message that item
                                      is already in list
                            Else
                                 count ← count + 1
                                 For k = count to j + 1 by −1 do
                                      x(k) ← x(k − 1)
                                 x(j) ← new value
                            Return
```

The structure chart for the solution is shown next, along with the FORTRAN program.

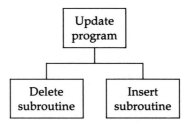

```
*-------------------------------------------------------------*
      PROGRAM  UPDATE
*
*  This program updates a computer access list.
*
      INTEGER   J, CODE, COUNT, OLD, NEW, SSN(500), LIMIT
      LOGICAL   DONE
*
      OPEN (UNIT=8,FILE='ACCESS',STATUS='OLD')
      OPEN (UNIT=9,FILE='NEWACCES',STATUS='NEW')
*
      DONE = .FALSE.
      LIMIT = 500
      J = 1
    5 IF (.NOT.DONE) THEN
          READ (8,*) SSN(J)
          IF (SSN(J).EQ.999999999) THEN
             DONE = .TRUE.
          ELSE
             J = J + 1
          ENDIF
          GO TO 5
      ENDIF
      COUNT = J
      DONE = .FALSE.
*
   10 IF (.NOT.DONE) THEN
          PRINT*, 'ENTER -1 FOR DELETION, 1 FOR INSERTION, ',
     +            '0 TO QUIT'
          READ*, CODE
          IF (CODE.EQ.-1) THEN
             PRINT*, 'ENTER SSN FOR DELETION'
             READ*, OLD
             CALL DELETE(OLD,COUNT,SSN)
          ELSEIF (CODE.EQ.1) THEN
             IF (COUNT.EQ.500) THEN
                PRINT*, 'LIST IS FULL - DO DELETIONS FIRST'
             ELSE
                PRINT*, 'ENTER SSN FOR INSERTION'
                READ*, NEW
                CALL INSERT(LIMIT,NEW,COUNT,SSN)
             ENDIF
          ELSE
             DONE = .TRUE.
          ENDIF
          GO TO 10
      ENDIF
*
      DO 15 J=1,COUNT
         WRITE (9,*) SSN(J)
   15 CONTINUE
*
      END
*-------------------------------------------------------------*
             DELETE subroutine from page 326 goes here
*-------------------------------------------------------------*
```

```
      SUBROUTINE  INSERT (LIMIT,NEW,COUNT,X)
*
*   This subroutine inserts an element in an ordered list.
*
      INTEGER  NEW, COUNT, X(LIMIT), J, K, LIMIT
      LOGICAL  DONE
*
      DONE = .FALSE.
      J = 1
    5 IF (.NOT.DONE) THEN
         IF (X(J).LT.NEW) THEN
            J = J + 1
         ELSE
            DONE = .TRUE.
         ENDIF
         GO TO 5
      ENDIF
*
      IF (X(J).EQ.NEW) THEN
         PRINT*, 'SSN ALREADY IN FILE'
      ELSE
         COUNT = COUNT + 1
         DO 10 K=COUNT,J+1,-1
            X(K) = X(K-1)
   10    CONTINUE
         X(J) = NEW
      ENDIF
*
      RETURN
      END
*-------------------------------------------------------------*
```

TESTING

Testing this program is much simpler since we used procedures that have already been tested independently. We know that the procedures work properly by themselves, so we can spend most of our testing time checking the interaction between the modules and the program. Of course, since we modified the insert procedure, it must be carefully tested again.

The terminal screen interaction and the input and output file contents from the hand example follow:

```
ENTER -1 FOR DELETION, 1 FOR INSERTION, 0 TO QUIT
1
ENTER SSN FOR INSERTION
122899823
ENTER -1 FOR DELETION, 1 FOR INSERTION, 0 TO QUIT
1
ENTER SSN FOR INSERTION
244448353
ENTER -1 FOR DELETION, 1 FOR INSERTION, 0 TO QUIT
1
ENTER SSN FOR INSERTION
595959591
ENTER -1 FOR DELETION, 1 FOR INSERTION, 0 TO QUIT
-1
ENTER SSN FOR DELETION
289129430
ENTER -1 FOR DELETION, 1 FOR INSERTION, 0 TO QUIT
0
```

File ACCESS	203294433
	289129430
	319330022
	450123452
	999999999
File NEWACCES	122899823
	203294433
	244448353
	319330022
	450123452
	595959591
	999999999

Note that the trailer signal was kept in the array along with the Social Security numbers. This was convenient because we always are inserting values within the array, instead of at the end of the array, since all values would be less than 999999999. Also, by including it in the list of values, it is automatically written to the data file at the end of the program.

7-6 COMMON BLOCKS

As you modularize your programs, you will find that the argument lists can become lengthy as you pass more and more data to functions and subroutines. FORTRAN allows you to set up a block of memory that is accessible, or common, to the main program and to all its subprograms — a *common block*. The variables in this block of memory do not have to be passed through argument lists and cannot be used as arguments in subprograms.

FORTRAN allows two types of common blocks: *blank common* and *named common*. Blank common is set up with the specification statement shown:

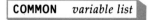

> **COMMON**   *variable list*

Each subprogram that uses data in this common block must also contain a COMMON statement. Although the data names do not have to match in every subprogram, the type and order of the names are important. Consider these COMMON statements from a main program and a subprogram, respectively:

```
PROGRAM   TEST1
INTEGER   J
REAL   A, B, X, Y
COMMON   A, J, B
      .
      .
      .
CALL ANSWR(X,Y)
      .
      .
      .
END
SUBROUTINE   ANSWR(X,Y)
INTEGER   KTOT
REAL   TEMP, SUM, X, Y
COMMON   TEMP, KTOT, SUM
      .
      .
      .
END
```

In these statements, the main program communicates with the subroutine using two arguments, X and Y. In addition, the main program and the subroutine share a memory area. A and TEMP represent the same memory location; J and KTOT represent the same memory location; and B and SUM represent the same memory location, as shown in the following diagram below

Common Memory Area

A	57.63	TEMP
J	−25	KTOT
B	0.007	SUM

Named common, also referred to as *labeled common,* is established if the list of variable names in the COMMON statement is preceded by a name enclosed in slashes:

COMMON   /*name*/ *variable list*

The purpose of establishing different blocks of common with unique names is to allow subprograms to refer to the named common block with which they wish to share data without listing all the other variables in the other common blocks.

For example, one group of variables may be used in a set of computations, and another group of variables may be used in generating graphs to be plotted. The first group of variables could comprise one common area named CALC, and the other group of variables could comprise another common area named GRAPH. Both named COMMON statements appear in the main program; then individual subprograms include either or both named COMMON statements depending on the variables they need to access. The argument lists for the individual subprograms include other input and output variables that are not in the common areas. A variable cannot appear in more than one block of named common, and thus a variable could not appear in both the CALC and GRAPH common blocks; if the variable is needed in the computations and the graphics, it should be passed through the argument list of the subprograms or in a third named common block.

Arrays may be included in the COMMON statement. The COMMON statement can be used to define the storage for these arrays as shown:

```
COMMON   X(50), INCOME(4)
```

An array size can be specified in the COMMON statement, as shown in the previous statement, or it can be specified in an explicit type statement as in

```
INTEGER   SUM
REAL   TIME(25), DIST(25)
COMMON   SUM, TIME, DIST
```

The size of an array cannot be specified in both a type statement and a COMMON statement.

Variables in blank common cannot be initialized with DATA statements. They can be initialized with READ statements or assignment statements. Variables in named common can be initialized with READ statements, assignment statements, or with a special subprogram called a BLOCK DATA subprogram. This subprogram is nonexecutable and serves only to assign initial values to variables in a named common block. An example of a BLOCK DATA subprogram to initialize two named common blocks is

```
BLOCK DATA
COMMON   /EXPER1/ TEMP(100)
COMMON   /EXPER2/ TIME, DIST, VEL(10)
DATA   TEMP, TIME, DIST, VEL /100*0.0, 50.5, 0.5, 10*0.0/
END
```

Both of the COMMON statements must be in the main program. Either or both of the statements also appear in any subprogram that uses variables in these common blocks of memory.

Unless extremely large amounts of data must be passed to subprograms, the use of common blocks is discouraged because they weaken the independence of modules; the module can be affected not only by its arguments but also by variables in common. If you do use common blocks, pay attention to the order of the variables on all COMMON statements. Also look for omitted variables; if a variable is left out of a COMMON statement in a subprogram, incorrect values are used for all variables following it in the COMMON statement. These errors can cause problems that are difficult to locate.

SUMMARY

The subroutine is a subprogram that allows us to return multiple values to the main program, such as when we want to sort an array, or to return no values to the main program, such as when we want to print an error message. Functions and other subroutines can also call a subroutine, in addition to the main program. The subroutine, along with the function, allows us to structure our programs by breaking them into modules that can be written and tested independently of each other. Not only do programs become simpler, but the same module can also be used in other programs without retesting. In this chapter we developed subroutines that are useful in many applications — a sort routine, an insert routine, and a delete routine.

DEBUGGING AIDS

Subroutine testing, like function testing, is the same as program testing: It generally involves writing a special main program or driver to initialize values and call the subroutine. The specific guides that we enumerate refer to the argument list, which is the link between the subroutine and the main program:

1. In general, use the argument list to pass information back and forth between the program and the subroutine, as opposed to using common blocks.
2. Be sure that the variables or expressions listed in the argument list match in type and in order the argument list in the SUBROUTINE statement.
3. Include all variables in the subroutine in type statements to avoid incorrect default typing.
4. Use PRINT statements in the subroutine for debugging, just as you do in the main program.
5. Test each subroutine separately before combining it in a program with other subprograms.
6. Test each of the subroutines with several sets of data to check any special conditions.

Separating a long program into modules that transfer control smoothly from one to another becomes easier with practice. Although different sets of subprograms may solve the same problem, some choices are more logical and readable than others; these are the solutions that you want to develop. Once you have selected a segment that is to be made into a subroutine, you must decide what arguments are needed. Listed are a few style suggestions to keep in mind as you make these decisions:

1. Choose descriptive names for your subroutines.
2. Use comments in the subroutines as you would in the program. In particular, use comments at the beginning of a subroutine to describe its purpose and to define its arguments, if necessary.
3. For clarity, use the same variables in the argument list of the subroutine as those used in the main program, if possible. If the subroutine is called several times with different arguments, choose completely different variable names in the subroutine to avoid confusion with variables in the main program.
4. List input parameters before output parameters in the argument list.

KEY WORDS

blank common	named common
BLOCK DATA subprogram	software tools
common block	subroutine
deletion	user-friendly
insertion	user interface

PROBLEMS

We begin our problem set with modifications to programs developed earlier in this chapter. Give the decomposition, refined pseudocode or flowchart, and FORTRAN solution for each problem.

Problems 1–5 modify the program SIGGEN, given on page 310, which generated a data file composed of a sine wave plus random noise.

1. Modify the signal generating program so that it increments the time by 0.25 instead of 0.01.
2. Modify the signal generating program so that it reads the time increment from the terminal.

3. Modify the signal generating program so that it reads the number of data points that are to be generated from the terminal, instead of generating 101 points.

4. Modify the signal generating program so that it multiplies the noise value generated by the random number generator by a constant that is read from the terminal.

5. Modify the signal generating program so that it adds the noise value to a cosine, instead of a sine wave.

For problems 6–10 modify the program STREAM, given on page 317, which determines the maximum oxygen deficit for each stream in a data file.

6. Modify the oxygen deficit program so that it determines the minimum oxygen deficit for each stream in a data file.

7. Modify the oxygen deficit program so that it determines the maximum oxygen deficit for each stream in a data file using 0.25 day increments.

8. Modify the oxygen deficit program so that it determines the maximum oxygen deficit for each stream in a data file using a daily increment that is entered from the terminal.

9. Modify the oxygen deficit program so that it determines the overall maximum oxygen deficit for the group of streams in a data file, and prints this maximum at the end of the summary.

10. Modify the oxygen deficit program so that it determines the maximum oxygen deficit for each stream in a data file and prints the day on which it occurred as an integer, instead of a real number. Thus, if the maximum deficit occurred at day 2.8, the program would indicate that it occurred on day 2.

For problems 11–15 modify the program UPDATE, given on page 334, which updates a computer access list.

11. Modify the computer access program so that it writes the number of additions and deletions performed by the program on the terminal screen before exiting the program.

12. Modify the computer access program so that it writes the number of valid users in the access file on the terminal screen before exiting the program.

13. Modify the computer access program so that it writes the number of valid users in the original access file on the terminal screen before beginning the update process.

14. Modify the computer access program so that it assumes that the access file is in descending order instead of ascending order and has a trailer value of zero.

15. Modify the computer access program so that it prints a report that lists all the valid access numbers after the access list is updated.

For problems 16–21, assume that TIME, a one-dimensional array of 100 real values, has already been filled with data.

16. Write a subroutine to determine the maximum value in the array TIME and to subtract that value from each value in the array.

17. Write a subroutine to determine the minimum value in the array TIME and to add that value to each value in the array.

18. Write a subroutine to replace each negative value in the array TIME with 0.0.

19. Write a subroutine to determine the average of the values in the array TIME. Add 1.0 to all values above the average; subtract 1.0 from all values below the average.

20. Write a subroutine to replace all values in the array TIME with the absolute value of the corresponding value.

21. Write a subroutine to return a logical value of true if all the values in the array TIME are zero; otherwise, the values returned should be false.

For problems 22–25, assume that Z, a two-dimensional array with 5 rows and 4 columns of real values, has already been filled with data.

22. Write a subroutine that fills an array W (the same size as Z) with the absolute value of the corresponding element in Z.

23. Write a subroutine that fills an array W (the same size as Z) with a value based on the corresponding element in Z, where

$$W(I,J) = 0.0 \qquad \text{if } Z(I,J) = 0$$
$$W(I,J) = -1.0 \qquad \text{if } Z(I,J) < 0$$
$$W(I,J) = 1.0 \qquad \text{if } Z(I,J) > 0$$

24. Write a subroutine that fills an array W (the same size as Z) in the following manner: W should contain the same values of Z unless the corresponding values in Z are greater than the average value of Z. In these cases, the corresponding value of W should contain the average value of Z.

25. Write a subroutine that fills an array W (the same size as Z) with numbers such that each element of W is the corresponding value of Z rounded up to the next multiple of 10. Thus, 10.76 rounds to 20.0; 18.7 rounds to 20.0; 0.05 rounds to 10.0; 10.0 rounds to 10.0; and −5.76 rounds to 0.0.

Develop these programs and subroutines. Use the five-phase design process.

26. Write a subroutine called RANGE that receives an integer array with 50 elements and returns the maximum and minimum values.

27. Write a subroutine that reads a group of test measurements from a data file until it finds a negative measurement. The subroutine should return the number of test measurements read before the negative value was encoun-

tered and the average of those test measurements. Assume that the data file has been opened and assigned to unit 12.

28. Write a subroutine that computes the average, the variance, and the standard deviation of an array X of 100 data values. Use the following formulas:

$$\text{Average} \qquad \overline{X} = \frac{\sum\limits_{i=1}^{100} X_i}{100}$$

$$\text{Variance} \qquad \sigma^2 = \frac{\sum\limits_{i=1}^{100} (\overline{X} - X_i)^2}{99}$$

$$\text{Standard deviation} \qquad \sigma = \sqrt{\sigma^2}$$

29. Rewrite the subroutine in problem 28 so that it computes the average, variance, and standard deviation for an array with 500 values. Assume that N contains the number of actual values in the array. The denominator of the expression for the variance should then be $N - 1$, instead of 99.

30. Write a subroutine called BIAS that is called with the following statement:

$$\text{CALL BIAS(X,Y,N)}$$

where X is an input array of 200 real values; N is an integer that specifies how many of the values represent actual data values; and Y is an output array the same size as X whose values should be the values of X with the minimum value of the X array subtracted from each one. For example,

if $X =$
10
2
36
8

, then $Y =$
8
0
34
6

Thus, the minimum value of Y is always zero. (This operation is referred to as removing the bias in X or adjusting for bias in X.)

FORTRAN STATEMENT SUMMARY

Blank COMMON Statement:

COMMON *variable list*

Example:

COMMON   A, B, X(100)

Discussion:
The blank COMMON statement defines variables that are stored in a block of memory accessible to all subprograms that also contain the COMMON statement, without the variables being listed as arguments in the subprograms.

BLOCK DATA Statement:

BLOCK DATA

Discussion:
The BLOCK DATA statement is the first statement in a BLOCK DATA subprogram. This subprogram contains only DATA statements and is used to initialize variables in common blocks.

CALL Statement:

CALL *subroutine name (argument list)*

Examples:

CALL MERGE(X,Y)

CALL ERROR

Discussion:
The CALL statement is used to transfer control to a subroutine. The inputs and outputs to the subroutine must be listed in the argument list and must match in type and in number those used in the SUBROUTINE statement.

Labeled COMMON Statement:

COMMON   /*name*/ *variable list*

Example:

COMMON   /REPORT/ DATE, PAGENO, TOTAL

Discussion:
The labeled COMMON statement allows us to define several blocks of memory available to subprograms. The subprogram must include the labeled COMMON statement that contains the variables to be used in that subprogram. The main program must include all labeled COMMON statements.

SUBROUTINE Statement:

SUBROUTINE   *name (argument list)*

Examples:

SUBROUTINE   SORT(A,B,N)

SUBROUTINE   HEADING

Discussion:

The SUBROUTINE statement assigns a name to a subroutine and lists the arguments that represent the input and output for the subroutine.

APPLICATION — Cryptography (Computer Science/Engineering)

Computers are widely used in *cryptography*, the encoding and decoding of information to prevent unauthorized use. Codes range from simple codes (one character represents another character) to complicated codes (multiple character substitutions). A key specifies the substitutions being used. This key is generally required to decode the information. Write a program to help decipher an encoded message without the key. (See Section 8–2 for the solution.)

8

ADDITIONAL DATA TYPES

INTRODUCTION

This chapter presents three data types: character, double precision, and complex. The character data type allows us to read and analyze character data such as names and addresses. With double-precision data, we can process numeric data more precisely than we could using previously discussed data types. With complex data, we can represent data as numbers that have a real portion and an imaginary portion. Although we don't use these data types routinely, they are special features of FORTRAN that help make it a powerful language for engineering and scientific applications.

8-1 CHARACTER DATA

In Chapter 1 we learned that computers use binary languages, an internal notation composed of 0's and 1's. Integers and real numbers are converted to binary numbers when they are used in a computer. If you study computer hardware or computer architecture, you learn how to convert values such as 56 and −13.25 to binary numbers — to use FORTRAN, however, it is not necessary to learn this conversion.

Characters also must be converted into binary form to be used in the computer; they are converted to *binary strings*, which are also series of 0's and 1's. Several codes convert character information to binary strings, but most computers use EBCDIC (Extended Binary Coded Decimal Interchange Code) or ASCII (American Standard Code for Information Interchange). In these codes, each character is represented by a binary string. Table 8–1 contains a few characters and their EBCDIC and ASCII equivalents.

TABLE 8-1 Binary Character Codes

CHARACTER	ASCII	EBCDIC
A	1000001	11000001
H	1001000	11001000
Y	1011001	11101000
3	0110011	11110011
+	0101011	01001110
$	0100100	01011011
=	0111101	01111110

You do not need to use the character binary codes to use the characters in your FORTRAN programs. However, you must be aware that the computer stores characters differently than the numbers used in arithmetic computations; that is, the integer number 5 and the character 5 are not stored the same. Thus, it is not possible to use arithmetic operations with character data even if the characters represent numbers.

We often refer to character data as character strings because we usually refer to groups or lists of characters that go together. For example, a city is usually given one variable name instead of a variable name for each letter in the city's name. Using character strings in FORTRAN is similar to using numeric data. We can have character string constants that always represent the same information. Character string variables have names and represent character strings that may remain constant or may change. Generally, these character string constants and variables contain characters from the FORTRAN character set, which is composed of the 26 alphabetic letters, the 10 numeric digits, a blank, and the following 12 symbols:

$$+ \ - \ * \ / \ = \ (\ ) \ , \ . \ ' \ \$ \ :$$

If other symbols are used, a program may not execute the same way on one computer as it does on another.

Character constants are always enclosed in apostrophes. These apostrophes are not counted when determining the length or number of characters in a constant. If 2 consecutive apostrophes (not a double quotation mark) are encountered within a character constant, they represent a single apostrophe. For example, the character constant for the word LET'S is 'LET''s'. The following list gives several examples of character constants and their corresponding lengths:

Constant	Length
'SENSOR 23'	9 characters
'TIME AND DISTANCE'	17 characters
' $ AMT.'	7 characters
' '	2 characters
'08:40-13:25'	11 characters
''''''	2 characters

A character string variable must always be defined with a specification statement whose general form is

CHARACTER*n variable list

where n represents the number of characters in the variable string. For instance, the statement

CHARACTER*8 CODE, NAME

identifies CODE and NAME as variables containing 8 characters each. Unlike numeric variable names, there is no significance to the first letter of a character variable's name. A variation of the CHARACTER statement allows you to specify character strings of different lengths in the same statement, as shown:

$$\text{CHARACTER} \quad \text{TITLE*10, STATE*2}$$

An array that contains characters can be defined as

$$\text{CHARACTER*4} \quad \text{NAME(50)}$$

or

$$\text{CHARACTER} \quad \text{NAME(50)*4}$$

The preceding specifications reserve memory for 50 elements in the array NAME, where each element contains 4 characters. A reference to NAME(18) references the character string that is the eighteenth element of the array, and it contains 4 characters.

Character strings can also be used as arguments in subprograms in which they must be specified in a CHARACTER statement in both the main program and in the subprogram. A subprogram can specify a character string without giving a specific length, as shown:

$$\text{CHARACTER*(*)} \quad \text{STRING}$$

This technique is similar to specifying the length of an array with an integer variable, as in

$$\text{INTEGER} \quad \text{SSN(N)}$$

It is also possible to define in a subprogram an array of N variables, each of which contains a character string. To make the character string more flexible, its length does not have to be specified in the CHARACTER statement. We use the following statement in the subprogram to accomplish this flexibility:

$$\text{CHARACTER*(*)} \quad \text{NAME(N)}$$

We discuss special operations and intrinsic functions for character strings later in this section. First, we illustrate how to use character strings in our input and output statements.

CHARACTER I/O

When a character string is used in a list-directed output statement, the entire character string is printed. Blanks are automatically inserted around the character string to separate it from other output on the same line. When a character string variable is used in a list-directed input statement, the corresponding data value must be enclosed in apostrophes. If the character string within the apostrophes is longer than the defined length of the character string variable, any extra characters to the right are ignored; if the character string within the apostrophes is shorter than the length of the character string variable, the extra positions to the right are automatically filled with blanks. In either instance, the character data is left-justified in the character string variable. To print a character string in a formatted output statement, we use A as the corresponding format specification to print the entire string.

EXAMPLE 8-1 Character I/O

Write a complete FORTRAN program to read an item description from the terminal and then print the description. Assume that the length of the description is no more than 20 characters.

Solution

Even though this is a simple program, we still use the decomposition and stepwise refinement method for developing the solution.

DECOMPOSITION

| Read description. |
| Print description. |

The following refinement indicates the conversation with the user.

REFINEMENT IN PSEUDOCODE

```
OUTPUT: Print message to user to enter description
        Read description
        Print description
```

Translating these steps into FORTRAN results in the following program:

FORTRAN PROGRAM

```
*------------------------------------------------------*
      PROGRAM   OUTPUT
*
*   This program reads and prints an item description.
*
      CHARACTER*20   ITEM
*
      PRINT*, 'ENTER ITEM DESCRIPTION IN APOSTROPHES'
      READ*, ITEM
      PRINT 5, ITEM
    5 FORMAT(1X,'ITEM DESCRIPTION IS ',A)
      END
*------------------------------------------------------*
```

A typical interaction when running this program is

```
ENTER ITEM DESCRIPTION IN APOSTROPHES
'COMPUTER MODEM'
ITEM DESCRIPTION IS COMPUTER MODEM
```

Note that the data entered was not 20 characters long. In this example, the padding of blanks on the end is not noticeable with the output; however, if the output FORMAT had been

```
      FORMAT(1X,A,' IS THE ITEM DESCRIPTION')
```

the interaction would have the following appearance:

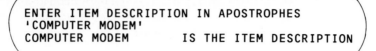

```
ENTER ITEM DESCRIPTION IN APOSTROPHES
'COMPUTER MODEM'
COMPUTER MODEM        IS THE ITEM DESCRIPTION
```

Another interaction that could come from the original program is

```
ENTER ITEM DESCRIPTION IN APOSTROPHES
'DIGITAL OSCILLOSCOPE WITH MEMORY'
ITEM DESCRIPTION IS DIGITAL OSCILLOSCOPE
```

In this case, the name exceeded the maximum number of characters specified for the description, thus part of the data was lost. To avoid this situation, carefully choose the length of your character variables based on the maximum length that you expect. You can also tell the program user what length you are expecting. In this example, you could use the following pair of PRINT statements:

```
PRINT*, 'ENTER ITEM DESCRIPTION IN APOSTROPHES'
PRINT*, '(MAXIMUM OF 20 CHARACTERS)'
```

CHARACTER OPERATIONS

Although character strings cannot be used in arithmetic computations, we can assign values to character strings, compare two character strings, extract a substring of a character string, and combine two character strings into one longer character string.

Assign Values Values can be assigned to character variables with the assignment statement and a character constant. The following statements initialize a character string array RANK with the 5 abbreviations for freshman, sophomore, junior, senior, and graduate:

```
CHARACTER*2  RANK(5)
RANK(1) = 'FR'
RANK(2) = 'SO'
RANK(3) = 'JR'
RANK(4) = 'SR'
RANK(5) = 'GR'
```

If a character constant in an assignment statement is shorter in length than the character variable, blanks are added to the right of the constant. If the following statement were executed, RANK(1) would contain the letter F followed by a blank:

```
RANK(1) = 'F'
```

That is, an equivalent statement would be

```
RANK(1) = 'F '
```

If a character constant in an assignment statement is longer than the character variable, the excess characters on the right are ignored. Thus, the following statement,

```
RANK(1) = 'FRESHMAN'
```

would store the letters FR in the character array element RANK(1). These examples emphasize the importance of using character strings that are the same length as the variables used to store them; otherwise, the statements can be misleading.

One character string variable can also be used to initialize another character string variable, as shown:

```
CHARACTER*4  GRADE1, GRADE2
GRADE1 = 'GOOD'
GRADE2 = GRADE1
```

Both variables, GRADE1 and GRADE2, contain the character string 'GOOD'.

Character strings can be initialized with DATA statements. The preceding examples can be performed with DATA statements, as shown:

```
CHARACTER  RANK(5)*2, GRADE1*4, GRADE2*4
DATA  RANK, GRADE1, GRADE2 /'FR', 'SO', 'JR', 'SR',
+                            'GR', 2*'GOOD'/
```

Compare Values An IF statement can be used to compare character strings. Assuming that the variable DEPT and the array CH are character strings, the following are valid statements:

```
IF (DEPT.EQ.'EECE') KT = KT + 1

IF (CH(I).GT.CH(I+1)) THEN
    CALL SWITCH(I,CH)
    CALL PRINT(CH)
ENDIF
```

To evaluate a logical expression using character strings, first look at the length of the two strings. If one string is shorter than the other, add blanks to the right of the shorter string so that you can proceed with the evaluation using strings of equal length.

The comparison of two character strings of the same length is made from left to right, one character at a time. Two strings must have exactly the same characters in the same order to be equal.

A *collating sequence* lists characters from the lowest to the highest value. Partial collating sequences for EBCDIC and ASCII are given in Table 8–2. Although the ordering is not exactly the same, some similarities include

1. Capital letters are in order from A to Z.
2. Digits are in order from 0 to 9.
3. Capital letters and digits do not overlap; digits either precede letters or letters precede digits.
4. The blank character is less than any letter or number. When necessary for clarity, we use ∅ to represent a blank.

TABLE 8-2 Partial Collating Sequences for Characters

ASCII
ƀ " # $ % & ( ) * + , — . /
0 1 2 3 4 5 6 7 8 9
: ; = ? @
A B C D E F G H I J K L M N O P Q R S T U V W X Y Z

EBCDIC
ƀ . (+ & $ *) ; — / , % ? : # @ = "
A B C D E F G H I J K L M N O P Q R S T U V W X Y Z
0 1 2 3 4 5 6 7 8 9

Several pairs of character strings are now listed, along with their correct relationships:

$$
\begin{array}{rcl}
\text{'A1'} & < & \text{'A2'} \\
\text{'JOHN'} & < & \text{'JOHNSTON'} \\
\text{'176'} & < & \text{'177'} \\
\text{'THREE'} & < & \text{'TWO'} \\
\text{'\$'} & < & \text{'DOLLAR'}
\end{array}
$$

If character strings contain only letters, their ordering is alphabetical — a *lexicographic* ordering.

Extract Substrings A *substring* of a character string is any string that represents a subset of the original string and maintains the original order. The following list contains all substrings of the string 'FORTRAN':

```
'F'  'FO'  'FOR'  'FORT'  'FORTR'  'FORTRA'  'FORTRAN'
'O'  'OR'  'ORT'  'ORTR'  'ORTRA'  'ORTRAN'
'R'  'RT'  'RTR'  'RTRA'  'RTRAN'
'T'  'TR'  'TRA'  'TRAN'
'R'  'RA'  'RAN'
'A'  'AN'
'N'
```

Substrings are referenced by using the name of the character string, followed by two integer expressions in parentheses, separated by a colon. The first expression in parentheses gives the position in the original string of the beginning of the substring; the second expression gives the position of the end of the substring. If the string 'FORTRAN' is stored in a variable LANG, some of its substring references are as shown:

REFERENCE	SUBSTRING
LANG(1:1)	'F'
LANG(1:7)	'FORTRAN'
LANG(2:3)	'OR'
LANG(7:7)	'N'

If the first expression in parentheses is omitted, the substring begins at the beginning of the string; thus, LANG(:4) refers to the substring 'FORT'. If the second expression in parentheses is omitted, the substring ends at the end of the string; thus, LANG(5:) refers to the substring 'RAN'.

The substring operation cannot operate correctly if the beginning and ending positions are not integers, are negative, or contain values greater than the number of characters in the substring. The ending position must also be greater than or equal to the beginning position of the substring.

The substring operator is a powerful tool, as the next two examples illustrate.

EXAMPLE 8-2   Propane-Heated Balloons

All aircraft including hot air balloons are assigned registration numbers by the Federal Aviation Agency. A new registration system for balloons has been proposed in which the registration number is a character string of 7 characters. The fifth character specifies balloon type: P, for propane-heated; S, for solar-heated; and H, for helium- or hydrogen-filled. Write a segment of FORTRAN code that counts the number of propane-heated hot air balloons using a character array of 500 registration numbers.

Solution

We need a loop to step through the array, checking each balloon registration number. We increment our count if the fifth character in the registration number is the letter P:

```
CHARACTER*7  REGNUM(500)
INTEGER  COUNT, I
DATA  COUNT /0/
   .
   .
   .
DO 10 I=1,500
    IF (REGNUM(I)(5:5).EQ.'P') COUNT = COUNT + 1
10 CONTINUE
```

EXAMPLE 8-3   Character Count

A string of 50 characters contains encoded information. The number of occurrences of the letter S represents a special piece of information. Write a loop that counts the number of occurrences of the letter S.

Solution

The loop index is used with the substring operator to allow us to test each character in the string:

```
CHARACTER*50  CODE
INTEGER  COUNT, I
DATA  COUNT /0/
        .
        .
        .
DO 20 I=1,50
    IF (CODE(I:I).EQ.'S') COUNT = COUNT + 1
20 CONTINUE
```

A reference to a substring can be used anywhere that a string can be used. For instance, if LANG contains the character string 'FORTRAN', the following statement changes the value of LANG to 'FORMATS':

```
LANG(4:7) = 'MATS'
```

If LANG contains 'FORMATS', the following statement changes the value of LANG to 'FORMASS':

```
LANG(6:6) = LANG(7:7)
```

When modifying a substring of a character string with a substring of the same character string, the substrings must not overlap: that is, do not use LANG(2:4) to replace LANG(3:5). Also, recall that if a substring is being moved into a smaller string, only as many characters as are needed to replace the smaller string are moved from left to right; if the substring is being moved into a larger string, the extra positions on the right are filled with blanks.

Combine Strings *Concatenation* is the operation of combining two or more character strings into one character string. It is indicated by two slashes between the character strings to be combined. The following expression concatenates the constants 'WORK' and 'ED' into one string constant 'WORKED':

```
'WORK'//'ED'
```

The next statement combines the contents of three character string variables MO, DA, and YR into one character string and then moves the combined string into a variable called DATE:

```
DATE = MO//DA//YR
```

If MO = '05', DA = '15', and YR = '86', then DATE = '051586'. Because concatenation represents an operation, it cannot appear on the left-hand side of an equal sign.

CHARACTER INTRINSIC FUNCTIONS

A number of intrinsic functions are designed for use with character strings:

INDEX locates specific substrings within a given character string.

LEN determines the length of a string and is used primarily in subroutines and functions that have character string arguments.

CHAR and ICHAR determine the position of a character in the collating sequence of the computer.

LGE, LGT, LLE, and LLT allow comparisons to be made based on the ASCII collating sequence, regardless of the collating sequence of the computer.

INDEX The INDEX function has two arguments, both of which are character strings. The function returns an integer value giving the position in the first string of the second string. Thus, if STRGA contains the phrase 'TO BE OR NOT TO BE', INDEX(STRGA,'BE') returns the value 4, which points to the first occurrence of the string 'BE'. To find the second occurrence of the string, we can use the following statements:

```
CHARACTER*18   STRGA
      .
      .
      .
K = INDEX(STRGA,'BE')
J = INDEX(STRGA(K+1:),'BE') + K
```

After execution, K would contain the value 4 and J would contain the value 17. (Note that we had to add K to the second reference of INDEX because the second use referred to the substring 'E OR NOT TO BE'; without K, the second INDEX reference would return a value of 13, not 17. The value of INDEX(STRGA,'AND') would be 0 because the second string 'AND' does not occur in the first string STRGA.)

LEN The input to the function LEN is a character string; the output is an integer that contains the length of the character string. This function is useful in a subprogram that accepts character strings of any length but needs the actual length within the subprogram. The statement in the subprogram that allows a character string to be used with any length is

```
CHARACTER*(*)   A, B, STRGA
```

This form can be used only in subprograms. Example 8-4 uses both the LEN function and the variable string length parameter in a subprogram.

EXAMPLE 8-4   Frequency of Blanks

Write a function subprogram that accepts a character string and returns a count of the number of blanks in the string.

Solution

To make this function flexible, we write it so that it can be used with any size character string:

```
*-------------------------------------------------------------*
      INTEGER FUNCTION  BLANKS(X)
*
*  This function counts the number
*  of blanks in a character string X.
*
      INTEGER  I
      CHARACTER*(*)  X
*
      BLANKS = 0
      DO 10 I=1,LEN(X)
         IF (X(I:I).EQ.' ') BLANKS = BLANKS + 1
   10 CONTINUE
*
      RETURN
      END
*-------------------------------------------------------------*
```

Character strings may also be used in user-written subroutines. In Example 8–5, we write a subroutine that combines input character strings into an output character string.

EXAMPLE 8–5 Name Editing

Write a subroutine that receives 3 character strings, FIRST, MIDDLE, and LAST, each containing 15 characters. The output of the subroutine is a character string 35 characters long that contains the first name followed by 1 blank, the middle initial followed by a period and 1 blank, and the last name. Assume that FIRST, MIDDLE, and LAST have no leading blanks and no embedded blanks. Thus, if

```
        FIRST = 'JOSEPH         '
        MIDDLE = 'CHARLES        '
        LAST = 'LAWTON         '
```

then

```
    NAME = 'JOSEPH C. LAWTON                   '
```

Solution

The solution to this problem is simplified by the use of the substring operation that allows us to look at individual characters and the INDEX function that is used to find the end of the first name. We move to NAME the characters in FIRST, then a blank, the middle initial, a period, another blank, and the last name. As you go through the solution, observe the use of the concatenation operation. Also, note that the move of the first name fills the rest of the character string NAME with blanks because FIRST is shorter than the field to which it is moved:

```
*--------------------------------------------------------*
*       SUBROUTINE  EDIT(FIRST,MIDDLE,LAST,NAME)
*
*  This subroutine edits a name to the form
*  first, middle initial, last.
*
        INTEGER  L
        CHARACTER*15  FIRST, MIDDLE, LAST
        CHARACTER*35  NAME
*
*  MOVE FIRST NAME
*
        NAME = FIRST
*
*  MOVE MIDDLE INITIAL
*
        L = INDEX(NAME,' ')
        NAME(L:L+3) = ' '//MIDDLE(1:1)//'. '
*
*  MOVE LAST NAME
*
        NAME(L+4:) = LAST
*
        RETURN
        END
*--------------------------------------------------------*
```

CHAR, ICHAR These functions refer to the collating sequence used in the computer. If a computer has 50 characters in its collating sequence, these characters are numbered from 0 to 49. For example, assume that the letter A corresponds to position 12. The function CHAR has an integer argument that specifies the position of a desired character in the collating sequence. The function returns the character in the specified position. The following statements print the character A:

```
        N = 12
        PRINT*, CHAR(N)
```

The ICHAR function is the inverse of the CHAR function. The argument to the ICHAR function is a character variable that contains one character. The function returns an integer that gives the position of the character in the collating sequence. Thus, the output of the following statements is the number 12:

```
        CHARACTER*1  INFO
        INFO = 'A'
        PRINT*, ICHAR(INFO)
```

Because different computers have different collating sequences, these functions can be used to determine the position of certain characters in the collating sequence.

EXAMPLE 8-6 Collating Sequence

Print each character in the FORTRAN character set along with its position in the collating sequence on your computer. The FORTRAN character set is given on page 349.

Solution

Note the use of the substring operator in initializing the character set:

```
*----------------------------------------------------------*
      PROGRAM  SEQNCE
*
*  This program prints the position in the collating
*  sequence of each FORTRAN character.
*
      CHARACTER*49  SET
*
      SET(1:26) = 'ABCDEFGHIJKLMNOPQRSTUVWXYZ'
      SET(27:36) = '0123456789'
      SET(37:49) = ' +-*/=(),.''$:'
*
      DO 10 I=1,49
         PRINT*, SET(I:I), ICHAR(SET(I:I))
   10 CONTINUE
*
      END
*----------------------------------------------------------*
```

Why did we put two apostrophes in the assignment for SET(37:49)? Remember that two apostrophes are converted into a single apostrophe when they are in a literal. If you have several computers available, run this program on each of them to see if they all use the same collating sequence for the FORTRAN character set.

LGE, LGT, LLE, LLT This set of functions allows you to compare character strings based on the ASCII collating sequence. These functions become useful if a program is going to be used on a number of different computers and is using character comparisons or character sorts. The functions represent a logical value, true or false. Each function has two character string arguments, STRG1 and STRG2. The function reference LGE(STRG1,STRG2) is true if STRG1 is lexically greater than or equal to STRG2; thus, if STRG1 comes after STRG2 in an alphabetical sort, this function reference is true. Remember, these functions are based on an ASCII collating sequence regardless of the sequence being used on the computer. The functions LGT, LLE, and LLT perform comparisons "lexically greater than," "lexically less than or equal to," and "lexically less than."

EXAMPLE 8-7 ASCII Sort

In a sort based on the collating sequence in a computer, we perform the following steps, where STRG represents a character array:

```
IF (STRG(I).GT.STRG(I+1)) THEN
   TEMP = STRG(I)
   STRG(I) = STRG(I+1)
   STRG(I+1) = TEMP
   SORTED = .FALSE.
ENDIF
```

Rewrite this loop so the switch of character strings occurs based on an ASCII collating sequence even if the computer does not use an ASCII code.

Solution

The solution involves replacing the character comparison with the character intrinsic function LGT:

```
IF (LGT(STRG(I),STRG(I+1))) THEN
    TEMP = STRG(I)
    STRG(I) = STRG(I+1)
    STRG(I+1) = TEMP
    SORTED = .FALSE.
ENDIF
```

SELF-TEST 8-1

This self-test allows you to check quickly to see if you have remembered some of the key points from Section 8-1. If you have any problems with the exercises, you should reread this section. The solutions are included at the end of the text.

For problems 1–10, give the substring referred to in each reference. Assume that a character string of length 25 called TITLE has been initialized with the statements:

```
CHARACTER*25  TITLE
TITLE = 'CONSERVATION OF ENERGY'
```

1. TITLE(1:25)
2. TITLE(1:12)
3. TITLE(13:23)
4. TITLE(16:16)
5. TITLE(17:)
6. TITLE(:12)
7. TITLE(:)
8. TITLE//'LAW'
9. TITLE(1:7)//'E'//TITLE(16:)
10. ''''//TITLE(1:4)//'ID'//TITLE(19:20)//'ATE'//''''

In problems 11–16, WORD is a character string of length 6. What is stored in WORD after each of the following statements?

11. WORD = 'DENSITY'
12. WORD = 'AREA'
13. WORD = 'CAN''T'
14. WORD = '''''''!'
15. WORD = 'FT'//'/SEC'
16. WORD = ' VOLUME'

8–2 APPLICATION — CRYPTOGRAPHY (Computer Science/Engineering)

Computers not only can encode and decode messages for a specific code, but they also can attempt to break unknown codes. One simple test used to analyze a code is to count the number of occurrences of each character in a coded message. In English text, the most common letter is the letter "e." If a code simply substitutes one letter for another, then the most frequently used letter is likely to be the letter e. Obviously, more complicated codes are more difficult to analyze.

In this application, we write a program to read a coded message and to count the number of occurrences of each of the vowels, a, e, i, o, and u. We then compare the number of occurrences using a bar graph. This program allows us to use characters for input data and also for printing the bar graph. Before we discuss the solution, we develop a subroutine for generating a bar graph. (The development of this subroutine is the main interest of this section. The program is just an extension of Example 8–4.)

Bar graphs are used frequently to compare a set of data points. For instance, a company with an 8-person sales staff can compare monthly sales in a bar graph, as shown:

We cannot draw lines such as these on the printer or on the terminal screen (unless the terminal is a graphics terminal), but we can make the bars with characters such as asterisks. We can develop a subroutine to print a bar graph from a set of data. The input to the subroutine is an array of numeric values. The procedure uses these values to generate and print a bar graph.

We begin by looking at a simple case. Suppose the data numbers are 1, 4, 2, and 3. We could then print a bar with 1 asterisk, with 4 asterisks, and so on, generating a pattern that represents a horizontal bar graph:

```
*
****
**
***
```

If the numbers were in an array NUM, this bar graph could be printed with the following statements:

```
DIMENSION  NUM(4)
CHARACTER*4  BAR
DATA  BAR /'****'/
   .
   .
   .
DO 10 I=1,4
    PRINT*, BAR(1:NUM(I))
10 CONTINUE
```

The value of NUM(I) is used to specify how many asterisks to print for each bar. Each time through the loop, another value in the NUM array is used to specify the number of asterisks to be printed. This solution works as long as we assume that the array of data values contains integer values greater than zero. Also, the data values cannot be greater than the number of asterisks in BAR or greater than the number of positions in our output line.

Printing bar graphs with large data values can be accomplished by scaling the data values. For instance, suppose that our data values are 20, 8, 40, and 32. We want the maximum bar length to be 20. Because 40 is the maximum value, we would print a bar with 20 asterisks; other bars would be scaled accordingly. The output would be

The code to perform this type of scaling follows. (Note that the scale factor is the length of the maximum bar divided by the maximum data value. If the maximum value is exactly the desired length of the maximum bar, the scale factor is 1, and none of the values are changed. If the maximum data value is less than the desired length of the maximum bar, then the quotient is greater than 1, and all the values increase proportionally. If the maximum data value is greater than the length of the maximum bar, the quotient is less than 1, and all the values decrease proportionally.)

```
*--------------------------------------------------------------*
      INTEGER  NUM(4), MAX, I
      REAL  SCALE
      CHARACTER*20  BAR
      DATA  BAR /'********************'/
          .
          .
          .
*
*  Find maximum value in num.
*
      MAX = NUM(1)
      DO 10 I=2,4
         IF (MAX.LT.NUM(I)) MAX = NUM(I)
   10 CONTINUE
*
*  Compute scale factor.
*
      SCALE = 20.0/REAL(MAX)
*
*  Print bar graph.
*
      DO 20 I=1,4
         PRINT*, BAR(1:INT(SCALE*REAL(NUM(I)))
   20 CONTINUE
*--------------------------------------------------------------*
```

Note that because SCALE is a real value, we used a real constant 20.0 and the function REAL to avoid an integer division. However, when the scale factor is multiplied by a data value to determine the number of asterisks to print, we want this result to be an integer—therefore, we used the INT function to truncate the result to an integer.

If we add two more modifications to the routine, we have a versatile bar graph routine. First, we allow the data to be real values. If we want to use the procedure with an integer array, we can simply move the values into a real array and then call the bar graph routine with the real array. The other modification involves the line length. The optimum line length for the maximum bar depends on the application and on the output device being used. If the output device is a line printer, we may want to use the entire line of 132 characters; if the output device is a small terminal screen, we may want to use only 30 or so characters.

To accommodate all these possibilities, we let an argument LINE specify the maximum bar length, up to a maximum of 130 characters. The number of asterisks to be printed for a data value is computed with the following expression:

$$\text{VALUE(I)}*(\text{REAL(LINE)}/\text{MAX})$$

(We look at this expression more closely in the hand-worked example.)

Before we describe the design steps, we want to mention a limitation of this routine: no negative data values are permitted. We must write the routine such that a value of zero causes a bar to be skipped, but a negative value causes the routine to be exited.

PROBLEM STATEMENT

Write a subroutine that prints a bar graph from a real array of N data values. Assume that the values are nonnegative. An argument LINE determines the maximum bar length.

INPUT/OUTPUT DESCRIPTION

The input to the subroutine is the real array of N values, the value of N, and the maximum bar length LINE. No output arguments are passed back through the subroutine.

HAND EXAMPLE

For our hand-worked example, we use the following data values:

$$
\begin{aligned}
\text{VALUE(1)} &= 15.0 \\
\text{VALUE(2)} &= 26.0 \\
\text{VALUE(3)} &= 4.0 \\
\text{VALUE(4)} &= 8.0 \\
\text{VALUE(5)} &= 15.8
\end{aligned}
$$

Assume that the line length is 30. The first step in computing the scale factor is to find the maximum data value. For our set of data, the maximum value is 26.0. The scale factor can then be computed as the maximum bar length divided by the maximum data value, or 30/26.0, which yields 1.15. We then multiply each data value by the scale factor to determine the number of asterisks to print for each bar. The result must be an integer because we cannot print a part of an asterisk; therefore, we can either truncate (drop) the fractional portion or round the fractional portion to the nearest integer. In this example, we choose rounding. The results are shown in the following table:

DATA VALUE	×	SCALE FACTOR	=	BAR LENGTH	→	ROUNDED
15.0	×	1.15	=	17.25	→	17
26.0	×	1.15	=	29.90	→	30
4.0	×	1.15	=	4.60	→	5
8.0	×	1.15	=	9.20	→	9
15.8	×	1.15	=	18.17	→	18

The corresponding bar graph is

```
*****************
******************************
*****
*********
******************
```

ALGORITHM DEVELOPMENT

Earlier discussions are summarized.

DECOMPOSITION

Scale data values to line size.
Print corresponding bars of asterisks.

REFINEMENT IN PSEUDOCODE

GRAPH(data values, N, LINE):
    Determine MAX and MIN data values
    If MIN < 0 or LINE < 0 or LINE > 130 then
        Print error message
    else
        Compute scale factor
        For each data value do
            Compute number of asterisks for bar
            Print bar

FORTRAN SUBROUTINE

```
*-----------------------------------------------------------------*
      SUBROUTINE  GRAPH(VALUE,N,LINE)
*
* This subroutine prints a bar graph using an array
* of N elements with a maximum line size.
*
      INTEGER  N, LINE, I, K
      REAL  VALUE(N), MAX, SCALE
      LOGICAL  NEGNUM
      CHARACTER*130  BAR
*
* Find maximum and check for error conditions.
*
      IF (LINE.GT.130.OR.LINE.LT.1) THEN
          PRINT*, 'LINE LENGTH ERROR ', LINE
      ELSE
          NEGNUM = .FALSE.
          MAX = VALUE(1)
          DO 10 I=1,N
             IF (VALUE(I).LT.0.0) THEN
                NEGNUM = .TRUE.
             ELSE
                IF (VALUE(I).GT.MAX) MAX = VALUE(I)
             ENDIF
   10     CONTINUE
```

```
*
*   Fill bar with asterisks.
*
          IF (.NOT.NEGNUM) THEN
              DO 20 I=1,LINE
                  BAR(I:I) = '*'
   20         CONTINUE
*
*   Scale data values and print bar.
*
              SCALE = REAL(LINE)/MAX
              DO 30 I=1,N
                  K = NINT(VALUE(I)*SCALE)
                  PRINT*, BAR(1:K)
   30         CONTINUE
          ENDIF
      ENDIF
*
      RETURN
      END
*----------------------------------------------------------------*
```

Note the use of the intrinsic function NINT to round to the nearest integer.

TESTING

A driver for testing this procedure is

```
*----------------------------------------------------------------*
      PROGRAM   DRIVER
*
*   This program tests the bar graph subroutine.
*
      INTEGER   LINE
      REAL    VALUE(5)
*
      PRINT*, 'ENTER 5 DATA VALUES'
      READ*, VALUE
      PRINT*, 'ENTER LINE SIZE'
      READ*, LINE
      PRINT*
      PRINT*, 'LINE = ',LINE
      CALL GRAPH(VALUE,5,LINE)
*
      END
*----------------------------------------------------------------*
      GRAPH subroutine goes here
*----------------------------------------------------------------*
```

Here are a few examples of output with different line sizes using the data values in the hand-worked example:

```
LINE = 10
******
*********
**
***
******
```

```
LINE = 20
***********
********************
***
******
************

LINE = 30
*****************
*****************************
*****
*********
******************

LINE = 40
**********************
****************************************
******
************
************************

LINE = 50
****************************
****************************************************
********
***************
*****************************
```

Can you think of ways to improve the appearance of the bar graph? How about double-row or triple-row bars instead of single-row bars? These bars could be separated by blank lines, and headings and scales on the sides might also help. This bar graph routine is general enough to be used with many types of data but simple enough to be customized for specific uses. Other types of printer plots (ones that do not use a graphics plotter but use the regular keyboard characters) are developed in problems 1–5 and 33 at the end of the chapter.

We now present a program that reads character strings from a data file. Each line in the data file contains a character string of 50 characters. In addition, each line begins and ends with an apostrophe so that we can read the file with list-directed statements. Assume that the first line in the data file specifies how many lines of text follow in the file. As we read the data, we keep track of the number of occurrences of each vowel and print the numbers along with a corresponding bar graph.

The structure chart for this program is:

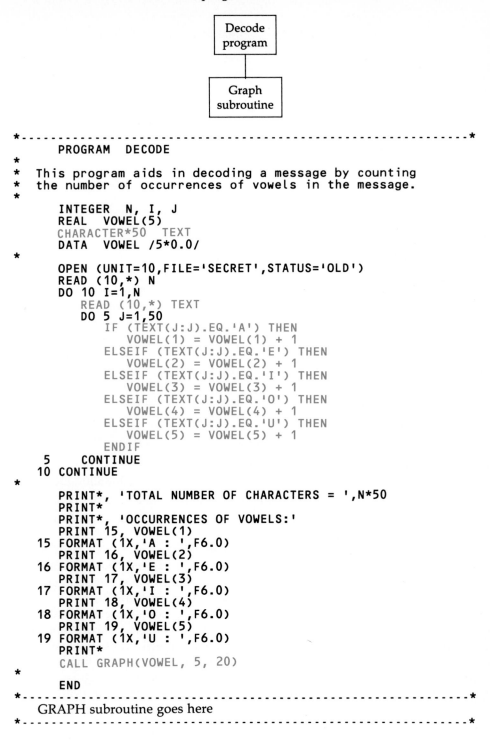

```
*------------------------------------------------------------------*
      PROGRAM  DECODE
*
*   This program aids in decoding a message by counting
*   the number of occurrences of vowels in the message.
*
      INTEGER  N, I, J
      REAL   VOWEL(5)
      CHARACTER*50   TEXT
      DATA   VOWEL /5*0.0/
*
      OPEN (UNIT=10,FILE='SECRET',STATUS='OLD')
      READ (10,*) N
      DO 10 I=1,N
         READ (10,*) TEXT
         DO 5 J=1,50
            IF (TEXT(J:J).EQ.'A') THEN
               VOWEL(1) = VOWEL(1) + 1
            ELSEIF (TEXT(J:J).EQ.'E') THEN
               VOWEL(2) = VOWEL(2) + 1
            ELSEIF (TEXT(J:J).EQ.'I') THEN
               VOWEL(3) = VOWEL(3) + 1
            ELSEIF (TEXT(J:J).EQ.'O') THEN
               VOWEL(4) = VOWEL(4) + 1
            ELSEIF (TEXT(J:J).EQ.'U') THEN
               VOWEL(5) = VOWEL(5) + 1
            ENDIF
   5     CONTINUE
  10  CONTINUE
*
      PRINT*, 'TOTAL NUMBER OF CHARACTERS = ',N*50
      PRINT*
      PRINT*, 'OCCURRENCES OF VOWELS:'
      PRINT 15, VOWEL(1)
  15  FORMAT (1X,'A : ',F6.0)
      PRINT 16, VOWEL(2)
  16  FORMAT (1X,'E : ',F6.0)
      PRINT 17, VOWEL(3)
  17  FORMAT (1X,'I : ',F6.0)
      PRINT 18, VOWEL(4)
  18  FORMAT (1X,'O : ',F6.0)
      PRINT 19, VOWEL(5)
  19  FORMAT (1X,'U : ',F6.0)
      PRINT*
      CALL GRAPH(VOWEL, 5, 20)
*
      END
*------------------------------------------------------------------*
      GRAPH subroutine goes here
*------------------------------------------------------------------*
```

A sample output from this program is

```
TOTAL NUMBER OF CHARACTERS = 250

OCCURRENCES OF VOWELS:
A:    15.
E:    26.
I:     4.
O:     8.
U:    16.
************
********************
***
******
************
```

8-3 DOUBLE-PRECISION DATA

Double-precision variables are necessary any time we want to keep more significant digits than are stored in real variables. Assume that a real variable can store 7 significant digits; this means that the real variable will keep 7 digits of accuracy, beginning with the first nonzero digit, in addition to remembering where the decimal point goes. A double-precision value can store more digits, with the exact number of digits dependent on the computer. For this discussion, assume that double-precision variables store 14 digits. The following table compares values that can be stored in real values (also called single-precision values) and in double-precision values.

VALUE TO BE STORED	SINGLE PRECISION	DOUBLE PRECISION
37.6892718	37.68927	37.689271800000
-1.60003	-1.600030	-1.6000300000000
820000000487.	820000000000.	820000000487.00
18268296.300405079	18268290.	18268296.300405

Note that we are doubling (or at least increasing) the precision of our values, but we are not doubling the range of numbers that can be stored. The same range of numbers applies to both single- and double-precision values, but double-precision values store those numbers with more digits of precision.

Many science and engineering applications use double-precision values to increase accuracy. For example, the study of solar systems, galaxies, and stars requires storing immense distances with as much precision as possible. Even economic models often need double precision. A model for predicting the gross national debt must handle numbers exceeding $1 trillion. With single precision, you cannot store the values with an accuracy to the nearest dollar. With double precision, amounts up to 10 trillion can be used and still have significant digits for all dollar amounts.

A double-precision constant is written in an exponential form, with a D in place of the E. Some examples of double-precision constants are

```
0.378926542D+04
1.4762D-02
0.25D+00
```

Always use the exponential form with the letter D for double-precision constants, even if the constant uses 7 or fewer digits of accuracy; otherwise, you may lose some accuracy because a fractional value that can be expressed evenly in decimal notation may not be expressed exactly in binary notation.

Double-precision variables are specified with a specification statement, whose general form is

> **DOUBLE PRECISION**   *variable list*

A double-precision array is specified as

```
DOUBLE PRECISION   DTEMP(50)
```

DOUBLE-PRECISION I/O

Double-precision variables can be used in list-directed output in the same manner that we list real values: The only distinction is that more digits of accuracy can be stored in a double-precision value; therefore, more digits of accuracy can be written from a double precision value.

In formatted input and output, double-precision values may be referenced with the F or E format specifications. Another specification, Dw.d, may also be used. Dw.d functions essentially like the E specification, but the D emphasizes that it is being used with a double-precision value. In output, the value in this exponential form is printed with a D, instead of an E. Thus, if the following statements were executed,

```
DOUBLE PRECISION   DX
    .
    .
    .
DX = 1.66587514521D+00
PRINT 10, DX
10 FORMAT (1X,'DX = ',D17.10)
```

the output would be

```
DX =   0.1665875145D+01
```

EXAMPLE 8-8   Solar Distances

Assume that a character array has been filled with the names of planets, moons, and other celestial bodies. A corresponding array has been filled with the distances of these objects from the sun in millions of miles. Both arrays have been defined to hold 200 values, and an integer N specifies how many elements are actually stored in the arrays. The array NAME is an array of character strings of length 20 and the array DIST is a double-precision array. Give the statements to print these names and distances.

Solution

Before printing the data in the arrays, we print a heading for the data. Next, a loop is executed N times and is used to print the object name and its corresponding distance from the sun in millions of miles. We use a D format for the output because the set of distances may cover a large range of values. The CHARACTER statement and the DOUBLE PRECISION statement are included with the statements to print the data:

```
      CHARACTER*20  NAME(200)
      DOUBLE PRECISION  DIST(200)
         .
         .
         .
      PRINT*, 'SOLAR OBJECTS AND DISTANCES FROM THE SUN'
      PRINT*, '                   (MILLIONS OF MILES)'
      PRINT*
      DO 10 I=1,N
         PRINT 5, NAME(I), DIST(I)
    5    FORMAT (1X,A,2X,D15.8)
   10 CONTINUE
```

A sample output from these statements is

```
        SOLAR OBJECTS AND DISTANCES FROM THE SUN
                      (MILLIONS OF MILES)

        JUPITER              0.43863717D+03
        MARS                 0.14151751D+03
        SATURN               0.88674065D+03
        VENUS                0.67235696D+02
        PLUTO                0.36662718D+04
        URANUS               0.17834237D+04
        MERCURY              0.35979176D+02
        NEPTUNE              0.27944448D+04
        EARTH                0.92961739D+02
```

DOUBLE-PRECISION OPERATIONS

When an arithmetic operation is performed with two double-precision values, the result is double precision. If an operation involves a double-precision value and a single-precision value or an integer, the result is a double-precision result. In such a mixed-mode operation, do not assume that the other value is converted to double precision; instead, think of the other value as being extended in length with zeros. To illustrate, the first two assignment statements that follow yield exactly the same values; the third assignment statement, however, adds a double-precision constant to DX and yields the most accurate result of the three statements:

```
DOUBLE PRECISION  DX, DY1, DY2, DY3
  .
  .
  .
DY1 = DX + 0.3872
DY2 = DX + 0.38720000000000
DY3 = DX + 0.3872D+00
```

The most accurate way to obtain a constant that cannot be written in a fixed number of decimal places is to perform a double-precision operation that yields the desired value. For instance, to obtain the double-precision constant one-third, use the following expression:

$$1.0D+00/3.0D+00$$

Using double-precision values increases the precision of our results, but there is a price for this additional precision — the execution time for computations is longer and more memory is required.

DOUBLE-PRECISION INTRINSIC FUNCTIONS

If a double-precision argument is used in a generic function, the function value is also double precision. Many of the common intrinsic functions for real numbers can be converted to double precision functions by preceding the function name with the letter D: for instance, DSQRT, DABS, DMOD, DSIN, DEXP, DLOG, and DLOG10 all require double-precision arguments and yield double-precision values. Double-precision functions can also be used to compute constants with double-precision accuracy. For instance, the following statements compute pi with double-precision accuracy:

```
DOUBLE PRECISION  DPI
  .
  .
  .
DPI = 4.0D+00*DATAN(1.0D+00)
```

(Recall that $\pi/4$ is equal to the arctangent of 1.0.)

Although Appendix A contains a complete list of the functions that relate to double-precision values, two functions, DBLE and DPROD, are specifically designed for use with double-precision variables. DBLE converts a REAL argument to a double-precision value by adding zeros. DPROD has two real arguments and returns the double-precision product of the two arguments.

EXAMPLE 8-9 Spherical Mirror Sag

The alignment of curved mirrors in a laser system is an extremely precise operation. The calculations may include computing the sag of the spherical mirror surface, which is calculated with the following equation, assuming that r is the radius of the spherical mirror and s is the distance from the center of the spherical mirror to its tangent plane:

$$\text{Sag} = \frac{rs^2}{1 + \sqrt{1 - r^2s^2}}$$

Assume that DR and DS represent double-precision values in the proper units for the radius *(DR)* of a spherical mirror and the distance *(DS)* from the center of the spherical mirror to its tangent plane. These two values have already been computed in a program. Give the statement to compute the sag to at least 10 digits of accuracy (assuming real values have 7 digits of accuracy).

Solution

```
DOUBLE PRECISION  DR, DS, DSAG
   .
   .
   .
DSAG = DR*DS*DS/(1.0D+00 + DSQRT(1.0D+00 - DR*DR*DS*DS))
```

SELF-TEST 8-2

This self-test allows you to check quickly to see if you have remembered some of the key points from Section 8-3. If you have any problems with the exercises, you should reread this section. The solutions are included at the end of the text.

In problems 1-6, show how to represent these constants as double precision constants.

1. 0.25
2. 0.58
3. 1/7
4. 1/13
5. 108.3
6. 2.0

In problems 7-9, show the output of the following PRINT statements if DX = 14.17862459, where DX is a double-precision variable.

```
7.    PRINT 4, DX
    4 FORMAT (1X,D14.6)
8.    PRINT 5, DX
    5 FORMAT (1X,D19.12)
9.    PRINT 6, DX
    6 FORMAT (1X,F10.6)
```

8-4 APPLICATION—TEMPERATURE DISTRIBUTION (Mechanical Engineering)

In this application, we consider the temperature distribution in a thin metal plate as it reaches a point of thermal equilibrium. The plate is constructed so that each edge is isothermal (maintained at a constant temperature). The temperature of an interior point on the plate is a function of the temperature of the surrounding material. If we consider the plate to be similar to a grid, then a two-dimensional array could be used to store the temperatures of the corresponding points on the plate. The following diagram contains an array that is used to store the temperatures of a plate that is being analyzed with 5 temperature measurements along the sides and 10 temperature measurements along the top and botton. A total of 50 temperature values are stored.

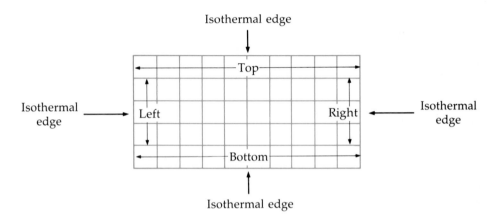

The isothermal temperatures at the top, bottom, left, and right would be given as inputs. The interior points are initially set to some arbitrary temperature, usually zero. The new temperature of each interior point is calculated as the average of its 4 surrounding points, as shown in the diagram:

$$T_0 = \frac{T_1 + T_2 + T_3 + T_4}{4}$$

After computing the new temperature for an interior point, the difference between the old temperature and the new temperature is computed. If the magnitude of a temperature change is greater than some specified tolerance value, the plate is not yet in thermal equilibrium, and the entire process is repeated.

We use two arrays for the temperatures, one for the old temperatures and one for the new temperatures. We need two arrays because we assume that the temperature changes for all the points are occurring simultaneously, even though we compute them one at a time. If we used only one array, we would be updating information before we were through with the old information. For example, suppose that we are computing the new temperature at position (3,3). The new value would be the average of temperatures in positions (2,3), (3,2), (3,4), and (4,3). When we move on to compute the new temperature at position (3,4), we again compute an average, but we want to use the old value in position (3,3), not its updated value.

Thus, we use a two-dimensional array of old temperatures to compute a two-dimensional array of new temperatures and, at the same time, to check if any of the temperature changes exceed the tolerance. We then move the new temperatures to the old array. When none of the temperature changes exceed the tolerance, we assume that equilibrium has been reached, and we print the final temperatures. We use double-precision values so that the equilibrium values can be determined accurately.

PROBLEM STATEMENT

Determine the equilibrium values for a metal plate.

INPUT/OUTPUT DESCRIPTION

The input values to the program include the number of rows and the number of columns in the temperature grid, the top temperature, the bottom temperature, the left temperature, the right temperature, and the tolerance value. The output from the program should be a grid of values representing the final temperature values when they have reached equilibrium.

HAND EXAMPLE

To be sure that we understand the process, we examine a simple case, studying each iteration. Assume that the array contains 4 rows and 4 columns. The isothermal edge temperatures are

$$
\begin{aligned}
\text{Top} &\leftarrow 100.0 \\
\text{Bottom} &\leftarrow 200.0 \\
\text{Left side} &\leftarrow 100.0 \\
\text{Right side} &\leftarrow 200.0
\end{aligned}
$$

The internal points are initialized to zero, and the tolerance value is 5.0.

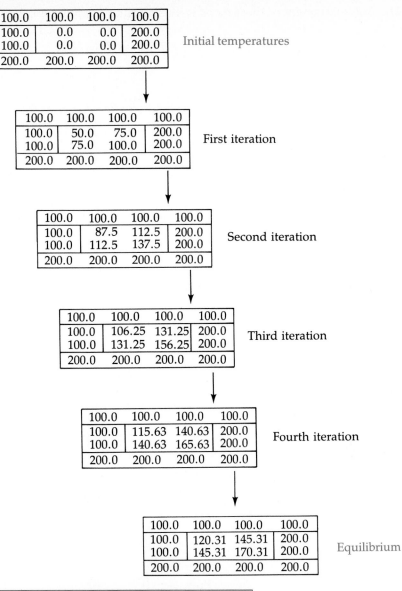

100.0	100.0	100.0	100.0
100.0	0.0	0.0	200.0
100.0	0.0	0.0	200.0
200.0	200.0	200.0	200.0

Initial temperatures

100.0	100.0	100.0	100.0
100.0	50.0	75.0	200.0
100.0	75.0	100.0	200.0
200.0	200.0	200.0	200.0

First iteration

100.0	100.0	100.0	100.0
100.0	87.5	112.5	200.0
100.0	112.5	137.5	200.0
200.0	200.0	200.0	200.0

Second iteration

100.0	100.0	100.0	100.0
100.0	106.25	131.25	200.0
100.0	131.25	156.25	200.0
200.0	200.0	200.0	200.0

Third iteration

100.0	100.0	100.0	100.0
100.0	115.63	140.63	200.0
100.0	140.63	165.63	200.0
200.0	200.0	200.0	200.0

Fourth iteration

100.0	100.0	100.0	100.0
100.0	120.31	145.31	200.0
100.0	145.31	170.31	200.0
200.0	200.0	200.0	200.0

Equilibrium

ALGORITHM DEVELOPMENT

The general decomposition of the steps in solving this problem are given.

DECOMPOSITION

Read isothermal edge temperatures and tolerance.
Update temperatures until equilibrium is reached.
Print equilibrium temperatures.

The first refinement of these steps is illustrated in the following general flowchart:

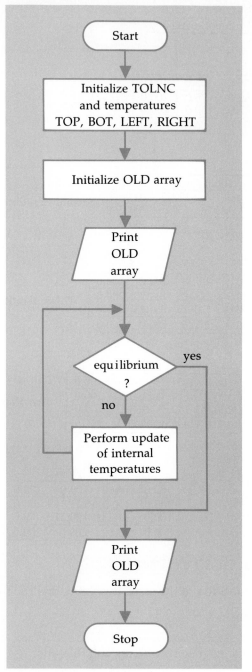

The portion of this flowchart that needs refinement before we can convert the solution into FORTRAN is the step "perform update of internal temperatures." It is in this step that we must compute the updated temperatures, determine if we have reached equilibrium, and move the new temperatures to the array of old temperatures. The refined portion of the flowchart follows:

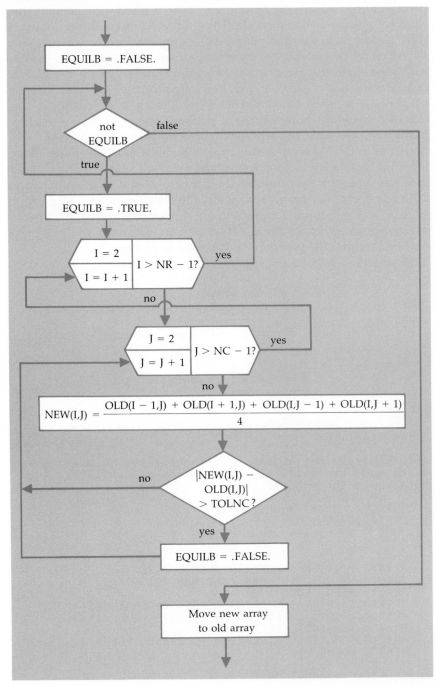

Before we convert the flowchart steps into FORTRAN, we must discuss data structures and subprograms. Clearly, the data that we are using is best represented by a two-dimensional array. We use a double-precision array to be able to work with tolerances that might be much smaller than the actual temperatures themselves. The arrays need to be defined with a maximum size, and we assume that 10 rows and 10 columns represent this maximum size.

The second issue we need to address is subprograms: As we developed the flowchart for this algorithm, there was no set of operations that needed to be performed in several places in the program. However, if we consider the overall program, it is getting lengthy; and long programs are harder to follow, even if they are properly structured. Therefore, you should look for operations that can easily be written in a subprogram, making our main programs more readable. In this program, the loop to move the new temperatures to the old temperature array is written as a subroutine. In addition, we write a subroutine to print the new temperatures. Even though the problem statement specifies that the temperatures are written only once, we definitely want to print them more often in the debugging stages; thus, it is useful to have a subroutine for printing out the temperatures at intermediate stages. In fact, we will print the initial set of temperatures in this program in order to be sure that the proper data was entered by the user.

The structure chart for this program is:

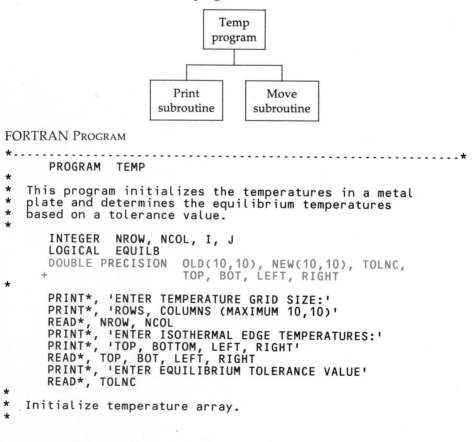

FORTRAN Program

```
*-------------------------------------------------------------------*
      PROGRAM  TEMP
*
*  This program initializes the temperatures in a metal
*  plate and determines the equilibrium temperatures
*  based on a tolerance value.
*
      INTEGER  NROW, NCOL, I, J
      LOGICAL  EQUILB
      DOUBLE PRECISION  OLD(10,10), NEW(10,10), TOLNC,
     +                  TOP, BOT, LEFT, RIGHT
*
      PRINT*, 'ENTER TEMPERATURE GRID SIZE:'
      PRINT*, 'ROWS, COLUMNS (MAXIMUM 10,10)'
      READ*, NROW, NCOL
      PRINT*, 'ENTER ISOTHERMAL EDGE TEMPERATURES:'
      PRINT*, 'TOP, BOTTOM, LEFT, RIGHT'
      READ*, TOP, BOT, LEFT, RIGHT
      PRINT*, 'ENTER EQUILIBRIUM TOLERANCE VALUE'
      READ*, TOLNC
*
*  Initialize temperature array.
*
```

```
      DO 5 J=1,NCOL
         NEW(1,J) = TOP
         NEW(NROW,J) = BOT
    5 CONTINUE
      DO 15 I=2,NROW-1
         NEW(I,1) = LEFT
         DO 10 J=2,NCOL-1
            NEW(I,J) = 0.0D+00
   10    CONTINUE
         NEW(I,NCOL) = RIGHT
   15 CONTINUE
      CALL MOVE(OLD,NEW,NROW,NCOL)
*
* Print initial temperature array.
*
      PRINT*
      PRINT*, 'INITIAL TEMPERATURES'
      PRINT*
      CALL PRINT(OLD,NROW,NCOL)
*
* Update temperatures until equilibrium.
*
      EQUILB = .FALSE.
   20 IF (.NOT.EQUILB) THEN
         EQUILB = .TRUE.
         DO 30 I=2,NROW-1
            DO 25 J=2,NCOL-1
               NEW(I,J) = (OLD(I-1,J) + OLD(I+1,J) +
     +                    OLD(I,J-1) + OLD(I,J+1))/4.0D+00
               IF (DABS(NEW(I,J) - OLD(I,J)).GT.TOLNC)
     +                    EQUILB = .FALSE.
   25       CONTINUE
   30    CONTINUE
         CALL MOVE(OLD,NEW,NROW,NCOL)
         GO TO 20
      ENDIF
*
* Print equilibrium temperature array.
*
      PRINT*
      PRINT*, 'EQUILIBRIUM TEMPERATURES'
      PRINT*
      CALL PRINT(OLD,NROW,NCOL)
*
      END
*-------------------------------------------------------------------*
*
*
      SUBROUTINE  PRINT(OLD,NROW,NCOL)
*
* This subroutine prints a double-precision
* array with NROW rows and NCOL columns.
*
      INTEGER  NROW, NCOL, I, J
      DOUBLE PRECISION  OLD(10,10)
*
      DO 10 I=1,NROW
         PRINT 5, (OLD(I,J), J=1,NCOL)
    5    FORMAT(1X,10(D12.5,1X))
   10 CONTINUE
*
      RETURN
      END
*-------------------------------------------------------------------*
```

```
*
*
      SUBROUTINE  MOVE(OLD,NEW,NROW,NCOL)
*
*  This subroutine moves the values in the new array
*  into the old array.
*
      INTEGER  NROW, NCOL, I, J
      DOUBLE PRECISION  OLD(10,10), NEW(10,10)
*
      DO 10 I=1,NROW
         DO 5 J=1,NCOL
            OLD(I,J) = NEW(I,J)
    5     CONTINUE
   10 CONTINUE
*
      RETURN
      END
*--------------------------------------------------------------*
```

TESTING

Testing this program is easier because of the subroutine that prints the values in the OLD array. You can call this subroutine just after the new temperatures are moved to the old temperatures (just before GO TO 20), which allows you to check the values after each update loop.

Note that the two subroutines used the variables NROW and NCOL as DO loop parameters but not as array dimensions. Remember that it is easy to cause problems with two-dimensional arrays when you use variable dimensioning; thus, we recommend that you use the maximum array size in all subprogram array definitions, as we did in this example. Then use variables to control the portion of the array that you actually use.

If we use the data from our hand-worked example in this program, our output is

```
INITIAL TEMPERATURES

   0.10000D+03  0.10000D+03  0.10000D+03  0.10000D+03
   0.10000D+03  0.00000D+00  0.00000D+00  0.20000D+03
   0.10000D+03  0.00000D+00  0.00000D+00  0.20000D+03
   0.20000D+03  0.20000D+03  0.20000D+00  0.20000D+03

EQUILIBRIUM TEMPERATURES

   0.10000D+03  0.10000D+03  0.10000D+03  0.10000D+03
   0.10000D+03  0.12031D+03  0.14531D+03  0.20000D+03
   0.10000D+03  0.14531D+03  0.17031D+03  0.20000D+03
   0.20000D+03  0.20000D+03  0.20000D+00  0.20000D+03
```

8-5 COMPLEX DATA

Complex numbers are needed to solve many problems in science and engineering, particularly in physics and electrical engineering. To help in their solutions, FORTRAN includes a special data type for complex variables and constants. (Recall that complex numbers have the form $a + bi$, where i is $\sqrt{-1}$ and a and b are real numbers. Thus, the real part of the number is represented by a, and the imaginary part of the number is represented by b.) These complex values are stored as an ordered pair of real values that represents the real and the imaginary portions of the value.

A complex constant is specified by two real constants separated by a comma and enclosed in parentheses. The first constant represents the real part of the complex value; the second constant represents the imaginary part of the complex value. Thus, the complex constant $3.0 + 1.5i$, where i represents the square root of -1, is written in FORTRAN as the complex constant (3.0, 1.5).

Complex variables are specified with a specification statement, whose general form is

COMPLEX   *variable list*

A complex array is specified as

```
COMPLEX   CX(100)
```

COMPLEX I/O

A complex value in list-directed output is printed as two real values separated by a comma and enclosed in parentheses. Two real values are read for each complex value in a list-directed input statement.

In formatted input, a complex value is read with two real specifications. For output, a complex value is printed with two real specifications. The real part of the complex value is read or printed before the imaginary portion. It is good practice to enclose the two parts printed in parentheses and separate them by a comma, or print them in the $a + bi$ form. Both forms are illustrated in the following statements:

```
COMPLEX  CX, CY
   .
   .
   .
CX = (1.5, 4.0)
CY = (0.0, 2.4)
   PRINT 5, CX, CY
 5 FORMAT (1X,'(',F4.1,',',F4.1,')'/1X,F4.1,' + ', F4.1,' I')
```

The output from the PRINT statement is

$$(\ 1.5, \ 4.0)$$
$$0.0 \ + \ \ 2.4 \ I$$

COMPLEX OPERATIONS

When an arithmetic operation is performed between two complex values, the result is also a complex value. In an expression containing a complex value and a real or integer value, the real or integer value is converted to a complex value whose imaginary part is zero. Expressions containing both complex values and double-precision values are not allowed.

The rules for complex arithmetic are not as familiar as those for integers or real values. The following display lists the results of basic operations on two complex numbers C_1 and C_2, where $C_1 = a_1 + b_1 i$ and $C_2 = a_2 + b_2 i$:

$$C_1 + C_2 = (a_1 + a_2) + i(b_1 + b_2)$$
$$C_1 - C_2 = (a_1 - a_2) + i(b_1 - b_2)$$
$$C_1 * C_2 = (a_1 a_2 - b_1 b_2) + i(a_1 b_2 + a_2 b_1)$$
$$\frac{C_1}{C_2} = \frac{a_1 a_2 + b_1 b_2}{a_2{}^2 + b_2{}^2} + i \ \frac{a_2 b_1 - b_2 a_1}{a_2{}^2 + b_2{}^2}$$
$$|C_1| = \sqrt{a_1{}^2 + b_1{}^2}$$
$$e^{C_1} = e^{a_1} \cos b_1 + i e^{a_1} \sin b_1$$
$$\cos C_1 = 1 - \frac{C_1{}^3}{3!} + \frac{C_1{}^5}{5!} - \frac{C_1{}^7}{7!} + \cdots$$

COMPLEX INTRINSIC FUNCTIONS

If a complex value is used in one of the generic functions, such as SQRT, ABS, SIN, COS, EXP, or LOG, the function value is also complex. The functions CSQRT, CABS, CSIN, CCOS, CEXP, and CLOG are all intrinsic functions with complex arguments. These function names begin with the letter C to emphasize that they are complex functions.

Although Appendix A contains a complete list of the functions that relate to complex values, four functions, REAL, AIMAG, CONJG, and CMPLX, are specifically designed for use with complex variables: REAL yields the real part of its complex argument; AIMAG yields the imaginary part of its complex argument; CONJG converts a complex number to its conjugate, where the conjugate of $(a + bi)$ is $(a - bi)$; COMPLX converts two real arguments, a and b, into a complex value $(a + bi)$. Note that while (2.0,1.0) is equal to the complex constant $2.0 + 1.0i$, we must use the expression CMPLX(A,B) to specify the complex variable $A + Bi$; the expression (A,B) by itself does not represent a complex variable in FORTRAN 77.

EXAMPLE 8-10 Quadratic Formula

The roots of a quadratic equation with real coefficients may be complex. Give the statements to compute and print the two roots of a quadratic equation, given the coefficients A, B, and C as shown:

$$AX^2 + BX + C = 0$$

$$X_1 = \frac{-B + \sqrt{B^2 - 4AC}}{2A} \qquad X_2 = \frac{-B - \sqrt{B^2 - 4AC}}{2A}$$

Solution

```
COMPLEX  DISCR, ROOT1, ROOT2
   .
   .
   .
DISCR = CMPLX(B*B - 4.0*A*C,0.0)
ROOT1 = (-B + SQRT(DISCR))/(2.0*A)
ROOT2 = (-B - SQRT(DISCR))/(2.0*A)
PRINT*, 'ROOTS TO THE QUADRATIC EQUATION ARE:'
PRINT 5, ROOT1, ROOT2
5 FORMAT (1X,F5.2,' + ',F5.2,' I',4X, F5.2,' + ',F5.2,' I')
```

Two sets of sample output are shown, one in which both roots are real
and one in which both roots are complex:

```
ROOTS TO THE QUADRATIC EQUATION ARE:
 1.56 +   0.00 I      2.00 +   0.00 I
```

```
ROOTS TO THE QUADRATIC EQUATION ARE:
-2.36 +   2.45 I  -2.36 +    -2.45 I
```

This self-test allows you to check quickly to see if you have remembered some of the key points from Section 8–5. If you have any problems with the exercises, you should reread this section. The solutions are included at the end of the text.

In problems 1–6, compute the value stored in CX if $CY = 1.0 + 3.0i$ and $CZ = 0.5 - 1.0i$. Assume CX, CY, and CZ are complex variables.

1. `CX = CY + CZ`
2. `CX = CY - CZ`
3. `CX = CONJG(CZ)`
4. `CX = REAL(CY) + AIMAG(CZ)`
5. `CX = CMPLX(5.0,0.2)`
6. `CX = ABS(CY)`

In problems 7–8, show the output of the following PRINT statements. Assume that $CX = 2.3 + 0.2i$.

```
7.    PRINT 5, CX
    5 FORMAT (1X,2F8.2)
```
```
8.    PRINT 6, CX
    6 FORMAT (1X,'(',F8.2,',',F8.2,')')
```

8–6   APPLICATION—ELECTRIC CIRCUIT MODEL (Electrical Engineering)

In the analysis of an electric circuit, we are often interested in the transfer function of the circuit. This transfer function can be used to determine the effect of the circuit on a sine function, in terms of magnitude changes and phase changes. The magnitude (absolute value) of the transfer function evaluated at the frequency of the sine wave is multiplied by the input magnitude to give the output magnitude. The phase (arctangent of the imaginary part divided by the real part) of the transfer function evaluated at the frequency of the sine wave is added to the input phase to give the output phase. For example, consider the following circuit that contains a capacitor C and a resistor R:

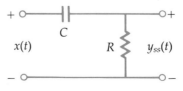

Kirchhoff's voltage law can be used to derive the transfer function for this system:

$$H(w) = \frac{\omega RCi}{1 + \omega RCi}$$

where ω represents frequency in radians per second and i represents the square root of -1. Write a program that determines the magnitude and phase changes caused by this circuit when a sine wave of a given frequency passes through the circuit.

PROBLEM STATEMENT

Write a program that determines the magnitude and phase changes of a sine wave after it passes through the given electric circuit.

INPUT/OUTPUT DESCRIPTION

There are three input values: the resistance R in ohms, the capacitance C in farads, and the frequency of the input sine wave. The output is the magnitude and phase of the transfer function evaluated at the input frequency.

HAND EXAMPLE

Assume that the input to the circuit is sine $100t$. The frequency of this sine wave is 100 radians per second. Also assume that R is equal to 10,000 ohms and that C is equal to 2.0 microfarads (or 0.000002 farads). The transfer function with these parameters is

$$H(100) = \frac{(100)(10000)(0.000002)i}{1 + (100)(10000)(0.000002)i} = \frac{2i}{1 + 2i}$$

$$= \frac{2i(1 - 2i)}{(1 + 2i)(1 - 2i)} = \frac{4 + 2i}{1 + 4} = 0.8 + 0.4i$$

The magnitude of $(0.8 + 0.4i)$ is .89, and the phase is 0.46 radians. Thus, a sine wave with a frequency of 100 radians per second has its magnitude multiplied by 0.89 and its phase changed by 0.46 radians when it passes through the circuit in this example.

ALGORITHM DEVELOPMENT

The decomposition of this problem solution involves reading the input values and then computing the corresponding transfer function magnitude and phase.

DECOMPOSITION

Read R, C, and ω.
Compute magnitude and phase.
Print ω, magnitude, and phase.

The refinement of this algorithm involves substituting the equations in the computation step.

REFINEMENT IN PSEUDOCODE

ELECT1: Read R, C, and ω
         Compute $H(\omega)$
         Determine magnitude of $H(\omega)$
         Determine phase of $H(\omega)$
         Print ω, magnitude, and phase

FORTRAN PROGRAM

```
*-------------------------------------------------------------*
      PROGRAM  ELECT1
*
*  This program determines the magnitude and phase
*  effects of an RC circuit on a sine wave.
*
      REAL  R, C, W, MAGN, PHASE
      COMPLEX  I, HW
*
      I = (0.0, 1.0)
*
      PRINT*, 'ENTER RESISTANCE IN OHMS'
      READ*, R
      PRINT*, 'ENTER CAPACITANCE IN FARADS'
      READ*, C
      PRINT*, 'ENTER THE SINE FREQUENCY IN RADIANS PER SEC'
      READ*, W
*
      HW = (W*R*C*I)/(1.0 + W*R*C*I)
      MAGN = CABS(HW)
      PHASE = ATAN(AIMAG(HW)/REAL(HW))
*
      PRINT 5, MAGN, PHASE
    5 FORMAT (1X,'MAGNITUDE EFFECT: ',F5.2,3X,
     +                'PHASE EFFECT: ',F5.2)
*
      END
*-------------------------------------------------------------*
```

TESTING

If we use the frequency from our hand-worked example to test this program, our output is

```
ENTER RESISTANCE IN OHMS
10000.
ENTER CAPACITANCE IN FARADS
0.000002
ENTER THE SINE FREQUENCY IN RADIANS PER SEC
100.0
MAGNITUDE EFFECT:  0.89   PHASE EFFECT:  0.46
```

An interesting modification to this program involves looking at the magnitude changes of the circuit over an interval of frequencies as opposed to a specific frequency. For example, some circuits are called low-pass circuits, which means that they pass frequencies below a certain frequency and reject frequencies above a certain frequency. When the magnitude effect is near 1.0, a frequency is being passed; when the magnitude effect is near 0.0, the frequency is being rejected. Other types of circuits are high-pass circuits, band-pass circuits, and band-reject circuits.

If we modify our program to read the starting and ending frequency for an interval of frequencies, we can look at the magnitude effect over that interval and determine the type of circuit being analyzed. In this program, we print 20 values over the frequency interval. The modified program and a sample output are given.

FORTRAN Program

```
*-------------------------------------------------------------*
      PROGRAM  ELECT2
*
*  This program determines the magnitude
*  effect of an RC circuit over a frequency interval.
*
      INTEGER  K
      REAL  W, R, C, WS, WE, STEP, MAGN
      COMPLEX  I, H, HW
*
      H(W) = (W*R*C*I)/(1.0 + W*R*C*I)
*
      I = (0.0, 1.0)
*
      PRINT*, 'ENTER RESISTANCE IN OHMS'
      READ*, R
      PRINT*, 'ENTER CAPACITANCE IN FARADS'
      READ*, C
      PRINT*, 'ENTER THE STARTING AND ENDING FREQUENCIES'
      PRINT*, '(RADIANS PER SEC)'
      READ*, WS, WE
*
      PRINT*
      PRINT*, 'FREQUENCY AND MAGNITUDE'
      STEP = (WE - WS)/20.0
      DO 20 K=1,20
         W = (K - 1)*STEP + WS
         HW = H(W)
         MAGN = CABS(HW)
         PRINT 10, W, MAGN
   10    FORMAT (1X,F6.2,5X,F5.2)
   20 CONTINUE
*
      END
*-------------------------------------------------------------*
```

```
ENTER RESISTANCE IN OHMS
10000.
ENTER CAPACITANCE IN FARADS
0.000002
ENTER THE STARTING AND ENDING FREQUENCIES
(IN RADIANS)
0.0 200.0

FREQUENCY AND MAGNITUDE
     0.00        0.00
    10.00        0.20
    20.00        0.37
    30.00        0.51
    40.00        0.62
    50.00        0.71
    60.00        0.77
    70.00        0.81
    80.00        0.85
    90.00        0.87
   100.00        0.89
   110.00        0.91
   120.00        0.92
   130.00        0.93
   140.00        0.94
   150.00        0.95
   160.00        0.95
   170.00        0.96
   180.00        0.96
   190.00        0.97
```

Note that this circuit rejects frequencies near zero and passes frequencies with little magnitude distortion when the frequency is above 150.00 radians per second.

SUMMARY

With the data types presented in this chapter, we now have a number of choices for defining our variables and constants. For numeric data, we can select integers, real values, or double-precision values. We have character data for information that is not going to be used in numeric computations. For special applications, we have complex variables. In addition to being able to choose the proper data type for our data, we also have special intrinsic functions and operations for simplifying our work with the data.

Many errors in character string manipulations occur because the character string is used incorrectly with numeric data. Some typical examples are:

Arithmetic expressions — Even if a character string contains numeric digits, it cannot be used in arithmetic operations.

Comparisons — Character strings should always be compared to other character strings and not to a numeric constant or variable.

Subprogram arguments — A character string used as an argument to a subprogram must be identified in CHARACTER statements in both the main program and in the subprogram.

Another source of errors may be introduced when moving or comparing strings of unequal length. For comparisons, the shorter string will be compared as if it had enough blanks on the right to be equal in length to the longer string. Character strings are always moved character by character from left to right, until the receiving string is filled. If there are too few characters in the sending string, blanks are moved into the right-most characters of the receiving string.

A final caution relative to the substring operation: Invalid results occur if the beginning or ending positions of the substring reference are outside the original string itself.

The primary debugging tool for double-precision and complex values is the PRINT statement. If an error is related to a double-precision value, print it out with an E21.14 format (assumes 14 digits of accuracy) each time it is used to be sure that you are not losing the extra accuracy. Also, be sure that you are not moving the value into a single-precision variable in an intermediate step in the program.

If your program errors relate to complex values, write the values of the complex numbers as soon as they are initialized and after each modification. Remember that if you move a complex value into a real variable, the imaginary portion is lost.

STYLE/TECHNIQUE GUIDES

A programmer who is comfortable and proficient with character string manipulations will find them extremely useful. The ability to display information clearly and simply is valuable in communication, and the use of character strings adds a new dimension to the method of both reading and displaying information.

Some guides for using character strings in your programs are:

1. Use character strings of the same length where possible.
2. Use the function INDEX instead of writing your own routines to find substrings in a string.

3. Become proficient with the substring and concatenation operators; these are powerful tools in manipulating and analyzing character strings.
4. Take advantage of the printer-plotting techniques described in this chapter and in the problems at the end of the chapter.

Finally, when you use a feature of FORTRAN (such as double-precision or complex variables) that is not commonly used, good documentation is important. More comment lines may be necessary to clarify your code. If a computation uses complex numbers, explain the computations in more detail than in regular arithmetic computations. Part of good documentation also includes choosing descriptive names.

KEY WORDS

ASCII code	double-precision value
character string	EBCDIC code
collating sequence	FORTRAN character set
complex value	lexicographical order
concatenation	substring

PROBLEMS

We begin our problem set with modifications to programs developed earlier in this chapter. Give the decomposition, refined pseudocode or flowchart, and FORTRAN solution for each problem.

Problems 1–5 modify the program DECODE, given on page 369, which generated a bar graph to compare the number of occurrences of vowels in a piece of text.

1. Modify the graph subroutine so that it prints two lines of asterisks for each bar.
2. Modify the graph subroutine so that it prints three lines of asterisks for each bar. Separate each group of three lines by a blank line.
3. Modify the decode program so that it includes lowercase or uppercase letters in each vowel count.
4. Modify the decode program so that it reads from the terminal the specific characters that it is going to count. The user first enters the number of specific characters and then the characters themselves. Assume that 30 characters is the upper limit.
5. Modify the graph subroutine so that it computes the average of the data values. In each bar, print asterisks up to the average value and plus signs for any part of the bar that is over the average. Thus, if a data value is below the average, its bar is entirely asterisks; if a data value is above the average, its bar is composed of asterisks and plus signs.

Problems 6–10 modify the program TEMP, given on page 380, which determined an equilibrium temperature distribution in a metal plate.

6. Modify the temperature distribution program so that it counts the number of iterations needed for the plate to reach equilibrium. Print this value after the final grid.

7. Modify the temperature distribution program so that the initialization of the temperature array is performed in a subroutine.

8. Modify the temperature distribution program so that the computation of the new temperature values is performed in a subroutine.

9. Modify the temperature distribution program so that the temperature iteration continues until equilibrium has been reached or until 10 iterations have been performed.

10. Modify the print subroutine so that it also prints the maximum and minimum temperatures and their positions in the temperature array.

Problems 11–15 modify the program ELECT1, given on page 388, which determines the magnitude and phase effects of an *RC* circuit on a sine wave.

11. Modify the program ELECT1 so that it prints the phase effect in degrees instead of in radians.

12. Modify the program ELECT1 so that it reads the resistance in units of thousands of ohms, or kilo-ohms.

13. Modify the program ELECT1 so that it reads the capacitance in units of microfarads. (one microfarad = 0.000001 farad)

14. Modify the program ELECT1 so that it reads the sine frequency in hertz (or cycles per second) instead of in radians per second. (1 hertz = 2*pi radians per second)

15. Add a loop to the program ELECT1 so it continues computing magnitude and phase effects until a negative value is entered for the sine frequency.

In problems 16–35, develop programs and modules using the five-phase design process.

16. Write a complete program that reads a data file ADDR containing 50 names and addresses. The first line for each person contains the first name (10 characters), the middle name (6 characters), and the last name (21 characters). The second line contains the address (25 characters), the city (10 characters), the state abbreviation (2 characters), and the zip code (5 characters). Print the information in the following label form:

```
First Initial. Middle Initial. Last Name
Address
City, State   Zip
```

Skip four lines between labels. The city should not contain any blanks before the comma that follows it. A typical label might be

```
J. D. Doe
117 Main St.
Taos, NM   87166
```

For simplicity, assume there are no embedded blanks in the individual data values. For example, San Jose would be entered as SanJose and printed in the same manner.

17. Write a subroutine CNDNS that receives a character array of 50 characters and returns a character array OUT, also of 50 characters, which has no adjacent blanks except at the end of the string. Thus, if IN was composed of 'HELLO THERE' followed by blanks, then the output array OUT should contain 'HELLO THERE' followed by blanks.

18. Write a complete program to read a double-precision value from the terminal. Compute the sine of the value using the following series:

$$\sin X = X - \frac{X^3}{3!} + \frac{X^5}{5!} - \frac{X^7}{7!} + \cdots$$

Continue using terms until the absolute value of a term is less than 1.0D−09. Print the computed sine and the value obtained from the function DSIN for comparison.

19. Write a complete program that reads the coefficients A, B, and C of a quadratic equation from a data line. Compute and print the two roots of the equation. If the roots are real values, use an F format to print them. If the roots are complex, use the $a + bi$ form for output. If the value of A is zero, print a message stating that the equation is linear and not quadratic.

20. Write a program that reads the complex coefficients for a general transfer function with the following equation:

$$H(\omega) = \frac{A*\omega*\omega + B*\omega + C}{\omega*\omega + D*\omega + E}$$

Read an input frequency ω and determine the magnitude and phase effects of this transfer function on a sinusoid with frequency ω.

21. Modify the program in problem 20 to read a beginning and ending frequency from the terminal. Compute and print the magnitude effects for 20 frequency points spaced evenly over the interval.

22. Modify the program in problem 20 to read a beginning and ending frequency from the terminal. Also read the number of points desired in the frequency interval. Print the magnitude effects for these frequency points spaced evenly over the interval.

23. Write a program that prints a table of values for exp(x) where x varies from 0.1 to 2.0 in increments of 0.1. Print 3 columns: x, exp(x) using the single-precision intrinsic function, and exp(x) using the double-precision intrinsic function.

24. Write a subroutine DELETE that has an argument list composed of a character array TEXT of 100 characters and a pointer PTR. The subroutine should delete the character in position PTR. The characters in the positions following PTR should be moved one position to the left. A blank should be added at the end of TEXT to keep the length of TEXT at 100 characters.

25. Write a subroutine INSERT that has an argument list composed of a character string TEXT of 100 characters, a pointer PTR, and a single character CHAR1. The subroutine should insert CHAR1 in the position pointed to by PTR. The rest of the characters should be moved one position to the right, with the last character truncated to keep the length of TEXT at 100 characters.

26. A data file called CARS contains the license plate number and the number of gallons of gas that can be put into the car for each car in a certain state. The license plate is composed of 3 characters, followed by a space, and then 3 digits. Each line in the file contains a license number and a real number that gives the corresponding gallons of gas. The last line in the file has a license number of ZZZ 999 and is not a valid data line. Write a complete program that helps analyze the feasibility of gas rationing based on whether the license plate number is odd or even. The data to be computed and printed is the following:

```
SUM OF GAS FOR ODD CARS    XXXXX GALLONS    XX.X%
SUM OF GAS FOR EVEN CARS   XXXXX GALLONS    XX.X%
```

27. A palindrome is a word or piece of text that is spelled the same forward and backward. The word 'RADAR' is an example of a palindrome, but ' RADAR' is not a palindrome because of the unmatched blank. 'ABLE ELBA' is another palindrome. Write a logical function PALIND that receives a character variable X of length 20. The function should be true if the character array is a palindrome; otherwise, it should be false.

28. Write a subroutine ALPHA that receives an array of 50 letters. The subroutine should alphabetize the list of letters.

29. Modify the subroutine in problem 28 to remove duplicate letters and to add blanks at the end of the array for the letters removed.

30. Write a subroutine whose input is a character array of length 50. Change all punctuation marks (commas, periods, exclamation points, and question marks) to blanks. Assume that the program calls the subroutine with the following statement:

CALL EDIT(STRING)

31. Write a subroutine that receives a piece of text called PROSE that contains 200 characters. The subprogram should print the text in lines of 30 characters each. Do not split words between two lines. Do not print any lines that are completely blank.

32. Write a function CONSNT that receives a character array of 100 alphabetic letters. Count the number of consonants and return that number to the main program. (It might be easiest to count the number of vowels and subtract that number from 100.)

33. Write a subroutine that receives an array of N real values (maximum value of N is 200) and prints a printer plot. Use an output line of 101 characters. Scale the line from the minimum value to the maximum value. The first line of output should be 101 periods representing the Y-axis. All the following lines should contain a period in the column representing $X = 0$ (if this point is included in the graph), and the letter X in the position of each data point, as shown in the following diagram. (In this diagram, the minimum and the maximum values have the same absolute value.)

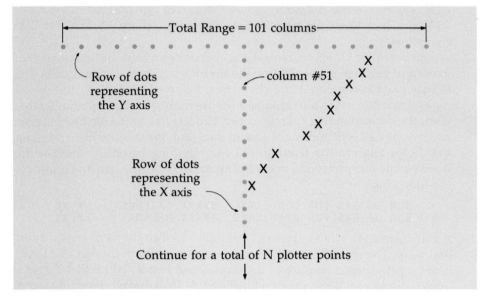

34. Write a complete program that reads and stores the following two-dimensional array of characters:

```
ATIDEB
LENGTH
ECPLOT
DDUEFS
OUTPUT
CGDAER
HIRXJI
KATIMN
BHPARG
```

Now read the 11 strings that follow and find the same strings in the preceding array. Print the positions of characters of these hidden words that may appear forward, backward, up, down, or diagonally. For instance, the word EDIT is located in positions (1,5), (1,4), (1,3), and (1,2).

HIDDEN WORDS

PLOT	STRING
CODE	TEXT
EDIT	READ
LENGTH	GRAPH
INPUT	BAR
OUTPUT	

35. Modify the subprogram of problem 31 such that the length of the output line is an argument of the subroutine. Distribute any blanks between words on a line such that every line begins and ends with a nonblank character. Thus, if the character string PROSE contained a portion of the Gettysburg Address and the line length is 23, then the first three lines of output should be

```
FOUR   SCORE   AND   SEVEN
YEARS AGO   OUR   FATHERS
BROUGHT FORTH UPON THIS
```

36. Text material is sometimes analyzed very carefully to determine quantities such as average word length. Such a quantity can be used to recommend the level of reading ability necessary to read the text. Average word length can even be used to help determine authorship of a literary work; it has been applied to the works of Shakespeare in an attempt to indicate whether Sir Frances Bacon authored some of the plays attributed to Shakespeare. Write a function that receives a character string and returns the average word length of the string. Assume that all words are separated from adjacent words by at least one blank. The first and last characters may or may not be blanks.

37. Write a subroutine that sorts a complex array of N values into a descending order based on the absolute value of the complex values. Assume that the subroutine is called with the statement

```
CALL ORDER(CDATA,N)
```

where CDATA is an array of N complex values.

38. Write a subroutine ENCODE that receives a character string KEY containing 26 characters and a character string MESSGE of an unspecified size. The subroutine should encode MESSGE, using a substitution code where the first letter in KEY is substituted for the letter A in MESSGE, the second letter in KEY is substituted for the letter B in MESSGE, and so on. Thus, if KEY contained the character string

'YXAZKLMBJOCFDVSWTREGHNIPUQ'

and MESSGE contained the character string

'MEET AT AIRPORT SATURDAY'

then the encoded character string would be

'DKKG YG YJRWSRG EYGHRZYU'

The encoded character string should be stored in a character string called SECRET. The subroutine is called with the following statement:

CALL ENCODE(KEY,MESSGE,SECRET)

39. Write a subroutine DECODE that receives a character string KEY containing 26 characters and a character string SECRET of an unspecified size. The subroutine should decode SECRET, which has been encoded with a substitution key where the first letter in KEY was substituted for the letter A, the second letter in KEY was substituted for the letter B, and so on. Blanks were not changed in the coding process. Thus, if KEY contained the character string

'YXAZKLMBJOCFDVSWTREGHNIPUQ'

and SECRET contained the character string

'DKKG YG YJRWSRG EYGHRZYU'

then the decoded character string would be

'MEET AT AIRPORT SATURDAY'

The decoded character string should be stored in a character string called MESSGE. The subroutine is called with the statement

CALL DECODE(KEY,SECRET,MESSGE)

40. Write a subroutine to sort a character string array into alphabetical order. Assume that each character string in the array contains 4 characters. Remove any leading blanks from the character strings before sorting. The input is a character array with N values. The output is the same array, but with the character strings reordered into alphabetical order and the leading blanks removed. Use the following statement to call the subroutine:

CALL ALPHA(NAME,N)

The following example illustrates the reason for removing leading blanks:

ORIGINAL ORDER	ALPHABETICAL ORDER WITH BLANKS	ALPHABETICAL ORDER WITHOUT BLANKS
SAM b	bb ED	AL bb
bb ED	b AL b	AMY b
b SUE	b SUE	BEV b
MARY	AMY b	ED bb
JOSE	BEV b	JOHN
JOHN	JOHN	JOSE
AMY b	JOSE	LISA
b AL b	LISA	MARY
LISA	MARY	SAM b
BEV b	SAM b	SUE b

FORTRAN STATEMENT SUMMARY

CHARACTER Statement:

> **CHARACTER**   *variable list*

Examples:

> **CHARACTER*5   NAME, DESC(10)**
>
> **CHARACTER   CITY*20, LOCATION*35**

Discussion:
The CHARACTER statement defines variables that store character information. It also specifies the number of characters in the variable.

COMPLEX Statement:

> **COMPLEX**   *variable list*

Example:

> **COMPLEX   I, CX, Z(10)**

Discussion:
The COMPLEX statement defines variables that represent complex values. Each complex variable consists of two real values: the first representing the real part of the complex value and the second representing the imaginary part of the complex value. When a COMPLEX value is read or printed, two real values correspond to the COMPLEX value.

DOUBLE PRECISION Statement:

> **DOUBLE PRECISION**   *variable list*

Example:

> **DOUBLE PRECISION   X, Y, ACCEL(25)**

Discussion:
The DOUBLE PRECISION statement defines variables that have more significant digits of accuracy than real variables. The exact number of significant digits of accuracy in a double-precision variable depends on the computer system. Typically, a real value contains 7 digits of accuracy and a double-precision value contains 14 digits of accuracy.

APPLICATION — Voyager Spacecraft Data Analysis (Electrical Engineering)

The pictures of Saturn sent back by Voyager II were spectacular. However, these pictures were initially transmitted as long strings of numbers which represented light intensities detected by the cameras on Voyager II. Sophisticated image processing techniques were used to turn the strings of numbers into recreated images of the surface of Saturn. Write a program to read a data file of light intensities and perform a simple type of digital image processing called edge detection, where an edge detector distinguishes between different surfaces in a two-dimensional image. (See Section 9–3 for the solution.)

Photo courtesy of NASA.

9

ADDITIONAL FILE HANDLING

INTRODUCTION

In previous chapters, we used files extensively. For example, READ* and PRINT* statements that referred to input and output on the terminal screen (or a line printer) caused the input and output files to be connected automatically to your program. Using the OPEN statement introduced in Chapter 4, we could also connect other data files. These types of files are called *external files* because they are external to the memory area reserved by our program.

External files can also be read from other devices such as magnetic tape drives or magnetic disk drives; on these devices, these files have special properties that determine the types of statements used to process them. Processing magnetic tape or magnetic disk files also requires some knowledge of sequential access and direct access. In both of these access methods, we use the term *record* to describe a unit of information in the file; in a data file, one line represents a *record*. Each record contains *fields* of information. For instance, a payroll file contains individual payroll records, and each record could contain fields such as a name, hours worked, and hourly rate.

Sequential access of a file involves processing records from the physical beginning of the file. Throughout this text, we have used this type of access. We read the first data line, then the second data line, and so on. In *direct access*, information is not necessarily accessed in its physical order. We may reference the tenth record, then the last record, and then the second record, all without reading the records in between. This type of access is also called random access because we can access the records in a random order.

External files are often used because they are *portable* — they can be used not only on another computer of the same manufacturer, but also on computers made by different manufacturers. For example, a magnetic tape file created on a Digital Equipment Corporation VAX computer can be read on a Control Data Corporation 7600 computer. But for these files to be portable, standard procedures must be observed when creating and using them; for example, because list-directed input and output are system dependent with regard to the formats used, all input and output stored on external devices must use formats to guarantee consistency from one computer to another. You may want to refer to some of the formatting material in Chapter 4 as you study this chapter.

FORTRAN also has a feature called *internal files* that allows us to use a character string as if it were a file to manipulate the data internally.

9-1 INTERNAL FILES

When the unit number in an input or output statement is the name of a character variable, the statement transfers data from one internal storage area to another. These storage areas are called internal files. For instance, we can read data from a character string instead of a data line; the input and output statements function exactly as if the contents of the character string were actually entered in a data line, as shown:

```
CHARACTER*13  DATA
DATA = '127 65   42.17'
READ (DATA,*) I, J, X
```

After execution, the value of I is 127, the value of J is 65, and the value of X is 42.17.

The internal file feature is useful if you want to perform some type of editing on the data before using it. For example, suppose you are reading information from a data file that contains amounts entered with dollar signs to the left of the amounts. If the fields are read directly into real variables, execution errors occur. Using internal files, you can read the data into an internal character file, edit the data by changing all dollar signs to blanks, and then read the number values from the internal file. The following statements read 10 positions from a data line, change any leading dollar sign to a blank, and then read the value into a real variable:

```
      INTEGER  PTR
      REAL   AMOUNT
      CHARACTER*10  TEMP
      .
      .
      .
      READ (12,5) TEMP
    5 FORMAT (A)
      IF (INDEX(TEMP,'$').NE.0) THEN
          PTR = INDEX(TEMP,'$')
          TEMP(PTR:PTR) = ' '
      ENDIF
      READ (TEMP,*) AMOUNT
```

A similar use of internal files is beneficial if you want to edit lines of an output report before printing. For example, you might want to insert dollar signs next to real values to be printed; with internal files, you can insert the dollar sign next to the digits, as in $_{bbb}$$146.21, instead of next to the output field, as in $_{bbb}$146.21.

9-2 SEQUENTIAL FILES

Sequential files are typically built by one program and then accessed by other programs. Once a sequential file is created, individual records cannot be updated. When changes need to be made to the information, the updating is usually done by reading the information in a record, updating it if desired, and then writing the information to an output record. The process is repeated for each record in the file. Sometimes this technique is referred to as *father-son updating*. (The original file is the father file, and the updated file is the son.)

When we use sequential files, the same READ and WRITE statements are used, but other statements may also be needed: an extended form of the OPEN statement; and statements to close the file, to reposition the record pointer to the first record in the file, to backspace one record in the file, and to add an end-of-file indicator to a new file.

OPEN STATEMENT

The OPEN statement connects an external file to a program. The OPEN statement is executable but typically is placed at the beginning of the program because it should generally be executed only once. A simplified form of the OPEN statement was introduced in Chapter 4. The complete form of the OPEN statement is

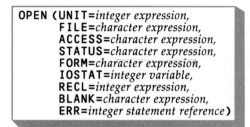

```
OPEN (UNIT=integer expression,
      FILE=character expression,
      ACCESS=character expression,
      STATUS=character expression,
      FORM=character expression,
      IOSTAT=integer variable,
      RECL=integer expression,
      BLANK=character expression,
      ERR=integer statement reference)
```

UNIT Number The integer expression in this specification is usually a constant. This value is used in READ or WRITE statements to specify the file to be used. The following example illustrates the use of unit number 13 to open the file DIST and write information into it with a WRITE statement:

```
    OPEN (UNIT=13,FILE='DIST',STATUS='NEW')
    WRITE (13,10) X, Y
 10 FORMAT (F8.3,F5.1)
```

FILE The character expression in this file specification is the name of the file; all references to the file must use the same name. Filenames typically consist of 1 – 6 alphabetic letters or numbers, with an alphabetic letter as the first character.

ACCESS The character string in this specification must be either 'SEQUENTIAL' or 'DIRECT'. If this specification is omitted, 'SEQUENTIAL' is assumed.

STATUS The character string in this specification must be 'NEW', 'OLD', or 'SCRATCH'. 'NEW' specifies that the file is being created through WRITE statements. 'OLD' specifies that the file is already built, and its records are accessed with READ statements. 'SCRATCH' specifies that the file is an output file that is not being used after the program has been executed; hence, it will be deleted.

FORM The character string in this specification must be either 'FORMATTED' or 'UNFORMATTED'. A FORMATTED file uses either formatted READ and WRITE statements or list-directed input/output statements. All examples used in this text have been formatted. UNFORMATTED input/output is used for transfer of data with no data conversion; the data is transferred as binary strings, not as numbers or characters. One of the main uses of UNFORMATTED input/ output is to transfer tape or disk data to another tape or disk file. If this specification is omitted, the default is 'FORMATTED' for sequential files and 'UNFORMATTED' for direct files.

IOSTAT The IOSTAT specification is not required but can be used to provide error-recovery. If no errors occur in attaching the specified file to the program, the value of the integer variable is zero. If an error occurs, such as when an input file with the proper name is not found, a value specified by the computer system is stored in the variable. You can test this variable in your program and specify what action is to be taken if it is nonzero. In this next example, an error in opening the file causes IERR to be nonzero. An error message can be printed, and execution then continues. If the IOSTAT specification were not used and an error occurred in opening the file, execution would be terminated with an execution error:

```
OPEN (UNIT=15,FILE='XYDATA',STATUS='OLD',
+      IOSTAT=IERR)
IF (IERR.NE.O) PRINT*, IERR
```

The IOSTAT specification can also be used with READ and WRITE statements.

RECL The RECL specification is required for direct-access files and specifies the record length. It is not used with sequential-access files. This specification is discussed further in Section 9–5.

BLANK The character string in this specification must be either 'NULL' or 'ZERO' and cannot be used with unformatted files. If the specification is 'NULL', blanks are usually ignored in numeric fields, but this is system dependent; if the specification is 'ZERO', blanks are assumed to be zeros in numeric fields. If the specification is omitted, 'NULL' is assumed.

ERR This specification is optional and provides error-recovery. If an error occurs during execution of a statement that contains this ERR specification, control passes to the statement referenced by this specification instead of causing an execution error. The ERR specification can also be used with READ and WRITE statements.

CLOSE STATEMENT

The CLOSE statement is an executable statement that disconnects a file from a program. Its general form is

```
CLOSE (UNIT=integer expression,
       STATUS=character expression,
       IOSTAT=integer variable,
       ERR=integer statement reference)
```

The CLOSE statement is optional because all files are closed automatically upon termination of program execution. The STATUS, IOSTAT, and ERR specifications are also optional. The STATUS specification options for the CLOSE statement are not the same as for the OPEN statement. When a file is closed, the default option is 'KEEP', which indicates that the file is to be kept. The option 'DELETE' may be chosen to indicate that the file is no longer needed and should be deleted.

REWIND STATEMENT

The REWIND statement is an executable statement that repositions a sequential file at the first record of the file. Its general form is

```
REWIND (UNIT=integer expression,
        IOSTAT=integer variable,
        ERR=integer statement reference)
```

Some systems require a REWIND statement before reading an input file.

BACKSPACE STATEMENT

The BACKSPACE statement is an executable statement that repositions a sequential file to the last record read; thus, it backs up one record in the file. Its general form is

```
BACKSPACE (UNIT=integer expression,
           IOSTAT=integer variable,
           ERR=integer statement reference)
```

ENDFILE STATEMENT

When a sequential file is being built, a special end-of-file record must be written to specify the end of the file. This special record is written when the ENDFILE statement is executed. The general form of the executable ENDFILE statement is

```
ENDFILE (UNIT=integer expression,
         IOSTAT=integer variable,
         ERR=integer statement reference)
```

The CLOSE statement automatically performs this function on most systems.

This self-test allows you to check quickly to see if you have remembered some of the key points from Section 9−2. If you have any problems with the exercise, you should reread this section. The solution is included at the end of the text.

1. Write a program to count the number of records in a file called XYDATA. Assume that the file is sequential and each record contains 2 real values in the following format:

   FORMAT (F6.2,1X,F6.2)

   Print the number of records. If an error occurs in opening the file, print an error message.

9−3 APPLICATION—VOYAGER SPACECRAFT DATA ANALYSIS (Electrical Engineering)

The pictures of Saturn sent back by Voyager II were spectacular. However, these pictures were not discernible by the human eye because they were transmitted as a long string of numbers or digital intensities that had to be processed and reassembled to compose the pictures that we saw. In this application we will write a program to perform a simple type of digital image processing called edge detection, where an edge detector distinguishes between the different surfaces in a two-dimensional image.

In the program, we will assume that we have a data file similar to that which might have been sent by Voyager II. Although it takes a very sophisticated procedure to recreate the original image, you can often determine the major features of the image by locating major differences in the digital intensities. If a major difference occurs between the intensities represented by the data points, an edge has been encountered. The actual calculation to determine if an edge has been encountered is performed as follows (assuming that we are trying to determine if point P5 is part of an edge):

P1	P2	P3
P4	P5	P6
P7	P8	P9

$$DIF = \frac{|P5 - P2| + |P5 - P4| + |P5 - P6| + |P5 - P8|}{4}$$

If DIF is greater than some specified threshold, such as 1.25, then you may have detected an edge. The threshold may be changed depending on the amount of detail you wish to have in your reconstructed image.

Assume that the image intensities are represented by integers from 0 to 9, with 0 representing white and 9 representing black, and the integers in between representing shades of gray. Furthermore, assume that the spacecraft camera converts its images into two-dimensional information with a maximum of 50 values per line and a maximum of 40 lines. The number of values per line and the number of lines per image depends on the resolution desired for the particular image. The data is sent back to earth in streams of integers that are stored one row per line in a data file. Each image is preceded by a line that gives an identification number for the image and the number of rows and the number of columns in that image. In order to store the information efficiently, no blanks or commas are used between the integers that represent the intensities, or shades of gray in the image; therefore, this information will need to be read with a formatted READ statement. A trailer line in the file will contain an identification number of 9999 followed by two zero values.

The output from your program is to be a picture of the edges in a specified image. Thus, at each point in the image that corresponds to an edge, print the symbol #; at each point in the image that is not an edge, print a blank. Allow the user to enter the threshold for edge detection.

The program should ask the user for the name of the data file to be used by the program. Since there might be many images stored in the same data file, the program should first scan the file and print the identification and size of all images in the file. Because there might be many images, it is not feasible to store them all in memory as you read them; only print the identification and size of the images. Then, ask the user which image is to be analyzed and the threshold to be used. After reading this information from the terminal, rewind the file and locate the desired image. Read the image data into an array and perform the edge analysis using the threshold specified by the user.

PROBLEM STATEMENT

Write a program to read a two-dimensional image from a data file. The program should determine the location of edges in the file and print the edge image.

INPUT/OUTPUT DESCRIPTION

The user will specify the name of the data file that will be assumed to contain images. The program will list the identification and size of all images in the file, and the user will enter the identification number of the file to be analyzed and the threshold value. The intensity information is represented by integers that are not separated by blanks or commas. The output will be a two-dimensional image of the edges generated using the symbol # and blanks.

We will use a small image for our example. Consider the following two-dimensional array of intensities:

3	7	8	8	8	7
4	5	7	8	8	6
4	5	5	5	5	6
4	4	4	5	6	6

In general, we assume that points on the top, bottom, and sides of the array are not edges because we do not have complete data on these points. Therefore, we consider only "interior" points in our analysis. Call the array P, and then for the point in $P(2,2)$, we compute the difference DIF to be the following:

$$DIF = (|5 - 7| + |5 - 4| + |5 - 7| + |5 - 5|)/4 = 1.25$$

If our threshold is 1.25 or below, then $P(2,2)$ corresponds to an edge; otherwise it is not an edge. If we generate an image with the symbol #, using a threshold of 0.9, our image is the following:

	#	#	#	#	
				#	

ALGORITHM DEVELOPMENT

DECOMPOSITION

Read file name.
Read desired intensity data.
Determine and print edge information.

REFINEMENT IN PSEUDOCODE:

EDGE: Read filename
       Print a list of all images in file
       Read desired intensity data
       Read threshold
       Determine edge information
       Print edge information

The step to produce the list of images in the file will require reading and printing the identification and size of an image, reading past its image data, reading and printing the identification and size of the next image, and so on until we reach the identification number of 9999. Since we know that each line of an image starts on a new line in the file, we only have to read the first value of the line as we skim through the file looking for the next image. We need the complete data only for the image that we are going to analyze.

As we convert the pseudocode to FORTRAN, we want to ask ourselves if any of the steps involved should be implemented as functions or subroutines. The step to determine the edge information is one that is a good candidate for a subroutine because it involves a number of steps that will make our program longer and harder to read if we include them in the main program. If we use a subroutine, we can reference it in the main program and put the details in the subroutine itself. The structure chart for this program is:

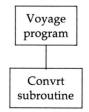

```
*--------------------------------------------------------------*
      PROGRAM  VOYAGE
*
*  This program detects edges in a two-dimensional image.
*
      INTEGER  I, J, IMAGE(40,50), ID, NR, NC, NEWID
      REAL  LIMIT
      CHARACTER  FILENM*6, EDGE(40)*50
      LOGICAL  DONE
*
      PRINT*, 'ENTER NAME OF IMAGE FILE ENCLOSED IN QUOTES'
      READ*, FILENM
      OPEN (UNIT=8,FILE=FILENM,STATUS='OLD')
```

```
*
      PRINT*
      PRINT*,'IMAGES IN THIS FILE'
      READ(8,*) ID, NR, NC
   5  IF (ID.NE.9999) THEN
         PRINT 10, ID, NR, NC
  10     FORMAT (1X,'ID = ',I4,' SIZE = (',I2,',',I2,')')
         DO 20 I=1,NR
            READ(8,15)IMAGE(I,1)
  15        FORMAT (50I1)
  20     CONTINUE
         READ(8,*)ID, NR, NC
         GO TO 5
      ENDIF
*
      PRINT*
      PRINT*, 'ENTER ID OF IMAGE TO BE ANALYZED'
      READ*, NEWID
      PRINT*, 'ENTER THRESHOLD FOR EDGE DETECTION'
      READ*, LIMIT
*
      REWIND (UNIT=8)
      READ(8,*) ID, NR, NC
      DONE = .FALSE.
  25  IF (.NOT.DONE) THEN
         IF (ID.EQ.NEWID) THEN
            DO 30 I=1,NR
               READ (8,15) (IMAGE(I,J),J=1,NC)
  30        CONTINUE
            CALL CONVERT(LIMIT,IMAGE,EDGE,NR,NC)
            PRINT*
            PRINT 35, LIMIT
  35        FORMAT (1X,'THRESHOLD VALUE = ',F5.2)
            DO 45 I=1,NR
               PRINT 40, EDGE(I)(1:NC)
  40           FORMAT (1X,A)
  45        CONTINUE
            DONE = .TRUE.
         ELSEIF (ID.EQ.9999) THEN
            DONE = .TRUE.
            PRINT*, 'IMAGE NOT FOUND'
         ELSE
            DO 50 I=1,NR
               READ(8,15) IMAGE(I,1)
  50        CONTINUE
            READ(8,*) ID, NR, NC
         ENDIF
         GO TO 25
      ENDIF
      END
*------------------------------------------------------------------*
```

continued

```
      SUBROUTINE   CONVRT  (LIMIT,IMAGE,EDGE,NR,NC)
*
*   This subroutine converts a two-dimensional image
*   to a character array containing edge information.
*
      INTEGER   IMAGE(40,50),  I,  J,  NR,  NC
      REAL   LIMIT,  DIF
      CHARACTER   EDGE(40)*50
*
      DO 5 J=1,NC
         EDGE(1)(J:J) = ' '
    5 CONTINUE
      DO 20 I=2,NR-1
         EDGE(I)(1:1) = ' '
         DO 15 J=2,NC-1
            DIF = (ABS(IMAGE(I-1,J)-IMAGE(I,J)) +
     +              ABS(IMAGE(I,J-1)-IMAGE(I,J)) +
     +              ABS(IMAGE(I,J+1)-IMAGE(I,J)) +
     +              ABS(IMAGE(I+1,J)-IMAGE(I,J)))/4.0
            IF  (DIF.GT.LIMIT) THEN
               EDGE(I)(J:J) = '#'
            ELSE
               EDGE(I)(J:J) = ' '
            ENDIF
   15    CONTINUE
         EDGE(I)(NC:NC) = ' '
   20 CONTINUE
      DO 25 J=1,NC
         EDGE(NR)(J:J) = ' '
   25 CONTINUE
*
      RETURN
      END
*-------------------------------------------------------*
```

Note that the first DO loop in the subroutine fills the top row of the image
with blanks, and that the last DO loop in the subroutine fills the bottom row
of the image with blanks. The first statement of the DO 20 loop fills the left
side of the other rows with a blank, and the last statement of the DO 20 loop
fills the right side of the other rows with a blank.

TESTING

The following data file called IMAGES was used to test the edge detection program:

```
87  4  6
378887
457886
455556
444566
25  12  28
1111111111111111311111111331
1333111111111111131111111311
1111311111111111113311111131
1111113111111111111133111113
1111113111111111111111311111
1111111311111111111111411111
1111111411111111111111311111
1111111131111111111111131111
1111111131111111111111113111
1111111113111111111111111311
1111111111311111111111113111
1111111111311111111111111111
34  5  4
22435
22444
23334
24244
24333
9999  0  0
```

The output from the program is shown below:

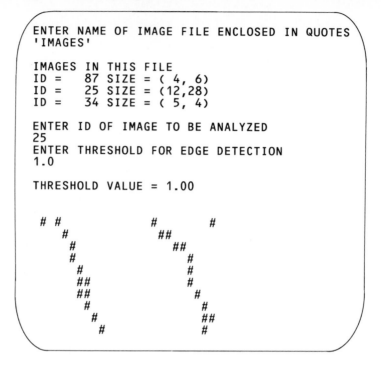

9-4 APPLICATION—WHOOPING CRANE MIGRATION (Biology)

Several operations are commonly encountered as we process data. For instance, we have seen a number of applications that use sorting algorithms. Other operations frequently used include finding the minimum value or maximum value in a set of data, computing the average value in a set of data, inserting or deleting values in a list, and searching for a value in a list.

In this application, we use the merge operation, which is the combining of an ordered list (the current whooping crane migration information) with another list that preserves the same order (the new sightings information). We assume that we are merging only two lists.

Assume that arrays A and B have each been sorted into ascending order, as shown:

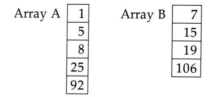

If these arrays are merged into an array C, the result is

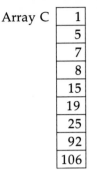

Array C

| 1 |
| 5 |
| 7 |
| 8 |
| 15 |
| 19 |
| 25 |
| 92 |
| 106 |

Note that array C is larger than either array A or B; in fact, if array A contains N elements and array B contains M elements, array C should contain N + M elements.

Data to be merged must have some order, such as ascending or descending. Alphabetical data can also be merged. In either case, what should you do about items that appear in both lists? Should the duplicate item appear once or twice in the merged list?

The answer depends on the application. If the merged data represents an alphabetical mailing list that has been put together from several sources, we would not want to duplicate a name on both lists. However, if we are merging bank transactions that are received in the mail with transactions processed at the teller windows, we would want to keep transactions with the same account number because they represent different transactions. Therefore, a specific requirement on how to handle duplicates must be included in the problem statement for a problem that includes a merging operation.

In this application, recall that the whooping crane migration problem involved printing the sightings information collected by the Wildlife Service. We want to print this information in the order of the sightings, which requires merging the master file with new sightings information received by the Wildlife Service. Assume that each sighting record contains the following information:

Sighting date (month, day, year)
Sighting time (time using a 24-hour clock)
Grid location (2 integer coordinates)
Number of birds

We assume that the data in the master file CRANES is stored as a series of integers (month, day, year, time, grid1, grid2, and birds) with the following format:

FORMAT (3I2,1X,I4,1X,2I2,1X,I4)

The new sightings information in the file SIGHTS is stored in the same format.

PROBLEM STATEMENT

Write a program to merge data in two files: the current whooping crane migration information file with the new sightings information file.

INPUT/OUTPUT DESCRIPTION

The migration data is in a data file CRANES that contains the sightings information in ascending order by date and time. The new information is to be merged with this information to generate an updated file, also called CRANES. After updating the data, an ordered listing of the sightings information is to be printed.

HAND EXAMPLE

For a hand-worked example, we use the following data for the master file and the file of new sightings information:

MASTER FILE CRANES

DATE	TIME	GRID	NUMBER OF BIRDS
040386	0920	21 07	5
040886	0830	21 07	4
050186	1805	22 08	4
051086	0915	22 09	4
051586	0730	23 07	5

UPDATE FILE SIGHTS

DATE	TIME	GRID	NUMBER OF BIRDS
040586	0815	21 09	4
051086	0800	22 09	4

If we merge these files by the date and time, the migration file CRANES and the corresponding report should contain the following information:

```
WHOOPING CRANE MIGRATION

CURRENT SIGHTINGS

04-03-86    0920
        GRID LOCATION:  21  7
        NUMBER OF BIRDS     5

04-05-86    0815
        GRID LOCATION:  21  9
        NUMBER OF BIRDS     4

04-08-86    0830
        GRID LOCATION:  21  7
        NUMBER OF BIRDS     4

05-01-86    1805
        GRID LOCATION:  22  8
        NUMBER OF BIRDS     4

05-10-86    0800
        GRID LOCATION:  22  9
        NUMBER OF BIRDS     4

05-10-86    0915
        GRID LOCATION:  22  9
        NUMBER OF BIRDS     4

05-15-86    0730
        GRID LOCATION:  23  7
        NUMBER OF BIRDS     5
```

Note that we may need to use part or all of the values for year, month, day, and time to order the sightings correctly.

ALGORITHM DEVELOPMENT

The general steps in the algorithm are simple to list. We want to merge the two data files, generate a new master file, and print the contents of the master file.

DECOMPOSITION

Merge sightings file and master file into new master file.
Print the data in the new master file.

We now need to develop an algorithm for merging two lists. One algorithm might be to move one list (with M elements) into the first part of a larger array with $M + N$ elements, and then move the other array (with N elements) into the last part of the larger array. We could sort the large array and have the data items in the desired order. This idea could be extended to three or more lists. However, there are two reasons why this is not a good algorithm: It is inefficient because each individual array or list is already sorted; and, it requires that all the data to be merged reside in memory at one time, which is impractical with large files.

If we reexamine the hand-worked example, we see that we need only the next value on each list to determine which record should be moved to the output file: The record with the smaller date is moved to the output file, and the next record of that file is read. A trailer signal simplifies the algorithm's logic development because we do not need to worry about what to do when we reach the end of a data file while there are still records left in the other file. When we read a trailer record with 999999 as the date, it is larger than the other valid dates and thus forces the rest of the records to be moved to the output file until we are positioned at the trailer signal of each file. We then write a trailer signal to the output file.

Let's try some simple data with this algorithm. Assume that we want to merge File 1 and File 2. Both files contain a trailer signal 999. The arrows point to the current record (the one we have just read for the input files or the one we have just written for output files).

File 1	File 2	Output File
→ 5	→ 2	
10	51	
82	999	
107		
999		

File 1	File 2	Output File
→ 5	2	→ 2
10	→ 51	
82	999	
107		
999		

File 1	File 2	Output File
5	2	2
→ 10	→ 51	→ 5
82	999	
107		
999		

File 1	File 2	Output File
5	2	2
10	→ 51	5
→ 82	999	→ 10
107		
999		

File 1	File 2	Output File
5	2	2
10	51	5
→ 82	→999	10
107		→ 51
999		

(continued)

File 1	File 2	Output File
5	2	2
10	51	5
82	→ 999	10
→ 107		51
999		→ 82

File 1	File 2	Output File
5	2	2
10	51	5
82	→ 999	10
107		51
→ 999		82
		→ 107

File 1	File 2	Output File
5	2	2
10	51	5
82	→ 999	10
107		51
→ 999		82
		107
		→ 999

We develop the pseudocode for the merge separately, and then add it to the pseudocode for the whooping crane migration algorithm. We assume that a merge of two files is always sufficient: If you have three files to merge, merge two of them, and then merge the combined file with the third file. If you have more than three files, continue merging two at a time until you have combined them all.

MERGE REFINEMENT IN PSEUDOCODE

MERGE: Read first record in both files
       While more data do
         Write information from file with smaller code
         Read new information from file with smaller code
       Write trailer signal

We now return to our whooping crane migration problem and include the steps for the merge.

Refinement in Pseudocode

```
MIGRAT: Read first master record
            Read first update record
            While more sightings do
               If update date < master date then
                  Write update record
                  Read new update record
               else
                  Write master record
                  Read new master record
            Write trailer signal      ·
            Copy merged file to master file and print report
```

Because we are reading data that represents the same types of information from both files, we would like to choose names that indicate which file contained the data. Thus, for the day from the file CRANES, we use the variable CDA; for the day from the file SIGHTS, we use the variable SDA. When we copy the output file back into the file CRANES, we use the variable DA because it is not being compared to other variables.

Before we convert the refined pseudocode into FORTRAN, we need to discuss one more item in the algorithm. We compare the date from one record with the date in another record to determine which date occurred first: This comparison first involves comparing the years. If the years are equal, we compare the months. If the months are equal, we compare the days. If the days are equal, we compare the times. This process is easy to understand, but it is cumbersome to translate into FORTRAN. Thus, we use a statement function to recombine the month, day, year, and time into a number that can make all the comparisons simultaneously; for example, if month = 09, day = 25, year = 86, and time = 0845, we create a number equal to the value 8609250845. If we compare another date in this new form, we need only one comparison to determine which date occurred first. This new number that we compute cannot be an integer because its value is typically greater than the maximum integer in many computers (approximately 2 billion for a VAX computer). We also cannot use a real number because we need 10 digits of precision. Thus, we must use a double precision number to store the number that combines the year, month, day, and time information.

```
*--------------------------------------------------------------*
      PROGRAM  MIGRAT
*
*  This program merges new sighting information into the
*  master file of migration information on whooping cranes.
*
      INTEGER   M,D,Y,T,MO,DA,YR,TIME,GRID1,GRID2,BIRDS,
     +          SMO,SDA,SYR,STIME,SGRID1,SGRID2,SBIRDS,
     +          CMO,CDA,CYR,CTIME,CGRID1,CGRID2,CBIRDS
      DOUBLE PRECISION  DATE, CDATE, SDATE
      LOGICAL  DONE
*
      DATE(M,D,Y,T) = DBLE(REAL(Y)*1.0D08) +
     +                DBLE(REAL(M)*1.0D06) +
     +                DBLE(REAL(D)*1.0D04) +
     +                DBLE(REAL(T))
*
      OPEN (UNIT=10,FILE='SIGHTS',STATUS='OLD')
      OPEN (UNIT=11,FILE='CRANES',STATUS='OLD')
      OPEN (UNIT=12,FILE='TEMP',STATUS='NEW')

      READ (10,5) SMO,SDA,SYR,STIME,SGRID1,SGRID2,SBIRDS
    5 FORMAT (3I2,1X,I4,1X,2I2,1X,I4)
      READ (11,5) CMO,CDA,CYR,CTIME,CGRID1,CGRID2,CBIRDS
      SDATE = DATE(SMO,SDA,SYR,STIME)
      CDATE = DATE(CMO,CDA,CYR,CTIME)
      IF (SMO.EQ.99.AND.CMO.EQ.99) THEN
         DONE = .TRUE.
      ELSE
         DONE = .FALSE.
      ENDIF
*
   10 IF (.NOT.DONE) THEN
         IF (CDATE.LT.SDATE) THEN
            WRITE (12,5) CMO,CDA,CYR,CTIME,CGRID1,
     +                   CGRID2,CBIRDS
            READ (11,5) CMO,CDA,CYR,CTIME,CGRID1,
     +                  CGRID2,CBIRDS
            CDATE = DATE(CMO,CDA,CYR,CTIME)
         ELSE
            WRITE (12,5) SMO,SDA,SYR,STIME,SGRID1,
     +                   SGRID2,SBIRDS
            READ (10,5) SMO,SDA,SYR,STIME,SGRID1,
     +                  SGRID2,SBIRDS
            SDATE = DATE(SMO,SDA,SYR,STIME)
         ENDIF
         IF (SMO.EQ.99.AND.CMO.EQ.99) DONE = .TRUE.
         GO TO 10
      ENDIF
      WRITE (12,5) SMO,SDA,SYR,STIME,SGRID1,SGRID2,SBIRDS
      CLOSE (UNIT=11,STATUS='DELETE')
      CLOSE (UNIT=12)

      OPEN (UNIT=11,FILE='CRANES',STATUS='NEW')
      OPEN (UNIT=12,FILE='TEMP',STATUS='OLD')
      PRINT*, 'WHOOPING CRANE MIGRATION'
      PRINT*
      PRINT*, 'CURRENT SIGHTINGS'
      PRINT*
*
```

continued

```
15 READ (12,5,END=50) MO,DA,YR,TIME,GRID1,GRID2,BIRDS
      IF (MO.NE.99) THEN
          PRINT 20, MO,DA,YR,TIME
20        FORMAT (1X,I2,'-',I2,'-',I2,4X,I4)
          PRINT 25, GRID1,GRID2
25        FORMAT (1X,5X,'GRID LOCATION: ',2I3)
          PRINT 30, BIRDS
30        FORMAT (1X,5X,'NUMBER OF BIRDS',1X,I5)
      ENDIF
      WRITE (11,5) MO,DA,YR,TIME,GRID1,GRID2,BIRDS
      GO TO 15
*
50 STOP
   END
*-------------------------------------------------------------*
```

TESTING

If we use the data from the hand-worked example in this program, the output
from our program is

```
WHOOPING CRANE MIGRATION

CURRENT SIGHTINGS

4- 3-86    0920
            GRID LOCATION:  21  7
            NUMBER OF BIRDS     5

4- 5-86    0815
            GRID LOCATION:  21  9
            NUMBER OF BIRDS     4

4- 8-86    0830
            GRID LOCATION:  21  7
            NUMBER OF BIRDS     4

5- 1-86    1805
            GRID LOCATION:  22  8
            NUMBER OF BIRDS     4

5-10-86    0800
            GRID LOCATION:  22  9
            NUMBER OF BIRDS     4

5-10-86    0915
            GRID LOCATION:  22  9
            NUMBER OF BIRDS     4

5-15-86    0730
            GRID LOCATION:  23  7
            NUMBER OF BIRDS     5
```

Throughout this text, we have emphasized the importance of carefully
selecting test data. If you look at the updates in this set of test data, you see
that it includes data in an order that causes insertions to be made at two

---

different points in the file. Also, the program is not thoroughly tested until the test data includes insertions that occur both at the beginning and at the end of the master file. Finally, because the date and time are involved in determining the correct order of the sightings, we include some sightings with the same date but different times to test this part of the program.

9–5 DIRECT-ACCESS FILES

Records in direct-access files are not accessed sequentially; they are accessed in the order specified. You specify that you want to read the tenth record, then the second record, and so forth. (However, you could read them sequentially by specifying that you want to read the first record, then the second record, and so on.)

When a direct file is opened, the ACCESS specification in the OPEN statement must be set to 'DIRECT' and a record length must be given with the RECL specifier. The READ and WRITE statements must include a REC specification to give the record number of the record to be addressed. The general form of a direct-access READ or WRITE is

| READ | *(unit number,format reference,*REC=*integer expression)* | *variable list* |

| WRITE | *(unit number,format reference,*REC=*integer expression)* | *variable list* |

The integer expression on the REC specification is evaluated to give the record number to be accessed. The ERR and IOSTAT specifications may also be used with the direct-access READ or WRITE statement. The END option may be used only with the READ statement.

Applications that use direct files usually have an account number or identification number that is part of each record, which can be used as the record number. For example, student identification numbers in a university often start at 00001 and increase in steps of 1; thus, the information for student number 00210 could be stored in record 210. Sometimes a numerical computation is performed on a field in the record to yield its record number: Suppose an inventory file contains records for items with stock numbers 500 through 1000. If 499 is subtracted from the stock number, we have the record number for the record that stores information about that stock item. When the steps to convert a value into a record number for a direct file reference become more complicated, the steps are called a *hash code*, the value computed as the record number is often called a *key*.

A direct file is usually built by loading the information into the file sequentially, with the record number starting at 1 and increasing by 1 each time a new record is written. The file can be accessed in a sequential order by varying the record number from 1 through the total number of records. However, the real power of a direct file is apparent when we want to update information in some of its records. Instead of reading each record sequentially, looking for the one we want to update, we specify the record number and that record is accessed automatically. Once we have updated the information in that record, we can write that new information into the record. Note that this is not father-son updating — we are actually updating information in the direct file itself, which can be considered a master file, because it contains all the updated information. If we specify a record number in a READ statement for a record that does not exist, an error occurs. To recover, the ERR specification can be included in the WRITE statement to provide a controlling branch to an error routine. These concepts are illustrated in Section 9–6.

SELF-TEST 9–2

This self-test allows you to check quickly to see if you have remembered some of the key points from Section 9–5. If you have any problems with the exercise, you should reread this section. The solution is included at the end of the text.

1. A direct-access file called STORES contains 100 records. Each record contains an item number that varies from 1 through 100 and is used as the record key. Each record also contains the number of items in the warehouse. The format of each record is

    FORMAT (I5,2X,I5)

    Write a program to print the item number of all items in which the record indicates that there are fewer than 5 items in the warehouse.

9–6 APPLICATION—COMPUTER PARTS INVENTORY (Computer Science/Engineering)

In this application, we develop a program to update an inventory file for the automated warehouse of a computer manufacturing plant. The inventory file is a direct-access file with the following record format:

Stock number	Item description	Quantity	Unit price

Stock number is a numeric value that can range from 001 to 999. Item description is a 10-character description of the item. The quantity or number of units of that piece of equipment is a 4-digit integer. The unit price of one

---

item is stored in a real value with a format of F6.2. Thus, the total record length is 23 characters and will appear as RECL = 23 in the OPEN statement.

The file that we use to update the inventory file PARTS is a transaction file called TRANS that contains information on items received and shipped out. The order of the transactions is the order in which they occurred. The transaction record consists of a stock number and a quantity: If the quantity is positive, the transaction represents items received; if the quantity is negative, the transaction represents items sent to the assembly lines. The transaction file is a sequential file with the following record format:

| Stock number | Quantity |

The stock number is a 3-digit integer, and the quantity is a 4-digit integer. Two blanks separate the fields. Assume that a trailer line in the transaction file contains 999 in the stock number.

Write a program to update the computer parts inventory file using this transaction file. (Note that we are not adding new records to the inventory file. We are only updating the records currently in the inventory file.)

PROBLEM STATEMENT

Write a program to update the quantity in a direct-access file.

INPUT/OUTPUT DESCRIPTION

The input to the program is two files: the direct-access master inventory file and the sequential transaction file.

HAND EXAMPLE

Assume that the two files contain this computer equipment information:

MASTER INVENTORY FILE

STOCK NUMBER	ITEM DESCRIPTION	QUANTITY	UNIT PRICE
1	microprocessor	10	586.92
2	modem	5	85.00
3	power supply	3	299.50
4	cable	12	24.95

TRANSACTION FILE

STOCK NUMBER	QUANTITY
1	-2
3	-1
2	8
1	15
1	-2
2	-2

After the update, the master inventory file should be updated to contain the following information:

MASTER INVENTORY FILE

STOCK NUMBER	ITEM DESCRIPTION	QUANTITY	UNIT PRICE
1	microprocessor	21	586.92
2	modem	11	85.00
3	power supply	2	299.50
4	cable	12	24.95

ALGORITHM DEVELOPMENT

The steps used to solve this problem are straightforward, as shown in the following decomposition. The primary reason that this solution is simple is because of the power of direct-access file processing.

DECOMPOSITION

> Read transaction records and update master file.

In the initial refinement we show the WHILE loop that is executed as long as there are transactions to process.

INITIAL REFINEMENT IN PSEUDOCODE

UPDATE: While more transactions do
        Read transaction record
        Read corresponding inventory record
        Update quantity
        Write updated inventory record

In further refining the solution, we add an error routine to print a message on the terminal screen if a match cannot be found between the inventory stock number and the transaction stock number.

FINAL REFINEMENT IN PSEUDOCODE

UPDATE: Read stock number, update
      If stock number = 999 then
         more ← false
      else
         more ← true
      While more do
         Read corresponding inventory record
         If no match then
            Print error message
         else
            new quantity ← old quantity + update
            Write inventory record
         Read stock number, update
         If stock number = 999 then
            more ← false

The program for performing this update for a direct-access file follows.

FORTRAN PROGRAM

```
*---------------------------------------------------------------*
      PROGRAM  UPDATE
*
*  This program updates a direct file
*  using a stock number as the key.
*
      INTEGER  STOCK, CHANGE, QUANT, KEY
      REAL   PRICE
      LOGICAL  MORE
      CHARACTER*10  DESC
*
      DATA  MORE /.TRUE./
*
      OPEN (UNIT=10,FILE='TRANS',ACCESS='SEQUENTIAL',
     +      STATUS='OLD',FORM='FORMATTED')
      OPEN (UNIT=11, FILE='PARTS',ACCESS='DIRECT',
     +      STATUS='OLD',FORM='FORMATTED',RECL=23)
*
      READ (10,5) KEY, CHANGE
    5 FORMAT (I3,2X,I4)
      IF (KEY.EQ.999) MORE = .FALSE.
*
   10 IF (MORE) THEN
         READ (11,15,REC=KEY,ERR=20,END=20)
     +         STOCK, DESC, QUANT, PRICE
   15    FORMAT (I3,A10,I4,F6.2)
         QUANT = QUANT + CHANGE
         WRITE (11,15,REC=KEY) STOCK, DESC, QUANT, PRICE
   20    IF (KEY.NE.STOCK) PRINT*, 'NO MATCH FOR', KEY
         READ (10,5) KEY, CHANGE
         IF (KEY.EQ.999) MORE = .FALSE.
         GO TO 10
      ENDIF
*
      END
*---------------------------------------------------------------*
```

TESTING

Before you can test this program, you must create the direct-access master file.
A program to build the direct-access file from data entered from the terminal
follows: The program closes the file after it is built, reopens it as an input file,
and prints the data. Try this with the initial set of hand-worked data; then, try
the update program. After you are comfortable with the steps, develop some
new test data. Be sure to try transactions without a match in the master
inventory file.

FORTRAN PROGRAM

```
*------------------------------------------------------------*
      PROGRAM  CREATE
*
*  This program creates an inventory direct file
*  from terminal input data.
*
      INTEGER  STOCK, QUANT, N
      CHARACTER*10  DESC
*
      OPEN (UNIT=9,FILE='PARTS',ACCESS='DIRECT',
     +      STATUS='NEW',FORM='FORMATTED',RECL=23)
      PRINT*, 'ENTER NUMBER OF RECORDS FOR MASTER FILE'
      READ*, N
      DO 10 I=1,N
         PRINT*, 'ENTER STOCK NUMBER'
         READ*, STOCK
         PRINT*, 'ENTER DESCRIPTION IN APOSTROPHES'
         READ*, DESC
         PRINT*, 'ENTER INITIAL QUANTITY'
         READ*, QUANT
         PRINT*, 'ENTER PRICE (NO DOLLAR SIGN)'
         READ*, PRICE
         WRITE (9,5,REC=STOCK) STOCK, DESC, QUANT, PRICE
    5    FORMAT (I3,A,I4,F6.2)
   10 CONTINUE
*
      CLOSE (UNIT=9)
      OPEN (UNIT=9,FILE='PARTS',ACCESS='DIRECT',
     +      STATUS='OLD',FORM='FORMATTED',RECL=23)
      DO 15 I=1,N
         READ (9,5,REC=I,ERR=12) STOCK, DESC, QUANT, PRICE
         PRINT*, STOCK, DESC, QUANT, PRICE
   12    IF (I.NE.STOCK) PRINT*, 'NO RECORD NUMBER', I
   15 CONTINUE
*
      END
*------------------------------------------------------------*
```

9-7 INQUIRE STATEMENT

Our final statement used with files is the INQUIRE statement. It has two general forms:

> INQUIRE (FILE=*character expression,inquiry specifier list*)

> INQUIRE (UNIT=*integer expression,inquiry specifier list*)

This executable statement gains information about a file or a unit number. For example, suppose that we are going to allow a user to enter the name of a data file to be used in a program, as we did in the edge detection program in Section 9-3. If the user enters the name of a file that does not exist, then the program will terminate with an execution error. If we use the INQUIRE statement, we can determine whether the file exists, and if it does not exist, we can ask the user to enter a different file name. The following statements illustrate this type of interaction with the user:

```
      DONE = .FALSE.
      FOUND = .FALSE.
      PRINT*, 'ENTER FILE NAME OF IMAGE FILE IN QUOTES'
      READ*, FILENM
    5 IF (.NOT.DONE) THEN
          INQUIRE (FILE=FILENM, EXIST=THERE)
          IF (.NOT.THERE) THEN
              PRINT*, 'FILE DOES NOT EXIST'
              PRINT*, 'ENTER NEW FILE NAME OR QUIT IN QUOTES'
              READ*, FILENM
              IF (FILENM.EQ.'QUIT') DONE = .TRUE.
          ELSE
              DONE = .TRUE.
              FOUND = .TRUE.
          ENDIF
          GO TO 5
      ENDIF
      IF (FOUND) THEN
          OPEN (UNIT=10,FILE=FILENM,STATUS='OLD')
          .
          .
          .
```

These statements assume that FOUND, DONE, and THERE have been specified to be logical variables, and that FILENM has been specified to be a character variable.

The INQUIRE statement is also useful when we are writing a module (function or subroutine) that uses a file, and we don't know whether the file has been opened. We will assume that the main program and the modules using the file all use the value 15 for the unit number. The following pair of statements could then be used in a module to determine whether the file had been opened, and to then open the file if it was not already open:

```
      INQUIRE (UNIT=15,OPENED=AVAIL)
      IF (.NOT.AVAIL) OPEN(UNIT=15,FILE='FLIGHT',STATUS='OLD')
```

These statements would assume that AVAIL had been specified to be a logical variable.

Table 9–1 contains a complete list of the inquiry specifiers that can be used with the INQUIRE statement.

TABLE 9–1 Inquiry Specifiers

Inquiry Specifier	Variable Type	Value for File Inquiry	Value for Unit Inquiry
ACCESS =	character	'SEQUENTIAL' 'DIRECT'	'SEQUENTIAL' 'DIRECT'
BLANK =	character	'NULL' 'ZERO'	'NULL' 'ZERO'
DIRECT =	character	'YES' 'NO' 'UNKNOWN'	—
ERR =	integer	statement number of error routine	statement number of error routine
EXIST =	logical	.TRUE. .FALSE.	.TRUE. .FALSE.
FORM =	character	'FORMATTED' 'UNFORMATTED'	'FORMATTED' 'UNFORMATTED'
FORMATTED =	character	'YES' 'NO' 'UNKNOWN'	—
IOSTAT =	integer	error code	error code
NAME =	character	—	name of the file if it is not a scratch file
NAMED† =	logical	—	.TRUE. .FALSE.
NEXTREC =	integer	next record number in direct-access file	next record number in direct-access file
NUMBER† =	integer	unit number	—
OPENED =	logical	.TRUE. .FALSE.	.TRUE. .FALSE.
RECL =	integer	record length	record length
SEQUENTIAL =	character	'YES' 'NO' 'UNKNOWN'	—
UNFORMATTED =	character	'YES' 'NO' 'UNKNOWN'	—

† These specifiers do not refer to scratch files.

SUMMARY

In this chapter we presented a complete discussion of file processing with both sequential and direct files. Data is often used by more than one program; thus, the data file makes the same data easily available to many programs. By carefully choosing the type of file (sequential or direct) and the order of the data in the file, we can handle large amounts of data with simple algorithms and programs.

DEBUGGING AIDS

When processing files, a useful subroutine prints the data in the current record in a highly readable form — you might call this routine SNAP because it gives you a snapshot of a record in the file. When you are debugging a program that uses the file, call the routine every time that you want to check the contents of the current record.

Another handy subroutine opens a file and reads through it, printing the key information in each record. This subroutine is useful before and after updating the file to see if the new information has been entered properly.

We also want to emphasize that proper handling of files must occur when one of the files that we are using is empty. Using trailer signals helps this situation because a file without data should still have the trailer signal. If you are concerned that a file may not exist, you can use the INQUIRE statement to determine whether or not it exists without causing a program execution error.

STYLE/TECHNIQUE GUIDES

Good documentation is always important when working with data files. The record format and its field descriptions should have the same names in all programs that use the file; for example, if a file contains a stock number, give it the same name in each program that uses it. It is also good to use all the specifications that relate to the file in the OPEN statement; they do not need to be repeated in the other statements that refer to the file, but they should all be included at the beginning of the OPEN statement.

KEY WORDS

direct-access file   master file

external file   merge

father-son update   random access

field   record

hash code   sequential-access file

internal file   transaction file

key

PROBLEMS

We begin our problem set with modifications to the programs developed earlier in this chapter. Give the decomposition, refined pseudocode or flowchart, and FORTRAN solution for each problem.

Problems 1–5 modify the program VOYAGE, given on page 410, which detects edges in a two-dimensional image.

1. Modify the edge-detection program so that it allows the user to specify the symbol used to indicate the edges when the edge image is printed.

2. Modify the edge-detection program so that asterisks are used to outline the edge image when it is printed.

3. Modify the edge-detection program so that it uses the diagonal elements in the computation for the difference. Then instead of using four elements, the computation will use eight elements.

4. Modify the edge-detection program so that it computes the number of points that are interior points, and prints the percentage of interior points that are also edge points after printing the edge image.

5. Modify the edge-detection program so that it allows points on the top, bottom, or sides to be edges by using the points on two or three sides for computing the difference, and then comparing the difference to one-half or three-fourths of the threshold.

Problems 6–10 modify the program MIGRAT, given on page 421, which merged the new whooping crane sightings information with the master data file.

6. Modify the migration program so that it prints a count of the total number of sightings at the end of the report.

7. Modify the migration program so that it prints the maximum number of birds that have been sighted in the current report.

8. Modify the migration program so that it prints a final list of all grid locations of sightings along with the number of sightings in that grid.

9. Modify the migration program so that it tracks only a certain size sighting group. For example, the program could ask the user to enter the size of group of cranes; if the user enters the number 5, then the program prints a report only for the data that included 5 birds in the sightings data.

10. Modify the migration program so that it prints the most sightings during one day in the file. Print this at the end of the report.

Problems 11–15 modify the computer parts inventory program UPDATE, given on page 427.

11. Write a program to create a direct-access file from a sequential data file.

12. Write a subroutine to print the data in the inventory file in a report form by stock number order.

13. Write a program to change the description for selected stock items in the inventory file, using input from the terminal.

14. Write a program to print a reorder report for items whose quantity has gone below 5 units. Include the number of items to be ordered to bring the total quantity to 10.

15. Write a function to compute the total value of all items in the warehouse.

Problems 16–22 use data in a data file called SENSOR that contains maintenance information on mechanical measurement equipment used in a new chemical plant. Each line in the file contains the following information:

> Work order number
> Identification code for type of measurement device

These values are stored with the following format:

FORMAT (I5,2X,I1)

The identification code is an integer that represents the following measuring devices:

1. Counter
2. Flowmeter
3. Pressure transducer
4. Thermocouple
5. Pyrometer

The order of the lines in the file correspond to the order in which the work orders were issued. If a repair involved more than one sensor, more than one line in the file has the same work order number; these lines are consecutive in the file. The following programs are needed by the plant engineers to analyze the reliability of process equipment.

16. Write a program that reads the data from the file SENSOR and prints a report that gives the total number of work orders for counters, flowmeters, and so on. Use the following report form:

```
WORK ORDER SUMMARY
SENSOR                  NUMBER OF WORK ORDERS
- - - - - - - - - - - - - - - - - - - - - - - - - - - - - - - - - - - - -
COUNTER                      XXXX
FLOWMETER                    XXXX
PRESSURE TRANSDUCER          XXXX
THERMOCOUPLE                 XXXX
PYROMETER                    XXXX
```

17. Write a program to print all the work orders for an identification code that is read from the terminal.

18. Write a function called COUNT that reads the data in the file and returns a count of the work orders required for a specified identification code, which is an input argument to the function.

19. Modify the program in problem 16 so that it also prints the total number of work orders.

20. Modify the program in problem 16 so that it includes the following analysis information in the summary report:

```
NUMBER OF SENSORS NEEDING MAINTENANCE          XXXX
NUMBER OF WORK ORDERS WITH ONE SENSOR          XXXX
NUMBER OF WORK ORDERS WITH MULTIPLE SENSORS    XXXX
```

21. Modify the program in problem 16 so that it includes the following summary information in the report:

```
NUMBER OF WORK ORDERS REQUIRING MAINTENANCE
ON BOTH PRESSURE TRANSDUCERS AND PYROMETERS IS    XXXX
```

22. Modify the program in problem 16 so that it prints the work order numbers for all requests of maintenance that includes thermocouples. Print four numbers per line using the following format:

```
WORK ORDER NUMBERS FOR THERMOCOUPLE MAINTENANCE
XXXX   XXXX    XXXX   XXXX
```

Problems 23–27 use the data in a direct-access file called TEST that contains the status of tests being performed at a materials testing laboratory. The testing lab offers four types of tests: compression, tensile, shear, and fatigue. The codes for these tests are, respectively, C, T, S, and F. Each time a test is completed on a material sample, the information is added to the test status file. The file TEST contains the sample number (integers 1–500); the material identification (30 characters); and four characters, which are initially blanks, but are updated to C, T, S, and F, as the material is tested. The format for each record in the file is

FORMAT (I3,1X,A30,1X,A4)

23. Write a program that reads the information in this file and prints a list of sample numbers for samples that have had the shear test completed. (The tests can occur in any order; thus, the four codes (C,T,S,F) can appear in any order in the string of characters.)

24. Write a program that reads the information in this file and prints a testing report. First list all samples that have been through the compression test, then all that have been through the tensile test, and so on. (The tests can occur in any order; thus the four codes (C,T,S,F) can appear in any order in the string of characters.) Put appropriate headers at the beginning of each list. If two tests have been completed on a sample, its sample number and identification will appear twice in the report, and so on.

25. Write a program that prints a summary report to give the percentages of materials that have been through each test. Use the following format:

```
SUMMARY OF MATERIAL TESTS
TEST                PERCENTAGE
- - - - - - - - - - - - - - - - - - - - - - - - - - -
COMPRESSION         XXX.X
TENSILE             XXX.X
SHEAR               XXX.X
FATIGUE             XXX.X
```

26. Modify the program in problem 25 so that it also prints the total number of samples in the test file and the total number of tests that have been completed.

27. Modify the program in problem 25 so that it also prints the number of samples that have had one test completed, the number of samples that have had two tests completed, the number of samples that have had three tests completed, and the number of samples that have had all four tests completed.

FORTRAN STATEMENT SUMMARY

BACKSPACE Statement:

$$\text{BACKSPACE (UNIT=}integer\ expression,optional\ file\ specifiers)$$

Examples:

$$\text{BACKSPACE (UNIT=10)}$$

$$\text{BACKSPACE (UNIT=12,IOSTAT=ERROR)}$$

Discussion:
The BACKSPACE statement allows you to back up to the previous record in an input file. When you execute a READ statement following the BACKSPACE statement, you are accessing the same information as the READ statement before the BACKSPACE statement. The file specifiers are discussed in Section 9–2.

CLOSE Statement:

$$\text{CLOSE (UNIT=}integer\ expression,optional\ file\ specifiers)$$

Examples:

$$\text{CLOSE (UNIT=10)}$$

$$\text{CLOSE (UNIT=15,ERR=99)}$$

Discussion:
The CLOSE statement closes a file. Files are automatically closed at the end of a program, so this statement is used primarily when the file is to be closed and reopened again in the same program.

ENDFILE Statement:

$$\text{ENDFILE (UNIT=}integer\ expression,optional\ file\ specifiers)$$

Example:

$$\text{ENDFILE (UNIT=12)}$$

Discussion:
The ENDFILE statement writes an end-of-file record to an output file. The CLOSE and END statements automatically perform this function on most systems.

INQUIRE Statement:

> **INQUIRE (FILE**=*character expression,inquiry specifier list***)**
> **INQUIRE (UNIT**=*integer expression,inquiry specifier list***)**

Examples:

> **INQUIRE (FILE='XYDATA',SEQUENTIAL=ANSWER)**
>
> **INQUIRE (UNIT=12,SEQUENTIAL=ANSWER)**

Discussion:

The INQUIRE statement has two forms: one to obtain information about a file with a specified name and one to obtain information about a file with a specified unit. The INQUIRY specifiers are listed in Table 9–1.

OPEN Statement:

> **OPEN (UNIT**=*integer expression,***FILE**=*character expression,*
> **STATUS**=*character expression,optional file specifiers***)**

Examples:

> **OPEN (UNIT=10,FILE='XYDATA',STATUS='OLD')**
>
> **OPEN (UNIT=15,FILE='EXPER1',ACCESS='DIRECT',STATUS='OLD')**

Discussion:

The OPEN statement must be used to connect data files to a program. The UNIT, FILE, and STATUS specifiers must also be used. Other optional file specifiers may be used to emphasize certain characteristics of the file or to change the default characteristics that are assumed when some file specifiers are omitted.

REWIND Statement:

> **REWIND (UNIT**=*integer expression,file specifiers***)**

Examples:

> **REWIND (UNIT=9)**
>
> **REWIND (UNIT=13,IOSTAT=ERROR,ERR=500)**

Discussion:

The REWIND statement repositions a sequential file at the first record of the file. Some systems require a REWIND statement after opening a file to begin reading information at the beginning of the file.

APPLICATION — Linear Regression Model
(Mechanical Engineering)

One of the greatest achievements of engineers and scientists has been the manned expeditions to the moon. Sophisticated sensors and computer equipment provide the astronauts and the NASA staff with the information they need to make decisions during the flights. Collecting data and then using that data to develop an equation or model is important in analyzing a complex system. Write a program to determine a linear model for a set of nozzle deflection data that has been collected for a spacecraft landing rocket. (See Section 10–2 for the solution.)

Photo courtesy of NASA.

10

NUMERICAL APPLICATIONS

INTRODUCTION

FORTRAN was specifically designed to perform the numerical computations needed by engineers and scientists. Although it is one of the oldest high-level languages, it continues to be one of the most popular because each new FORTRAN standard has kept the strengths of the numerical computations and has added new features that improve structure and data handling. In Chapters 1–9, we presented the major features of FORTRAN and illustrated them in a variety of applications. Some people incorrectly assume that using double precision will always improve the accuracy of computed values. However, if a poor choice is made in selecting a numerical technique, using double precision will not reduce the error. In this chapter, we discuss some of the common numerical techniques used in solving engineering and science problems along with some suggestions for avoiding or minimizing errors that are due to the precision of the computer.

10–1 APPROXIMATIONS

In this section we present several numerical techniques for approximating values or functions. As discussed in the chapter opening application, many engineering problems in complex environments use data samples to compute another value or to construct a model for the system being studied. For example, in weather forecasts the meteorologist uses the temperature and humidity values plus general weather conditions around the country to predict tomorrow's weather. Computer modeling is a similar process: We use the available information to determine an equation that "best fits" the data, and then we use that model to predict additional data values. When we use interpolation to find a logarithm or trigonometric value between entries in a table, we assume that the values are connected by a straight line. Interpolation computes a specific value on that line. In Section 10–2, we present an application in which we determine a *linear regression model* (or linear equation) for a set of data. We can use the model to determine values anywhere on the line. Other techniques to find polynomial models for a set of data are listed in the references at the end of this section.

An important aspect of creating a model for a set of data is evaluating the usefulness of the model. A linear model for a set of data may not work well if the data is better represented by a quadratic model (or quadratic equation). It is important that our techniques not only allow us to derive the model, but also to evaluate the quality of the model.

Approximations are also needed when we want to compute information related to the data. For example, a set of data may represent values of a function over a particular interval, and we want to approximate the area under this function in the interval. Although here we discuss this problem in terms of approximating an area, it is really a technique for numerical integration because an integral represents the area under a curve. Many techniques can approximate the area under a curve, but the most common is the *trapezoidal approximation*. In Section 10–3, we develop a program to read a set of data values from a data file and then approximate the area under the curve represented by the data.

Before we proceed, we discuss some general methods for minimizing *precision errors* in numerical calculations: These methods are presented through examples that do not include a detailed analysis of the error propagation. The discussion that follows assumes that you need to keep the same precision in the data storage as well as in the operations; otherwise, you can improve the accuracy of a numerical approximation by storing your data in double-precision values, and, after you have completed all the computations, moving the double-precision value back to a real value. Although most computer systems have 7- or 8-digit precision, our examples assume 3-digit precision for ease in computing.

Our first guideline relates to adding (or subtracting) long lists of numbers. To reduce precision errors, work with smaller numbers first. If you are concerned about keeping as much accuracy in the data as possible, you may want to sort the numbers and then begin adding with the smallest value; for example, consider the following set of numbers that have 3-digit precision (recall that the computer stores real values in exponential form, thus we begin counting digits of precision with the first nonzero digit):

$$0.0336$$
$$0.0356$$
$$0.3290$$
$$0.5190$$

If we add these values by hand, the sum is 0.9172. If we add these numbers as the computer would, we add them two at a time, with each partial sum being truncated to 3 digits of precision. This process is illustrated, with the addition starting with the smallest numbers on the left side and the addition starting with the largest numbers on the right side. As you can see, the more accurate sum started with the smaller numbers:

ADDING FROM TOP	ADDING FROM BOTTOM
0.0336	0.519
+ 0.0356	+ 0.329
0.0692	0.848
+ 0.329	+ 0.0356
0.398	0.883
+ 0.519	+ 0.0336
0.917	0.916

The second guideline relates to numbers of nearly equal value. If possible, avoid subtraction of nearly equal values. Sometimes, expressions can be written to avoid this subtraction; for example, consider the expression

$$a + b + (c - d)$$

If c and d are nearly equal in value, we can rewrite the expression as

$$(a + c) + (b - d)$$

As a specific example, assume that we are working with 3-digit precision and that the variables have the following values:

$$a = 0.919, \; b = 0.829, \; c = 0.0356, \; d = 0.0330$$

We now substitute these values in both expressions and truncate all intermediate steps to 3 digits. The correct value is 1.7506, but only one of the computations gives this result accurate to 3-digit precision:

$a + b + (c - d)$	$0.919 + 0.829$	$= 1.74$
	$0.0356 - 0.0330$	$= \underline{0.00260}$
		1.74
$(a + c) + (b - d)$	$0.919 + 0.0356$	$= 0.954$
	$0.829 - 0.0330$	$= \underline{0.796}$
		1.75

The third guideline minimizes the number of arithmetic operations. Because precision errors can occur with each operation, we minimize these effects when we minimize the number of operations. For example, the following expressions are equivalent, but the one on the left uses 2 operations and the one on the right uses 3 operations:

$$3.0*X*Y \qquad (X + X + X)*Y$$

If you use FORTRAN for numerical applications, you may want further information on numerical techniques and their analysis. The following list contains texts that provide detailed information on this topic:

1. Acton, F. *Numerical Methods That Work*. New York: Harper & Row, 1970.
2. Cheney, W., and D. Kincaid. *Numerical Mathematics and Computing*. Monterey, Calif.: Brooks/Cole, 1980.
3. Conte, S.D., and C. deBoor. *Elementary Numerical Analysis*. New York: McGraw-Hill, 1972.
4. Hornbeck, R. W. *Numerical Methods*. New York: Quantum, 1975.
5. James, M., G. Smith, and J. Wolford. *Applied Numerical Methods for Digital Computation*. New York: Harper & Row, 1985.
6. Pennington, R. H. *Introductory Computer Methods and Numerical Analysis*. London: Macmillan, 1970.
7. Shoup, T. *A Practical Guide to Computer Methods for Engineers*. Englewood Cliffs, N.J.: Prentice-Hall, 1979.

10-2 APPLICATION — LINEAR REGRESSION MODEL (Mechanical Engineering)

When working with experimental or empirical data, we often want to determine the equation of a straight line that represents a good fit to the data. If the data values are linear, a linear equation can estimate values for which we have no data. For instance, suppose that the following data represents the load-deflection curve of a coil spring, where the length of the spring is measured in millimeters and the load (or weight applied to the spring) is measured in dynes:

LOAD	LENGTH
0.28	6.62
0.50	5.93
0.67	4.46
0.93	4.25
1.15	3.30
1.38	3.15
1.60	2.43
1.98	1.46

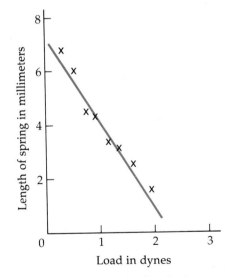

Given a linear equation that represents a good fit to the data, we could estimate the initial length of the spring by substituting a value of zero for the load in the equation. Similarly, the load that causes the spring to have a length of 5 millimeters could also be calculated. The following plot contains the original data points plus an estimate of the position of the straight line that represents a good fit to the data:

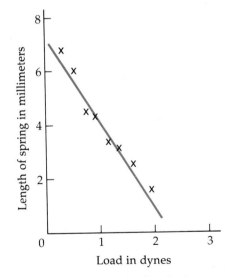

The *method of least squares* is a standard technique used for determining the equation of a straight line from a set of data. Recall that the equation of a straight line is

$$y = mx + b$$

where m is the slope of the line and b is the y-intercept. Given a set of data, such as the load-versus-length values for the spring problem, the slope and y-intercept for the least-squares line can be calculated using the following equations (derived from differential calculus). The symbol Σ represents summation. Therefore, given the set of points $\{(x_1,y_1), (x_2,y_2), \ldots, (x_n,y_n)\}$, let

$$\sum x = x_1 + x_2 + \cdots + x_n$$

$$\sum y = y_1 + y_2 + \cdots + y_n$$

$$\sum xy = x_1y_1 + x_2y_2 + \cdots + x_ny_n$$

$$\sum x^2 = x_1^2 + x_2^2 + \cdots + x_n^2$$

The slope and y-intercept can be calculated using these equations:

$$\text{Slope} = \frac{\sum x \sum y - n \sum (x \cdot y)}{\left(\sum x\right)^2 - n \sum (x^2)}$$

$$y\text{-intercept} = \frac{\sum y - \text{slope} \cdot \sum x}{n}$$

Once the slope and y-intercept have been calculated, the equation of the line can be obtained.

If the data points and the straight line were drawn on graph paper, it would be possible to see how closely the line fits the data. Another way to test how well the line fits the data would be to substitute an x value in the equation to calculate a new y value. This new y value, designated $\hat{y}$, would be an estimate for the value of y when x is given. For example, suppose the least-squares technique yielded the following linear equation for a set of data:

$$y = 4.2x - 3.1$$

Then, for the data coordinate (1.0,.9), the estimate for y would be

$$\hat{y} = 4.2(1.0) - 3.1 = 1.1$$

The *residual* for a data point is the difference between the actual data value for y and its estimated value, $y - \hat{y}$. The residual for the preceding data point is $(0.9 - 1.1)$, or -0.2. The sum of the squares of the residuals, called the residual sum, gives an estimate of the quality of fit of the data to the linear equation without plotting the data. When the data is exactly linear, the residual sum is zero. The residual sum becomes larger as the data deviates from the linear equation. If we want to compare two linear equations that both seem good estimates for the same data, we can compare residual sums to determine the better estimate.

The accelerometer used in a spacecraft to measure acceleration contains a spring that must be tested at different temperatures to determine the effects of temperature on the load-deflection model. Accurate measurements of this model are needed in order to determine accurate acceleration measurements for the spacecraft. Write a program to determine the load-deflection linear model from a set of data values.

PROBLEM STATEMENT

Find the linear equation that best fits a set of data values stored in a data file. Print a report that gives the linear equation and the residual sum.

INPUT/OUTPUT DESCRIPTION

The input is a data file XYDATA. We do not know how many values are in the file, and it does not contain a trailer signal. Each line of the file contains an experimentally measured x and y value. The output should be a report in the following form:

```
THE LINEAR EQUATION IS
Y = XXX.XX X + XXX.XX

ORIGINAL      ORIGINAL      ESTIMATED      RESIDUAL
   X             Y             Y

XXX.XX        XXX.XX        XXX.XX         XXX.XX
  .
  .
  .

RESIDUAL SUM = XXX.XX
```

HAND EXAMPLE

For a hand-worked example, we use the first 3 data values given for the load-deflection curve at the beginning of the section. The corresponding sums are

$$\sum x = 0.28 + 0.50 + 0.67 = 1.45$$

$$\sum y = 6.62 + 5.93 + 4.46 = 17.01$$

$$\sum xy = 0.28*6.62 + 0.50*5.93 + 0.67*4.46 = 7.8068$$

$$\sum x*x = 0.28*0.28 + 0.50*0.50 + 0.67*0.67 = 0.7773$$

Using the slope and y-intercept equations, we determine the following equation:

$$y = -5.42 x + 8.29$$

Using this equation to compute the residuals gives the following table:

```
THE LINEAR EQUATION IS
 Y =  -5.42 X +   8.29

 ORIGINAL      ORIGINAL      ESTIMATED      RESIDUAL
    X             Y             Y

   0.28          6.62          6.77          -0.15
   0.50          5.93          5.58           0.35
   0.67          4.46          4.66          -0.20

 RESIDUAL SUM =   0.19
```

ALGORITHM DEVELOPMENT

The decomposition of this problem solution into general steps is shown.

DECOMPOSITION

Read x and y data.
Compute slope and y-intercept.
Compute residuals.
Print report.

As we refine the decomposition, we recognize that we need a loop to read the x and y data. Because we are reading each pair of data values from a single line, at the same time we can add the values to the sums that we are going to need for the calculations. We also need to use arrays for the x and y data because the data is needed for the report. If we only wanted the values for the slope and y-intercept of the linear model, we would not need arrays for the x and y data.

The residuals are used for computing the residual sum and are printed in the report. However, we can compute the residual, add it to the sum, and print the corresponding residual in the same loop — thus, we do not need an array for the residual values.

REFINED PSEUDOCODE

LINEAR: $i \leftarrow 1$
       sumx $\leftarrow 0$
       sumy $\leftarrow 0$
       sumxy $\leftarrow 0$
       sumxx $\leftarrow 0$
       While more data do
         Read $x(i)$, $y(i)$
         sumx $\leftarrow$ sumx $+ x(i)$
         sumy $\leftarrow$ sumy $+ y(i)$
         sumxy $\leftarrow$ sumxy $+ x(i)y(i)$
         sumxx $\leftarrow$ sumxx $+ x(i)x(i)$
         $i \leftarrow i + 1$
       $n \leftarrow i - 1$
       Compute slope and y-intercept
       Print slope, y-intercept
       sumres $\leftarrow 0$
       For $i = 1$ to n do
         ynew $\leftarrow$ slope$*x(i) + y$-intercept
         res $\leftarrow y(i) -$ ynew
         sumres $\leftarrow$ sumres $+$ res$*$res
         Print $x(i)$, $y(i)$, ynew, res
       Print sumres

We can now convert the refined pseudocode into FORTRAN.

FORTRAN Program

```
*---------------------------------------------------------------*
      PROGRAM  LINEAR
*
*  This program computes a linear model for a set of data
*  and then computes the residual sum to evaluate the model.
*
      INTEGER  I,N
      REAL  X(500),Y(500),SLOPE,YINT,YNEW,RES,
     +      SUMX,SUMY,SUMXY,SUMXX,SUMRES
*
      DATA  I,SUMX,SUMY,SUMXY,SUMXX,SUMRES /1,5*0.0/
*
      OPEN (UNIT=10,FILE='XYDATA',STATUS='OLD')
*
    5 READ (UNIT=10,*,END=50) X(I), Y(I)
         SUMX = SUMX + X(I)
         SUMY = SUMY + Y(I)
         SUMXY = SUMXY + X(I)*Y(I)
         SUMXX = SUMXX + X(I)*X(I)
         I = I + 1
         GO TO 5
*
   50 N = I - 1
      SLOPE = (SUMX*SUMY - REAL(N)*SUMXY)/
     +        (SUMX*SUMX - REAL(N)*SUMXX)
      YINT = (SUMY - SLOPE*SUMX)/REAL(N)
*
      PRINT*, 'THE LINEAR EQUATION IS'
      PRINT 55, SLOPE, YINT
   55 FORMAT (1X,'Y = ',F6.2,' X + ',F6.2)
      PRINT*
      PRINT*,'ORIGINAL      ORIGINAL      ESTIMATED      RESIDUAL'
      PRINT*,'   X             Y              Y                 '
      PRINT*
*
      DO 65 I=1,N
         YNEW = SLOPE*X(I) + YINT
         RES = Y(I) - YNEW
         SUMRES = SUMRES + RES*RES
         PRINT 60, X(I), Y(I), YNEW, RES
   60    FORMAT (1X,F6.2,6X,F6.2,6X,F6.2,7X,F6.2)
   65 CONTINUE
*
      PRINT*
      PRINT 70, SUMRES
   70 FORMAT (1X,'RESIDUAL SUM = ',F6.2)
*
      END
*---------------------------------------------------------------*
```

TESTING

If we test this program with the data set given at the beginning of this section, the following report is printed:

```
THE LINEAR EQUATION IS
Y =  -2.93 X +    7.06

  ORIGINAL      ORIGINAL      ESTIMATED      RESIDUAL
     X             Y             Y

   0.28          6.62          6.24           0.38
   0.50          5.93          5.59           0.34
   0.67          4.46          5.10          -0.64
   0.93          4.25          4.33          -0.08
   1.15          3.30          3.69          -0.39
   1.38          3.15          3.02           0.13
   1.60          2.43          2.37           0.06
   1.98          1.46          1.26           0.20

RESIDUAL SUM =    0.88
```

(Note that the residual sum for the hand-worked example, which used the first 3 data points, was 0.19, and the residual sum for the full set of data was 0.88; this indicates that a linear equation better approximated the first 3 data points than the remaining data points.)

10-3   APPLICATION — NUMERICAL INTEGRATION (Electrical Engineering)

The operations of integration and differentiation give engineers and scientists important information about functions or data sets. For example, distance, velocity, and acceleration all relate to each other through integrals *(integration)* and derivatives *(differentiation)*. The derivative of distance is velocity, and the derivative of velocity is acceleration; the integral of acceleration is velocity, and the integral of velocity is distance. These topics are covered in detail in calculus courses, but the underlying principles are simple enough to apply independently. Integrating a function over an interval can be approximated by computing the area under the graph of the function; differentiation can be approximated by computing tangents to the graph of the function. Both of these numerical approximations are easily performed with FORTRAN.

In this application, we use a numerical technique to estimate the area under a curve. Problems 24–25 at the end of the chapter use a numerical technique to estimate tangents to a curve.

Assume that we want to estimate the area under the curve in the interval $[a,b]$, as shown in the diagram:

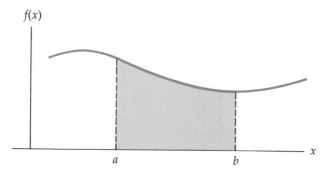

If we are given the function that represents the curve, we can evaluate that function at points spaced along the interval of interest, as shown:

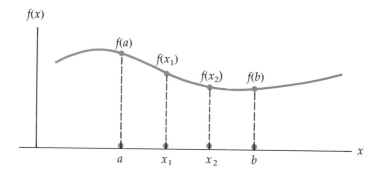

If we assume that the points on the curve that we have computed are joined by straight line segments, we have formed a group of trapezoids whose combined area approximates the area under the curve. As we compute points closer together on the curve, we have more trapezoids in the interval. The following two diagrams illustrate that our estimate of the area (which is the sum of the areas of the trapezoids) should improve as the number of trapezoids increases:

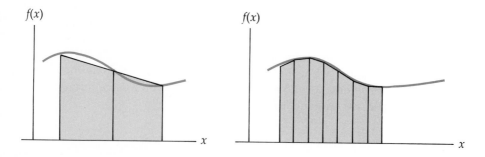

Consider a single trapezoid with a base and 2 heights. The equation for the area of the trapezoid is

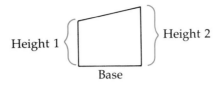

$$\text{area} = 0.5 \cdot \text{base} \cdot (\text{height1} + \text{height2})$$

If we assume that the base length represents the increment along the x-axis, this value is constant as we divide the interval into a number of equally spaced points. The heights represent the function value on the left- and right-hand sides of the small interval.

Before we develop this solution, we want to point out that the data points on the curve could come from several sources. If we have the equation for the curve, the program can compute the data points that we then use as sides for our trapezoids; in this case, we can choose the data points to be as close together or as far apart as we want. Another possibility is that the data represents experimentally collected data; in this case, we have a set of (x,y) coordinates but no general equation. We can use the increment in the x coordinates as the base values and the y coordinates as the heights of the trapezoids.

Both cases are important, and we give FORTRAN programs for both situations. Because the programs are similar, in the algorithm development phases, we assume the case where we have an equation for the curve.

Assume that the following equation describes the power in a signal with respect to frequency:

$$f(x) = y = 4e^{-(x-2)^2}$$

We can find the power of the signal over a band of frequencies by integrating or by computing the area under the curve in the desired frequency range. Write a program to compute the area under this curve between two specified points. Use the trapezoidal rule, and allow the user to choose the number of trapezoids used to approximate the area.

PROBLEM STATEMENT

Determine the area under the curve defined by the following equation:

$$f(x) = y = 4e^{-(x-2)^2}$$

INPUT/OUTPUT DESCRIPTION

The input values give the interval of x values to be used and the number of trapezoids in that interval. The output is the estimate of the area under the curve.

For a hand-worked example, we assume that we are interested in the area in the interval [1,2] and that we want to break the interval into 5 trapezoids, as shown:

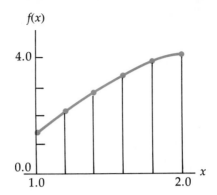

The following table shows the x and y coordinates and the computations for the areas of the 5 trapezoids:

x	y	TRAPEZOID AREA
1.0	1.47	
		$0.5*0.2*(1.47 + 2.11) = 0.36$
1.2	2.11	
		$0.5*0.2*(2.11 + 2.79) = 0.49$
1.4	2.79	
		$0.5*0.2*(2.79 + 3.41) = 0.62$
1.6	3.41	
		$0.5*0.2*(3.41 + 3.84) = 0.73$
1.8	3.84	
		$0.5*0.2*(3.84 + 4.00) = 0.78$
2.0	4.00	

Sum of Trapezoid Areas = 2.98

(The value of this integral is not easy to compute even using calculus because it does not have a closed form.)

ALGORITHM DEVELOPMENT

The decomposition of the solution into general steps is the following.

DECOMPOSITION

Read interval endpoints and number of trapezoids.
Compute estimate of area.
Print estimate of area.

We can compute the length of the entire interval by subtracting the left endpoint from the right endpoint. This length is then divided by the number of trapezoids, giving us the size of each base. For each trapezoid, we also need a left height and a right height; although, after computing the heights of the first trapezoid, we do not need to compute both heights for each trapezoid because the left height is computed as the right height of the previous trapezoid. We can develop the flowchart

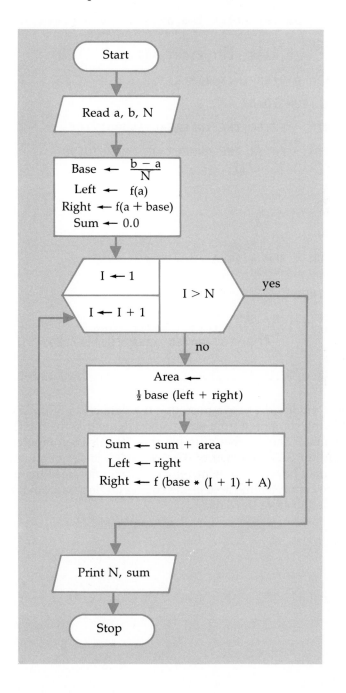

Converting the flowchart into FORTRAN gives the following program.

FORTRAN Program

```
*-------------------------------------------------------------------*
      PROGRAM  AREA1
*
*  This program estimates the area under a given curve.
*
      INTEGER  N, I
      REAL  A,B,BASE,LEFT,RIGHT,AREA,SUM
*
      F(X) = 4.0*EXP(-(X-2)**2)
*
      DATA  SUM /0.0/
*
      PRINT*, 'ENTER THE INTERVAL ENDPOINTS'
      READ*, A, B
      PRINT*, 'ENTER THE NUMBER OF TRAPEZOIDS'
      READ*, N
*
      BASE = (B - A)/REAL(N)
      LEFT = F(A)
      RIGHT = F(A + BASE)
*
      DO 10 I=1,N
         AREA = 0.5*BASE*(LEFT + RIGHT)
         SUM = SUM + AREA
         LEFT = RIGHT
         RIGHT = F(BASE*(I+1)+A)
   10 CONTINUE
*
      PRINT 15, N, SUM
   15 FORMAT (1X,'USING ',I3,' TRAPEZOIDS, '
     +            'THE ESTIMATED AREA IS ',F7.3)
*
      END
*-------------------------------------------------------------------*
```

We now modify the program so that the data is read from a data file instead of being computed from an equation. Note that the number of data points determines the number of trapezoids. We also recompute the base of the trapezoid for each new pair of data points because not all of the x coordinates may have the same increment. We do not need the data points after we have computed the area of the corresponding trapezoid; thus, no array is needed to store the data.

FORTRAN Program

```
*-------------------------------------------------------*
      PROGRAM  AREA2
*
*  This program estimates the area under a curve
*  using a set of data points in a data file.
*
      INTEGER  N
      REAL   XL,YL,XR,YR,BASE,AREA,SUM
*
      DATA  N, SUM /0, 0.0/
*
      OPEN (UNIT=12,FILE='XYDATA',STATUS='OLD')
*
      READ (12,*,END=5) XL, YL
    1 READ (12,*,END=5) XR, YR
         BASE = XR - XL
         AREA = 0.5*BASE*(YL + YR)
         SUM = SUM + AREA
         XL = XR
         YL = YR
         N = N + 1
         GO TO 1
*
    5 PRINT 15, N, SUM
   15 FORMAT (1X,'USING ',I3,' TRAPEZOIDS, '
      +              'THE ESTIMATED AREA IS ',F7.3)
*
      END
*-------------------------------------------------------*
```

TESTING

(We used the first version of the program for testing.) The following sets of output represent estimates of the function over the interval [1,2], using 5, 10, 50, and 100 trapezoids.

```
USING   5 TRAPEZOIDS, THE ESTIMATED AREA IS   2.977
```

```
USING  10 TRAPEZOIDS, THE ESTIMATED AREA IS   2.985
```

```
USING  50 TRAPEZOIDS, THE ESTIMATED AREA IS   2.987
```

```
USING 100 TRAPEZOIDS, THE ESTIMATED AREA IS   2.987
```

Note that we do not see any change from 50 trapezoids to 100 trapezoids when we use an F7.3 format specification to print our area.

This technique for numerical integration is referred to as integration using the Trapezoidal Rule. Another rule, called Simpson's Rule, is used in numerical integration to approximate the area under a curve by assuming that the points on the curve are joined by parabolas instead of straight lines. For the same number of divisions of a curve into smaller segments, Simpson's Rule gives a more accurate approximation than the Trapezoidal Rule. Simpson's Rule is slightly more complicated to compute; details can be found in the references given for numerical techniques at the end of Section 10–1.

10–4   ITERATIVE SOLUTIONS

In many of the applications in this text, the solution to the problem involved direct computation of a value or several values. Sometimes, an *iterative* or repetitive technique is needed to compute the desired information. For example, in Section 8–4 we computed the equilibrium temperatures of a metal plate, within a certain tolerance. In the problem solution, the temperatures were updated, and the temperature changes were compared to the tolerance value. As long as any of the temperature changes were greater than the tolerance value, we repeated the process to update all the temperatures in the plate. This iterative process continued until all the temperature changes were below the tolerance level. In several problems at the end of Chapter 6, we approximated the value of the cosine function by computing and adding terms of an infinite series that are equivalent to the cosine function; this technique is also iterative because we continue computing terms to add to our approximation until we have added a specified number of terms, or until the terms become so small that they are insignificant.

Iterative techniques are often used in situations not easily described with equations. For example, the following applications require computing the roots of polynomials: designing the control system for a robot arm, designing spring and shock absorbers in an automobile, analyzing the response characteristic of a motor, and analyzing the stability of an electric circuit. Recall that the roots are the values of x for which the polynomial $p(x)$ is equal to zero. If the polynomial is linear, it is easy to solve for the single root, as shown:

$$p(x) = 5x - 3$$
$$p(x) = 0 \rightarrow 5x = 3$$
$$x = 0.6$$

If the polynomial is quadratic, the quadratic formula can be used to determine the roots of polynomial: There could be no real roots (the quadratic curve does not cross the x-axis), 2 distinct real roots, or a double root. Thus, determining the roots for the linear or quadratic case is not difficult. However, suppose the polynomial equation is the one following:

$$p(x) = 4.5x^8 + 0.5x^4 - 2.1x^3 - 0.6$$

Finding the roots of this polynomial by hand is laborious; but if we use an iterative method, we have several techniques for finding the roots of a general polynomial. One of these techniques, called *interval halving*, or bisection, is presented in Section 10–5. Another common technique is the Newton Method (also called the Newton-Rhapson Method); this technique uses the derivative of the polynomial to determine the next approximation for the root—thus, to use the Newton Method, we must also be able to compute or approximate the derivative. The Secant Method is a variation of the Newton Method that uses linear interpolation to approximate the derivative. These techniques are discussed in the references listed at the end of Section 10–1.

Some of the root-finding techniques that we have discussed can also be applied to transcendental functions, which are not polynomials but are functions that contain trigonometric or other special functions such as logarithmic or exponential functions. For example, suppose that we wanted to solve the following equation:

$$x = \tan x$$

One way to solve for the value of x is to rewrite the equation as shown, and then to find the roots, or values, of x for which the equation is equal to zero:

$$f(x) = x - \tan x$$

These techniques do not always lead to a solution; a more detailed study of iterative solutions is required to solve for roots of transcendental functions.

10–5 APPLICATION — ROOTS OF EQUATIONS (Robotic Engineering)

Computers are often used to find the *roots of equations*. In a few cases, such as in the quadratic equation, simple formulas can find the roots. In most situations of practical interest, however, no such formulas exist, and it is necessary to use iterative (repetitive) methods that lead to an approximate answer. In this application, we study the simplest such method—interval halving.

Suppose we have an equation that is represented by the following curve on a given interval:

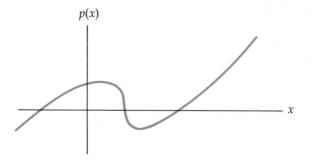

A root of the equation is a point at which the curve crosses the x-axis. At such a point, the y value of the curve is zero. Suppose that we have 2 points, a and b, such that p(a) and p(b) are of different signs, as shown:

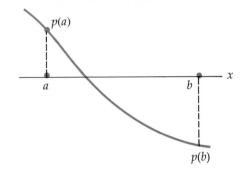

We can be sure that there is at least 1 root in the interval between a and b because the curve must cross the x-axis. There may also be 3 roots, or another odd number of roots, in the interval between a and b.

For now, assume that there is only 1 root in the interval between a and b. Also assume that p(a) is positive and that p(b) is negative. If the equation is evaluated at m, the midpoint of the interval, there are three possible outcomes: If the equation value at the midpoint is zero, it represents the root; if the equation value at the midpoint, represented by p(m), is negative, the root falls in the interval between a and m; if the equation value at the midpoint is positive, the root falls in the interval between m and b. We have halved the interval within which the root must lie. We now reperform the steps in this iterative algorithm, halving the interval of interest with each iteration.

There are many ways to decide when to stop the iterative process. In this application, we stop the process when we find the root or when the interval of interest is less than 0.01.

Because there can be more than 1 root in the overall interval being considered, we suggest starting at the left-hand side of the overall interval and begin moving across it in small intervals. If the left and right polynomial values for one of the small intervals have different signs, assume that there is 1 root in the interval and perform the iterations to narrow in on it; then proceed to the next interval, searching for new roots. There are special cases in which roots can be missed with this algorithm, but a completely general algorithm for root finding is too long for this example.

The design of a control system for a robot arm involves a careful analysis of the stability of the design. One step in the stability analysis uses the roots of polynomials that are used in the control system. Write a program to estimate the roots of a fourth-order polynomial over the interval [−5,5] by using the interval-halving technique.

PROBLEM STATEMENT

Write a program to determine the roots of a polynomial $p(x)$ within the interval $[-5,5]$, where $p(x)$ has the following form:

$$p(x) = Ax^4 + Bx^3 + Cx^2 + Dx + E$$

INPUT/OUTPUT DESCRIPTION

The input to the program is the polynomial coefficients A, B, C, D, and E. The output should be the equation for the polynomial and any roots that were found. If there are no roots for the polynomial in the given interval, print an appropriate message.

HAND EXAMPLE

We use small intervals of 0.25 for the initial test to determine whether or not a root is in the interval. For this test case, assume that the polynomial is

$$p(x) = 3x - 2.5$$

This is a linear equation, but it is also a special case of a quartic polynomial with the following coefficients:

$$A = 0, B = 0, C = 0, D = 3, E = -2.5$$

We begin by evaluating $p(x)$ at the endpoints of the following intervals:

$$[-5.0, -4.75], [-4.75, -4.5], \ldots$$

When the polynomial at the left endpoint, p(left), has a different sign than the polynomial at the right endpoint, p(right), there is a root in the interval. We also need to check the polynomial evaluated at the endpoints for the value of zero in case an endpoint is a root. For the specific example, both endpoints have negative polynomial values until we reach the interval $[0.75,1.00]$, where $p(0.75) = -0.25$ and $p(1.0) = 0.5$. The following steps halve the interval, determines which half contains the root, halves the new interval, and so on, until the root is found or the interval is less than 0.01:

Interval [0.75,1.0] $p(0.75) = -0.25$, $p(1.0) = 0.5$
Midpoint: $p(0.875) = 0.125$
Iteration 1: Interval [0.75,0.875]
$p(0.75) = -0.25$, $p(0.875) = 0.125$
Midpoint: $p(0.8125) = -0.0625$
Iteration 2: Interval [0.8125,0.875]
$p(0.8125) = -0.0625$, $p(0.875) = 0.125$
Midpoint: $p(0.8438) = 0.0314$
Iteration 3: Interval [0.8125,0.8438]
$p(0.8125) = -0.0625$, $p(0.8438) = 0.0314$
Midpoint: $p(.8282) = -0.0154$ *(continued)*

Iteration 4: Interval [0.8282,0.8438]
$$p(0.8282) = -0.0154, \; p(0.8438) = 0.0314$$
Midpoint: $p(.836) = .008$

Iteration 5: Interval [.8282,.836]

> This interval is less than 0.01; thus, our estimate of the root is the midpoint of this interval, or 0.8321. The polynomial value, $p(x)$, at this point is -0.0037.

ALGORITHM DEVELOPMENT

The decomposition of this algorithm involves reading coefficients and then finding roots.

DECOMPOSITION

Read coefficients.
Determine and print roots.

We develop this program so that it reads the coefficients of a polynomial, determines the roots in the interval [−5,5], and reads coefficients for another polynomial. We continue the process until the values of all the coefficients are zero.

REFINEMENT IN PSEUDOCODE

```
ROOTS: Read coefficients
       While all coefficients not zero do
           count ← 0
           left ← −5.0
           right ← −4.75
           For i = 1 to 40 do
             If p(left) = 0.0 then
               Print left
               count ← count + 1
             Else if p(left)*p(right) < 0.0 then
               Iterate for root
               Print root
               count ← count + 1
             left ← right
             right ← left + 0.25
           If p(left) = 0.0 then
             Print left
             count ← count + 1
           If count = 0 then
             Print 'no roots in interval'
           Read coefficients
```

We must further refine the iteration step. Recall that the iteration continues until the process finds the root or until the interval of interest is less than 0.01.

REFINEMENT IN PSEUDOCODE

```
ITERAT: done ← false
        size ← right − left
        while size > 0.01 and not done do
            mid ← (left + right)/2
            if p(mid) = 0 then
               done ← true
            elseif p(mid)*p(left) < 0.0 then
               right ← mid
            else
               left ← mid
        If size < 0.01 then
            root ← (left + right)/2
        else
            root ← mid
```

We are now ready to convert the pseudocode into FORTRAN. To keep the main program reasonably short, we implement the iteration process as a subroutine. The evaluation of the polynomial is implemented as a function; this function is referenced from both the main program and the iteration subroutine. It needs the 5 coefficients and the value of x for evaluating the polynomial as inputs; thus, the reference is $P(A,B,C,D,E,X)$. This large number of coefficients becomes cumbersome and not nearly as readable as the function reference $P(X)$. Therefore, we use a common block to store the coefficients of the polynomial so that we do not have to list them in the function reference.

The structure chart for this program is:

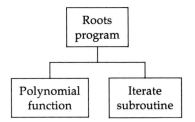

FORTRAN Program

```
*-------------------------------------------------------------*
      PROGRAM  ROOTS
*
*  This program determines the roots in the interval [-5,5]
*  for a quartic polynomial using interval halving.
*
      INTEGER  COUNT
      REAL  LEFT,RIGHT,P
*
      COMMON  /COEFF/ A,B,C,D,E
*
      PRINT*, 'ENTER COEFFICIENTS A, B, C, D, E'
      READ*, A,B,C,D,E
    1 IF (A.NE.0.0.OR.B.NE.0.0.OR.C.NE.0.0.OR.
     +    D.NE.0.0.OR.E.NE.0.0) THEN
*
         PRINT*
         PRINT*, 'POLYNOMIAL:'
         PRINT 5
    5    FORMAT (1X,'             4              3',
     +        '              2')
         PRINT 10, A,B,C,D,E
   10    FORMAT (1X,4(F7.3,' X  + '),F7.3)
         PRINT*
*
         COUNT = 0
         LEFT = -5.0
         RIGHT = -4.75
         DO 20 I=1,40
            IF (P(LEFT).EQ.0.0) THEN
               PRINT 15, LEFT, P(LEFT)
   15          FORMAT (1X,'ROOT = ',F7.3,
     +              '  P(ROOT) = ',F7.3)
               COUNT = COUNT + 1
            ELSEIF (P(LEFT)*P(RIGHT).LT.0.0) THEN
               CALL ITERAT(LEFT,RIGHT,ROOT)
               PRINT 15, ROOT, P(ROOT)
               COUNT = COUNT + 1
            ENDIF
            LEFT = RIGHT
            RIGHT = LEFT + 0.25
   20    CONTINUE
         IF (P(LEFT).EQ.0.0) THEN
            PRINT 15, LEFT, P(LEFT)
            COUNT = COUNT + 1
         ENDIF
         IF (COUNT.EQ.0) THEN
            PRINT*, 'NO ROOTS IN INTERVAL [-5,5]'
         ENDIF
         PRINT*
         PRINT*, 'ENTER COEFFICIENTS A, B, C, D, E'
         PRINT*, '(ALL ZEROS TO QUIT)'
         READ*, A,B,C,D,E
         GO TO 1
      ENDIF
*
      END
```

```
*----------------------------------------------------------------*
*
*
      REAL FUNCTION  P(X)
*
*  This function evaluates a quartic polynomial at X.
*
      REAL  X
*
      COMMON  /COEFF/ A,B,C,D,E
*
      P = A*X**4 + B*X**3 + C*X**2 + D*X + E
*
      RETURN
      END
*----------------------------------------------------------------*
*
*
      SUBROUTINE  ITERAT(LEFT,RIGHT,ROOT)
*
*  This subroutine uses interval halving to find a root.
*
      REAL  LEFT,RIGHT,ROOT,SIZE,MID
      LOGICAL  DONE
*
      DONE = .FALSE.
      SIZE = RIGHT - LEFT
    5 IF (SIZE.GT.0.01.AND..NOT.DONE) THEN
         MID = (LEFT + RIGHT)/2.0
         IF (P(MID).EQ.0.0) THEN
            DONE = .TRUE.
         ELSEIF (P(MID)*P(LEFT).LT.0.0) THEN
            RIGHT = MID
         ELSE
            LEFT = MID
         ENDIF
         SIZE = RIGHT - LEFT
         GO TO 5
      ENDIF
*
      IF (SIZE.GT.0.01) THEN
         ROOT = MID
      ELSE
         ROOT = (LEFT + RIGHT)/2.0
      ENDIF
*
      RETURN
      END
*----------------------------------------------------------------*
```

TESTING

Five different polynomials were used as test data. These polynomials covered the cases with no roots, 1 root, and 3 roots, and some of the roots fell on interval endpoints. The last polynomial is the one we used in the hand-worked example. The output from the program is shown. Following the output, we have also included plots of the polynomials in the same order as they were entered in the program.

```
ENTER COEFFICIENTS A, B, C, D, E
0. 1. -2.125 -25. 53.125

POLYNOMIAL:
   0.000  X⁴ +    1.000 X³ +  -2.125 X² + -25.000 X   +   53.125

ROOT =   -5.000    P(ROOT) =    0.000
ROOT =    2.125    P(ROOT) =    0.000
ROOT =    5.000    P(ROOT) =    0.000

ENTER COEFFICIENTS A, B, C, D, E
0. 0. 1. 14. 3.

POLYNOMIAL:
   0.000  X⁴ +    0.000 X³ +    1.000 X² +  14.000 X   +    3.000

ROOT =   -0.215    P(ROOT) =    0.038

ENTER COEFFICIENTS A, B, C, D, E
3. -12.4 -26.29 29.766 0.

POLYNOMIAL:
   3.000  X⁴ + -12.400 X³ + -26.290 X² +  29.766 X   +    0.000

ROOT =   -2.137    P(ROOT) =   -0.131
ROOT =    0.000    P(ROOT) =    0.000
ROOT =    0.855    P(ROOT) =    0.068

ENTER COEFFICIENTS A, B, C, D, E
0. 0. 1.234 -1.2 10.44

POLYNOMIAL:
   0.000  X⁴ +    0.000 X³ +    1.234 X² +  -1.200 X   +   10.440

NO ROOTS IN INTERVAL [-5,5]

ENTER COEFFICIENTS A, B, C, D, E
0. 0. 0. 3. -2.5

POLYNOMIAL:
   0.000  X⁴ +    0.000 X³ +    0.000 X² +   3.000 X   +   -2.500

ROOT =    0.832    P(ROOT) =   -0.004

ENTER COEFFICIENTS A, B, C, D, E
0. 0. 0. 0. 0.
```

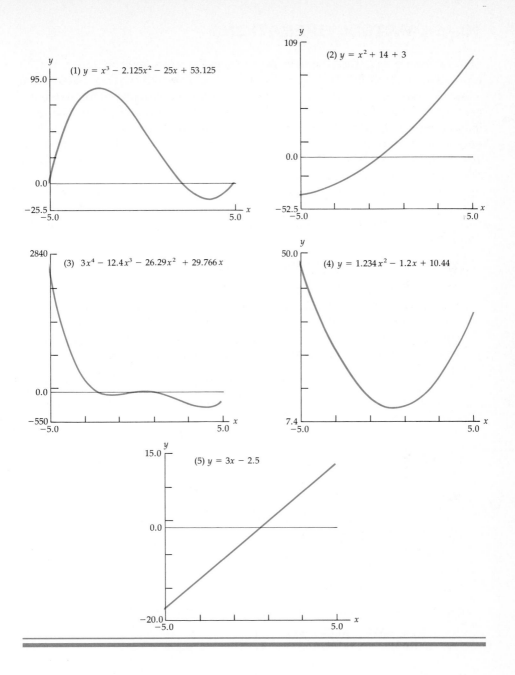

(1) $y = x^3 - 2.125x^2 - 25x + 53.125$

(2) $y = x^2 + 14 + 3$

(3) $3x^4 - 12.4x^3 - 26.29x^2 + 29.766x$

(4) $y = 1.234x^2 - 1.2x + 10.44$

(5) $y = 3x - 2.5$

10-6 MATRIX OPERATIONS

Many engineering and science computations use a *matrix* as a convenient way to represent data. In FORTRAN, a matrix is easily represented in a two-dimensional array. Operations performed with matrices require more than a single statement because the operations must be able to access all elements of the matrix; thus, loops are needed. In this section, we define a number of the common operations performed with matrices and develop subprograms to compute them in FOR-TRAN. (The next FORTRAN standard will include single-statement matrix operations; until then, however, we need to perform them using the techniques that follow.) In these examples, we assume that the size of the matrix is included as two parameters NROW and NCOL. Recall that these arguments should contain values that match the number of rows and columns used in the array definition in the main program.

EXAMPLE 10-1   Scalar Multiplication

Multiplying each element in a matrix by a scalar is referred to as scalar multiplication. Write a subroutine whose arguments are a matrix A, its size in terms of NROWS and NCOLS, and a scalar C. The subroutine should multiply the matrix A by the scalar C and return the result in the matrix A, as shown in the following matrix notation:

$$[a(i,j)] \leftarrow [c*a(i,j)]$$

To illustrate, matrix A is multiplied by a scalar value of 4, and the result is a new matrix:

$$A = \begin{bmatrix} 1.0 & 2.2 \\ 3.0 & 4.0 \\ -1.0 & 0.0 \end{bmatrix} \quad 4*A = \begin{bmatrix} 4.0 & 8.8 \\ 12.0 & 16.0 \\ -4.0 & 0.0 \end{bmatrix}$$

Solution

The steps in this solution involve defining a pair of nested loops to access each element of the array, then multiplying each element by the scalar or constant C:

```
*-------------------------------------------------*
      SUBROUTINE  SCALAR(A,NROW,NCOL,C)
*
*  This subroutine multiplies an array by a scalar.
*
      INTEGER  NROW, NCOL, I, J
      REAL  A(NROW,NCOL), C
*
      DO 10 I=1,NROW
         DO 5 J=1,NCOL
            A(I,J) = C*A(I,J)
    5    CONTINUE
   10 CONTINUE
*
      RETURN
      END
*-------------------------------------------------*
```

EXAMPLE 10-2   Matrix Addition

Matrix addition can be performed only with matrices of the same size. The result of the addition is another matrix of the same size in which the elements are the sum of the elements in the corresponding positions of the original matrices, as shown in the matrix notation:

$$[c(i,j)] \leftarrow [a(i,j)] + [b(i,j)]$$

To illustrate, matrix A is added to matrix B, and the result is a new matrix C:

$$A = \begin{bmatrix} 1.0 & 2.2 \\ 3.0 & 4.0 \\ -1.0 & 0.0 \end{bmatrix} \quad B = \begin{bmatrix} 4.0 & -3.0 \\ 2.0 & 6.0 \\ -4.0 & 0.5 \end{bmatrix}$$

$$A + B = C = \begin{bmatrix} 5.0 & -0.8 \\ 5.0 & 10.0 \\ -5.0 & 0.5 \end{bmatrix}$$

Write a subroutine called ADDMX that has 5 arguments: The first 3 arguments represent 3 matrices (two to be added and one to hold the sum), and the other 2 arguments give the size of the matrices.

Solution

This subroutine is written so that the matrix that represents the sum is a separate matrix; but, if we want to store the sum in one of the original matrices, we can list it also as the output matrix in the CALL statement, as shown:

```
CALL ADDMX(A,B,B,NROW,NCOL)
```

The subroutine is given:

```
*-----------------------------------------------------------------*
      SUBROUTINE  ADDMX(A,B,C,NROW,NCOL)
*
*  This subroutine adds matrices A and B and
*  stores the result in matrix C.
*
      INTEGER  NROW,NCOL,I,J
      REAL   A(NROW,NCOL),B(NROW,NCOL),C(NROW,NCOL)
*
      DO 10 I=1,NROW
         DO 5 J=1,NCOL
            C(I,J) = A(I,J) + B(I,J)
    5    CONTINUE
   10 CONTINUE
*
      RETURN
      END
*-----------------------------------------------------------------*
```

EXAMPLE 10-3 Matrix Subtraction

Matrix subtraction can also be performed only with matrices of the same size. The result of the subtraction is another matrix of the same size in which the elements are the difference of the elements in the corresponding positions of the original matrices, as shown in the matrix notation:

$$[c(i,j)] \leftarrow [a(i,j)] - [b(i,j)]$$

To illustrate, matrix B is subtracted from matrix A, and the result is a new matrix C:

$$A = \begin{bmatrix} 1.0 & 2.2 \\ 3.0 & 4.0 \\ -1.0 & 0.0 \end{bmatrix} \quad B = \begin{bmatrix} 4.0 & -3.0 \\ 2.0 & 6.0 \\ -4.0 & 0.5 \end{bmatrix}$$

$$A - B = C = \begin{bmatrix} -3.0 & 5.2 \\ 1.0 & -2.0 \\ 3.0 & -0.5 \end{bmatrix}$$

Although the order in adding matrices does not matter, the order in subtracting matrices is important.

Write a subroutine called SUBMX that has 5 arguments: The first 3 arguments represent 3 matrices (two to be subtracted and one to hold the difference), and the other 2 arguments give the size of the matrices.

Solution

This subroutine is written so that the matrix that represents the difference is a separate matrix, but if we want to store the difference in one of the original matrices, we can list it also as the output matrix in the call statement, as shown:

```
CALL SUBMX(A,B,A,NROW,NCOL)
```

The subroutine is given:

```
*----------------------------------------------------------*
       SUBROUTINE  SUBMX(A,B,C,NROW,NCOL)
*
*   This subroutine subtracts matrix B from matrix A
*   and stores the result in matrix C.
*
       INTEGER  NROW,NCOL,I,J
       REAL  A(NROW,NCOL),B(NROW,NCOL),C(NROW,NCOL)
*
       DO 10 I=1,NROW
          DO 5 J=1,NCOL
             C(I,J) = A(I,J) - B(I,J)
    5     CONTINUE
   10 CONTINUE
*
       RETURN
       END
*----------------------------------------------------------*
```

EXAMPLE 10-4   Dot Product

The dot product is an operation performed between two vectors, or one-dimensional arrays, with the same dimension. This is not actually a matrix operation; however, it is often used in computations that also involve matrices, so we will include it here. The dot product between two one-dimensional arrays of the same size is a number computed by adding the product of values in corresponding positions in the arrays, as shown in the summation equation:

$$\text{Dot product} \leftarrow \sum a(i)b(i)$$

To illustrate, the dot product of one-dimensional arrays A and B is computed:

$$A = \begin{bmatrix} 3.0 \\ 1.5 \\ -0.5 \end{bmatrix} \qquad B = \begin{bmatrix} 1.0 \\ 2.0 \\ 3.0 \end{bmatrix}$$

$$\begin{aligned}
\text{Dot product of A and B} &= 3.0*1.0 + 1.5*2.0 + -0.5*3.0 \\
&= 3.0 + 3.0 - 1.5 \\
&= 4.5
\end{aligned}$$

Write a function to compute the dot product of two arrays with a common size N.

Solution

Note that this subprogram is written as a function instead of as a subroutine because it returns a single value to the main program:

```
*-------------------------------------------------------*
      REAL FUNCTION  DOT(A,B,N)
*
*  This function computes the dot product of A and B.
*
      INTEGER  N, I
      REAL  A(N), B(N)
*
      DOT = 0.0
      DO 10 I=1,N
         DOT = DOT + A(I)*B(I)
   10 CONTINUE
*
      RETURN
      END
*-------------------------------------------------------*
```

EXAMPLE 10-5 Matrix Multiplication

Matrix multiplication is not computed by multiplying corresponding elements of the matrices. The value in position I,J of the product of two matrices is the dot product of row I of the first matrix and column J of the second matrix, as shown in the summation equation:

$$[c(i,j)] \leftarrow \sum_k a(i,k)*b(k,j)$$

In the equation, i and j are fixed values, and k varies in the summation.

Because dot products require that the arrays have the same number of elements, we must have the same number of elements in each row of the first matrix as we have in each column of the second matrix to compute the product of the two matrices. The product matrix has the same number of rows as the first matrix and the same number of columns as the second matrix. Thus, if A and B both have 5 rows and 5 columns, their product has 5 rows and 5 columns. If A has 3 rows and 2 columns, and B has 2 rows and 2 columns, their product has 3 rows and 2 columns. To illustrate, matrix A is multiplied by matrix B, and the result is a new matrix C:

$$A = \begin{bmatrix} 1.0 & 2.2 \\ 3.0 & 4.0 \\ -1.0 & 0.0 \end{bmatrix} \quad B = \begin{bmatrix} 4.0 & -3.0 \\ 2.0 & 6.0 \end{bmatrix}$$

$$A*B = C = \begin{bmatrix} 8.4 & 10.2 \\ 20.0 & 15.0 \\ -4.0 & 3.0 \end{bmatrix}$$

A subroutine to multiply two matrices must have the sizes of both input arrays in addition to the arrays themselves. The result of the multiplication must be an additional array because the original values are needed more than once in calculating the product.

Solution

In the subroutine, we print an error message if the input sizes are not correct:

```
*- - - - - - - - - - - - - - - - - - - - - - - - - - - - - - - - - - - - - - - - - - - *
      SUBROUTINE  MULTMX(A,AROW,ACOL,B,BROW,BCOL,
     +                   C,CROW,CCOL)
*
*   This subroutine multiplies arrays A and B
*   and stores the product in array C.
*
      INTEGER   AROW,ACOL,BROW,BCOL,CROW,CCOL,I,J,K
      REAL   A(AROW,ACOL),B(BROW,BCOL),C(CROW,CCOL)
      LOGICAL   ERROR
*
      ERROR = .FALSE.
      IF (ACOL.NE.BROW) ERROR = .TRUE.
      IF (AROW.NE.CROW) ERROR = .TRUE.
      IF (BCOL.NE.CCOL) ERROR = .TRUE.
*
```

```
      IF (ERROR) THEN
         PRINT*, 'ERROR IN ARRAY SIZES'
      ELSE
         DO 30 I=1,CROW
            DO 25 J=1,CCOL
               C(I,J) = 0.0
               DO 15 K=1,ACOL
                  C(I,J) = C(I,J) + A(I,K)*B(K,J)
15             CONTINUE
25          CONTINUE
30       CONTINUE
      ENDIF
*
      RETURN
      END
*------------------------------------------------------------*
```

In Section 10–7, our application solves simultaneous equations using matrices. Systems of simultaneous equations are often used in the stress analysis of mechanical systems, in the analysis of a fluid-flow system, and in the analysis of current or voltages in an electrical circuit. The design of airplane control systems also requires the solution of systems of simultaneous equations. The information from these applications is stored in a matrix, and we solve the system of simultaneous equations represented by this matrix to complete the desired analysis.

10–7 APPLICATION — DETERMINANTS (Electrical Engineering)

In this application, we develop a program to solve three simultaneous equations. A general set of three simultaneous equations can be written in the following form:

$$a(1) \, x + b(1) \, y + c(1) \, z = d(1)$$
$$a(2) \, x + b(2) \, y + c(2) \, z = d(2)$$
$$a(3) \, x + b(3) \, y + c(3) \, z = d(3)$$

There are many ways to solve a system of three simultaneous equations. We choose Cramer's Rule, which uses *determinants*. Recall that a determinant is a number that is computed from a matrix. Specifically, the determinant of the matrix formed from the set of coefficients of x, y, and z is computed as

$$\begin{vmatrix} a1 & b1 & c1 \\ a2 & b2 & c2 \\ a3 & b3 & c3 \end{vmatrix} = \begin{matrix} a1*b2*c3 + b1*c2*a3 + c1*a2*b3 \\ - a3*b2*c1 - b3*c2*a1 - c3*a2*b1 \end{matrix}$$

The x, y, and z values that form the solution of the set of three simultaneous equations can be computed from determinants, using Cramer's Rule, as shown:

$$x = \frac{\begin{vmatrix} d1 & b1 & c1 \\ d2 & b2 & c2 \\ d3 & b3 & c3 \end{vmatrix}}{\begin{vmatrix} a1 & b1 & c1 \\ a2 & b2 & c2 \\ a3 & b3 & c3 \end{vmatrix}} \qquad y = \frac{\begin{vmatrix} a1 & d1 & c1 \\ a2 & d2 & c2 \\ a3 & d3 & c3 \end{vmatrix}}{\begin{vmatrix} a1 & b1 & c1 \\ a2 & b2 & c2 \\ a3 & b3 & c3 \end{vmatrix}} \qquad z = \frac{\begin{vmatrix} a1 & b1 & d1 \\ a2 & b2 & d2 \\ a3 & b3 & d3 \end{vmatrix}}{\begin{vmatrix} a1 & b1 & c1 \\ a2 & b2 & c2 \\ a3 & b3 & c3 \end{vmatrix}}$$

Note that all three equations have the same denominator, which is the determinant formed from the coefficients of x, y, and z. When this determinant is equal to zero, a unique solution does not exist.

Write a program that will read the coefficients from three simultaneous equations with three variables that represent the current analysis equations in an electrical circuit. Solve the system of equations for the three unknown currents.

PROBLEM STATEMENT

Use determinants to find the x, y, and z values that solve a set of three simultaneous equations from an electrical circuit.

INPUT/OUTPUT DESCRIPTION

The input is the set of coefficients for the equations. There are 4 coefficients for each equation; thus, 12 coefficients are needed. The output is the set of values for x, y, and z that solve each equation.

HAND EXAMPLE

Assume that the following set of equations is to be solved using determinants:

$$2x + 3y - 1z = 1$$
$$3x + 5y + 2z = 8$$
$$1x - 2y - 3z = -1$$

We first compute the determinant of the matrix formed from the coefficients of x, y, and z to determine if a unique solution exists:

$$\begin{vmatrix} 2 & 3 & -1 \\ 3 & 5 & 2 \\ 1 & -2 & -3 \end{vmatrix} = -30 + 6 + 6 + 5 + 8 + 27 = 22$$

Because the determinant is nonzero, a unique solution exists. We now compute the specific values for x, y, and z.

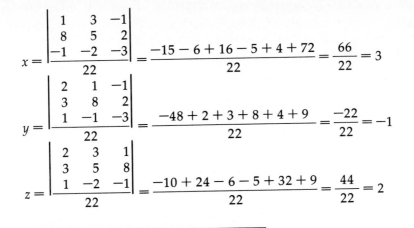

$$x = \frac{\begin{vmatrix} 1 & 3 & -1 \\ 8 & 5 & 2 \\ -1 & -2 & -3 \end{vmatrix}}{22} = \frac{-15 - 6 + 16 - 5 + 4 + 72}{22} = \frac{66}{22} = 3$$

$$y = \frac{\begin{vmatrix} 2 & 1 & -1 \\ 3 & 8 & 2 \\ 1 & -1 & -3 \end{vmatrix}}{22} = \frac{-48 + 2 + 3 + 8 + 4 + 9}{22} = \frac{-22}{22} = -1$$

$$z = \frac{\begin{vmatrix} 2 & 3 & 1 \\ 3 & 5 & 8 \\ 1 & -2 & -1 \end{vmatrix}}{22} = \frac{-10 + 24 - 6 - 5 + 32 + 9}{22} = \frac{44}{22} = 2$$

ALGORITHM DEVELOPMENT

The decomposition of our solution in general steps is the following:

DECOMPOSITION

Read coefficients.
Compute solution.
Print solution.

As we refine these steps, we realize that we need to compute several determinants in the solution. This computation can be performed in a function that is referenced each time that we need it. We want to think carefully about the arguments to this function — it is cumbersome to list 9 different variables that represent the matrix elements. Because the elements in the matrix vary with each computation, a two-dimensional array is not a good choice because we must change its values before each function reference. If you refer to the hand-worked example, you see that the matrix is composed of 3 columns, and each time the matrix changes, one of these columns changes. Therefore, if we send the 3 columns of the matrix to the determinant function as 3 one-dimensional arrays, we only need 3 arguments; it is also easy then to change arguments because we only change one-dimensional array names.

REFINEMENT IN PSEUDOCODE

EQN3: Read coefficients
    If coefficient determinant = 0 then
        Print 'NO UNIQUE SOLUTION'
    Else
        Compute x, y, z
        Print x, y, z

As we convert the pseudocode into FORTRAN, we want to make it as easy as possible to enter the coefficients—this is important because we have 12 values to enter, and if they are entered out of order, the solution is incorrect.

The structure chart for this program is:

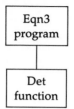

FORTRAN Program

```
*-------------------------------------------------------------------*
      PROGRAM  EQN3
*
*  This program computes the solution to three
*  simultaneous equations using determinants.
*
      REAL  A(3),B(3),C(3),D(3),DENOM,DET
*
      PRINT*, 'EACH EQUATION SHOULD BE IN THIS FORM:'
      PRINT*, 'A*X + B*Y + C*Z = D'
      PRINT*, 'ENTER A,B,C,D FOR EQUATION 1'
      READ*, A(1), B(1), C(1), D(1)
      PRINT*, 'ENTER A,B,C,D FOR EQUATION 2'
      READ*, A(2), B(2), C(2), D(2)
      PRINT*, 'ENTER A,B,C,D FOR EQUATION 3'
      READ*, A(3), B(3), C(3), D(3)
      PRINT*
*
      DENOM = DET(A,B,C)
      IF (DENOM.EQ.0.0) THEN
         PRINT*, 'NO UNIQUE SOLUTION EXISTS'
      ELSE
         X = DET(D,B,C)/DENOM
         Y = DET(A,D,C)/DENOM
         Z = DET(A,B,D)/DENOM
         PRINT 5, X
    5    FORMAT (1X,'SOLUTION: X = ',F7.2)
         PRINT 6, Y
    6    FORMAT (1X,'          Y = ',F7.2)
         PRINT 7, Z
    7    FORMAT (1X,'          Z = ',F7.2)
      ENDIF
*
      END
*-------------------------------------------------------------------*
```

```
*
*
      REAL FUNCTION  DET(P,Q,R)
*
*   This function computes the determinant of a 3X3 matrix
*   where P,Q,R represent the three columns of the matrix.
*
      REAL  P(3),Q(3),R(3)
*
      DET = P(1)*Q(2)*R(3)  +  Q(1)*R(2)*P(3)  +  R(1)*P(2)*Q(3)
     +      - P(3)*Q(2)*R(1)  -  Q(3)*R(2)*P(1)  -  R(3)*P(2)*Q(1)
*
      RETURN
      END
*- - - - - - - - - - - - - - - - - - - - - - - - - - - - - - - - - - - -*
```

Note that we did not use A, B, and C as variable names in the function. It would be confusing to use A, B, C, or D as variable names in the function because different combinations of those names were used as arguments.

TESTING

The output of this program with the data from the hand-worked example is

```
EACH EQUATION SHOULD BE IN THIS FORM:
A*X + B*Y + C*Z = D
ENTER A,B,C,D FOR EQUATION 1
2.0 3.0 -1.0 1.0
ENTER A,B,C,D FOR EQUATION 2
3.0 5.0 2.0 8.0
ENTER A,B,C,D FOR EQUATION 3
1.0 -2.0 -3.0 -1.0

SOLUTION:   X =      3.00
            Y =     -1.00
            Z =      2.00
```

This is a simple technique for solving systems of three equations, but it is not generally used for systems with four, five, or more equations because the determinant becomes more complicated to compute. The next section presents the Gauss elimination method that is commonly used when the number of equations is greater than three. In addition to the Gauss elimination method, the Gauss-Jordan Method for solving a system of equations can also be used to compute the inverse of a matrix; it requires a number of row manipulations to solve the system of equations. The Gauss-Siedel Method is an iterative technique that is often used for a sparse system (one in which many of the coefficients are zero). Both of these techniques are discussed in the references listed at the end of Section 10–1.

10-8 APPLICATION—GAUSS ELIMINATION (Optical Engineering)

One of the most interesting recent advances in the area of optics has been the development of "deformable" mirrors—mirrors whose surfaces can be reshaped by various techniques to correct for distortions in the optical path between the observer and the object being viewed. As an example, consider an astronomer who is observing the planet Saturn through a telescope, as shown in the following diagram:

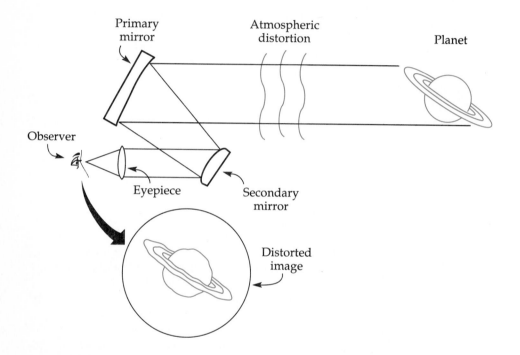

Because of atmospheric distortion caused by turbulence, pressure changes, and imperfections in the various optical elements of the telescope, the light rays are bent to various degrees such that the image of Saturn, as perceived by the astronomer, is distorted. The idea behind deformable mirrors, or "adaptive optics" as they are more generally called, is to somehow detect the distortion present and use that information to recontour one or more of the mirrors in the telescope to cancel the distortion, thereby presenting the viewer with an undistorted image.

One way this technique might be implemented is shown in the following diagram in which a few new optical elements have been added to the previous diagram:

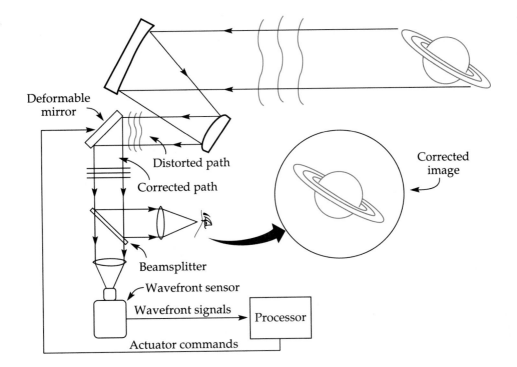

The new elements include a deformable mirror, a beamsplitter that enables a "wavefront sensor" to share the optical path with the observer, and a processor that provides the signals to shape the deformable mirror.

As seen in the diagram, the distorted image is reflected off the deformable mirror and sent to the beamsplitter. The beamsplitter, in turn, sends the image to the observer and the wavefront sensor. The wavefront sensor is a device that is capable of detecting the distortion in the image by measuring the departure of the incoming wavefront from the desired undistorted plane wavefront. The signals from the wavefront sensor, which contain the distortion, are then sent to a processor. The processor reconstructs the distorted wavefront, determines how the deformable mirror needs to be reshaped to cancel the distortion, and sends the commands to the mirror to reshape it.

The deformable mirror is one of the more interesting elements of the system. A sketch showing a square mirror having 25 actuators (movable elements) is shown in the following diagram:

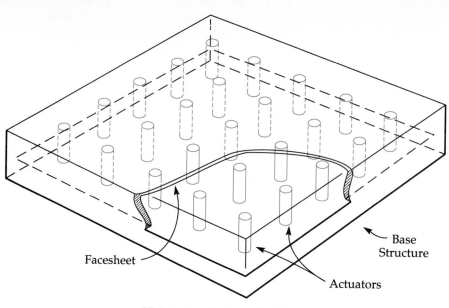

25-Actuator Deformable Mirror

The mirror uses a rigid base structure that supports the actuators. The actuators, along with the mirror's edge, support the relatively thin facesheet that is a highly polished, extremely flat, metal or glass surface. The actuators can expand or contract slightly when a voltage is applied, thereby moving the facesheet. When the actuators are used in unison, they are capable of producing the optical corrections needed to obtain an undistorted image.

The process used to obtain the correct shape for the facesheet of the deformable mirror involves a number of steps, which can be summarized in a system of equations that needs to be solved. The unknowns of the system represent the amounts of voltage needed for each actuator. Thus, the problem solution involves the solution of N simultaneous equations if there are N actuators in the mirror. The number of actuators in the deformable mirror in the diagram is 25, and thus a system of 25 equations with 25 unknowns would need to be solved in order to deform it properly. Clearly, the determinant method of Section 10–7 will not handle the complexity of this problem, so we develop another technique for solving a system of equations.

The *Gauss elimination* method of solving a system of equations is one in which we solve for the unknowns by combining equations. We first illustrate this method with an example. Specifically, we will use the set of equations used to illustrate Cramer's Method in Section 10–7.

$$2X + 3Y - Z = 1$$
$$3X + 5Y + 2Z = 8$$
$$1X - 2Y - 3Z = -1$$

Using Gauss elimination, we use the first equation in combination with the second equation in order to eliminate the first variable in the second equation;

that is, we want to eliminate the term $3X$ in the second equation. To do this, we multiply the first equation by $3/2$ (or 1.5) and subtract it from the second equation, as shown:

$$
\begin{array}{ll}
3X + 5Y + 2Z = 8 & \text{second equation} \\
3X + 4.5Y - 1.5Z = 1.5 & \text{first equation times 1.5} \\
\hline
0X + 0.5Y + 3.5Z = 6.5 & \text{difference}
\end{array}
$$

Thus, our new set of equations is:

$$
\begin{array}{l}
2X + 3Y - Z = 1 \\
0X + 0.5Y + 3.5Z = 6.5 \\
1X - 2Y - 3Z = -1
\end{array}
$$

We now eliminate the variable X in the third equation by multiplying the first equation by 0.5 and subtracting it from the third equation, as shown:

$$
\begin{array}{ll}
1X - 2Y - 3Z = -1 & \text{third equation} \\
1X + 1.5Y - .5Z = .5 & \text{first equation times 0.5} \\
\hline
0X - 3.5Y - 2.5Z = -1.5 & \text{difference}
\end{array}
$$

Our new set of equations is now:

$$
\begin{array}{l}
2X + 3Y - Z = 1 \\
0X + 0.5Y + 3.5Z = 6.5 \\
0X - 3.5Y - 2.5Z = -1.5
\end{array}
$$

Note that we have now eliminated all terms with X except in the first equation. We now move to the second variable, and eliminate it in all equations after the second equation. Thus, for our example, we multiply the second equation by -7 and subtract it from the third equation, which yields:

$$
\begin{array}{l}
2X + 3Y - Z = 1 \\
0X + 0.5Y + 3.5Z = 6.5 \\
0X + 0Y + 22Z = 44
\end{array}
$$

If we had N equations with N unknowns, we would eliminate the first unknown from all but the first equation, we would eliminate the second unknown from all but the first and second equations, and so on until the last equation has only one variable.

We now begin a back-substitution to solve for the unknowns. Using our example data, we know from the last equation that $22Z = 44$, or that $Z = 2$. Substituting this in the second equation, we know that $0.5Y + 3.5Z = 6.5$, or that $0.5Y + 3.5(2) = 6.5$, which implies that $Y = -1$. We now know the value of Y and Z, and we back-substitute these values in the first equation to determine the value of X. Since $2X + 3Y - Z = 1$, then $2X + 3(-1) - (2) = 1$, or $2X = 6$, which implies that $X = 3$.

If we had N equations with N unknowns, we would continue back-substituting, starting with the last equation, and backing up one equation each step, until we reach the first equation. After performing the back-substitution for each variable, we will have the final solution.

In order to improve the accuracy of this technique, we will add one modification to the algorithm discussed above. This modification requires that we reorder the set of equations such that the first equation is the equation with the largest coefficient (in absolute value) for the first variable. We then eliminate the first variable from the remaining equations. Starting with the second equation, we then reorder the equations such that the second equation has the largest coefficient (in absolute value) for the second variable. We then eliminate the second equation from all equations after the second equation. The reordering and elimination continues in this way until we reach the final equation, which will contain only one variable. The back-substitution then occurs as discussed previously in this section. If at some time in the reordering we find that all the coefficients for a variable are zero, or are close to zero, then the solution does not have a unique solution.

We now want to combine this algorithm with the problem relating to deformable mirrors. Assume that a data file named MIRROR has been created that contains the equations that describe the voltage settings needed to deform a mirror in order to remove a specific distortion. The first line of the data file will contain the number of actuators, with a maximum of 25. Each additional line in the file contains the coefficients for one equation. Thus, if there are five actuators, there will be five equations with six coefficients for each equation. Write a program to read the data and solve the system of equations in order to yield the voltages for the actuators. Print the solution.

PROBLEM DESCRIPTION

Write a program that will solve a system of simultaneous equations using Gauss elimination.

INPUT/OUTPUT DESCRIPTION

The input is contained in a data file MIRROR. The first line of the file contains the number of actuators for the mirror. Each following line of the file contains coefficients for one equation; thus if there are three actuators, there will be three rows of data, with four values in each row. The output is to be a report listing the corresponding voltage needed for each actuator.

HAND EXAMPLE

Using the example data from earlier in this section, the data file would contain the following information:

	MIRROR	3		
	2	3	-1	1
	3	5	2	8
	1	-2	-3	-1

Using the reorder and elimination process for each variable gives the following steps:

Select the first variable and reorder the equations if necessary:

$$3X + 5Y + 2Z = 8$$
$$2X + 3Y - Z = 1$$
$$1X - 2Y - 3Z = -1$$

We now eliminate the first variable from each of the equations after the first equation:

$$3X + 5Y + 2Z = 8$$
$$0X - 1/3\,Y - 7/3\,Z = -13/3$$
$$0X - 11/3\,Y - 11/3\,Z = -11/3$$

Starting with the second equation, we reorder the equations so that the second equation has the largest absolute value for the second coefficient:

$$3X + 5Y + 2Z = 8$$
$$0X - 11/3\,Y - 11/3\,Z = -11/3$$
$$0X - 1/3\,Y - 7/3\,Z = -13/3$$

We now eliminate the second variable from each equation after the second equation:

$$3X + 5Y + 2Z = 8$$
$$0X - 11/3\,Y - 11/3\,Z = -11/3$$
$$0X + 0Y - 2Z = - 4$$

We are now ready to do the back-substitution. We start at the last equation, and solve for the unknown in it. We then substitute that value in the next-to-last equation, and so on, moving up to the first equation:

$$3X + 5Y + 0Z = 4$$
$$0X - 11/3\,Y + 0Z = 11/3$$
$$0X + 0Y + 1Z = 2$$

We now solve the second-from-the-bottom equation, and substitute that value in all the equations previous to it:

$$3X + 0Y + 0Z = 9$$
$$0X + 1Y + 0Z = -1$$
$$0X + 0Y + 1Z = 2$$

We are now at the first equation, which we solve to get our final solution.

$$1X + 0Y + 0Z = 3$$
$$0X + 1X + 0Z = -1$$
$$0X + 0Y + 1Z = 2$$

```
DEFORMABLE MIRROR ACTUATOR SETTINGS

ACTUATOR SETTING 1 =  3
ACTUATOR SETTING 2 = -1
ACTUATOR SETTING 3 =  2
```

ALGORITHM DEVELOPMENT

The decomposition for this problem solution is the following:

DECOMPOSITION

Read distortion information.
Solve system of equations.
Print actuator settings.

Solving the system of equations requires reordering the equations, if r.ecessary, before each elimination process. The steps for reordering involve finding the equation with the maximum absolute value for the coefficient of the first unknown, and putting that equation first. We then combine equations to eliminate the first unknown in all equations after the first equation. As we think of the steps, it is helpful to use a pivot position. Our first pivot position is the first position. For all rows after the pivot row, we want to replace the row with a set of coefficients such that the pivot position has a value of zero. To do this, we determine a special factor. This factor is the value that we can multiply times the pivot equation to get a new equation that we can subtract from the current row in order to eliminate the pivot unknown. (Refer to the hand example again if necessary.) In general, this factor will be the coefficient of the pivot position in the current row divided by the coefficient of the pivot position in the pivot row.

Finally, we need to consider the back-substitution. We start at the bottom of the set of equations and divide the constant value on the right by the coefficient of the last unknown to get the solution for the last variable. We then back up one equation and use the value of the last variable to update this new equation by subtracting the term using the last variable from each side of the equation, thus giving a coefficient of zero for this last variable. We continue eliminating the last variable from each equation until we reach the first equation. We then go to the second equation from the bottom, solve for its variable, substitute back in all the equations above it, and so on.

As we consider combining these ideas into pseudocode, it is clear that we have several independent operations—the reordering step, the elimination step, and the back-substitution. We will implement these steps as subroutines in order to make our program more readable and easier to debug.

Refinement in Pseudocode

GAUSS: Read the coefficient array, a
      pivot ← 1
      error ← false
      While pivot < n and no error do
          Call order (a,n,pivot,error)
          If no error then
             Call elim (a,n,pivot)
             pivot ← pivot + 1
      If error then
          Print 'NO UNIQUE SOLUTION'
      Else
          Call backsb (a,n,soln)
          Print the solution array, soln

ORDER (a,n,pivot,error):
      rmax ← pivot
      For row = pivot + 1 to n do
          If abs(a(row,pivot)) > abs(a(rmax,pivot)) then
             rmax ← row
      If abs(a(rmax,pivot)) < 0.00001 then
          error ← true
      Else
          For k = 1,n + 1
             temp ← a(rmax,k)
             a(rmax,k) ← a(pivot,k)
             a(pivot,k) ← temp
      Return

ELIM (a,n,pivot):
      For row = pivot + 1 to n do
          factor ← a(row,pivot)/a(pivot,pivot)
          a(row,pivot) ← 0.0
          For col = pivot + 1 to n + 1 do
             a(row,col) ← a(row,col) − a(pivot,col)*factor
      Return

BACKSB (a,n,soln):
      For row = n to 1 in steps of −1 do
          For col = n to row + 1 in steps of −1 do
             a(row,n + 1) ← a(row,n + 1) − soln(col)*a(row,col)
          soln(col) ← a(row,n + 1)/a(row,row)
      Print soln, the solution array

The structure chart and FORTRAN program for this solution are the following:

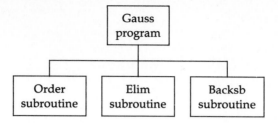

FORTRAN Program

```
*-------------------------------------------------------------*
      PROGRAM  GAUSS
*
*  This program uses the Gauss elimination method to
*  solve a set of simultaneous equations.
*
      INTEGER  N, I, J, PIVOT
      REAL  A(25,26), SOLN(25)
      LOGICAL  ERROR
*
      OPEN (UNIT=9,FILE='MIRROR',STATUS='OLD')
      READ (9,*) N
      DO 5 I=1,N
         READ(9,*) (A(I,J),J=1,N+1)
    5 CONTINUE
*
      PIVOT = 1
      ERROR = .FALSE.
   10 IF (PIVOT.LT.N.AND..NOT.ERROR) THEN
         CALL ORDER(A,N,PIVOT,ERROR)
         IF (.NOT.ERROR) THEN
            CALL ELIM(A,N,PIVOT)
            PIVOT = PIVOT + 1
         ENDIF
         GO TO 10
      ENDIF
*
      IF (ERROR) THEN
         PRINT*, 'NO UNIQUE SOLUTION EXISTS'
      ELSE
         CALL BACKSB(A,N,SOLN)
         PRINT*, 'DEFORMABLE MIRROR ACTUATOR SETTINGS'
         DO 20 I=1,N
            PRINT 15, I, SOLN(I)
   15       FORMAT (1X,'ACTUATOR SETTING ',I2,' = ',I2)
   20    CONTINUE
      ENDIF
      END
*-------------------------------------------------------------*
```

```
      SUBROUTINE  ORDER(A,N,PIVOT,ERROR)
*
*  This subroutine reorders the equations so that the pivot
*  position in the pivot equation has the maximum absolute value.
*
      INTEGER  N, ROW, RMAX, PIVOT, K
      REAL  A(25,26), TEMP
      LOGICAL  ERROR
*
      RMAX = PIVOT
      DO 10 ROW=PIVOT+1,N
          IF (ABS(A(ROW,PIVOT)).GT.ABS(A(RMAX,PIVOT))) RMAX = ROW
   10 CONTINUE
      IF (ABS(A(RMAX,PIVOT)).LT.1.0E-05) THEN
          ERROR = .TRUE.
      ELSE
          IF (RMAX.NE.PIVOT) THEN
              DO 20 K=1,N+1
                  TEMP = A(RMAX,K)
                  A(RMAX,K) = A(PIVOT,K)
                  A(PIVOT,K) = TEMP
   20         CONTINUE
          ENDIF
      ENDIF
      RETURN
      END
*-----------------------------------------------------------------*
      SUBROUTINE  ELIM(A,N,PIVOT)
*
*  This subroutine eliminates the element in the pivot
*  position from rows following the pivot equation.
*
      INTEGER  N, PIVOT, ROW, COL
      REAL  A(25,26), FACTOR
      DO 10 ROW=PIVOT+1,N
          FACTOR = A(ROW,PIVOT)/A(PIVOT,PIVOT)
          A(ROW,PIVOT) = 0.0
          DO 5 COL=PIVOT+1,N+1
              A(ROW,COL) = A(ROW,COL) - A(PIVOT,COL)*FACTOR
    5     CONTINUE
   10 CONTINUE
      RETURN
      END
*-----------------------------------------------------------------*
      SUBROUTINE  BACKSB(A,N,SOLN)
*
*  This subroutine performs the back-substitution to
*  determine the solution to the system of equations.
*
      INTEGER  N, ROW, COL
      REAL  A(25,26), SOLN(25)
*
      DO 20 ROW=N,1,-1
          DO 10 COL=N,ROW+1,-1
              A(ROW,N+1) = A(ROW,N+1) - SOLN(COL)*A(ROW,COL)
   10     CONTINUE
          SOLN(ROW) = A(ROW,N+1)/A(ROW,ROW)
   20 CONTINUE
      RETURN
      END
*-----------------------------------------------------------------*
```

TESTING

Using the sample set of data in this program gives the following results:

```
DEFORMABLE MIRROR ACTUATOR SETTINGS

ACTUATOR SETTING  1 =   3
ACTUATOR SETTING  2 =  -1
ACTUATOR SETTING  3 =   2
```

In an algorithm as complicated as this one, you want to print the values in the array A each time through the different loops as you debug the steps in order to follow the execution of the program. It would be very useful to have a subroutine that would print the values in A in an easily readable form. Then, each time you want to see the values in A, you just insert the following statement in your program:

```
CALL PRINT(A,N)
```

In fact, you would probably want to include it in each loop initially. Then, as you verify that certain loops are working properly, you could remove the subroutine reference from those loops.

There are ways to combine some of the steps outlined in this algorithm, but we have chosen not to combine them in order that the algorithm be easier to follow. For additional information on combining some of the steps, and for information on the types of roundoff error generated by this algorithm, refer to the references in the first section of this chapter.

SUMMARY

Some of the numerical techniques commonly used by engineers and scientists were introduced in this chapter. A set of data was modeled using a linear equation, and the model was evaluated using a sum of squared residuals. Numerical integration was discussed, and a program for estimating the integral of a function over a given interval was developed using the trapezoidal technique. Iterative techniques were illustrated with a program for finding the roots of a general polynomial. A number of matrix operations were implemented in FORTRAN. A program for solving a system of three linear equations was developed using determinants, and a program for solving larger systems of equations was developed using the Gauss elimination method.

DEBUGGING AIDS

Some important suggestions to ensure accuracy in your computations were presented in the chapter. We list these again:

1. When adding or subtracting long lists of numbers, work with the smaller numbers first.
2. If possible, avoid subtraction of nearly equal values.
3. Minimize the number of arithmetic operations.
4. Use double-precision variables to reduce the effects of precision errors.

At the end of Section 10–1, we gave a reference list for further information on numerical techniques—these references not only describe a number of numerical techniques but also discuss the limitations that apply to the techniques.

STYLE/TECHNIQUE GUIDES

Numerical applications may often use techniques that are not familiar to all programmers; thus, be sure to document the program and its modules carefully. If certain numerical applications are going to be used frequently, develop a set of modules that apply to the application. For example, if you are using matrices frequently, develop a set of modules to perform the operations that you need, and use this set consistently.

FORTRAN does not have a standard set of numerical approximation functions and subroutines; thus, in this chapter we wrote our own programs and subprograms. However, a number of excellent packages exist that are written in FORTRAN and thus are accessible from a FORTRAN program. These packages include routines to find matrix inverses, to solve differential equations and large systems of simultaneous equations, and to fit curves to a set of data. In general, if a routine exists in a numerical package to perform the operation that you need, it is better to use that routine than to write one yourself because the general routine is written to handle special cases and to perform operations so that precision errors are minimized.

KEY WORDS

approximation	matrix
determinant	numerical differentiation
Gauss elimination	numerical integration
interval-halving technique	residual
iterative technique	roots of an equation
linear model	

PROBLEMS

We begin our problem set with modifications to programs developed earlier in this chapter. Give the decomposition, refined pseudocode or flowchart, and FORTRAN solution for each problem.

Problems 1–5 modify the program LINEAR, given on page 448, which computed a linear model for a set of data.

1. Modify the linear model program so that it prints the point that has the largest residual (in absolute value)—this is the point that deviates the most from the approximate straight line.

2. Modify the linear model program so that it computes the residual sum as the sum of the absolute value of the difference between the actual data value for y and its estimated value.

3. Modify the linear model program so that it computes the slope and y-intercept in a subroutine.

4. Modify the linear model program so that it reads a data file that has a trailer record containing (−999,−999) as the coordinates of the data point.

5. Modify the linear model program so that it asks the user to enter an x value, and then uses the linear equation that has been computed to predict the corresponding y value.

Problems 6–10 modify the program AREA1, given on page 454, which estimated the area under a curve.

6. Modify the area program so that the user can continue specifying the number of trapezoids until the user is satisfied with the accuracy of the area estimate.

7. Modify the area program so that the number of trapezoids is initially set to 10 and the corresponding area is computed. Then, the number of trapezoids is doubled and the area is recomputed. This process continues until the change in the area is less than 0.01.

8. Modify the area program so that the number of trapezoids is initially set to 10 and the corresponding area is computed. Then, the number of trapezoids is doubled and the area is recomputed. This process continues until the change in the area is less than a user-entered tolerance.

9. Modify the area program so that the function value is computed in a function subprogram instead of a statement function.

10. Modify the area program so that it stores the x and y coordinates of the endpoints of the trapezoids in a data file so that they can be plotted later.

Problems 11–15 modify the program ROOTS, given on page 462, which determines the roots of a polynomial in a given interval.

11. Modify the polynomial program so that it allows the user to enter the interval endpoints instead of using $[-5,5]$.

12. Modify the polynomial program so that it allows the user to enter the size of the small intervals used to search initially for the roots.

13. Modify the polynomial program so that it prints the maximum and minimum polynomial values over the interval.

14. Modify the polynomial program so that it prints the number of iterations performed to find the root.

15. Modify the polynomial program so that it continues halving the interval until the absolute function value for the root is less than 0.01.

Problems 16–18 modify the program EQN3, given on page 474, which determines a solution for three linear equations.

16. Modify the linear equation program so that the data is read from a data file instead of from the terminal.

17. Modify the linear equation program so that it solves a system of two simultaneous equations. The determinant of a matrix with 2 rows and 2 columns is defined as

$$\begin{vmatrix} a(1) & b(1) \\ a(2) & b(2) \end{vmatrix} = a(1)*b(2) - a(2)*b(1)$$

18. Modify the linear equation program so that it determines if two of the equations represent the same plane when the determinant is equal to zero. In these cases, print an additional message that specifies which of the planes are the same. Recall that a plane can be represented by two different equations if one is a constant multiplied by the other. Thus, the following equations represent the same plane:

$$3x + 2y - z = 5$$
$$6x + 4y - 2z = 10$$

Problems 19–21 modify the program GAUSS, given on page 484, which uses Gauss elimination to solve a set of simultaneous equations.

19. Modify the Gauss elimination program so that the reorder subroutine prints a message specifying which rows were switched.

20. Modify the Gauss elimination program so that it includes a debugging subroutine PRINT that will print the values in the A array in an easily readable form.

21. Modify the Gauss elimination program so that it writes the solution to the set of simultaneous equations to a data file. The first line of the data file should contain the number of actuators, and each actuator number and its corresponding setting should be on a separate line in the file.

In problems 22–23, use the five-phase design process to develop programs.

22. Write a subroutine to compute the transpose of an integer matrix, where a transpose is defined to be another matrix that is generated by moving the rows of the original matrix to the columns of a new matrix. An example of a matrix A and its transpose is

$$A = \begin{bmatrix} 2 & 5 & 1 & 1 \\ 3 & 1 & 0 & 5 \\ 8 & 9 & 9 & 4 \end{bmatrix} \qquad \text{Transpose of } A = \begin{bmatrix} 2 & 3 & 8 \\ 5 & 1 & 9 \\ 1 & 0 & 9 \\ 1 & 5 & 4 \end{bmatrix}$$

The subroutine would be called with the following statement:

```
CALL TRANSP(A,AROW,ACOL,T,TROW,TCOL)
```

23. Write a subroutine that will normalize the values in a matrix to values between 0 and 1. Thus, the maximum value is scaled to 1, the minimum value is scaled to 0, and all values in between are scaled accordingly. Assume that the subroutine is called with the following statement where NA represents the normalized matrix:

```
CALL NORM(A,AROW,ACOL,NA)
```

Problems 24–26 refer to the following algorithm for computing pi. The area of a circle with radius 1 is equal to pi, and thus the area of a quarter circle with radius 1 is equal to pi/4. If we compute an estimate of the area of this quarter circle and multiply that value by 4, we have an estimate for the value of pi. To compute the area of the quarter circle, we sum the area of the subsections of the circle that are approximated by trapezoids, as shown in the following diagram. The values for Y_1 and Y_2 can be computed using the Pythagorean Theorem because they represent the length of one side of a right triangle. If we assume that the areas of the subsections are added, starting with the subsections on the right, the appropriate equations are

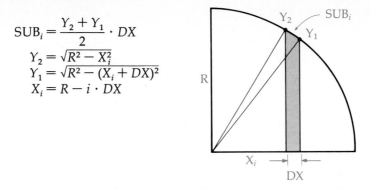

$$SUB_i = \frac{Y_2 + Y_1}{2} \cdot DX$$
$$Y_2 = \sqrt{R^2 - X_i^2}$$
$$Y_1 = \sqrt{R^2 - (X_i + DX)^2}$$
$$X_i = R - i \cdot DX$$

24. Write a program to compute pi using the technique just described. Let the number of subsections be entered by the user.

25. Modify the program in problem 24 so that the variables and all computations are performed in double precision.

26. Modify the program in problem 24 so that the number of subsections is initialized to 100. Print the number of subsections and the estimate of pi, then repeat the process increasing the number of subsections by 100. Continue until the number of subsections is equal to 1000.

Problems 27–28 refer to the following discussion on numerical differentiation. A derivative of a function at a given point can be approximated by the tangent or slope of the function at the given point, as shown in the diagram:

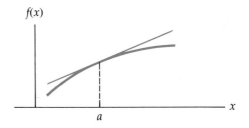

If we are given the x and y coordinates of two points on a curve, we can compute the slope of the line joining the two points, and this slope is then an estimate of the derivative of the function at the midpoint of the two given points, as shown in the diagram:

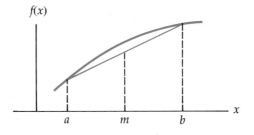

This technique uses a *symmetric difference* to approximate the derivative because it computes the derivative at a point using the function values on both sides of it. Other common techniques for approximating the derivative use a forward difference (which computes the derivative at a point using function values at that point and at the next point) or a backward difference (which computes the derivative at a point using function values at that point and at the previous point).

27. Write a program to read a set of (x,y) coordinates and compute the slope between consecutive pairs of points. Print the x coordinate of the midpoint of the interval generated by each pair of points and the value of the slope that corresponds to it.

28. Modify the program in problem 27 so that instead of printing a table of values, it prints a message that says: 'POINT OF MAXIMUM OR MINIMUM IN CURVE OCCURS NEAR X COORDINATE VALUE XXX.XX' when the sign of the slope changes.

APPENDIX A

FORTRAN 77 INTRINSIC FUNCTIONS

In the following table of intrinsic functions, the names of the arguments specify their type as indicated below:

ARGUMENT		TYPE
X	$\longrightarrow$	real
CHX	$\longrightarrow$	character
DX	$\longrightarrow$	double precision
CX	$\longrightarrow$	complex, a + bi
LX	$\longrightarrow$	logical
IX	$\longrightarrow$	integer
GX	$\longrightarrow$	generic

Function type, the second column of the table of intrinsic functions, specifies the type of value returned by the function.

Generic function names are printed in maroon. Any type argument that is applicable can be used with generic functions, and the function value returned will be the same type as the input arguments, except for type conversion functions such as REAL and INT.

FUNCTION NAME	FUNCTION TYPE	DEFINITION
SQRT(X)	Real	$\sqrt{X}$
DSQRT(DX)	Double precision	$\sqrt{DX}$
CSQRT(CX)	Complex	$\sqrt{CX}$
ABS(X)	Real	$|X|$
IABS(IX)	Integer	$|IX|$
DABS(DX)	Double precision	$|DX|$
CABS(CX)	Complex	$|CX|$
EXP(X)	Real	e^X
DEXP(DX)	Double precision	e^{DX}
CEXP(CX)	Complex	e^{CX}
LOG(GX)	Same as GX	$\log_e GX$
ALOG(X)	Real	$\log_e X$
DLOG(DX)	Double precision	$\log_e DX$
CLOG(CX)	Complex	$\log_e CX$
LOG10(GX)	Same as GX	$\log_{10} GX$
ALOG10(X)	Real	$\log_{10} X$
DLOG10(DX)	Double precision	$\log_{10} DX$
REAL(GX)	Real	Convert GX to real value
FLOAT(IX)	Real	Convert IX to real value
SNGL(DX)	Real	Convert DX to single precision
ANINT(X)	Real	Round to nearest whole number
DNINT(DX)	Double precision	Round to nearest whole number
NINT(X)	Integer	Round to nearest integer
IDNINT(DX)	Integer	Round to nearest integer
AINT(X)	Real	Truncate X to whole number
DINT(DX)	Double precision	Truncate DX to whole number
INT(GX)	Integer	Truncate GX to an integer
IFIX(X)	Integer	Truncate X to an integer
IDINT(DX)	Integer	Truncate DX to an integer
SIGN(X, Y)	Real	Transfer sign of Y to $|X|$
ISIGN(IX, IY)	Integer	Transfer sign of IY to $|IX|$
DSIGN(DX, DY)	Double precision	Transfer sign of DY to $|DX|$
MOD(IX, IY)	Integer	Remainder from IX/IY
AMOD(X, Y)	Real	Remainder from X/Y
DMOD(DX, DY)	Double precision	Remainder from DX/DY
DIM(X, Y)	Real	X − (minimum of X and Y)
IDIM(IX, IY)	Integer	IX − (minimum of IX and IY)
DDIM(DX, DY)	Double precision	DX − (minimum of DX and DY)
MAX(GX,GY, . . .)	Same as GX, GY, . . .	Maximum of (GX,GY, . . .)
MAX0(IX,IY, . . .)	Integer	Maximum of (IX,IY, . . .)
AMAX1(X,Y, . . .)	Real	Maximum of (X,Y, . . .)
DMAX1(DX,DY, . . .)	Double precision	Maximum of (DX,DY, . . .)
AMAX0(IX,IY, . . .)	Real	Maximum of (IX,IY, . . .)
MAX1(X,Y, . . .)	Integer	Maximum of (X,Y, . . .)

FUNCTION NAME	FUNCTION TYPE	DEFINITION
MIN(GX,GY, . . .)	Same as GX, GY, . . .	Minimum of (GX,GY, . . .)
MIN0(IX,IY, . . .)	Integer	Minimum of (IX,IY, . . .)
AMIN1(X,Y, . . .)	Real	Minimum of (X,Y, . . .)
DMIN1(DX,DY, . . .)	Double precision	Minimum of (DX,DY, . . .)
AMIN0(IX,IY, . . .)	Real	Minimum of (IX,IY, . . .)
MIN1(X,Y, . . .)	Integer	Minimum of (X,Y, . . .)
SIN(X)	Real	Sine of X, assumes radians
DSIN(DX)	Double precision	Sine of DX, assumes radians
CSIN(CX)	Complex	Sine of CX
COS(X)	Real	Cosine of X, assumes radians
DCOS(DX)	Double precision	Cosine of DX, assumes radians
CCOS(CX)	Complex	Cosine of CX
TAN(X)	Real	Tangent of X, assumes radians
DTAN(DX)	Double precision	Tangent of DX, assumes radians
ASIN(X)	Real	Arcsine of X
DASIN(DX)	Double precision	Arcsine of DX
ACOS(X)	Real	Arccosine of X
DACOS(DX)	Double precision	Arccosine of DX
ATAN(X)	Real	Arctangent of X
DATAN(DX)	Double precision	Arctangent of DX
ATAN2(X,Y)	Real	Arctangent of X/Y
DATAN2(DX,DY)	Double precision	Arctangent of DX/DY
SINH(X)	Real	Hyperbolic sine of X
DSINH(DX)	Double precision	Hyperbolic sine of DX
COSH(X)	Real	Hyperbolic cosine of X
DCOSH(DX)	Double precision	Hyperbolic cosine of DX
TANH(X)	Real	Hyperbolic tangent of X
DTANH(DX)	Double precision	Hyperbolic tangent of DX
DPROD(X,Y)	Double precision	Product of X and Y
DBLE(X)	Double precision	Convert X to double precision
CMPLX(X)	Complex	$X + 0i$
CMPLX(X,Y)	Complex	$X + Yi$
AIMAG(CX)	Real	Imaginary part of CX
REAL(CX)	Real	Real part of CX
CONJG(CX)	Complex	Conjugate of CX, $a - bi$
LEN(CHX)	Integer	Length of character string CHX
INDEX(CHX,CHY)	Integer	Position of substring CHY in string CHX
CHAR(IX)	Character string	Character in the IXth position of collating sequence
ICHAR(CHX)	Integer	Position of the character CHX in the collating sequence
LGE(CHX,CHY)	Logical	Value of (CHX is lexically greater than or equal to CHY)

Function Name	Function Type	Definition
LGT(CHX,CHY)	Logical	Value of (CHX is lexically greater than CHY)
LLE(CHX,CHY)	Logical	Value of (CHX is lexically less than or equal to CHY)
LLT(CHX,CHY)	Logical	Value of (CHX is lexically less than CHY)

APPENDIX B

ADDITIONAL FORTRAN 77 TOPICS

This appendix summarizes a number of features of FORTRAN that were not introduced in earlier chapters but that should be included for completeness. We have divided these additional features into specification statements, control statements, subprogram features and formatting features. Most of these features are from older versions of FORTRAN. In general, the use of these features is discouraged because they make programs more difficult to debug and to understand. For example, the control structures discussed employ multiple branches from a single statement and thus no longer yield structures with one entrance and one exit.

SPECIFICATION STATEMENTS

Three specification statements, and thus nonexecutable statements, are included here. The IMPLICIT statement is used to specify the beginning letters of variable names that are to be associated with a particular type, such as REAL or CHARACTER. The PARAMETER statement is used to assign names to constants. The EQUIVALENCE statement allows the sharing of data storage.

IMPLICIT STATEMENT

We have discussed six different specification statements: INTEGER, REAL, LOGICAL, CHARACTER, DOUBLE PRECISION, and COMPLEX. Only two of these statements, INTEGER and REAL, have default values. That is, variable names beginning with letters I–N specify integer variables by default, and all other variable names specify real variables by default. The IMPLICIT statement allows us to specify defaults for variables of all types. Its general form is

> **IMPLICIT** *type 1 (default), type 2 (default), . . .*

For instance, if a program contained only integers, you could specify that any variable is an integer with this statement:

```
IMPLICIT  INTEGER(A-Z)
```

Or you might want to specify that the first half of the alphabet represents beginning letters of integer names and the last half represents real names:

```
IMPLICIT  INTEGER(A-M), REAL(N-Z)
```

If you are following the convention of beginning all double-precision variable names with the letter D instead of listing all the names in a DOUBLE PRECISION statement, you could use the following:

```
IMPLICIT  DOUBLE PRECISION(D)
```

An implicit declaration can be overridden with a specification statement, as shown here:

```
IMPLICIT  COMPLEX(C), LOGICAL(L)
CHARACTER*10  CHAR
```

The variable CHAR should be a complex variable according to the IMPLICIT statement, but instead it is defined as a character string by the CHARACTER statement.

If you type all variables used in your programs, as we have recommended and as we have done in our sample programs, the IMPLICIT statement is unnecessary.

PARAMETER STATEMENT

The PARAMETER statement is a specification statement used to assign names to constants, with the following general form:

> **PARAMETER** *(name 1 = expression, name 2 = expression, . . .)*

The expression after the equal sign typically is a constant, although it can be an expression consisting of other constants and operations. A specific example of the PARAMETER statement is

```
PARAMETER  (PI = 3.141593, N = 75)
```

Type statements should precede the PARAMETER statement in order to assign the proper type to the constant name. Thus, the previous statement should be used with type statements as shown:

```
INTEGER  N
REAL   PI
PARAMETER   (PI = 3.141593, N = 75)
```

The DATA and PARAMETER statements are similar, but there are some significant differences. A DATA statement assigns an initial value to a variable, and the value may or may not be changed by other statements when the program is executed. The PARAMETER statement assigns a name to a constant, and the value of a constant cannot be changed by other statements within the program. A name assigned to a constant by a PARAMETER statement can be used anywhere in a program that a constant is used except in FORMAT statements. For example, the following statements are valid at the beginning of a main program. Although it is not valid to use a variable to specify the dimension of an array in the main program, these statements are correct because N is a constant and not a variable:

```
INTEGER  N
REAL   PI
PARAMETER   (PI = 3.141593, N = 75)
REAL   TEMP(N,N)
```

Note that we needed two REAL statements. The first statement was necessary in order to specify that PI represented a real constant. This statement had to be listed before the constant PI was given a value. Because the array TEMP used the constant N in its specification, it could not be specified before the PARAMETER statement.

A PARAMETER statement can be used to assign names to constants of any type, as shown in the next pair of statements:

```
CHARACTER*6  DATE
PARAMETER   (DATE = '090287')
```

Because the PARAMETER statement must be included at the beginning of a program (or a subprogram), it is easy to locate if we want to change the value of the constant. For example, in the statements above we can change the date used in all references to DATE simply by changing the constant value in the PARAMETER statement.

EQUIVALENCE STATEMENT

The EQUIVALENCE statement, a specification statement that permits data storage to be shared by several variables, has the following general form:

EQUIVALENCE *(variable list 1), (variable list 2),* . . .

The variable list may contain variable names, array names, and character substring names. The EQUIVALENCE statement causes all the names enclosed in a set of parentheses to reference the same storage location. Character variables cannot be equivalenced with noncharacter variables. In fact, it is best to use the same type in all equivalence lists. The entire arrays are involved when array elements are equivalenced, as shown in the next example, because an array is always stored sequentially in memory. Two variables in a common block or in two different common blocks cannot be made equivalent, and two variables in the same array cannot be made equivalent.

Consider the following EQUIVALENCE statement:

```
INTEGER  HEIGHT, DIST
REAL   A(5), B(9), C(2,2)
EQUIVALENCE  (HEIGHT,DIST), (A(1),B(4),C(1,1))
```

The first variable list specifies that HEIGHT and DIST are to occupy the same location that can be referenced by either variable name. The equivalence of storage locations specified by the second variable list is best explained using the following diagram of computer memory:

	B(1)	
	B(2)	
	B(3)	
A(1)	B(4)	C(1,1)	← All three variables share the same storage location.
A(2)	B(5)	C(2,1)
A(3)	B(6)	C(1,2)
A(4)	B(7)	C(2,2)
A(5)	B(8)	
	B(9)	

By specifying that A(1) and B(4) share the same location, we also have implicitly specified that A(2) and B(5) share the same location, and so on through A(5) and B(8). Furthermore, we have equated the location that stores A(1) and B(4) with C(1,1), and hence other implicit equivalences have been specified as shown in the diagram. When using two-dimensional arrays in equivalence statements, it is important to remember that they are stored by columns.

CONTROL STATEMENTS

The control structures mentioned in this section contain multiple branches and therefore have multiple exits. Because these statements do not follow a one-entrance, one-exit path of execution, we discourage their use. The main reason that multiple branch statements are included in the language is so that programs written in earlier versions can still be used without modifications. (Older versions of FORTRAN did not include all forms of the IF statements that were presented in Chapter 3, and thus multiple branching could not always be avoided.)

ARITHMETIC IF STATEMENT

The general form of the arithmetic IF statement is

> **IF** *(arithmetic expression) label 1, label 2, label 3*

Labels 1, 2, and 3 must be references to executable statements in the program. The arithmetic expression is evaluated, and if it represents a negative value, control passes to the statement referenced by label 1. If the expression represents zero, then control passes to the statement referenced by label 2. Finally, if the expression represents a positive value, control passes to the statement referenced by label 3. In the following arithmetic IF statement, control will pass to statement 10 if A is greater than B, to statement 15 if A is equal to B, and to statement 20 if A is less than B.

$$\text{IF (B - A) 10, 15, 20}$$

Thus, the arithmetic IF statement is a three-way branch, equivalent to the following statements:

```
IF (arithmetic expression.LT.0.0) GO TO label 1
IF (arithmetic expression.EQ.0.0) GO TO label 2
GO TO label 3
```

Early versions of FORTRAN did not include even the simple IF statement presented in Chapter 3. Hence, all IF statements were written in the form of arithmetic IF statements at that time.

COMPUTED GO TO STATEMENT

The general form of the computed GO TO statement is

> **GO TO** *(label 1, label 2, . . . , label n), integer expression*

Labels 1, 2, . . . , and *n* must be references to executable statements in your program. The computed GO TO statement is used for a multi-way branch of control. For example, if we wish to execute a different set of statements dependent on the rank of a student, we could use the following computed GO TO statement, where RANK = 1 for freshman, 2 for sophomore, 3 for junior, 4 for senior, and 5 for graduate. Assume RANK is an integer variable.

```
INTEGER  RANK
    .
    .
    .
GO TO (11, 15, 20, 17, 17), RANK
PRINT*, 'RANK VALUE IN ERROR'
```

If RANK = 1 (representing a freshman), then the computed GO TO statement will be executed as if it were

GO TO 11

Similar branches would occur for RANK = 2 and RANK = 3. For seniors and graduate students (RANK = 4 and RANK = 5), control will transfer to statement 17, thus illustrating the fact that the statement labels do not have to be unique. If the value of RANK is such that it does not cause a branch (in this case, less than 1 or greater than 5), control passes to the next statement, which we have used to print an error message.

This type of multi-way branch is also sometimes called a CASE statement, because it tests a number of cases and then branches depending on the results of the tests. The IF-ELSEIF statement provides a structured way of implementing an algorithm that performs different steps depending on a series of tests.

ASSIGNED GO TO STATEMENT

The ASSIGN statement and the assigned GO TO statement work together to yield a multi-branch structure. The general forms of these two statements are

ASSIGN *integer constant* **TO** *integer variable*

GO TO *integer variable, (label 1, label 2, . . . , label n)*

The assigned GO TO statement looks very similar to the computed GO TO statement, but there are some significant differences.

1. The integer variable referenced in the assigned GO TO must have been initialized with the ASSIGN statement.
2. The integer variable can be used only to store statement references.
3. If the value of the integer variable is not in the list of labels, an execution error occurs.

In the next example, the value 3 has been initially assigned to K. The IF statements may change the value stored in K to either 11 or 20. When the assigned GO TO statement is executed, control will transfer to statement 11 if K = 11, statement 20 if K = 20, or statement 3 if K = 3. Otherwise, an execution error occurs.

```
        ASSIGN 3 TO K
        .
        .
        .
        IF (A.LT.B) ASSIGN 20 TO K
        IF (A.GE.C) ASSIGN 11 TO K
        .
        .
        .
        GO TO K, (3, 11, 20)
```

Again, the IF-ELSEIF statement provides a structured alternative to this multi-way branch statement.

SUBPROGRAM FEATURES

This section discusses additional features of FORTRAN that relate to subprograms. The SAVE, INTRINSIC, and EXTERNAL statements are not frequently used but can be very useful, as pointed out in the following discussions. The ENTRY statement and alternate return point from a subprogram are covered so that the coverage of FORTRAN 77 is complete, but their use is discouraged, again because they do not support a one-entrance, one-exit path of execution that is simple to follow.

SAVE

Local variables are those used in a subprogram that are not arguments; thus, they tend to be totals, loop indexes, and counters. The values of these local variables are generally lost when a RETURN statement is executed. A SAVE specification statement will, however, save the values of local variables so they will contain the same values as they did at the end of the previous reference. This nonexecutable statement appears only in the subprogram. The general form of the SAVE statement is

SAVE   *variable list*

The values of all local variables will be saved if the list of variables is omitted.

To illustrate the use of the SAVE statement, suppose you wanted to know how many times a subprogram was accessed. The following statements would initialize the counter COUNTR to zero at the beginning of the program and increment COUNTR each time the subprogram was used. Recall that the DATA statement does not reinitialize COUNTR each time the function is used.

```
*- - - - - - - - - - - - - - - - - - - - - - - - - - - - - - - - - - - - -*
        REAL FUNCTION   AVE(X,Y)
        .
        .
        .
        INTEGER   COUNTR
        SAVE   COUNTR
        DATA   COUNTR /0/
        .
        .
        .
        COUNTR = COUNTR + 1
        .
        .
        .
        RETURN
        END
*- - - - - - - - - - - - - - - - - - - - - - - - - - - - - - - - - - -*
```

INTRINSIC, EXTERNAL

The INTRINSIC and EXTERNAL statements are specification statements used when subprogram names are to be used as arguments in another subprogram. The general forms of these nonexecutable statements are

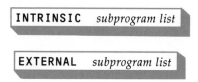

These statements appear only in the module that sends the arguments representing the subprogram names. If the argument is an intrinsic function, use the INTRINSIC statement. If the argument is a user-written function or a subroutine, use the EXTERNAL statement.

We reference a subroutine twice in the following statements. In one reference, the subroutine replaces each value in an array with its natural logarithm. The other reference replaces each value in an array with its logarithm, using base 10.

```
*--------------------------------------------*
       PROGRAM   TEST1
       .
       .
       .
       REAL   X(10), TIME(10)
       INTRINSIC   ALOG, ALOG10
       .
       .
       .
       CALL COMPUT(X,ALOG)
       .
       .
       .
       CALL COMPUT(TIME,ALOG10)
       .
       .
       .
       END
*--------------------------------------------*
*
       SUBROUTINE   COMPUT(R,F)
*
*   This subroutine applies a function
*   to the real array R.
*
       INTEGER   I
       REAL   R(10)
*
       DO 10 I=1,10
          R(I) = F(R(I))
    10 CONTINUE
*
       RETURN
       END
*--------------------------------------------*
```

ENTRY

The ENTRY statement is used to define entry points into a subprogram other than the entry point at the beginning of the subprogram. The general form of the statement is

> **ENTRY**   *entry name (argument list)*

The ENTRY statement is placed at the point in the subprogram that is to be an alternative entry. The argument list does not have to be the same as that for the original entry point. The ENTRY statement is nonexecutable and will not affect execution of the subprogram if it is in the statements being executed from a previous entry point.

The following statements illustrate references to a subroutine through two different entry points:

```
*-----------------------------------------*
          PROGRAM  TEST2
          .
          .
          .
          CALL SUBAA(X)
          .
          .
          .
          CALL SUBAB(X,K)
          .
          .
          .
          END
*-----------------------------------------*
*
          SUBROUTINE  SUBAA(T)
          .
          .
          .
          ENTRY  SUBAB(T,J)
          .
          .
          .
*
          RETURN
          END
*-----------------------------------------*
```

One of the fundamental advantages of structured programming lies in the simplicity of the interface between modules. The use of multiple entry points to a subprogram complicates that linkage; their usage is therefore not generally recommended. If you want to use a portion of a subprogram, define that portion as a subprogram itself. It can then be referenced by other subprograms in addition to the main program, and the simple interface between modules is maintained.

ALTERNATE RETURNS

Normally, the execution of a RETURN statement in a subroutine returns control to the first statement following the CALL statement; however, a return point can be specified with an argument in the subroutine. The argument list in the SUBROUTINE statement contains asterisks in the locations of arguments that are the alternate return points. The RETURN statement has this expanded general form:

RETURN   *integer expression*

If the value of the integer expression is 1, the return point is the statement number that corresponds to the first asterisk in the argument list. If the value of the integer expression is 2, the return point is the statement nunber that corresponds to the second asterisk, and so on. The following statements will help clarify this process:

```
*-------------------------------------------*
      PROGRAM   TEST3
      .
      .
      .
      CALL SUB1(A,B,*20,*50)
      .
      .
      .
   20 PRINT 25, A
      .
      .
      .
   50 COUNT = COUNT + 1
      .
      .
      .
      END
*-------------------------------------------*
*
      SUBROUTINE   SUB1(X,Y,*,*)
      .
      .
      .
*
      RETURN I
      END
*-------------------------------------------*
```

If the value of I is 1 in the subroutine, then control will return to statement 20. If the value of I is 2, then control returns to statement 50. An execution error occurs if the value of I is not 1 or 2.

Again, multiple return points also complicate the linkage between modules and generally should be avoided. Structured alternatives can be developed using the IF structures.

FORMATTING FEATURES

The formatting features discussed here are rarely used. If you do use them or work with programs that use them, be sure to document their use carefully.

ADDITIONAL FORMAT SPECIFICATIONS

The following FORMAT specifications are not routinely used but occassionally simplify the input and output steps in a program.

Gw.d The G format code is a generalized code to transmit real data. The width w specifies the number of positions in the input or output that are used. Input data can be entered in an F or E format. The real advantage of the G format is in output formats. If the exponent of the data value is negative or larger than d, the output is performed with an Ew.d specification; if the exponent is between 0 and d, the output is performed with an F specification that will print d significant digits followed by 4 spaces. Thus, very large or small values are automatically printed with an E format, and values of reasonable size are printed with an F format. For example, if the G specification is G10.3, then the value 26.8 is printed as $_{bb}26.8_{bbbb}$, and the value 1248.1 is printed as $_b0.125E_b04$.

wH Literal data can be specified in an output format with an H, or Hollerith, specification. The width w specifies that total number of positions in the literal. The literal itself immediately follows the H. The following two formats are equivalent:

```
10 FORMAT (1X,'EXPERIMENT NO. 1')
10 FORMAT (1X,16HEXPERIMENT NO. 1)
```

Specifying literals with apostrophes is easier than using an H format because we do not need to count the characters in the literal; hence, H formats are rarely used.

Lw Logical variables can be read or printed with an L specification. In an input specification, the first non-blank character (in the w characters read) must be T or F; the variable receives the corresponding true or false value. In an output specification, the letter T or F is printed, again corresponding to whether the variable is true or false.

FORMAT EXTENSIONS

The following FORMAT extensions are not specifications that correspond to a variable; they are modifiers that affect the performance of the specifications already presented.

Ew.dEe and Gw.dEe The addition of Ee to an exponential or generalized format specifies that e positions are to be printed in the exponent. The Ee affects only output specifications.

nP The addition of nP to an F, E, or G format code specifies a scale factor n that is applied to subsequent specifications until another scale factor is encountered. The actual value stored is multiplied by 10**n to give the number read or printed when the scale factor n is in effect. For instance, if the following READ statement is

```
        READ 5, A, B
      5 FORMAT (2PF4.1,F5.1)
```

and the data line read is

```
        12.1362.4
```

then the value stored in A is 0.121 and the value stored in B is 3.624. Any computations with A and B use the values 0.121 and 3.624.

The output statement

```
        PRINT 10, A,B
     10 FORMAT (1X,F4.1,1X,F5.1)
```

generates the following data line:

$$00.1_{bbb}3.6$$

The scale factor might be useful in applications that use percentages — the input could be in the form XX.X; but, the internal values used in calculations and the output would use the form .XXX.

S, SP, and SS These options affect I, F, E, and G specifications during execution of output statements. If a numeric value is negative, the minus sign is printed in the first position to the left of the data value. If the numeric value is positive, the printing of the plus sign is system dependent. If SP precedes a specification, in the value to be printed and in all subsequent values, a sign is printed, whether the value is positive or negative. If SS precedes a specification, in the value to be printed and all subsequent values, only a minus sign is printed. If S precedes a specification, the system designation of producing signs is restored. The following example illustrates the use of the SP modifier. If these statements are executed

```
        A = 36.2
        PRINT 5, A, A, A
      5 FORMAT (1X,F5.1,1X,SPF5.1,1X,F5.1)
```

the output line is

$$_{b}36.2_{b}+36.2_{b}+36.2$$

BN and BZ The BN and BZ modifiers specify the interpretation of nonleading blanks in numeric data fields during execution of input statements. Normally, leading and nonleading blanks are converted to zeros in numeric input fields. The modifier BN, however, specifies that blanks be considered null characters or ignored in the current and all succeeding specifications. The BZ modifier restores the interpretation of all blanks as zeros in numeric fields. If the data line

$$_{b}21_{bb}21_{b}$$

is read with the statement

```
      READ 15, I, J
   15 FORMAT (I4,BNI4)
```

the value stored in I is 210 and the value stored in J is 21.

Colon A colon terminates the format if there are no more items in the input or output list. The following statements and their corresponding output illustrate the usefulness of this feature:

```
         MAX = 20
         MIN = -5
         PRINT 10, MAX
         PRINT 10, MAX, MIN
      10 FORMAT (1X,'MAX =',I3,:,2X,'MIN =',I3)
```

The output from the first PRINT statement is

```
MAX = 20
```

The output from the second PRINT statement is

```
MAX = 20   MIN = -5
```

Without the colon, the output from the first PRINT statement would be

```
MAX = 20   MIN =
```

VARIABLE FORMATTING

In input and output statements up to this point, the format identifier has always been a statement number reference. However, this format identifier can also be an integer variable that has been initialized by an ASSIGN statement (defined earlier in this appendix) with the number of the desired FORMAT statement. The format identifier can also be a character constant, character array element, character array, or character expression.

GLOSSARY OF KEY WORDS

algorithm A stepwise procedure for solving a problem.

approximation An estimate of a value that is used instead of the actual value.

argument An expression used in a function or subroutine reference.

arithmetic expression An expression of variables, constants, and arithmetic operations that can be evaluated as a single numerical value.

arithmetic logic unit (ALU) A fundamental computer component that performs all the arithmetic and logic operations.

array A group of variables that share a common name and are specified individually with subscripts.

ascending order An order from lowest to highest.

ASCII code A binary code (American Standard Code for Information Interchange) commonly used by computers to store information.

assembler A program that converts an assembly language program into machine language.

assembly language A programming language that is unique to an individual computer system.

assignment statement A FORTRAN statement that assigns a value to a variable.

batch processing A method of interacting with the computer in which programs are executed in generally the same order in which they are submitted.

binary A term used to describe something that has two values, such as a binary digit that can be 0 or 1.

binary search   An algorithm that searches an ordered list by continually dividing the array in half as it looks for a specific value.

binary string   A string or group of binary values, such as 11011000.

blank common   A single group of storage locations that is accessible to subprograms without being specified as subprogram arguments.

BLOCK DATA subprogram   A subprogram that is used to assign initial values to variables in named common using DATA statements.

branch   A change in the flow of a program such that the steps are not executed in the sequential order in which they are written.

bubble sort   Another name for a multipass sort algorithm that generally requires more than one pass through the list in order to guarantee that the list is sorted into the desired order.

buffer   An internal storage area used to store input and output information.

bug   An error in a computer program.

carriage control   A character used at the beginning of a buffer of printed output that specifies the page spacing desired before the line is printed.

cathode ray tube (CRT) terminal   A terminal that uses a video screen for its input and output.

central processing unit (CPU)   The combination of the processor unit, the ALU, and the internal memory that forms the basis of a computer.

character string   A string or group of characters that contains numerical digits, alphabetical letters, or special characters.

collating sequence   The ascending order of characters specified by a particular code.

comment line   A statement included in FORTRAN programs to document the program but not translated into machine language.

common block   A block or group of storage locations that is accessible to subprograms without being specified as subprogram arguments.

compilation   The process of converting a program written in a high-level language into machine language.

compiler   The program that converts a program written in a high-level language into machine language.

complex value   A numerical value that is of the form $a + bi$; where $i = \sqrt{-1}$.

compound logical expression   A logical expression formed by combining two single logical expressions with the connectors .AND. or .OR.

computer network   A network that links computers so they can communicate with each other.

concatenation   An operation that connects two strings together to form one string.

condition   An expression that can be evaluated to be true or false.

constant   A specific value used in arithmetic or logical expressions.

continuation line   A statement used to continue a FORTRAN statement that extends past column 72; the continuation statement must contain a non-blank character in column 6 to signify that it is a continuation line.

control structure A structure that controls the order of execution of a series of steps.

conversational computing A method of interacting with the computer in which the computer seems to converse with the user in an English-like manner.

counting loop A loop that is repeated a specific number of times.

data The information used by a program or generated by a program.

data file A file used to store information used by a program or generated by a program.

debug The process of eliminating bugs or errors from a program.

decomposition Dividing a problem solution into a series of smaller problems.

deletion A technique for removing an element from an ordered list.

descending order An order from highest to lowest.

design phases A procedure for solving a problem by dividing the solution into a series of phases that begin with the problem description and end with the problem solution.

determinant A real number that is computed from a matrix.

diagnostic A message that describes an error in a program that has been located in either the compilation or execution step.

direct-access file A file whose information can be accessed in nonsequential order.

DO loop An iterative loop specified in FORTRAN with the DO statement.

double-precision value A real value that has been specified to have more precision than the standard real value.

driver A main program written specifically to test a subprogram.

EBCDIC code A binary code (Extended Binary-Coded-Decimal Interchange Code) commonly used by computers to store information.

echo A debugging aid in which the values of variables are printed immediately after they are read.

editor A program in a time-sharing system that allows the user to modify programs entered into the system.

element A specific storage location in an array.

END option An option that can be used in a READ statement to generate a branch to a specified program statement if the end of the data (or data file) is reached.

executable statement A statement specifying action to be taken in a program that is translated into machine language by the compiler.

execution The process of executing the steps specified by a program.

explicit typing A specification of the type of information to be stored in a variable with a REAL or INTEGER statement.

exponential notation A notation for real values that uses the letter E to separate the mantissa and the exponent.

external file A file that is available to a program through an external device such as a disk drive or tape drive.

father-son update A type of file updating that uses a transaction (son) file to update information on the master (father) file.

field A unit of information in a record.

flowchart A graphical diagram used to describe the steps in an algorithm.

formatted I/O The input or output statements that use FORMAT statements to describe the spacing.

FORTRAN character set The set of characters accepted by FORTRAN compilers.

FORTRAN 77 The version of FORTRAN established in 1977 that includes a number of new features, such as the IF-ELSE structure.

function A subprogram that returns a single value to the main program.

Gauss elimination A technique for solving a system of equations in which we solve for the unknowns by combining equations.

generic function A function that returns a value of the same type as its input argument.

hardware The physical components of a computer.

hash code A code used to compute a record number for accessing a direct-access file.

high-level language An English-like language that must be converted into machine language before it can be executed.

IF-ELSEIF structure A structure that tests one condition and executes a set of steps if the condition is true; if the condition is false, another condition is tested, and if it is true, a different set of steps is executed.

IF-ELSE structure A structure that tests a condition and executes one set of steps if the condition is true and another set of steps if the condition is false.

IF structure A structure that tests a condition and executes a set of steps if the condition is true.

implicit typing The specification of the type of information (real or integer) to be stored in a variable by the beginning letter of the variable name.

implied DO loop A DO loop that can be specified completely on an I/O statement or a DATA statement.

increment value   The parameter in a DO loop that specifies the increment to be added to the index each time the loop is executed.

index   The variable used as a loop counter in a DO loop.

initial value   The parameter in a DO loop that specifies the initial value of the index.

initialize   To give an initial value to a variable.

input/output (I/O)   The information that a program reads or writes.

insertion   A technique for adding an element in an ordered list.

insertion sort   A sort that begins at the top of the list, comparing adjacent elements. If an element is out of order, it is continually exchanged with the value above it in the list until it is in its proper place.

integer value   A value that contains no fractional portion.

interactive computing   Computing in which the user interacts with the program by answering questions and entering data.

intermediate result   A result used in evaluating an expression to get the final result.

internal file   A file defined on information stored in the internal memory of the computer.

interval halving technique   A technique for approximating roots of a function by determining an interval in which the function crosses the x axis and then halving the interval to find a new smaller interval in which the function crosses the x axis.

intrinsic function   A function used so frequently that its code is included in a library available to the compiler.

iterative loop   A loop that is controlled by the value of a variable called the index of the loop or the loop counter.

iterative technique   A technique that is repeated to give better and better approximations to a value that cannot be computed through a direct computation.

job control information   The information that must accompany a program submitted to a batch-processing system.

key   An integer used to specify the record number for accessing records in a direct-access file.

left-justified   No blanks on the left side.

lexicographic order   Dictionary order.

library function   A function used so frequently that its code is available in a library available to the compiler.

limit value   The parameter in a DO loop that specifies the value used to determine completion of the DO loop.

linear model A linear equation that approximates the relationship between two variables.

list-directed I/O The input or output statements that do not use FORMAT statements to describe the spacing.

literal A character string.

logic error An error in the logic used to define an algorithm.

logical expression An expression of variables, constants, and operations that can be evaluated as a single logical value.

logical operator One of the operators .NOT., .AND., and .OR. that is used with logical expressions.

logical value A value that is either true or false.

loop A group of statements that are executed repeatedly.

machine language The binary language understood by computers.

magnitude limitation A limitation on the size of value that can be used in a specific computer.

main program A complete program that may access functions and subroutines.

master file A file that contains the master information or most accurate information.

matrix A group of values that can be represented by a two-dimensional array.

memory The storage available for the variables and constants needed in a program.

merge An operation that combines two ordered lists into one ordered list.

mixed-mode operation An operation between values that are not of the same type.

module A function or a subroutine.

multidimensional array A group of variables that share the same name and whose elements are specified by more than one subscript.

multipass sort A sort algorithm that generally requires more than one pass through the list in order to guarantee that the list is sorted into the desired order.

named common A group of storage locations that is accessible to subprograms by name without being specified as subprogram arguments.

nested function A function argument that is the value of another function.

nested loop A loop that is completely contained within another loop.

nonexecutable statement A statement that affects the way memory is used by a program although it is not converted into machine language by the compiler.

numerical differentiation Numerical techniques for estimating the derivative (or slope) of a function at a specified point.

numerical integration   Numerical techniques for estimating the integral of a function (or the area under the graph of the function) over a specified interval.

object program   A program in machine-language form.

one-dimensional array   A group of variables that share the same name and whose elements are specified by one subscript.

overflow   An error condition that occurs when the result of an arithmetic operation yields a result that is too large to be stored in the computer's memory.

parameter   A value or variable used in the DO statement to specify the DO loop.

problem solving   The process of determining a solution to a problem.

processor   A fundamental computer component that controls the operation of the other parts of the computer.

program   A set of statements that specify a complete algorithm in a computer language.

pseudocode   The English-like statements used to describe the steps in an algorithm.

random access   A file-access technique in which records can be accessed in any order.

real value   A value that may contain a fractional or decimal portion.

record   The basic unit of information related to a data file.

relational operator   An operator used to compare two arithmetic expressions.

repetition   A structure in which steps are repeated, such as in a WHILE loop or a counting loop.

residual   A value used to determine the quality of a linear model for a set of data.

right-justified   No blanks on the right side.

roots of an equation   Values that yield a result of zero when substituted for the unknowns of the equation.

rounding   A technique that approximates a value.

scientific notation   A notation for real values that expresses the value as a number between 1 and 10 multiplied by a power of 10.

search algorithm   An algorithm that searches a list looking for a specific value.

selection   A structure that tests a condition to determine which steps are to be performed next.

selection sort   A sort that is based on finding the minimum value and placing it first in the list, finding the next smallest value and placing it second in the list, and so on.

sentinel signal   A signal at the end of a data file that indicates that no more data follows.

sequence   A structure in which steps are performed one after another, or sequentially.

sequential access file   A file whose information can be accessed only in a sequential order.

software   The programs used to specify the operations in a computer.

sort   To put in a specific order.

source program   A program in a high-level language form.

specification statement   A statement that specifies the nature of the values to be stored in a variable.

statement function   A function that can be defined in a single assignment statement that is placed before any executable statement in a program.

statement label   A number that appears in columns 1–5 of a FORTRAN statement and that can be used by other statements to reference the statement.

stepwise refinement   A process for converting a general algorithm to one that is detailed enough to be converted into a computer language.

structure chart   A diagram that outlines the module structure of a program.

structured programming   Programming with a top-down flow that is easy to follow and modify because of its structure.

subprogram   A function or subroutine.

subroutine   A subprogram that may return many values, a single value, or no value to the main program.

subscript   An integer variable or constant used to specify a unique element in an array.

substring   A string that is a subset of another string and that maintains the original order of characters.

syntax error   An error in a FORTRAN statement.

time-sharing   A method of interacting with the computer in which a number of programs are being executed at the same time although the user appears to have the complete attention of the computer.

top-down design   Technique for problem solving in which the solution is first decomposed into a set of smaller steps, which are then refined individually in more and more detail until the problem is solved.

trailer signal   A signal at the end of a data file that indicates that no more data follows.

transaction file   A file that contains information to update a master file.

truncation   A technique that approximates a value by dropping its fractional value and using only the integer portion.

two-dimensional array   A group of variables that share the same name and whose elements are specified by two subscripts.

underflow   An error condition that occurs when the result of an arithmetic operation yields a result that is too small to be stored in the computer's memory.

user-friendly   A term used to describe a program that is easy to use.

user interface   The part of the program that interfaces the user to the steps in the program itself. The user interface usually consists of the input and output portion of the program.

variable   A memory location referenced with a name whose value can be changed within a program.

variable dimensioning   A technique that permits the size of an array in a subprogram to be specified by an argument to the subprogram.

WHILE loop   A loop that is executed as long as a specified condition is true.

workstation   A computer that can function as a computer itself or that functions as a terminal to other computers through a computer network.

ANSWERS TO SELF-TESTS

Self-test 2-1, page 18

1. valid
2. invalid (too long)
3. valid
4. valid
5. invalid character (—)
6. invalid character (—)
7. invalid characters (parentheses)
8. invalid (starts with a digit)
9. valid
10. invalid character ($)
11. not the same (2300, 23000)
12. not the same (0.000007, 7000.0)
13. same
14. not the same (110.0, 110.1)
15. not the same (−34.7, −34.0)
16. not the same (−0.76, 0.76)

Self-test 2-2, page 25

1. $Y = -4.0$
2. $A = 2.0, K = 2$
3. $T = 4.25$

Self-test 2-3, page 28

1. SLOPE = (Y2-Y1)/(X2-X1)
2. FACTOR = 1 + B/V + C/V**2
3. FRICTN = V*V/(30.0*S)
4. CENTER = 38.1972*(R**3 - S**3)*SIN(A)/((R*R - S*S)*A)
5. LOSS = F*P*(L/D)*(V*V/2.0)
6. REQ = 1.0/(1.0/X1 + 1.0/X2 + 1.0/X3 + 1.0/X4)
7. $\text{MOTION} = \sqrt{VI^2 + 2AX}$
8. $\text{FREQ} = \dfrac{1.0}{\sqrt{2\pi \cdot \frac{1}{XL} \cdot C}}$
9. $\text{RANGE} = \dfrac{2VI^2\sin(B)\cos(B)}{G}$
10. $\text{LENGTH} = LI\,\sqrt{1-(V/C)^2}$
11. $\text{ENERGY} = 1.6747 \times 10^{-24}\,(2.99 \times 10^{10})^2$
12. $\text{VOLUME} = 2\pi X^2\,((1-\pi/4)Y - (0.8333-\pi/4)X)$

Self-test 2-4, page 44

1. 57.8290ᵇᵇᵇ23
2. DISTANCEᵇ=ᵇ15.6832
   VELOCITYᵇ=ᵇᵇᵇ0.27E-01

Here subscripts represent blanks:

1. 57.8290_bbb_23
2. DISTANCE_b_=_b_15.6832
   VELOCITY_b_=_bbb_0.27E-01

Self-test 3-1, page 90

1. true
2. true
3. true
4. false
5. true
6. true
7. true
8. false
9. IF (TIME.GT.15.0) TIME = TIME + 1.0
10. IF (SQRT(POLY).LT.0.5) PRINT*, POLY
11. IF (ABS(VOLT1 - VOLT2).GT.10.0) PRINT*, VOLT1, VOLT2
12. IF (DEN.LT.0.005) PRINT*, 'DENOMINATOR IS TOO SMALL'
13. IF (ALOG(X).GE.3.0) THEN
        TIME = 0.0
        COUNT = COUNT + 1
    ENDIF
14. IF (DIST.LT.50.0.AND.TIME.GT.10.0) THEN
        TIME = TIME + 2.0
    ELSE
        TIME = TIME + 2.5
    ENDIF

```
15. IF (DIST.GE.100.0) THEN
        TIME = TIME + 2.0
    ELSEIF (DIST.GT.50.0) THEN
        TIME = TIME + 1.0
    ELSE
        TIME = TIME + 0.5
    ENDIF
```

Self-test 3-2, page 114

1. 18 times
2. 17 times
3. 9 times
4. 11 times
5. 0 times
6. 0 times
7. COUNT = 10
8. COUNT = 55
9. COUNT = 0
10. COUNT = −15
11. COUNT = 0

Self-test 3-3, page 129

1. COUNT = 100
2. COUNT = 16
3. COUNT = 12

Self-test 4-1, page 172

1. ID = 1456
   HT = 14.6
   WIDTH = 0.7
2. ID = 0
   HT = 13.7
   WIDTH = 0.865
3. one data line: col 1−6   TIME
                   col 7−12   DIST
                   col 13−18 VEL
                   col 19−24 ACCEL
4. four data lines: line 1: col 1−6 TIME
                    line 2: col 1−6 DIST
                    line 3: col 1−6 VEL
                    line 4: col 1−6 ACCEL
5. four data lines: line 1: col 1−3 TIME
                    line 2: col 1−4 DIST
                    line 3: col 1−3 VEL
                    line 4: col 1−4 ACCEL

6. two data lines: line 1: col 1–6   TIME
    col 7–12 DIST
    line 2: col 1–6   VEL
    col 7–12 ACCEL

7. single space:${}_{bb}$4.55${}_{bbbbbb}$0.000756.8300

8. single space:TIME${}_{b}$=${}_{bb}$4.55${}_{bb}$RESPONSE${}_{b}$1${}_{b}$=${}_{bb}$0.00074
   single space:TIME${}_{b}$=${}_{bb}$4.55${}_{bb}$RESPONSE${}_{b}$2${}_{b}$=${}_{b}$56.83000

9. single space:EXPERIMENT RESULTS
   single space:
   single space:TIME${}_{bb}$RESPONSE${}_{b}$1${}_{bb}$RESPONSE${}_{b}$2
   single space:4.55${}_{bbb}$0.740E−03${}_{bbb}$0.568E+02

Self-test 5-1, page 199

1. ARRAY VALUES:
    2
    3
    4
    5
    6
    7
    8
    9
   10
   11

2. ${}_{bbbb}{}^{8}{}_{bbbb}{}^{7}{}_{bbbb}{}^{6}{}_{bbbb}{}^{5}{}_{bbbb}{}^{4}$

3. TIME   1 = 0.00
   TIME   5 = 2.00
   TIME   9 = 4.00
   TIME 13 = 6.00
   TIME 17 = 8.00

Self-test 5-2, page 213

1. Array contents after each switch:

16	9	9	9	9
83	83	16	16	16
91	91	91	25	25
25	25	25	91	72
9	16	83	83	83
72	72	72	72	91

2. Array contents after each switch:

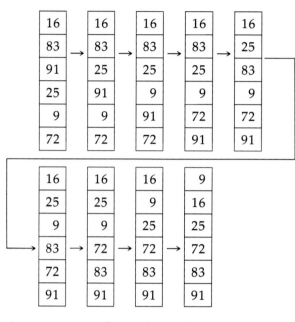

3. Array contents after each switch:

Self-test 5-3, page 222

1.
1	2	3	4
2	4	6	8
3	6	9	12
4	8	12	16
5	10	15	20

bbbb^{3}bbbb^{6}bbbb^{9}bbb^{12}

2.
5	-5	0
5	-5	0
5	-5	0

bbb^5
bb^{-5}
bbb^0

3.
11.5	17.5	23.5
13.0	19.0	25.0
14.5	20.5	26.5
16.0	22.0	28.0

b$^{11.5}$b$^{17.5}$b$^{23.5}$
b$^{13.0}$b$^{19.0}$b$^{25.0}$
b b b

Self-test 6-1, page 249

1. `AREA(R) = 3.14159*R*R`
2. `RADIAN(DEGREE) = (180.0/3.14159)*DEGREE`
3. `DEGREE(RADIAN) = (3.14159/180.0)*RADIAN`
4. `T(M,W,A,S) = M*W*W*A*A*S/4.0`
5. `RADIUS(X,Y) = SQRT(X*X÷Y*Y)`

Self-test 6-2, page 270

1. $X = -0.5$
2. $X = 0.5$
3. $X = 0.5$
4. $X = -0.5$

Self-test 7-1, page 305

1. `NEW VALUES OF K ARE:`
   bbbb^{2}bbbb^{4}bbbb^{6}bbbb^{8}bbb^{10}
   bbb^{12}bbb^{14}bbb^{16}bbb^{18}bbb^{20}

2. NEW VALUES OF K ARE:
bbbb^{2}bbbb^{4}bbbb^{6}bbbb^{8}bbb^{10}
bbbb^{6}bbbb^{7}bbbb^{8}bbbb^{9}bbb^{10}

Self-test 7-2, page 329

```
*
        INTEGER X(10), COUNT, J, HOLD(10)
*
.
.
.
*
        DO 1 J=1,COUNT
            HOLD(J) = X(J)
      1 CONTINUE
        DO 5 J=2,10
            CALL INSERT (10,HOLD(J),J-1,X)
      5 CONTINUE
*
```

Self-test 8-1, page 361

1. CONSERVATION OF ENERGY$_{bbb}$

2. CONSERVATION

3. $_b$OF$_b$ENERGY$_b$

4. $_b$

5. ENERGY$_{bbb}$

6. CONSERVATION

7. CONSERVATION$_b$ OF$_b$ ENERGY$_{bbb}$

8. CONSERVATION$_b$ OF$_b$ ENERGY$_{bbb}$LAW

9. CONSERVE$_b$ ENERGY$_{bbb}$

10. 'CONSIDERATE'

11. DENSIT

12. AREA$_{bb}$

13. CAN'T$_b$

14. ''''!$_{bb}$

15. FT/SEC

16. $_{bb}$VOLU

Self-test 8-2, page 374

1. 1.0D+00/4.0D+00
2. 0.58D+00
3. 1.0D+00/7.0D+00
4. 1.0D+00/13.0D+00
5. 108.3D+00
6. 2.0D+00
7. single space: bb 0.141786D+02
8. single space: b 0.141786245900D+02
9. single space: 14.178625

Self-test 8-3, page 386

1. $CX = 1.5 + 2.0i$
2. $CX = 0.5 + 4.0i$
3. $CX = 0.5 + 1.0i$
4. $CX = 1.0 - 1.0i$
5. $CX = 5.0 + 0.2i$
6. $CX = 3.162278 + 0.0i$
7. single space: bbbb 2.30 bbbb 0.20
8. single space: (bbbb 2.30, bbbb 0.20)

Self-test 9-1, page 407

```
*-----------------------------------------------------------------*
      PROGRAM   COUNT
*
*  This program counts the number of records
*  in a data file called XYDATA.
*
      INTEGER   N
      DATA   N /0/
*
      OPEN (UNIT=10,FILE='XYDATA',STATUS='OLD',ERR=100)
*
    1 READ (10,5,END=98) X, Y
    5     FORMAT (F6.2,1X,F6.2)
          N = N + 1
          GO TO 1
*
   98 PRINT 99, N
   99 FORMAT (1X,'FILE CONTAINS',I5,' RECORDS')
      STOP
*
```

```
 100 PRINT*, 'ERROR IN OPENING DATA FILE'
     STOP
     END
```

Self-test 9-2, page 424

```
     PROGRAM  ORDER
*
*  This program prints the item numbers for items that
*  have less than 5 items in the warehouse.
*
     INTEGER  I, ITEM, INVEN
*
     OPEN (UNIT=10,FILE='STORES',ACCESS='DIRECT',
    +       STATUS='OLD',FORM=FORMATTED,RECL=12)
*
     DO 15 I=1,100
        READ (10,5,REC=I) ITEM, INVEN
  5     FORMAT (I5,2X,I5)
        IF (INVEN.LT.5) THEN
           PRINT 10, ITEM
 10        FORMAT ('ITEM NUMBER ',I5,' HAS LESS THAN 5 ',
    +               'ITEMS IN THE WAREHOUSE.')
        ENDIF
 15  CONTINUE
     END
```

ANSWERS TO SELECTED PROBLEMS

Answers that contain FORTRAN statements are not usually unique. Although these answers represent good solutions to the problems, they are not necessarily the only valid solutions.

Chapter 2

5.
```
*--------------------------------------------------------------*
      PROGRAM   CONVRT
*
*  This program converts kilowatt-hours to calories.
*
      REAL  KWH, JOULES, CALRS
*
      PRINT*, 'ENTER ENERGY IN KILOWATT HOURS'
      READ*, KWH
      JOULES = 3.6E+06*KWH
      CALRS = JOULES/4.19
      PRINT 5, KWH, CALRS
    5 FORMAT (1X,F6.2,' KILOWATT-HOURS = ',E9.2,' CALORIES')
      END
*--------------------------------------------------------------*
```

9.
```
*--------------------------------------------------------------*
      PROGRAM   GROWTH
*
*  This program predicts bacteria growth.
```

```
*
      REAL  TIME1, TIME2, POP1, POP2, CHANGE
*
      PRINT*, 'ENTER TIME1 (HOURS)'
      READ*, TIME1
      PRINT*, 'ENTER TIME2 (>TIME1)'
      READ*, TIME2
      POP1 = EXP(1.386*TIME1)
      POP2 = EXP(1.386*TIME2)
      CHANGE = POP2 - POP1
      PRINT 5, CHANGE
    5 FORMAT (1X,'AMOUNT OF GROWTH = ',F8.2)
      END
*------------------------------------------------------------*
```

13.
```
*------------------------------------------------------------*
      PROGRAM  DATE
*
*  This program estimates the age of an artifact from
*  the proportion of carbon remaining in the artifact.
*
      REAL  CARBON, AGE, CENTRY
*
      PRINT*, 'ENTER PROPORTION REMAINING FOR CARBON DATING'
      READ*, CARBON
      AGE = (-LOG(CARBON))/0.0001216
      CENTRY = AGE/100.0
      PRINT 5, CENTRY
    5 FORMAT (1X,'ESTIMATED AGE OF ARTIFACT IS ',F6.2,
     +          ' CENTURIES')
      END
*------------------------------------------------------------*
```

19.
```
*------------------------------------------------------------*
      PROGRAM  TRAIN
*
*  This program computes the horizontal force
*  generated by a train on a level curve.
*
      INTEGER  FORCE
      REAL  WEIGHT, MPH, RADIUS
*
      PRINT*, 'ENTER WEIGHT OF TRAIN IN TONS'
      READ*, WEIGHT
      PRINT*, 'ENTER SPEED OF TRAIN IN MILES PER HOUR'
      READ*, MPH
      PRINT*, 'ENTER RADIUS OF CURVE IN FEET'
      READ*, RADIUS
*
      FORCE = NINT((WEIGHT*2000.0/32.0)*
     +          ((MPH*1.4667)**2/RADIUS))
*
      PRINT 10, WEIGHT
   10 FORMAT (1X,'TRAIN WEIGHT - ',F8.2,' TONS')
      PRINT 20, MPH
   20 FORMAT (1X,'TRAIN SPEED - ',F8.2,' MPH')
      PRINT 30, RADIUS
   30 FORMAT (1X,'CURVE RADIUS - ',F8.2,' FEET')
      PRINT*
      PRINT 40, FORCE
```

```
    40 FORMAT (1X,'RESULTING HORIZONTAL FORCE - ',
      +           I8,' POUNDS')
       END
```
--

23.
--
```
       PROGRAM  RELY
*
*  This program computes the reliability of
*  instrumentation using a Bernoulli equation.
*
       INTEGER  N
       REAL  P1, P2, P3, PARALL, SERIES
*
       PRINT*, 'ENTER RELIABILITY OF COMPONENTS 1, 2, 3'
       PRINT*, '(USE PERCENTAGE BETWEEN 0.0 and 100.0)'
       READ*, P1, P2, P3
*
       PARALL = (P2/100.0 + P3/100.0 -
      +          (P2/100.0)*(P3/100.0))*100.0
       SERIES = (P1/100.0)*(PARALL/100.0)*100.0
*
       PRINT*, 'PERCENT OF THE TIME THAT THE EQUIPMENT'
       PRINT 5, SERIES
     5 FORMAT (1X,'SHOULD WORK WITHOUT FAILURE IS ',
      +          F6.2,'%')
       END
```
--

29.
--
```
       PROGRAM  CONVRT
*
*  This program converts meters to kilometers to miles.
*
       REAL  METERS, KMETER, MILES
*
       PRINT*, 'ENTER METERS'
       READ*, METERS
       KMETER = METERS/1000.0
       MILES = KMETER/1.609
       PRINT 5, METERS
     5 FORMAT (1X,F8.2,' METERS')
       PRINT 10, KMETER
    10 FORMAT (1X,F8.2,' KILOMETERS')
       PRINT 15, MILES
    15 FORMAT (1X,F8.2,' MILES')
       END
```
--

Chapter 3

5.
--
```
       PROGRAM  ROCKET
*
*  This program simulates a rocket flight.
*
       REAL  TIME, HEIGHT, NEWHT
*
       TIME = 0.0
       HEIGHT = 60.0
       PRINT 5
```

```
    5 FORMAT (1X,'TIME (SEC.)        HEIGHT (FT.)')
      PRINT*
*
   10 IF (HEIGHT.GT.0.0.AND.TIME.LE.100.0) THEN
         NEWHT = 60.0 + 2.13*TIME**2 - 0.0013*TIME**4
      +          + 0.000034*TIME**4.751
         IF (NEWHT.LT.HEIGHT) THEN
            PRINT 15, TIME
   15       FORMAT (1X,'ROCKET BEGINS RETURNING AT '
      +              F5.1,' SECONDS')
         ENDIF
         HEIGHT = NEWHT
         TIME = TIME + 0.01
         GO TO 10
      ENDIF
      IF (TIME.LE.100.0) THEN
         PRINT 20, TIME
   20    FORMAT (1X,'ROCKET IMPACTED AT ',F5.1,' SECONDS')
      ELSE
         PRINT*, 'TIME LIMIT OF 100 SECS EXCEEDED'
      ENDIF
      END
```

7.

```
      PROGRAM  SEALS
*
*  This program analyzes data on batches of sutures that have
*  not been properly sealed, and then prints a report.
*
      INTEGER  BATCH, COUNT, REJCTT, REJCTP, REJCTD
      REAL   TEMP, PRESSR, DWELL, PERCT, PERCP, PERCD
*
      COUNT = 0
      REJCTT = 0
      REJCTP = 0
      REJCTD = 0
*
      PRINT*, 'ENTER BATCH NUMBER, TEMPERATURE, PRESSURE, DWELL'
      PRINT*, 'FOR BATCHES THAT HAVE BEEN REJECTED'
      PRINT*, '(NEGATIVE BATCH NUMBER TO STOP)'
      READ*, BATCH, TEMP, PRESSR, DWELL
*
    5 IF (BATCH.GE.0)  THEN
         IF (TEMP.LT.150.0.OR.TEMP.GT.170.0) REJCTT = REJCTT + 1
         IF (PRESSR.LT.60.0.OR.PRESSR.GT.70.0) REJCTP = REJCTP + 1
         IF (DWELL.LT.2.0.OR.DWELL.GT.2.5) REJCTD = REJCTD + 1
         COUNT = COUNT + 1
         PRINT*, 'ENTER NEXT SET OF DATA'
         READ*, BATCH, TEMP, PRESSR, DWELL
         GO TO 5
      ENDIF
      PERCT = REAL(REJCTT)/REAL(COUNT)*100.0
      PERCP = REAL(REJCTP)/REAL(COUNT)*100.0
      PERCD = REAL(REJCTD)/REAL(COUNT)*100.0
*
      PRINT*
      PRINT*, 'SUMMARY OF BATCH REJECT INFORMATION'
      PRINT*
      PRINT 10, REJCTT, PERCT
   10 FORMAT (1X,I4,' BATCHES OR ',F6.2,
      +        ' % REJECTED DUE TO TEMPERATURE')
```

```
          PRINT 15, REJCTP, PERCP
       15 FORMAT (1X,I4,' BATCHES OR ',F6.2,
                 ' % REJECTED DUE TO PRESSURE')
          PRINT 20, REJCTD, PERCD
       20 FORMAT (1X,I4,' BATCHES OR ',F6.2,
                 ' % REJECTED DUE TO DWELL')
          END
```

--

12.

--

```
      PROGRAM  TIMBER
*
*  This program computes a reforestation summary
*  for an area which has not been completely harvested.
*
      INTEGER  ID, YEAR
      REAL  TOTAL, UNCUT, RATE, REFOR
*
      PRINT*, 'ENTER LAND IDENTIFICATION (INTEGER)'
      READ*, ID
      PRINT*, 'ENTER TOTAL NUMBER OF ACRES'
      READ*, TOTAL
      PRINT*, 'ENTER NUMBER OF ACRES UNCUT'
      READ*, UNCUT
      PRINT*, 'ENTER REFORESTATION RATE'
      READ*, RATE
*
      IF (UNCUT.GT.TOTAL) THEN
          PRINT*, 'UNCUT AREA LARGER THAN ENTIRE AREA'
      ELSE
          PRINT*
          PRINT*, 'REFORESTATION SUMMARY'
          PRINT*
          PRINT 5, ID
    5     FORMAT (1X,'IDENTIFICATION NUMBER ',I5)
          PRINT 10, TOTAL
   10     FORMAT (1X,'TOTAL ACRES = ',F10.2)
          PRINT 20, UNCUT
   20     FORMAT (1X,'UNCUT ACRES = ',F10.2)
          PRINT 30, RATE
   30     FORMAT (1X,'REFORESTATION RATE = ',F5.3)
          PRINT*
          PRINT*, 'YEAR  REFORESTED   TOTAL REFORESTED'
          DO 50 YEAR=1,20
              REFOR = UNCUT*RATE
              UNCUT = UNCUT + REFOR
              IF (MOD(YEAR,2).EQ.0) THEN
                  PRINT 40, YEAR, REFOR, UNCUT
   40             FORMAT (1X,I3,F11.3,F17.3)
              ENDIF
   50     CONTINUE
      ENDIF
      END
```

--

20.

--

```
      PROGRAM  CABLE
*
*  This program computes the velocity of a cable car
*  on a thousand-foot cable with three towers.
*
```

```
      INTEGER TOTDIS, DIST, TOWER
      REAL    VEL
*
      PRINT 1
   1  FORMAT (1X,9X,'CABLE CAR REPORT')
      PRINT*
      PRINT 2
   2  FORMAT (1X,'DISTANCE  NEAREST TOWER   VELOCITY')
      PRINT 3
   3  FORMAT (1X,'  (FT)',19X,'(FT/SEC)')
      PRINT*
*
      DO 50 TOTDIS=0,1000,10
         IF (TOTDIS.LE.150) THEN
            TOWER = 1
            DIST = TOTDIS
         ELSEIF (TOTDIS.LE.500) THEN
            TOWER = 2
            DIST = ABS(TOTDIS - 300)
         ELSEIF (TOTDIS.LE.850) THEN
            TOWER = 3
            DIST = ABS(TOTDIS - 700)
         ELSE
            TOWER = 4
            DIST = 1000 - TOTDIS
         ENDIF
         IF (DIST.LE.30) THEN
            VEL = 2.425 + 0.00175*DIST*DIST
         ELSE
            VEL = 0.625 + 0.12*DIST - 0.00025*DIST*DIST
         ENDIF
         PRINT 30, TOTDIS, TOWER, VEL
  30     FORMAT (1X,I4,11X,I1,9X,F7.2)
  50  CONTINUE
      END
*-------------------------------------------------------------*


24.        .
*-------------------------------------------------------------*
      PROGRAM  TABLE
*
*  This program prints a table of function values.
*
      INTEGER  I, J
      REAL   X, Y, F
*
      PRINT*, 'TABLE OF FUNCTION VALUES'
      PRINT*
      PRINT*, 'X          Y          F'
      PRINT*
      DO 15 I = 1,9
         DO 10 J = 1,9
            X = REAL(I)
            Y = (J + 1)*0.25
            F = (X*X - Y*Y)/(2.0*X*Y)
            PRINT 5, X, Y, F
   5        FORMAT (1X,F3.1,5X,F5.2,5X,F5.2)
  10     CONTINUE
  15  CONTINUE
      END
*-------------------------------------------------------------*
```

Chapter 4

3.
```
*------------------------------------------------------------*
      PROGRAM  PATH
*  This program determines the critical path
*  information for a project.
*
      INTEGER  EVENT, TASK, DAYS, TOTAL, NUMBER, MIN, MAX,
     +         WEEKS, PLUS, SUMTSK, NUMTSK
      LOGICAL  DONE
*
      OPEN (UNIT=8,FILE='PROJECT',STATUS='OLD')
      TOTAL = 0
      SUMTSK = 0
      NUMTSK = 0
      PRINT*, 'PROJECT COMPLETION TIMETABLE'
      PRINT*
      PRINT*, 'EVENT NUMBER     MINIMUM TIME     MAXIMUM TIME'
*
      READ (8,*) EVENT, TASK, DAYS
      NUMBER = EVENT
      MIN = DAYS
      MAX = DAYS
      IF (EVENT.EQ.99) THEN
         DONE = .TRUE.
      ELSE
         DONE = .FALSE.
      ENDIF
*
    5 IF (.NOT.DONE) THEN
         IF (EVENT.EQ.NUMBER)  THEN
            IF (DAYS.LT.MIN)  THEN
               MIN = DAYS
            ELSE IF (DAYS.GT.MAX) THEN
               MAX = DAYS
            ENDIF
         ELSE
            PRINT 10, NUMBER, MIN, MAX
   10       FORMAT (1X,I2,14X,I3,13X,I3)
            TOTAL = TOTAL + MAX
            NUMBER = EVENT
            MIN = DAYS
            MAX = DAYS
         ENDIF
         SUMTSK = SUMTSK + DAYS
         NUMTSK = NUMTSK + 1
         READ (8,*) EVENT, TASK, DAYS
         IF (EVENT.EQ.99) DONE = .TRUE.
         GO TO 5
      ENDIF
      PRINT 10, NUMBER, MIN, MAX
      TOTAL = TOTAL + MAX
*
      WEEKS = TOTAL/5
      PLUS = TOTAL - WEEKS*5
      PRINT*
      PRINT 15, TOTAL
   15 FORMAT (1X,'TOTAL PROJECT LENGTH = ',I3,' DAYS')
      PRINT 20, WEEKS, PLUS
   20 FORMAT (1X,'                        = ',I3,' WEEKS',
     +         I2,' DAYS')
```

```
          PRINT*
          PRINT 25, REAL(SUMTSK)/REAL(NUMTSK)
       25 FORMAT (1X,'AVERAGE NUMBER OF DAYS PER TASK = ',F5.1)
          END
*---------------------------------------------------------------*
```

7.
```
*---------------------------------------------------------------*
      PROGRAM  CENSUS
*
*  This program reads 101 population values and determines
*  the years of greatest percentage increase in population.
*
      INTEGER  YROLD, YRNEW, POPOLD, POPNEW,
     +         GPIYR, YR1, YR2, MINPOP, I
      REAL  PERC, GPI
*
      OPEN (UNIT=15,FILE='PEOPLE',STATUS='OLD')
      GPI = 0.0
      READ (15,*) YROLD, POPOLD
      MINPOP = POPOLD
      DO 50 I=1,100
         READ (15,*) YRNEW, POPNEW
         IF (POPNEW.LT.MINPOP) MINPOP = POPNEW
         PERC = (POPNEW - POPOLD)*100.0/POPOLD
         IF (I.EQ.1.OR.PERC.GT.GPI) THEN
            GPI = PERC
            GPIYR = YRNEW
         ENDIF
         YROLD = YRNEW
         POPOLD = POPNEW
   50 CONTINUE
      YR1 = GPIYR - 1
      YR2 = GPIYR
      PRINT 55, YR1, YR2
   55 FORMAT (1X,'GREATEST PERCENT INCREASE OCCURRED',
     +        ' BETWEEN ',I4,' AND ',I4)
      CLOSE (UNIT=15)
      OPEN (UNIT=15,FILE='PEOPLE',STATUS='OLD')
      DO 70 I=1,101
         READ(15,*) YROLD, POPOLD
         IF (POPOLD.EQ.MINPOP) THEN
            PRINT 65, YROLD
   65       FORMAT(1X,I4,' HAS MINIMUM POPULATION')
         ENDIF
   70 CONTINUE
      END
*---------------------------------------------------------------*
```

13.
```
*---------------------------------------------------------------*
      PROGRAM  QUALTY
*
*  This program uses defect data to print
*  a Quality Analysis Report.
*
      INTEGER  BOARDS, BDDEF, BDWIRE, BDIC, BDNON, WIRE,
     +         IC, NON, ID, NWIRE, NIC, NNON, DEFECT
      REAL  PERCW, PERCIC, PERCNO
*
```

```
         BDDEF = 0
         BDWIRE = 0
         BDIC = 0
         BDNON = 0
         WIRE = 0
         IC = 0
         NON = 0
         OPEN (UNIT=10,FILE='REPORT',STATUS='OLD')
         READ (10,*) BOARDS
*
         PRINT*, '              MONTHLY QUALITY ANALYSIS REPORT'
         PRINT*
         PRINT*, 'IDENTIFICATION NUMBERS OF BOARDS WITH ',
       +         'THREE OR MORE DEFECTS:'
         PRINT*
*
         READ (10,*) ID, NWIRE, NIC, NNON
    10   IF (ID.NE.99999)  THEN
            IF (NWIRE + NIC + NNON.GE.3) PRINT 15, ID
    15      FORMAT (1X,I8)
            BDDEF = BDDEF + 1
            IF (NWIRE.GT.0) BDWIRE = BDWIRE + 1
            IF (NIC.GT.0) BDIC = BDIC + 1
            IF (NNON.GT.0) BDNON = BDNON + 1
            WIRE = WIRE + NWIRE
            IC = IC + NIC
            NON = NON + NNON
            READ (10,*) ID, NWIRE, NIC, NNON
            GO TO 10
         ENDIF
*
         PRINT 20, BOARDS, BDDEF, BDWIRE, BDIC, BDNON
    20   FORMAT (/,1X,'TOTAL NUMBER OF BOARDS ASSEMBLED = ',I4,//,
       +          1X,'TOTAL BOARDS WITH DEFECTS = ',I4,//,
       +          1X,5X,I4,' BOARDS WITH BROKEN WIRES',/,
       +          1X,5X,I4,' BOARDS WITH DEFECTIVE IC COMPONENTS',/,
       +          1X,5X,I4,' BOARDS WITH DEFECTIVE NON-IC COMPONENTS')
         DEFECT = WIRE + IC + NON
         PERCW = REAL(WIRE)*100.0/REAL(DEFECT)
         PERCIC = REAL(IC)*100.00/REAL(DEFECT)
         PERCNO = REAL(NON)*100.0/REAL(DEFECT)
         PRINT 30, DEFECT, PERCW, PERCIC, PERCNO
    30   FORMAT (/,1X,'DEFECT ANALYSIS',//,
       +          1X,5X,'TOTAL NUMBER OF DEFECTS = ',I5,/,
       +          1X,5X,F5.1,'% OF DEFECTS ARE BROKEN WIRES',/,
       +          1X,5X,F5.1,'% OF DEFECTS ARE DEFECTIVE ',
       +                     'IC COMPONENTS',/,
       +          1X,5X,F5.1,'% OF DEFECTS ARE DEFECTIVE ',
       +                     'NON-IC COMPONENTS')
         END
*-------------------------------------------------------------------*

18.
*-------------------------------------------------------------------*
      PROGRAM  TESTS
*
*  This program analyzes pressure data from three chambers.
*
      INTEGER  PRESS1, PRESS2, PRESS3, MAX1, MAX2, MAX3, I
*
      OPEN (UNIT=10,FILE='RESULTS',STATUS='OLD')
      READ (10,*) MAX1, MAX2, MAX3
```

```
          DO 5 I=1,19
             READ (10,*) PRESS1, PRESS2, PRESS3
             IF (PRESS1.GT.MAX1) MAX1 = PRESS1
             IF (PRESS2.GT.MAX2) MAX2 = PRESS2
             IF (PRESS3.GT.MAX3) MAX3 = PRESS3
        5 CONTINUE
*
          PRINT 10, 1, MAX1
          PRINT 10, 2, MAX2
          PRINT 10, 3, MAX3
       10 FORMAT (1X,'MAXIMUM PRESSURE IN CHAMBER ',I1,' = ',I4)
*
          END
*-------------------------------------------------------------*
```

Chapter 5

1.
```
*-------------------------------------------------------------*
          PROGRAM  SNOFAL
*
*    This program computes the average snowfall
*    for January and counts the number of days
*    with above-average snowfall.
*
          INTEGER  COUNT, NOSNOW, I
          REAL  SNOW(31), TOTAL, AVE
          DATA  TOTAL, COUNT, NOSNOW /0.0, 0, 0/
*
          OPEN (UNIT=10,FILE='JAN',STATUS='OLD')
          READ (10,*) SNOW
          PRINT 5, SNOW
        5 FORMAT (1X,4F8.1)
*
          DO 10 I=1,31
             TOTAL = TOTAL + SNOW(I)
             IF (SNOW(I).EQ.0.0) NOSNOW = NOSNOW + 1
       10 CONTINUE
          AVE = TOTAL/31.0
          PRINT 20, AVE
       20 FORMAT (1X,'AVERAGE SNOWFALL IS ',F5.2,' INCHES')
*
          DO 30 I=1,31
             IF (SNOW(I).GT.AVE) COUNT = COUNT + 1
       30 CONTINUE
          PRINT 40, COUNT
       40 FORMAT (1X,I2,' DAYS WITH ABOVE-AVERAGE SNOWFALL')
          PRINT 45, NOSNOW
       45 FORMAT (1X,I2,' DAYS WITH NO SNOWFALL')
*
          END
*-------------------------------------------------------------*
```

9.
```
*-------------------------------------------------------------*
          PROGRAM  EARTH
*
*    This program will read a file of earthquake data
*    and sort and print it in ascending order.
*
          INTEGER  LOCATE, I, N, J, PTR, LAST, FIRST, K
          REAL  QUAKE(200), HOLD, MEDIAN
*
```

```
      OPEN (UNIT=9,FILE='MOTION',STATUS='OLD')
      READ (9,*) LOCATE
      PRINT 5, LOCATE
    5 FORMAT (1X,'LOCATION NUMBER: ',I5)
*
      I = 1
   10 READ (9,*,END=20) QUAKE(I)
          I = I + 1
          GO TO 10
*
   20 N = I - 1
      LAST = N
      DO 40 J=1,N-1
          PTR = J
          FIRST = J + 1
          DO 30 K = FIRST, LAST
              IF (QUAKE(K).LT.QUAKE(PTR)) PTR = K
   30     CONTINUE
          HOLD = QUAKE(J)
          QUAKE(J) = QUAKE(PTR)
          QUAKE(PTR) = HOLD
   40 CONTINUE
*
      DO 60 I=1,N
          PRINT 50, I, QUAKE(I)
   50     FORMAT (1X,I3,'.',3X,F6.4)
   60 CONTINUE
      IF (MOD(N,2).EQ.1) THEN
          MEDIAN = QUAKE(N/2+1)
      ELSE
          MEDIAN = (QUAKE(N/2) + QUAKE(N/2+1))/2.0
      ENDIF
      PRINT 65, MEDIAN
   65 FORMAT (1X,'MEDIAN EARTHQUAKE VALUE IS ',F6.4)
*
      END
*-------------------------------------------------------------------*
```

13.
```
*-------------------------------------------------------------------*
      PROGRAM  PWRPLT
*
*  This program computes and prints a composite report
*  summarizing several weeks of power plant data.
*
      INTEGER  POWER(20,7), MIN, TOTAL, COUNT, I, J, N
      REAL    AVE
      DATA    TOTAL, COUNT /0, 0/
*
      PRINT*, 'ENTER NUMBER OF WEEKS FOR ANALYSIS'
      READ*, N
      OPEN (UNIT=12,FILE='PLANT',STATUS='OLD')
      DO 5 I=1,N
          READ (12,*) (POWER(I,J), J=1,7)
    5 CONTINUE
*
      MIN = POWER(1,1)
      DO 15 I=1,N
          DO 10 J=1,7
```

```
                  TOTAL = TOTAL + POWER(I,J)
                  IF (POWER(I,J).LT.MIN) MIN = POWER(I,J)
   10       CONTINUE
   15 CONTINUE
      AVE = REAL(TOTAL)/REAL(N*7)
*
      DO 25 I=1,N
          DO 20 J=1,7
              IF (POWER(I,J).GT.AVE) COUNT = COUNT + 1
   20     CONTINUE
   25 CONTINUE
*
      PRINT 30
   30 FORMAT (1X,15X,'COMPOSITE INFORMATION')
      PRINT 35, AVE
   35 FORMAT (1X,'AVERAGE DAILY POWER OUTPUT = ',F5.1,
     +         ' MEGAWATTS')
      PRINT 40, COUNT
   40 FORMAT (1X,'NUMBER OF DAYS WITH GREATER THAN ',
     +         'AVERAGE POWER OUTPUT = ',I2)
      PRINT 45
   45 FORMAT (1X,'DAY(S) WITH MINIMUM POWER OUTPUT:')
      DO 60 I=1,N
          DO 55 J=1,7
              IF (POWER(I,J).EQ.MIN) PRINT 50, I, J
   50         FORMAT (1X,12X,'WEEK ',I2,'   DAY ',I2)
   55     CONTINUE
   60 CONTINUE
*
      END
*--------------------------------------------------------------*

19.
*--------------------------------------------------------------*
      PROGRAM  NAVIG
*
*  This program reads the elevation data for a set of land
*  grids and determines the number of peaks in each grid.
*
      INTEGER  MAP(100,100), I, J, ID, NROWS, NCOLS, COUNT,
     +         MAX, MIN
*
      PRINT 5
    5 FORMAT (1X,'SUMMARY OF LAND GRID ANALYSIS')
      PRINT 10
   10 FORMAT (1X,'IDENTIFICATION    NUMBER OF POINTS   ',
     +         'NUMBER OF PEAKS')
*
      OPEN (UNIT=15,FILE='ELEVTN',STATUS='OLD')
      READ (15,*) ID
   15 IF (ID.NE.99999) THEN
          READ (15,*) NROWS, NCOLS
          DO 20 I=1,NROWS
              READ (15,*) (MAP(I,J), J=1,NCOLS)
   20     CONTINUE
          COUNT = 0
          DO 30 I=2,NROWS-1
              DO 25 J=2,NCOLS-1
                  IF ((MAP(I-1,J).LT.MAP(I,J)).AND.
     +                (MAP(I+1,J).LT.MAP(I,J)).AND.
     +                (MAP(I,J-1).LT.MAP(I,J)).AND.
     +                (MAP(I,J+1).LT.MAP(I,J))) THEN
```

```
                         COUNT = COUNT + 1
                 ENDIF
     25          CONTINUE
     30      CONTINUE
         PRINT 35, ID, NROWS*NCOLS, COUNT
     35      FORMAT (1X,I7,10X,I7,10X,I7)
         READ (15,*) ID
         GO TO 15
     ENDIF
*
     MAX = MAP(1,1)
     MIN = MAP(1,1)
     DO 45 I=1,NROWS
         DO 40 J=1,NCOLS
             IF (MAP(I,J).GT.MAX) MAX = MAP(I,J)
             IF (MAP(I,J).LT.MIN) MIN = MAP(I,J)
     40      CONTINUE
     45 CONTINUE
     PRINT 50, MAX, MIN
     50 FORMAT (1X,'MAXIMUM ELEVATION = ',I6,5X,
     +           'MINIMUM ELEVATION = ',I6)
*
     END
*----------------------------------------------------------------*
```

25.

```
     INTEGER  TIME(30)
         .
         .
         .
     DO 50 I=2,30,2
         PRINT 45, I, TIME(I)
     45      FORMAT (1X,'TIME(',I2,') CONTAINS ',I4,' SECONDS')
     50 CONTINUE
```

Chapter 6

5.

```
*----------------------------------------------------------------*
     PROGRAM  TABLE1
*
*  This program generates a temperature conversion table.
*
     INTEGER  IN, OUT
     REAL  FIRST, CHANGE, LAST, NEXT, NEW, TEMP,
     +       CTOF, KTOF, RTOF, FTOC, FTOK, FTOR, HOLD
*
*  Conversion functions use Fahrenheit
*  as the base temperature unit.
*
     CTOF(TEMP) = 1.8*TEMP + 32.0
     KTOF(TEMP) = CTOF(TEMP - 273.15)
     RTOF(TEMP) = TEMP - 459.67
     FTOC(TEMP) = (TEMP - 32.0)*0.5555556
     FTOK(TEMP) = FTOC(TEMP) + 273.15
     FTOR(TEMP) = TEMP + 459.67
*
     PRINT*, 'CODE TEMPERATURE AS FOLLOWS:'
     PRINT*, '1-FAHRENHEIT'
     PRINT*, '2-CENTIGRADE'
     PRINT*, '3-KELVIN'
```

```
         PRINT*, '4- RANKIN'
         PRINT*, 'ENTER CODE FOR TABLE INPUT'
         READ*, IN
         PRINT*, 'ENTER CODE FOR TABLE OUTPUT'
         READ*, OUT
         PRINT*, 'ENTER NUMBER OF DEGREES FOR FIRST LINE: '
         READ*, FIRST
         PRINT*, 'ENTER CHANGE IN DEGREES BETWEEN LINES: '
         READ*, CHANGE
         PRINT*, 'ENTER NUMBER OF DEGREES FOR LAST LINE: '
         READ*, LAST
*
         PRINT 5
       5 FORMAT (1X,5X,'TEMPERATURE CONVERSION TABLE')
         PRINT 10
      10 FORMAT (1X,'DEGREES, INPUT',10X,
         +         'DEGREES, OUTPUT')
         NEXT = FIRST
      20 IF (NEXT.LE.LAST) THEN
            IF (IN.EQ.1) THEN
               HOLD = NEXT
            ELSEIF (IN.EQ.2) THEN
               HOLD = CTOF(NEXT)
            ELSEIF (IN.EQ.3) THEN
               HOLD = KTOF(NEXT)
            ELSE
               HOLD = RTOF(NEXT)
            ENDIF
            IF (OUT.EQ.1) THEN
               NEW = HOLD
            ELSEIF (OUT.EQ.2) THEN
               NEW = FTOC(HOLD)
            ELSEIF (OUT.EQ.3) THEN
               NEW = FTOK(HOLD)
            ELSE
               NEW = FTOR(HOLD)
            ENDIF
            PRINT 25, NEXT, NEW
      25    FORMAT (1X,F9.2,18X,F9.2)
            NEXT = NEXT + CHANGE
            GO TO 20
         ENDIF
*
         END
*--------------------------------------------------------------*

   7.
*--------------------------------------------------------------*
      PROGRAM  REPORT
*
*  This program generates a report from the daily
*  production information for a set of oil wells.
*
      INTEGER  MO, DA, YR, ID, N, I
      REAL  OIL(7), TOTAL, AVE, INDAVE, MAX
      DATA  N, TOTAL, MAX /0, 0.0, 0/
*
      OPEN (UNIT=12,FILE='WELLS',STATUS='OLD')
      READ (12,*) MO, DA, YR
      PRINT*, 'OIL WELL PRODUCTION'
      PRINT 5, MO, DA, YR
    5 FORMAT (1X,'WEEK OF ',I2,'-',I2,'-',I2)
```

```
      PRINT*
      PRINT*, 'WELL ID      AVERAGE PRODUCTION'
      PRINT*, '             (IN BARRELS)'
*
      READ (12,*) ID, (OIL(I), I=1,7)
   10 IF (ID.NE.99999) THEN
         INDAVE = AVE(OIL,7)
         PRINT 15, ID, INDAVE
   15    FORMAT (1X,I5,9X,F6.2)
         N = N + 1
         TOTAL = TOTAL + INDAVE
         IF (INDAVE.GT.MAX) MAX = INDAVE
         READ (12,*) ID, (OIL(I), I=1,7)
         GO TO 10
      ENDIF
*
      PRINT*
      PRINT 20, N, TOTAL/REAL(N)
   20 FORMAT (1X,'OVERALL AVERAGE FOR ',I3,
     +        ' WELLS IS ',F6.2)
      PRINT 25, MAX*7.0
   25 FORMAT (1X,'MAXIMUM WEEKLY PRODUCTION IS ',F8.2)
*
      END
*------------------------------------------------------------*
                (no changes in function AVE)
*------------------------------------------------------------*


15.
*------------------------------------------------------------*
                (no changes in main program ANALYZ)
*------------------------------------------------------------*
*
      INTEGER FUNCTION  MINUTE(BEGIN,END)
*
*  This function computes the number of minutes
*  between the beginning time and the ending time.
*
      INTEGER  BEGIN, END, BEGHR, BEGMIN, ENDHR, ENDMIN
*
      BEGHR = BEGIN/100
      BEGMIN = MOD(BEGIN,100)
      ENDHR = END/100
      ENDMIN = MOD(END,100)
      IF (BEGIN.LT.END) THEN
         MINUTE = (ENDHR*60 + ENDMIN) - (BEGHR*60 + BEGMIN)
      ELSE
         MINUTE = (ENDHR*60+ENDMIN)+1440 - (BEGHR*60+BEGMIN)
      ENDIF
*
      RETURN
      END
*------------------------------------------------------------*


25.
*------------------------------------------------------------*
      INTEGER FUNCTION  INVERT(NUM)
*
*  This function  reverses the
*  digits in a two-digit number.
*
```

```
      INTEGER  NUM, DIGIT1, DIGIT2
*
      DIGIT1 = NUM/10
      DIGIT2 = MOD(NUM,10)
      INVERT = DIGIT2*10 + DIGIT1
*
      RETURN
      END
*-----------------------------------------------------------*
```

Chapter 7

3.
```
*-----------------------------------------------------------*
      PROGRAM  SIGGEN
*
*  This program generates a signal composed
*  of a sine wave plus random noise.
*
      INTEGER  SEED, I, N
      REAL  PI, T, NOISE, X
      DATA  PI, T /3.141593, 0.0/
*
      PRINT*, 'ENTER A POSITIVE INTEGER SEED: '
      READ*, SEED
      OPEN (UNIT=15,FILE='SIGNAL',STATUS='NEW')
*
      PRINT*, 'ENTER NUMBER OF DATA POINTS TO GENERATE'
      READ*, N
      DO 10 I=1,N
         CALL RANDOM (SEED, NOISE)
         X = 2*SIN(2*PI*T) + NOISE
         WRITE (15,*) T, X
         T = T + 0.01
   10 CONTINUE
*
      END
*-----------------------------------------------------------*
            (no changes in subroutine RANDOM)
*-----------------------------------------------------------*
```

8.
```
*-----------------------------------------------------------*
      PROGRAM  STREAM
*
*  This program computes the maximum oxygen deficit for
*  a group of waste water discharge streams.
*
      INTEGER  N, J, NUM
      REAL  DAYS, QD, QS, BODD, BODS, TMIX, KR, DOXYGN,
     +      DEFMAX, DEFDAY
*
      OPEN (UNIT=10,FILE='STREAMS',STATUS='OLD')
      PRINT*, 'ENTER TIME PERIOD FOR STREAM ANALYSIS IN DAYS'
      READ*, DAYS
      PRINT*, 'ENTER NUMBER OF ANALYSES PER DAY (INTEGER)'
      READ*, NUM
      PRINT*
      PRINT*, 'OXYGEN DEFICIT ANALYSIS OF ',
     +        'WASTE WATER DISCHARGE STREAMS'
      PRINT*
*
```

```
      READ (10,*) N
      DO 30 J=1,N
          READ (10,*) QD, QS, BODD, BODS, TMIX, KR, DOXYGN
          CALL CALC(NUM,QD,QS,BODD,BODS,TMIX,KR,DOXYGN,
     +                DAYS,DEFMAX,DEFDAY)
          PRINT 10, J, DEFMAX
  10      FORMAT (1X,'STREAM ',I3,':',' MAXIMUM DEFICIT = ',F6.3)
          PRINT 20, DEFDAY
  20      FORMAT (1X,12X,'OCCURRED AT DAY ',F3.1)
          PRINT*
  30  CONTINUE
*
      END
*-------------------------------------------------------------*
      SUBROUTINE CALC(NUM,QD,QS,BODD,BODS,TMIX,KR,DOXYGN,
     +                DAYS,DEFMAX,DEFDAY)
*
* This subroutine calculates the maximum oxygen deficit for a
* stream along with the day that it occurred.
*
      INTEGER  STEPS, J, NUM
      REAL  QD, QS, BODD, BODS, TMIX, KR, DOXYGN,
     +      FSMIX, KD, BODMIX, DEFCT, INCR,
     +      DAYS, DEFMAX, DEFDAY, T, TEMP1, TEMP2, TEMP3
*
      BODMIX = ((BODS*QS) + (BODD*QD))/(QS + QD)
      FSMIX = BODMIX*(0.02*TMIX + 0.6)/0.68
      KD = 0.1*(1.047**(TMIX  - 20.0))
*
      DEFMAX = 0.0
      DEFDAY = 0.0
      STEPS = INT(DAYS)*NUM
      INCR = 1.0/REAL(NUM)
*
      DO 10 J=1,STEPS
          T = REAL(J)*INCR
          TEMP1 = (KD*FSMIX)/(KR -  KD)
          TEMP2 = 10.0**(-KD*T)  - 10.0**(-KR*T)
          TEMP3 = DOXYGN*(10.0**(-KR*T))
          DEFCT = (TEMP1*TEMP2)  + TEMP3
          IF (J.EQ.1.OR.DEFCT.GT.DEFMAX)  THEN
              DEFMAX = DEFCT
              DEFDAY = T
          ENDIF
  10  CONTINUE
*
      RETURN
      END
*-------------------------------------------------------------*

12.
*-------------------------------------------------------------*
      PROGRAM  UPDATE
*
* This program updates a computer access list.
*
      INTEGER  J, CODE, COUNT, OLD, NEW, SSN(500)
      LOGICAL  DONE
*
      OPEN (UNIT=8,FILE='ACCESS',STATUS='OLD')
      OPEN (UNIT=9,FILE='NEWACCES',STATUS='NEW')
*
```

```
            DONE = .FALSE.
         J = 1
       5 IF (.NOT.DONE) THEN
            READ (8,*) SSN(J)
            IF (SSN(J).EQ.999999999)   THEN
               DONE = .TRUE.
            ELSE
               J = J + 1
            ENDIF
            GO TO 5
         ENDIF
         COUNT = J
         DONE = .FALSE.
*
      10 IF (.NOT.DONE) THEN
            PRINT*, 'ENTER -1 FOR DELETION, 1 FOR INSERTION, ',
         +            '0 TO QUIT'
            READ*, CODE
            IF (CODE.EQ.-1)   THEN
               PRINT*, 'ENTER SSN FOR DELETION'
               READ*, OLD
               CALL DELETE(OLD,COUNT,SSN)
            ELSE IF (CODE.EQ.1) THEN
               IF (COUNT.EQ.500) THEN
                  PRINT*, 'LIST IS FULL - DO DELETIONS FIRST'
               ELSE
                  PRINT*, 'ENTER SSN FOR INSERTION'
                  READ*, NEW
                  CALL INSERT(LIMIT,NEW,COUNT,SSN)
               ENDIF
            ELSE
               DONE = .TRUE.
            ENDIF
            GO TO 10
         ENDIF
*
         DO 15 J=1,COUNT
            WRITE (9,*) SSN(J)
      15 CONTINUE
         PRINT 20, COUNT-1
      20 FORMAT (1X,'NUMBER OF VALID USERS = ',I4)
*
         END
*-------------------------------------------------------------*
               (no changes in subroutine DELETE)
*-------------------------------------------------------------*
               (no changes in subroutine INSERT)
*-------------------------------------------------------------*


24.
*-------------------------------------------------------------*
      SUBROUTINE  GREAT(Z,W)
*
*  This subroutine moves corresponding values of
*  Z into W unless the value is less than
*  the average of all values in Z.  In these
*  cases the average value of Z is used in W.
*
      INTEGER  I, J
      REAL  Z(5,4) W(5,4), SUM, AVE
*
```

```
          SUM = 0.0
          DO 10 I=1,5
              DO 5 J=1,4
                  SUM = SUM + Z(I,J)
    5         CONTINUE
   10     CONTINUE
          AVE = SUM/20.0
          DO 20 I=1,5
              DO 15 J=1,4
                  IF (Z(I,J).LE.AVE) THEN
                      W(I,J) = Z(I,J)
                  ELSE
                      W(I,J) = AVE
                  ENDIF
   15         CONTINUE
   20     CONTINUE
*
          RETURN
          END
*--------------------------------------------------------------*
```

Chapter 8

3.
```
*--------------------------------------------------------------*
      PROGRAM  DECODE
*
*  This program aids in decoding a message by counting
*  the number of occurrences of vowels in the message.
*
      INTEGER  N, I, J
      REAL   VOWEL(5)
      CHARACTER*50  TEXT
      DATA  VOWEL /5*0.0/
*
      OPEN (UNIT=10,FILE='SECRET',STATUS='OLD')
      READ (10,*) N
      DO 10 I=1,N
          READ (10,*) TEXT
          DO 5 J=1,50
              IF (TEXT(J:J).EQ.'A'.OR.TEXT(J:J).EQ.'a') THEN
                  VOWEL(1) = VOWEL(1) + 1
              ELSEIF (TEXT(J:J).EQ.'E'.OR.TEXT(J:J).EQ.'e') THEN
                  VOWEL(2) = VOWEL(2) + 1
              ELSEIF (TEXT(J:J).EQ.'I'.OR.TEXT(J:J).EQ.'i') THEN
                  VOWEL(3) = VOWEL(3) + 1
              ELSEIF (TEXT(J:J).EQ.'O'.OR.TEXT(J:J).EQ.'o') THEN
                  VOWEL(4) = VOWEL(4) + 1
              ELSEIF (TEXT(J:J).EQ.'U'.OR.TEXT(J:J).EQ.'u') THEN
                  VOWEL(5) = VOWEL(5) + 1
              ENDIF
    5     CONTINUE
   10 CONTINUE
*
      PRINT*, 'TOTAL NUMBER OF CHARACTERS = ',N*50
      PRINT*
      PRINT*, 'OCCURRENCES OF VOWELS:'
      PRINT 15, VOWEL(1)
   15 FORMAT (1X,'A: = ',F6.0)
      PRINT 16, VOWEL(2)
   16 FORMAT (1X,'E: = ',F6.0)
```

```
          PRINT 17, VOWEL(3)
       17 FORMAT (1X,'I: = ',F6.0)
          PRINT 18, VOWEL(4)
       18 FORMAT (1X,'O: = ',F6.0)
          PRINT 19, VOWEL(5)
       19 FORMAT (1X,'U: = ',F6.0)
          PRINT*
          CALL GRAPH (VOWEL,5,20)
*
          END
*--------------------------------------------------------------*
                    (no changes in subroutine GRAPH)
*--------------------------------------------------------------*


   7.
*--------------------------------------------------------------*
          PROGRAM  TEMP
*
*   This program initializes the temperatures in a metal
*   plate and determines the equilibrium temperatures
*   based on a tolerance value.
*
          INTEGER  NROW, NCOL, I, J
          LOGICAL  EQUILB
          DOUBLE PRECISION  OLD(10,10), NEW(10,10), TOLNC,
         +                  TOP, BOT, LEFT, RIGHT
*
          PRINT*, 'ENTER TEMPERATURE GRID SIZE:'
          PRINT*, 'ROWS, COLUMNS  (MAXIMUM 10,10) '
          READ*, NROW, NCOL
          PRINT*, 'ENTER ISOTHERMAL EDGE TEMPERATURES:'
          PRINT*, 'TOP, BOTTOM, LEFT, RIGHT '
          READ*, TOP, BOT, LEFT, RIGHT
          PRINT*, 'ENTER EQUILIBRIUM TOLERANCE VALUE: '
          READ*, TOLNC
*
*   INITIALIZE TEMPERATURE ARRAY
*
          CALL FIRST(NEW,NROW,NCOL,TOP,BOT,LEFT,RIGHT)
          CALL MOVE(OLD,NEW,NROW,NCOL)
*
*   PRINT INITIAL TEMPERATURE ARRAY
*
          PRINT*
          PRINT*, 'INITIAL TEMPERATURES'
          PRINT*
          CALL PRINT(OLD,NROW,NCOL)
*
*   UPDATE TEMPERATURES UNTIL EQUILIBRIUM
*
          EQUILB = .FALSE.
       20 IF (.NOT.EQUILB) THEN
             EQUILB = .TRUE.
             DO 30 I=2,NROW-1
                DO 25 J=2,NCOL-1
                   NEW(I,J) = (OLD(I-1,J) + OLD(I+1,J) +
         +                     OLD(I,J-1) + OLD(I,J+1))/4.0+00
                   IF (DABS(NEW(I,J) - OLD(I,J)).GT.TOLNC)
         +                     EQUILB = .FALSE.
       25       CONTINUE
       30    CONTINUE
```

```
          CALL MOVE(OLD,NEW,NROW,NCOL)
          GO TO 20
      ENDIF
*
*   PRINT EQUILIBRIUM TEMPERATURE ARRAY
*
      PRINT*
      PRINT*, 'EQUILBRIUM TEMPERATURES'
      PRINT*
      CALL PRINT(OLD,NROW,NCOL)
*
      END
*-----------------------------------------------------------------*
                  (no changes in subroutine PRINT)
*-----------------------------------------------------------------*
                  (no changes in subroutine MOVE)
*-----------------------------------------------------------------*
*
      SUBROUTINE  FIRST(NEW,NROW,NCOL,TOP,BOT,LEFT,RIGHT)
*
*   This subroutine initializes the temperature array.
*
      INTEGER  NROW, NCOL, I, J
      DOUBLE PRECISION  NEW(10,10), TOP, BOT, LEFT, RIGHT
*
      DO 5 J=1,NCOL
          NEW(1,J) = TOP
          NEW(NROW,J) = BOT
    5 CONTINUE
      DO 15 I=2,NROW-1
          NEW(I,1) = LEFT
          DO 10 J=2,NCOL-1
              NEW(I,J) = 0.0D+00
   10     CONTINUE
          NEW(I,NCOL) = RIGHT
   15 CONTINUE
*
      RETURN
      END
*-----------------------------------------------------------------*
13.
*-----------------------------------------------------------------*
      PROGRAM  ELECT1
*
*   This program determines the magnitude and phase
*   of an RC circuit on a sine wave.
*
      REAL  R, MC, C, W, MAGN, PHASE
      COMPLEX  I, HW
*
      I = (0.0, 1.0)
*
      PRINT*, 'ENTER RESISTANCE IN OHMS'
      READ*, R
      PRINT*, 'ENTER CAPACITANCE IN MICROFARADS'
      READ*, MC
      PRINT*, 'ENTER THE SINE FREQUENCY IN RADIANS PER SEC'
      READ*, W
*
      C = MC*1.0E-06
      HW = (I*W*R*C)/(1.0 + I*W*R*C)
```

```
      MAGN = CABS(HW)
      PHASE = ATAN(AIMAG(HW)/REAL(HW))
*
      PRINT 5, MAGN, PHASE
    5 FORMAT (1X,'MAGNITUDE EFFECT:',F5.2,3X,
     +              'PHASE EFFECT:', F5.2)
*
      END
```
--

17.
--
```
      SUBROUTINE  CNDNS(IN,OUT)
*
*  This subroutine removes all groups
*  of multiple blanks from IN and
*  stores in OUT.
*
      INTEGER  I, K
      CHARACTER*50  IN, OUT
*
      OUT = ' '
      K = 1
      DO 10 I=1,49
         IF (IN(I:I).NE.' ') THEN
            OUT(K:K) = IN(I:I)
            K = K + 1
         ELSE
            IF (IN(I+1:I+1).NE.' ') THEN
               OUT(K:K) = IN(I:I)
               K = K + 1
            ENDIF
         ENDIF
   10 CONTINUE
      OUT(K:K) = IN(50:50)
*
      RETURN
      END
```
--

Chapter 9

2.
--
```
      PROGRAM  VOYAGE
*
*  This program detects edges in a two-dimensional image.
*
      INTEGER  I, J, IMAGE(40,50), ID, NR, NC, NEWID
      REAL   LIMIT
      CHARACTER  FILENM*6, EDGE(40)*50, LINE*50
      LOGICAL  DONE
*
      DO 3 I=1,50
         LINE(I:I) = '*'
    3 CONTINUE
      PRINT*, 'ENTER NAME OF IMAGE FILE ENCLOSED IN QUOTES'
      READ*, FILENM
      OPEN (UNIT=8,FILE=FILENM,STATUS='OLD')
*
```

```
      PRINT*
      PRINT*,'IMAGES IN THIS FILE'
      READ(8,*) ID, NR, NC
    5 IF (ID.NE.9999)  THEN
         PRINT 10, ID,NR,NC
   10    FORMAT (1X,'ID = ',I4,' SIZE = (',I2,',',I2,')')
         DO 20 I=1,NR
            READ(8,15)  IMAGE(I,1)
   15       FORMAT (50I1)
   20    CONTINUE
         READ(8,*) ID, NR, NC
         GO TO 5
      ENDIF
*
      PRINT*
      PRINT*, 'ENTER ID OF IMAGE TO BE ANALYZED'
      READ*, NEWID
      PRINT*, 'ENTER THRESHOLD FOR EDGE DETECTION'
      READ*, LIMIT
*
      REWIND (UNIT=8)
      READ(8,*) ID, NR, NC
      DONE = .FALSE.
   25 IF (.NOT.DONE)  THEN
         IF (ID.EQ.NEWID)  THEN
            DO 30 I=1,NR
               READ (8,15) (IMAGE(I,J),J=1,NC)
   30       CONTINUE
            CALL CONVERT(LIMIT,IMAGE,EDGE,NR,NC)
            PRINT*
            PRINT 35, LIMIT
   35       FORMAT (1X,'THRESHOLD VALUE = ',F5.2)
            PRINT 40, LINE(1:NC)
            DO 45 I=1,NR
               PRINT 40, EDGE(I)(1:NC)
   40          FORMAT (1X,'*',A,'*')
   45       CONTINUE
            PRINT 40, LINE(1:NC)
            DONE = .TRUE.
         ELSEIF (ID.EQ.9999)  THEN
            DONE = .TRUE.
            PRINT*, 'IMAGE NOT FOUND'
         ELSE
            DO 50 I=1,NR
               READ(8,15) IMAGE(I,1)
   50       CONTINUE
            READ(8,*) ID, NR, NC
         ENDIF
         GO TO 25
      ENDIF
      END
*--------------------------------------------------------*
                (no changes in subroutine CONVRT)
*--------------------------------------------------------*


10.
*--------------------------------------------------------*
      PROGRAM  MIGRAT
*
*  This program merges new sighting information into the
*  master file of migration information on whooping cranes.
*
```

```
      INTEGER   M,D,Y,T,MO,DA,YR,TIME,GRID1,GRID2,BIRDS,
     +          SMO,SDA,SYR,STIME,SGRID1,SGRID2,SBIRDS,
     +          CMO,CDA,CYR,CTIME,CGRID1,CGRID2,CBIRDS,COUNT,
     +          MAXCT,HOLDM,HOLDD
      DOUBLE PRECISION  DATE, CDATE, SDATE
      LOGICAL   DONE
*
      DATE(M,D,Y,T) = DBLE(REAL(Y)*1.0D08) +
     +                DBLE(REAL(M)*1.0D06) +
     +                DBLE(REAL(D)*1.0D04) +
     +                DBLE(REAL(T))
*
      OPEN (UNIT=10,FILE='SIGHTS',STATUS='OLD')
      OPEN (UNIT=11,FILE='CRANES',STATUS='OLD')
      OPEN (UNIT=12,FILE='TEMP',STATUS='NEW')
*
      READ (10,5) SMO,SDA,SYR,STIME,SGRID1,SGRID2,SBIRDS
    5 FORMAT (3I2,1X,I4,1X,2I2,1X,I4)
      READ (11,5) CMO,CDA,CYR,CTIME,CGRID1,CGRID2,CBIRDS
      SDATE = DATE(SMO,SDA,SYR,STIME)
      CDATE = DATE(CMO,CDA,CYR,CTIME)
      IF (SMO.EQ.99.AND.CMO.EQ.99) THEN
         DONE = .TRUE.
      ELSE
         DONE = .FALSE.
      ENDIF
*
   10 IF (.NOT.DONE) THEN
         IF (CDATE.LT.SDATE) THEN
            WRITE (12,5) CMO,CDA,CYR,CTIME,CGRID1,
     +                   CGRID2,CBIRDS
            READ (11,5) CMO,CDA,CYR,CTIME,CGRID1,
     +                   CGRID2,CBIRDS
            CDATE = DATE(CMO,CDA,CYR,CTIME)
         ELSE
            WRITE (12,5) SMO,SDA,SYR,STIME,SGRID1,
     +                   SGRID2,SBIRDS
            READ (10,5) SMO,SDA,SYR,STIME,SGRID1,
     +                   SGRID2,SBIRDS
            SDATE = DATE(SMO,SDA,SYR,STIME)
         ENDIF
         IF (SMO.EQ.99.AND.CMO.EQ.99) DONE = .TRUE.
         GO TO 10
      ENDIF
      WRITE (12,5) SMO,SDA,SYR,STIME,SGRID1,SGRID2,SBIRDS
      CLOSE (UNIT=11,STATUS='DELETE')
      CLOSE (UNIT=12)
*
      OPEN (UNIT=11,FILE='CRANES',STATUS='NEW')
      OPEN (UNIT=12,FILE='TEMP',STATUS='OLD')
      PRINT*, 'WHOOPING CRANE MIGRATION'
      PRINT*
      PRINT*, 'CURRENT SIGHTINGS'
      PRINT*
*
      HOLDM = 0
      HOLDD = 0
      COUNT = 0
      MAXCT = 0
   15 READ (12,5,END=35) MO,DA,YR,TIME,GRID1,GRID2,BIRDS
      IF (MO.NE.99) THEN
         PRINT 20, MO,DA,YR,TIME
```

```
      20        FORMAT (1X,I2,'-',I2,'-',I2,4X,I4)
                PRINT 25, GRID1,GRID2
      25        FORMAT (1X,5X,'GRID LOCATION: ',2I3)
                PRINT 30, BIRDS
      30        FORMAT (1X,5X,'NUMBER OF BIRDS',1X,I5)
                IF (MO.EQ.HOLDM.AND.DA.EQ.HOLDD) THEN
                   COUNT = COUNT + 1
                ELSE
                   IF (COUNT.GT.MAXCT) MAXCT = COUNT
                   COUNT = 1
                   HOLDM = MO
                   HOLDD = DA
                ENDIF
            ENDIF
            WRITE (11,5) MO,DA,YR,TIME,GRID1,GRID2,BIRDS
            GO TO 15
      35 PRINT 40, MAXCT
      40 FORMAT (1X,'MAXIMUM NUMBER OF SIGHTINGS IN ONE DAY = ',I4)
*
      50 STOP
         END
*------------------------------------------------------------------*

12.
*------------------------------------------------------------------*
      SUBROUTINE  REPORT
*
*  This subroutine prints the inventory file
*  in stock number order.
*
      INTEGER  KEY, STOCK, QUANT
      REAL   PRICE
      CHARACTER*10  DESC
*
      CLOSE (UNIT=11)
      OPEN  (UNIT=11,FILE='PARTS',ACCESS ='DIRECT',
     +       STATUS='OLD',FORM ='FORMATTED',RECL=23)
      PRINT*, 'INVENTORY REPORT'
      PRINT*
      PRINT*, 'NUMBER  DESCRIPTION  QUANTITY  PRICE'
      KEY = 1
   10 READ (11,15,REC=KEY,ERR=25,END=25) STOCK,DESC,QUANT,PRICE
   15    FORMAT (I3,A10,I4,F6.2)
         PRINT 20, STOCK, DESC, QUANT, PRICE
   20    FORMAT (1X,I3,5X,A10,5X,I4,5X,F6.2)
         KEY = KEY + 1
         GO TO 10
   25 CLOSE (UNIT=11)
*
      RETURN
      END
*------------------------------------------------------------------*

17.
*------------------------------------------------------------------*
      PROGRAM  PLANT
*
*  This program prints the work orders
*  for specified pieces of equipment.
*
      INTEGER  TYPE, ORDER, CODE
      LOGICAL  DONE
*
```

```
          OPEN (UNIT=8,FILE='SENSOR',STATUS='OLD')
          DONE = .FALSE.
      5 IF (.NOT.DONE)  THEN
            PRINT*, 'ENTER SENSOR TYPE (1 THROUGH 5)'
            PRINT*, 'OR ENTER 9 TO QUIT'
            READ*, TYPE
            IF (TYPE.NE.9) THEN
               PRINT*
               PRINT*, 'WORK ORDERS:'
               REWIND (UNIT=8)
     10        READ (8,15,END=20) ORDER, CODE
     15           FORMAT (I5,2X,I1)
                  IF (CODE.EQ.TYPE) PRINT*, ORDER
                  GO TO 10
     20        PRINT*,'END OF FILE REACHED'
            ELSE
               DONE = .TRUE.
            ENDIF
            GO TO 5
          ENDIF
*
          END
*-------------------------------------------------------------------*
```

Chapter 10

1.
```
*-------------------------------------------------------------------*
      PROGRAM  LINEAR
*
*  This program computes a linear model for XY data and
*  then computes the residual sum to evaluate the model.
*
      INTEGER  I, N
      REAL   X(500),Y(500),SLOPE,YINT,YNEW,RES,
     +       SUMX,SUMY,SUMXY,SUMXX,SUMRES,DEVX,DEVY,MAXDEV
*
      DATA   I,SUMX,SUMY,SUMXY, SUMXX, SUMRES /1,5*0.0/
*
      OPEN (UNIT=10,FILE='XYDATA',STATUS='OLD')
      5 READ (10,*,END=50) X(I), Y(I)
          SUMX = SUMX + X(I)
          SUMY = SUMY + Y(I)
          SUMXY = SUMXY + X(I)*Y(I)
          SUMXX = SUMXX + X(I)*X(I)
          I = I + 1
          GO TO 5
*
     50 N = I - 1
        SLOPE = (SUMX*SUMY - REAL(N)*SUMXY)/
     +          (SUMX*SUMX - REAL(N)*SUMXX)
        YINT = (SUMY - SLOPE*SUMX)/REAL(N)
*
        PRINT*, 'THE LINEAR EQUATION IS'
        PRINT 55, SLOPE, YINT
     55 FORMAT (1X,'Y = ',F6.2,' X + ',F6.2)
        PRINT*
        PRINT*, 'ORIGINAL    ORIGINAL     ESTIMATED     RESIDUAL'
        PRINT*, '   X           Y             Y                 '
        PRINT*
*
```

```
         DO 65 I=1,N
             YNEW = SLOPE*X(I) + YINT
             RES = Y(I) - YNEW
             SUMRES = SUMRES + RES*RES
             PRINT 60, X(I), Y(I), YNEW, RES
     60      FORMAT (1X,F6.2,6X,F6.2,6X,F6.2,7X,F6.2)
             IF (I.EQ.1) THEN
                 MAXDEV = ABS(RES)
                 DEVX = X(I)
                 DEVY = Y(I)
             ELSE
                 IF (MAXDEV.LT.ABS(RES)) THEN
                     MAXDEV = ABS(RES)
                     DEVX = X(I)
                     DEVY = Y(I)
                 ENDIF
             ENDIF
     65  CONTINUE
*
     PRINT*
     PRINT 70, SUMRES
     70 FORMAT (1X, 'RESIDUAL SUM = ', F6.2)
     PRINT 75, DEVX, DEVY
     75 FORMAT (1X,'POINT (',F6.2,',',F6.2,') DEVIATES THE MOST',
     +          ' FROM THE LINE')
*
     END
*-------------------------------------------------------------*

  7.
*-------------------------------------------------------------*
     PROGRAM  AREA1
*
*  This program estimates the area under a given curve.
*
     INTEGER  N, I
     REAL  A, B, BASE, LEFT, RIGHT, AREA, SUM, OLD
     LOGICAL  DONE
*
     F(X) = 4.0*EXP(-(X - 2.0)**2)
*
     DATA  SUM, DONE /0.0, .FALSE./
*
     PRINT*, 'ENTER THE INTERVAL ENDPOINTS: '
     READ*, A, B
     N = 10
   5 IF (.NOT.DONE) THEN
         BASE = (B - A)/REAL(N)
         LEFT = F(A)
         RIGHT = F(A + BASE)
         DO 10 I=1,N
             AREA = 0.5*BASE*(LEFT + RIGHT)
             SUM = SUM + AREA
             LEFT = RIGHT
             RIGHT = F(BASE*(I + 1) + A)
     10      CONTINUE
         IF (N.EQ.10) THEN
             OLD = SUM
             N = N*2
             SUM=0.0
         ELSE
             IF (ABS(SUM - OLD).LT.0.01) THEN
```

```
                    DONE = .TRUE.
               ELSE
                    OLD = SUM
                    N = N*2
                    SUM=0.0
               ENDIF
            ENDIF
            GO TO 5
         ENDIF
         PRINT 15, N, SUM
      15 FORMAT (1X,'USING ',I3,' TRAPEZOIDS, ',
        +          'THE ESTIMATED AREA IS ',F7.3)
*
         END
```
--

11.
--
```
      PROGRAM  POLY
*
*  This program determines the roots in an interval
*  for a quartic polynomial using interval halving.
*
      INTEGER  COUNT, N
      REAL  LEFT, RIGHT, ENDL, ENDR, P
*
      COMMON  /COEFF/ A, B, C, D, E
*
      PRINT*, 'ENTER LEFT AND RIGHT INTERVAL ENDPOINTS'
      REAL*, ENDL, ENDR
      PRINT*, 'ENTER COEFFICIENTS A, B, C, D, E'
      READ*, A, B, C, D, E
    1 IF (A.NE.0.0.OR.B.NE.0.0.OR.C.NE.0.0.OR.
       +    D.NE.0.0.OR.E.NE.0.0) THEN
*
         PRINT*
         PRINT*, 'POLYNOMIAL:'
         PRINT 5
    5    FORMAT (1X,'              4              3',
       +         '                             2')
         PRINT 10, A, B, C, D, E
   10    FORMAT (1X,4(F7.3,' X  + '),F7.3)
         PRINT*
*
         COUNT = 0
         LEFT = ENDL
         RIGHT = ENDL + 0.25
         N = NINT((ENDR - ENDL)/0.25)
         DO 20 I=1,N
            IF (P(LEFT).EQ.0.0) THEN
               PRINT 15, LEFT, P(LEFT)
   15          FORMAT (1X,'ROOT = ',F7.3,
       +               '   P(ROOT) = ',F7.3)
               COUNT = COUNT + 1
            ELSEIF (P(LEFT)*P(RIGHT).LT.0.0) THEN
               CALL ITERAT (LEFT,RIGHT,ROOT)
               PRINT 15, ROOT, P(ROOT)
               COUNT = COUNT + 1
            ENDIF
            LEFT = RIGHT
            RIGHT = LEFT + 0.25
   20    CONTINUE
```

```
              IF (P(LEFT).EQ.0.0) THEN
                  PRINT 15, LEFT, P(LEFT)
                  COUNT = COUNT + 1
              ENDIF
          IF (COUNT.EQ.0) THEN
              PRINT*, 'NO ROOTS IN INTERVAL'
          ENDIF
          PRINT*
          PRINT*, 'ENTER COEFFICIENTS A, B, C, D, E'
          PRINT*, '(ALL ZEROS TO QUIT) '
          READ*, A, B, C, D, E
          GO TO 1
      ENDIF
*
      END
*-------------------------------------------------------------*
                (no changes in function P)
*-------------------------------------------------------------*
              (no changes in subroutine ITERAT)
*-------------------------------------------------------------*


17.
*-------------------------------------------------------------*
      PROGRAM  EQN3
*
*  This program computes the solution to two
*  simultaneous equations using determinants.
*
      REAL A(2), B(2), C(2), DENOM, DET
*
      PRINT*, 'EACH EQUATION SHOULD BE IN THIS FORM:'
      PRINT*, 'A*X + B*X = C'
      PRINT*, 'ENTER A, B, C FOR EQUATION 1: '
      READ*, A(1), B(1), C(1)
      PRINT*, 'ENTER A, B, C FOR EQUATION 2: '
      READ*, A(2), B(2), C(2)
      PRINT*
*
      DENOM = DET(A,B)
      IF (DENOM.EQ.0.0) THEN
          PRINT*, 'NO UNIQUE SOLUTION EXISTS'
      ELSE
          X = DET(C,B)/DENOM
          Y = DET(A,C)/DENOM
          PRINT 5, X
    5     FORMAT (1X,'SOLUTION: X = ',F7.2)
          PRINT 6, Y
    6     FORMAT (1X,'          Y = ',F7.2)
      ENDIF
*
      END
*-------------------------------------------------------------*
*
      REAL FUNCTION  DET(P,Q)
*
*  This function computes the determinant of a 2X2 matrix
*  where P, Q represent the two columns of the matrix.
*
      REAL  P(2), Q(2)
*
      DET = P(1)*Q(2) - P(2)*Q(1)
*
```

```
      RETURN
      END
*-------------------------------------------------------------------*

19.
*-------------------------------------------------------------------*
               (no changes in main program GAUSS)
*-------------------------------------------------------------------*
      SUBROUTINE  ORDER(A,N,PIVOT,ERROR)
*
*  This subroutine reorders the equations so that the pivot
*  position in the pivot equation has the maximum absolute value.
*
      INTEGER  N, ROW, RMAX, PIVOT, K
      REAL  A(25,26), TEMP
      LOGICAL  ERROR
*
      RMAX = PIVOT
      DO 10 ROW=PIVOT+1,N
         IF (ABS(A(ROW,PIVOT)).GT.ABS(A(RMAX,PIVOT)))  RMAX = ROW
   10 CONTINUE
      IF (ABS(A(RMAX,PIVOT)).LT.1.0E-05)  THEN
         ERROR = .TRUE.
      ELSE
         IF (RMAX.NE.PIVOT)  THEN
            DO 20 K=1,N+1
               TEMP = A(RMAX,K)
               A(RMAX,K)  = A(PIVOT,K)
               A(PIVOT,K)  = TEMP
   20       CONTINUE
            PRINT 25, PIVOT, RMAX
   25       FORMAT (1X,'ROWS INTERCHANGED:',I3,2X,I3)
         ENDIF
      ENDIF
      RETURN
      END
*-------------------------------------------------------------------*
               (no changes in subroutine ELIM)
*-------------------------------------------------------------------*
               (no changes in subroutine BACKSB)
*-------------------------------------------------------------------*

22.
*-------------------------------------------------------------------*
      SUBROUTINE  TRANSP(A,AROW,ACOL,T,TROW,TCOL)
*
*  This subroutine transposes
*  matrix A into matrix T.
*
      INTEGER  AROW, ACOL, A(AROW,ACOL), TROW, TCOL,
     +         T(TROW,TCOL), I, J
*
      DO 10 I=1,AROW
         DO 5 J=1,ACOL
            T(J,I) = A(I,J)
    5    CONTINUE
   10 CONTINUE
*
      RETURN
      END
*-------------------------------------------------------------------*
```

INDEX

SS format specification, 508
Statement
  executable, 16
  function, 245
  nonexecutable, 16
  number, 14
STATUS specifier, 145, 404
Stepwise refinement, 8
STOP statement, 45
String
  binary, 4
  character, 349
Structure chart, 255
Structured
  algorithm, 72
  program, 72
Style/technique guides, 59, 131, 180,
    234, 291, 340, 391, 431, 487
Subprogram
  block data, 338
  function, 256
  subroutine, 300
Subroutine
  alternate entry, 505
  alternate return, 506
  argument, 300
  call, 300
  name, 300
  user-written, 245, 256
SUBROUTINE statement, 300
Subscript, 192, 218
Substring, 354
Syntax error, 6

T

.TRUE., 83
Tab specification, 171
Temporary workspace, 7
Technique. *See* Style/technique
    guides
Terminals, 7
Testing, 10
THEN, 85
Time-sharing, 7
TLn format specification, 171
Tn format specification, 171
Top-down design, 8, 254
Trailer signal, 148
Transaction file, 425
Transfer statement, 91
TRn format specification, 171
Truncation, 23
Two-dimensional array
  initialization, 218

Two-dimensional array *(continued)*
  I/O, 221
  specification, 218
  storage, 218
Type statement
  character, 349
  complex, 383
  double-precision, 371
  explicit, 15
  implicit, 15
  integer, 16
  logical, 84
  real, 16

U

Unconditional GO TO statement, 430
Underflow, 25
Unformatted file, 404
UNFORMATTED specifier, 430
Unit number, 145
UNIT specifier, 145, 404
User-written function, 245, 256

V

Variable, 15
  character, 349
  complex, 383
  dimensioning, 262
  double-precision, 371
  formatting, 509
  integer, 15
  local, 503
  logical, 84
  name, 15
  real, 15
Vertical spacing, 34

W

WHILE loop, 76, 91
Width of format specification, 40
Workspace, 7
Workstation, 7
WRITE statement
  formatted, 145, 423
  list-directed, 144

X

X format specification, 37